D1452565

THE LIMITS OF LIBERTY

Borderlands and Transcultural Studies

Series Editors   Pekka Hämäläinen, Paul Spickard

THE LIMITS OF LIBERTY

Mobility and the Making of the
Eastern U.S.-Mexico Border

JAMES DAVID NICHOLS

University of Nebraska Press
LINCOLN AND LONDON

For Alma and Abel

CONTENTS

    and Cooperation in the Age of Vidaurri   189

    Conclusion: Mobility Interrupted   217

    Notes   233
    Bibliography   263
    Index   281

Illustrations

Acknowledgments

This work would not have been possible without the help of many giving and talented individuals. First, I must thank the three people most responsible for my intellectual development as a graduate student at Stony Brook University. April F. Masten was always there to encourage me and to push me to embrace new and challenging ideas. As my dissertation adviser, her assistance with writing made my work much better than it would have been otherwise. She has been both an inspiration and a friend during the long journey from idea to book. Kathleen Wilson is the person most responsible for my abiding interest in cultural theory. Her deeply thoughtful and provocative classes on methods and comparative slavery were fundamental to developing my way of seeing and interpreting the past. Paul Gootenberg is the professor behind my dive into Latin American studies. I would not have learned about, visited, or done research in Mexico without his help. He has been both a mentor and a friend—and he can play a pretty mean saxophone. Others professors who helped me during my graduate school career were Nancy Tomes, Herman Lebovics, and Shirley Lim, among many others. Last, I must acknowledge the seminal importance of a class I took with Walter Johnson at New York University in 2005, U.S. Culture in the Age of the Mexican War, for the development of my thesis.

While doing research in both Texas and Mexico I continued to accrue debts of both the personal and financial sorts. First, I must thank various research institutions and archives and their staffs for their assistance and availability: the Briscoe Center for American History, the Archivo

General de la Nación in Mexico City, the Archive for the Secretary of Foreign Relations, the Texas State Archives, the municipal archives of Saltillo, and the Secretary of National Defense in Mexico City. In Monterrey, the late, great Artemio Benavides helped me find dusty volumes until the day the swine flu interrupted my research. In Saltillo, the staff at the state archives gave their time, resources, advice, and even supplies. I want to thank particularly Francisco Javier Gutierrez Rodríguez, who was head of the archive when I was there in 2009. I would also like to thank the research team at the New York Public Library, where I did my final editorial work in the quiet comfort of the Wertheim Study Room. Finally, I must thank the Social Science Research Council and the Texas State Historical Association for making my dissertation research in both Mexico and the United States possible financially.

While conducting researching for my dissertation I also gained invaluable insights from expert Mexicanists in both Mexico and the United States. I wish to thank Josefina Zoraida Vásquez, Froylan Enciso, Miguel Ángel González Quiroga, and Luis Alberto García. Cyrila Quintero at the Colegio de la Frontera Norte and Clara Lida at the Colegio de México served as my advisers and occasional dinner companions while I was in Mexico. Karl Jacoby, meanwhile, proved immensely helpful as my outside reader, and he has supported me in ways too numerous to count. The field of borderlands studies is richer for having him, and I personally owe him a tremendous intellectual debt. At CUNY Queensborough Community College, my colleague Megan Elias enthusiastically proofread a number of drafts of this work. Tom McDonald, author of a definitive forthcoming biography of James Hughes Callahan, also helped me as I turned my dissertation into a monograph. Likewise, Nicole Lopez-Jantzen, Mark Van Ells, and Cameron Hawkins have proven themselves wonderful colleagues and friends who do not shy away from scholarly conversations.

As I turned the dissertation into a book, I continued to accrue personal debts. Benjamin H. Johnson served as a guide into borderlands studies. He led a National Endowment for the Humanities Summer Seminar on borderlands in 2014 at Chicago's Newberry Library in which I enthusiastically participated. Ben has also read my work and offered helpful insights and criticisms. In addition, he invited me to participate in a wonderful workshop at the Newberry Library alongside David Sartorius, Brian DeLay, and Geraldo L. Cadava. Julian Lim and Ryan Hall are other friends I made at the Newberry Library, and they have become consistent companions at academic conferences. I am also grateful for the opportunity to have participated in the Conference on Remaking North American Sovereignty in the majestic Rocky Mountain town of Banff, organized by Frank Towers and sponsored by the Ann Richards Civil War Era Center. While there, I also had the pleasure of meeting Alice Baumgartner. She is involved in her own exhaustive research on runaway slaves to Mexico that I anticipate reading, and she has kindly shared sources with me.

In addition, I must thank the staff at the *Western Historical Quarterly*, including Anne Hyde and David Rich Lewis, for publishing an article on my early research and helping me win two awards for it. I am also grateful for two PSC-CUNY grants for professional development that helped me finish my work in the summers of 2015 and 2016, relieving me of the duty to teach. And, last but not least, at the University of Nebraska Press, Matt Bokovoy has been a kind and patient advocate for my work. I also thank the reviewers and editorial staff at the University of Nebraska Press for their feedback and help.

Finally, this work would not have existed had it not been for the kind and loving support of my family. I could not have conceived, finished, or published this book without their help. My parents, Jim and Della, were always there to lend a hand with the kids or read drafts of chapters. My dad is probably responsible for my interest in history to begin with; he is a Civil War buff, and we have passed many pleasant, lazy afternoons debating the military history of that war. My wife, Lilla Tőke, has been with me for this entire journey, even as we have undertaken our own journey into a life together. She has been my best editor and has read every chapter in multiple forms. If it had not been for her, I would not have gotten rid of all those filler words—"indeed," "although," and "one must consider"—that pepper my first drafts. *Szivem, nagyon szeretlek.* My children are too young to know what this book is about, but the happiness they have given me has made its way into these pages.

THE LIMITS OF LIBERTY

Introduction: The Making of Borderlands Mobility

In April 1836, the Republic of Texas won its independence from Mexico. One of the most storied events in the early history of the U.S.-Mexico borderlands, this seminal victory was celebrated by those who felt the stirring of republicanism in their breasts as a stroke won for liberty. For too long, the Mexican government had neither provided stability for the far northern areas, like Texas, nor allowed them the autonomy for which they yearned. To escape a government that many in the far north of Mexico felt had grown despotic, a group of men in Texas declared their independence, fought for it, and then consummated it at the battle of San Jacinto. But even as the victors of San Jacinto celebrated their victory over the forces of General Antonio López de Santa Anna, there were some people who lived in Texas who despaired of the republic's newfound independence. Many Native Americans felt that the train of events that the victory of white Texans and their handful of *tejano* (Latino/a Texan; Tejano) allies put into motion would not ultimately work in their favor. The governments of Texas and Mexico remained at loggerheads for another decade as they squabbled over the location of the new border separating their republics. Texas claimed that the Rio Grande—known as the Río Bravo to Mexicans—separated the two countries. Mexico, meanwhile, claimed the Nueces River as the border. The only consensus to emerge was that somewhere, either within or below the vast tract of land known on maps as the Wild Horse Desert, the Texas Revolution had given birth to a new border. This new border— though no one knew where it was—immediately set people opposed to the recent independence of Texas in motion.

In the ensuing years, a large number of Indians sought to escape the newly independent Republic of Texas, and they mobilized routes across the borderlands in search of new possibilities. Many Kadohadacho and Hasinai Caddos—among a vast array of Native peoples mobilized by the war and the new border it created—moved from their old homes near the Texas-Louisiana frontier and dispersed in different directions beyond the pale of Anglo settlement. Fearful of what a Texan victory would mean for them and looking to escape white whiskey traders and Texan land lust, Caddos migrated in search of new options. Many went toward Indian Territory to the north, seeking out some sort of rapprochement with the U.S. government. Another small group found themselves camped outside Shreveport, Louisiana, in a pitiful state, living alongside other Native peoples left behind from the great removals of the 1820s and 1830s.[1] Another group of Caddos chose a less politically neutral option than migrating to Indian Territory. They headed to Mexico in order to find refuge and help the Mexican officers there keep up a running war with the Texans. Rafael de la Fuente, prefect of Monclova in far northern Coahuila, was one such officer, and he welcomed a great number of Caddos into his jurisdiction on April 27, 1841. These Caddos had just made the long and difficult journey from eastern Texas into his frontier district and, by extension, the sovereign republic of Mexico. Theirs was a large migration comprising mainly Nadaco Caddos, and the group consisted of thirty armed warriors and two hundred women and children who— exactly five years after the "disgrace" at San Jacinto when the Texans consummated their independence—found their paths crossing with those of Mexican officers who held a similar grudge against the Texans.[2]

After greeting the Caddos and welcoming them into his district, de la Fuente sent them on to Lampazos in the neighboring state of Nuevo León—the nerve center of military operations in the Mexican North— where they would at last get their opportunity for revenge against the Texans. The officers in charge of preparing war parties in Mexico outfitted them for an expedition against their common enemy. They probably even made up part of the forces under Adrián Woll, who briefly recaptured San Antonio the following year.[3] Those Caddos who chose to leave Texas in this case were far from politically neutral.[4] Alongside other dissident Indians, they had already intrigued with Mexican agents and spies from within Texas for years after the battle of San Jacinto. Upon crossing into Mexico they found refuge and a more practical "staging ground"—to borrow Willem Van Schendel's trenchant metaphor for troubled borders—for their resistance to the Texans who had arrogated their old homelands to themselves.[5]

Long before anyone could locate its final position on a map, the international border already had a strange drawing power. During the fluid borderlands stage that preceded the final placement of the border in 1848, and before the Rio Grande separated two "bordered lands" from one another officially, the frontier still divided people from one another and served as a partition of sorts. Texan whites generally lived above the Colorado River and Mexicans and Tejanos below it, in Goliad, Béxar (San Antonio), and along the Rio Grande.[6] Even in this early stage, the boundary line that lay between these two distinct peoples beckoned the Caddos across the contested zone of the Nueces Strip, attracting them to the other side of the Rio Grande in search of refuge, succor, and revenge. The Caddos knew they had made it to the other side only when Mexican officers hostile to the Texan cause greeted them. The Caddos found a border already in 1841, and they looked to take advantage of the contradictions between Mexico and the United States that registered along the geographically ill-defined international border.

This book demonstrates that the U.S.-Mexico border, which to this day beckons people across in search of opportunity, has had a long history of conducting movement. This division between the two countries is so powerful that the runaway slaves, Indians, fugitives, immigrants, and other mobile people discussed in this book found themselves enticed across the new international border even before it showed up on maps. Most took a route that led them into Mexico, opposite the direction we are most accustomed to hearing about today. In Mexico they found liberty, which for the purpose of this book, meant independence and the ability to follow one's life path as one deemed best. In the case of runaway slaves, the meaning of liberty was quite clear: it was the absence of slavery. Native Americans and migrant Mexican laborers also sought greater freedom across the line, to escape harsh masters and bad circumstances. Runaways from slavery, fleeing debt peons, and migrant Indians may all have found agency through mobility, but they deployed transnational movement in very different ways and moved in opposing directions across the border. For runaway slaves and debt peons, liberty entailed setting up semipermanently on the other side of the border, enjoying the protection offered by the laws on that side and starting over. For Native Americans, on the other hand, mobility was often a means to liberty itself. This dynamic is illustrated amply throughout the book, beginning

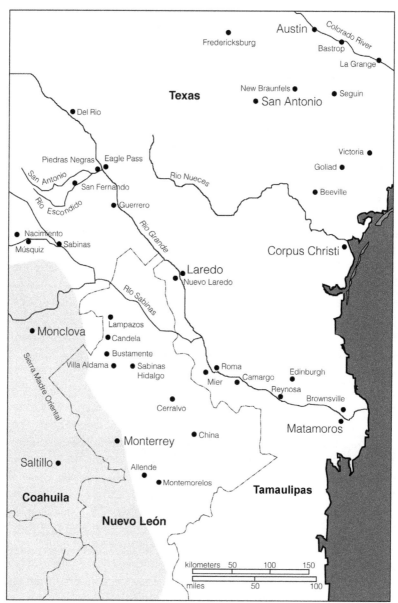

The Eastern U.S.-Mexico Borderlands. Map by author.

in chapter 1. Lipan Apaches, the main subject of that chapter, refused to become sedentary and instead found freedom by continually crossing borders. For these mobile people it was the journey itself that mattered more than the destination. Movement afforded them all sorts of opportunities to play people and governments off one another. The type of mobility and migration deployed by Native peoples contrasted sharply with that used by runaways and fugitives. Still, all of these mobile people invested in and lent meaning to the nascent international border as a limit of liberty in its earliest stages.

It is the emphasis on the different types of mobility deployed by different social groups in the Texas-Mexico borderlands that sets this work apart from those of other scholars who have written about borders and freedom. Omar S. Valerio-Jiménez, Rosalie Schwartz, Samuel Truett, Juan Mora-Torres, and Miguel Ángel González Quiroga have also found that the border meant hope, freedom, or increased opportunity for many of those who crossed it. Many of these scholars write about a migration path that we are not used to hearing about today, from the United States into Mexico. In conducting their research, these authors add subaltern voices to the history of the making of the border. Schwartz, who writes about runaway slaves, theorizes the border as a gateway to freedom. Valerio-Jiménez, meanwhile, imagines a "river of hope" that allowed *mexicano* (Mexican) and Tejano runaways and peons, including women, an opportunity to escape into a country that was under foreign governance but still very similar culturally. Truett uncovers many forgotten transnational connections that tied the borderlands together, even as the arrival of an international border pushed people farther apart.[7]

My book differs from these works in a couple of significant ways. Unlike the works that concentrate on Tejanos or mexicanos, I theorize that the cultural and political milieu that runaways and renegades entered on the other side of the border could be quite markedly different. Drawing upon research conducted on both sides of the border, the stories of runaway slaves, fleeing debt peons, and renegade Indians do not cease at the border in this book, riding off into historiographical oblivion. I contend that these refuge seekers remained important on the other side of the border, and I have used multinational archives to discover what happened to them there and what impact they had on their adopted societies. I also highlight the way that the border brought out differences on either side rather than similarities. Frequently, freedom was not everything it was hoped to be, of course—hence the double meaning of the word *limits* in my title. Nevertheless, and as Sean Kelley has so elegantly written about enslaved people in Texas, the border was a powerful draw in the imaginations of marginalized people.[8] I demonstrate that it was not only the enslaved in Texas who invested so heavily in the emancipatory significance of the international line but Indians, peons, and others as well.

Another way that my work differs from others is that I theorize the act of border crossing as an important aspect of the construction of national differences. Like Truett, I discover routes that mobile people continually pursued across the border. And like Valerio-Jiménez, I find that people could cross back and forth continually, adding an unexpected transnational dimension to lives that were otherwise intensely local. But I suggest that the act of border crossing was important in another way: it allowed mobile people to drive the creation of national contrasts across the boundary. Unlike Truett or Valerio-Jiménez, I am most interested in how border crossers influenced the political discourse on both sides and lent meaning to embryonic national differences.

Yet these meanings were hardly monolithic, and they remained contested as long as mobile people stayed in motion. The journey for most mobile people was seldom a one-way trip, and only infrequently did they cross over the border and stay put for a long period. Many Indians continually crossed over the border, pursuing a sort of play-off diplomacy that guaranteed their freedom more than any mass relocation might have. In mobility lay freedom for migrant Native Americans, but immigrants, Mexican peons, and others also returned to their points of origin in large numbers—even if they did not remain in continual motion as many horseback Indians did. After the Civil War, for instance, many blacks returned to Texas. So too did some immigrant Indians. Some of these groups maintain a presence on both sides of the border today. The Kickapoos, Black Seminoles, and migrant Mexican laborers in South Texas are examples of those whose lives are transnational and in continual motion.[9] Mobile peoples have contributed to the making of major national differences across the line, but the process whereby borders mutually constitute sharply contrasting nations is a dynamic one. That "liberty" lay on the Texas side for some and on the Mexican side for others amply illustrates just how central the border was (and is) in marking national differences.

My work also differs from others that have teased out subaltern contributions to the making of the border in that it covers a wide range of mobile people who crossed in both directions. Cattle rustlers, vigilantes, Texas Rangers, Mexican militias, and others also had a part to play in the making of the border and transnational mobility. To demonstrate the power of the border to set people in motion and dramatically affect nearby societies, I tell as comprehensive a story as possible and include many different people not often considered together. In uncovering this history, I bring together many different groups to suggest that their presence (and sometimes absence) in the borderlands affected histories of migrancy and mobility besides their own. Taken together, all of these mobile people had an important effect in the aggregate. They worked together to lend potentially subversive meanings to the newly devised dividing line, meanings that the border carries to this day.

I uncover stories about the people whom the great heroes of Texas independence sought to assign to the dustbin of history. By mobilizing routes across the international divide, they contributed to the elaboration of the international borderlands and, after 1848, to the making of the border itself. The arrival of a definitive border in 1848—a result of the Treaty of Guadalupe Hidalgo, which ended the U.S.-Mexico War—did not put a stop to transnational mobility but rather invited it. Many examples in the pages that follow demonstrate this point.

This book also contends that borders accrue significance not just from above. They also gain meaning from below, from groups like mobile Indians, runaway slaves, and migrant laborers, who sought shelter, asylum, and opportunity by crossing to the other side. Set afoot by circumstances that greatly reduced their life options, the border attracted outsiders, creating a vast array of mobile people in the U.S.-Mexico borderlands in the trade. In this scenario, borders encouraged international migration. Borders were meaningful, important, and stark—and many marginal figures quite literally lived and died by them. Newly "bordered lands" did not stop the movement of "people-in-between" as the state might have hoped. Quite the opposite. Newly reified borders encouraged transgression. And mobile people were especially important in constructing an unintended meaning of the border as an escape hatch.[10]

The coming of the border certainly did not end borderlands mobility. We have become used to thinking of imperial borderlands as offering all sorts of options for play-off diplomacy and social—as well as physical—mobility for the people in between empires and nations. After the coming of the border, however, opportunities supposedly disappear and formerly mobile people find themselves hemmed in on one side or the other, living lives of quiet desperation wholly within the steel-trap-like boundaries of their governing states. This is the formulation of Jeremy Adelman and Stephen Aron's deeply thoughtful and influential essay on borderlands. This book tells a very different story, however. Borders, rather than reducing opportunities, created them—setting people afoot, sending them to the other side in search of a better life for themselves. The arrival of borders created a "great system of roaming" and set an entire landscape in motion. This goes against the grain of the popular understanding of borders, that they end the autonomy of the people who used to live on far-flung frontiers. Some people persist in believing that leaky borders—that is, those that do not end transnational movement—are the result of insufficient attention from the state, that somehow resources or even a giant wall can fix the problem. It is the contention of this book that borders by nature leak, no matter how many resources governments expend to stop the flow of unauthorized border crossers.[11]

That transnational mobile people were important to the making of the border should become clear early on, but this book also traces their impact on the other side of the border in their host societies. Most significantly, this book argues that people who crossed the international line contributed to statecraft in Mexico. Their departure from Texas (and later the United States) was not neutral, and the lives they led in Mexico had political consequence. Mobile border crossers not only helped to construct a meaningful border that separated two young republics from one another. They also built a transnational network that invited further transgression. On the Mexican side, they contributed to building sovereignty in the distant, underpopulated, and underdeveloped northern Mexican frontier. They became great allies to the officials, diplomats, and officers who sought to tie the northern borderlands to the center of Mexico since they had similar interests and enemies. Local citizens, on the other hand, generally did not have the same appreciation for border crossers. Many *vecinos*—a word that translates as "neighbor" but more accurately means citizen and resident—saw outsiders as interlopers in their locally bounded worlds. They recognized the tremendous threat border crossers represented, and how they were at the root of continuing conflicts between the United States, Texas, and Mexico. Hence, mobile border-crossing people not only brought out conflicts with people on the other side of the border. They also brought strife between people who inhabited the same side of the border and their officials.

In considering the tensions caused by streams of cross-border migrants, this book has a dimension of political history. In statecraft, and the role that mobile people played in it, the major actors on the Mexican side are officials, politicians, officers, and diplomats. These were the people most vested in the Mexican national project and the people who sought out potential allies wherever they could find them. The Mexican nation was an abstract and distant concept in the Mexican North, and many locals saw federal officials as alien oppressors—especially when they invited troublesome outsiders to settle their territory. National authorities' attitudes to immigrants could contrast quite sharply with the local vecinos (and some local officials) who lived on the frontier and had the difficult task of inhabiting an area constantly under siege by invaders of both the Native American and filibusterer varieties. *Norteños* (northern Mexicans) generally fell within the "Federalist" (and later, Liberal) camp in Mexican politics, and they resented the heavy-handed "Centralist" (later, Conservative) policies enacted by authorities in Mexico City. Centralist leaders like Anastasio Bustamente or Santa Anna all too often wanted to strip the norteños of their cherished autonomy in the interest of yoking them more firmly to national projects. Not only did Centralists want to eliminate slavery, but they also wanted to abolish militias, disarm vecinos, enact tariffs, and regulate commerce. This was the reason that Zacatecas rebelled and Texas seceded in 1836.

Nevertheless, up until 1855—and despite a great number of military coup d'états—Centralists tended to dominate the political conversation in Mexico City, and this was an unhappy fact in the Mexican North. In exchange for following directives from Mexico City, northern vecinos received very little. Neither the local nor the state nor the national government had the resources to improve life or security for them. Norteños would have preferred autonomy, to decide their own course of action free from the meddling of Mexico City. Projects to attract immigrants and alleged troublemakers from Texas did not gain much traction among vecinos either. Many of the attempts where Centralists officers sought to enact policies that harnessed mobile people to national projects alienated local vecinos and brought on the fury of the Texans. Locals did not want more trouble in borderlands that already had woes enough, and national immigration projects all too often made their lives even more insecure.[12]

Yet we are very quick to write off any sort of positive effects that Centralism and Conservatism might have had—which is a legacy of a Mexican historiography largely centered on the rise of caudillos, dictators, and, later, a leviathan-like state or party in the early twentieth century. Many vecinos disliked the overreach of the state in the North and saw very little benefit in its presence there. There were a number of mobile people who used the border for leverage, however, and they saw things quite differently. More often than not, they tied their fates to the promises of officers and officials in the borderlands who said that they would enforce federal laws banning slavery, give citizenship to Native Americans, grant *amparo* (protection) and even, on occasion, ameliorate the worst abuses of debt servitude. Whether they actually fulfilled these promises or not is a different story, of course. Nevertheless, we should not completely dismiss the cause of Centralism and, later, Conservatism in the North as an alien and aggressive force implanted on fiercely independent vecinos who strained under the yoke of a tyrannical government. Runaway slaves and others in Mexico certainly did not feel this way. Neither did all vecinos.

The role that mobile people played in the elaboration of the borderlands, of setting national political and local actors off from one another, and in the making of the border between two distinct nations is the theme of this book. It is also a theme that has the potential to join histories of the nation-state and migration between the United States and Mexico, tracing them to the early nineteenth century. Brian DeLay's seminal *War of a Thousand Deserts* connects the histories of Mexico and the United States by locating the movement of international mobile people—in his case, raiding horseback Comanches.[13] Yet, in DeLay's work, we see how transnational movement actually undid Mexican sovereignty in the North—and ultimately cost the Mexicans a large swath of territory that they claimed. In *The Limits of Liberty* we see a case where some mobile people actually helped maintain Mexico's sovereignty in the North by, most obviously, taking up guns in defense of it. There were other ways that migrants to Mexico helped establish a federal presence in the Mexican North as well. Runaway slaves and immigrant Indians proved the greater magnanimity of Mexican laws toward racial others and might even have played a small role in shaping a more fluid Mexican racial identity. They lent meaning to a new international line dividing two starkly different racial regimes—well in advance of the invention of "Latin America" in the 1850s and the racial populist movements of the first half of the twentieth century.[14] When Mexican officials sheltered runaways, they demonstrated official Mexican liberality on issues of race, which was in itself a bold assertion of Mexico's independence and sovereignty.[15] This book argues for an important national presence in the Mexican borderlands that historians have for too long overlooked.

Further, nation building wrought by runaways was not limited to the Mexican side. On the other side of the border, in Texas, runaway debt peons from Mexico made Texans differentiate their freer labor conditions (for nonblacks anyway) from those on the Mexican side of the border. This too contributed to the making of meaningful national differences. It was the fact that oppressed people crossed the border, not the direction they were headed, that lent the international line meaning and by extension shaped nationalities on either side.

International migration made the nations facing each other across the Rio Grande dig in deep in defense of what they considered national principles. In most of the stories told in this book, the state actively discouraged international cooperation on the issue of runaways, something that might have had the effect of making things more peaceful along the border. Proposals for extradition treaties came and went, and the United States and Mexico would not come to terms until the early 1880s—a couple of decades beyond the scope of this book. There was a good reason for this failure to cooperate: getting along with the folks on the other side of the borderlands would have erased the very significant dividing line that Mexican and Texan officials alike were trying to put in place, to separate themselves from one another in an attempt to assert sovereignty and even define their national identities by way of contrast. (Of course locals did not see major differences as they traversed the border almost daily and met with people very similar to themselves on the other side. But this was not the way that either Texan or Mexican authorities intended the border to operate.)

As far as the Mexican North is concerned, this book tells a novel story—one of people who invested in the state and lived at the frontier, and one about people who found the border very meaningful. This should stand in stark contrast to studies that emphasize the fluidity of Tejano and mexicano lives along the border. It also traces the importance of Centralism and Conservatism in the Mexican North. Scholars generally frame the period between the highly centralist *siete leyes* (Seven Laws) of 1835 and the rise of Liberalism in Monterrey about twenty years later as a sort of dark age in the Mexican North, when local desires went unheeded, militias were unarmed, and autonomy dwindled to nothing in the face of detached and disinterested Centralist officials.[16] But there were some at least who did not see things this way, and this book tells their stories.

To sum up these thoughts on borders and mobilities, let us return to my example of the migrant Caddos. Alongside the Native Americans who immigrated to Coahuila in 1841, there was also a young black man. This runaway, a formerly enslaved person who escaped his former master on the other side of the Colorado River, approached the Caddo chief Coyote when his convoy passed near the headwaters of the Río Frío en route to Mexico. The young black man informed the chief that he wanted to join their migration into Mexico as he was "looking for a country in which he could acquire liberty." Coyote introduced him into the caravan, and they made the trip across the Rio Grande together. When they arrived in the district of Monclova, the prefect, de la Fuente, sent the black man off to town to earn his keep while the authorities figured out what to do with him. He would almost certainly not be returned to his former master. Mexico had abolished slavery (with the exception of the Anglo colonies in Texas) in 1829, and runaway slaves immediately took advantage of the more liberal laws in Mexico. Furthermore, Mexicans were highly unlikely to return fugitives from American slavery to their former masters as they wanted to demonstrate their magnanimity on issues of race. Already in 1833, just four years after emancipation in Mexico, the sheer number of runaways from Louisiana instigated some Americans in New Orleans to try to come up with some sort of extradition treaty with Mexico. But nothing came of these efforts to achieve comity.[17] Despite what the historian Sarah Cornell has contended, when runaways crossed over into Mexico, generally they were safe—even if they found that other types of insecurity dogged their lives.[18] There is no greater example of how strongly people invested in the border from the moment of its very inception than runaway slaves.

In the narrative that follows, I uncover an alternative epistemology of the international boundary. Many of the meanings that mobile people— often working in tandem with the Mexican state—lent to the border are now lost to us, sedimented over by time and doomed to condescension by history, but some of them are still with us. In either case, many uncounted generations have invested heavily in the border, lending it novel meanings and reimagining its significance. I show that the idea and the reality of the border were not always the same thing. As much as the border was flexible, fungible, and elastic, some people still willingly and even gratefully lived in accordance with its fictions.

Terminology

There are a number of terms used in this book that, though they may not have been used at the time, lend historical precision to the analysis. Most controversially, this book uses the term "Anglo Texan" to refer to white transplant and native-born Texans of Anglo origin. I use the term "Tejano/a" to refer to Texans of Latino/a ancestry. Both terms are anachronistic. The victors of San Jacinto referred to themselves as "Texians" in order to differentiate themselves from Latino/a Texans, but I do not use that antiquated term in this book. "Tejano" is also problematic since in the lower strata of society it is very difficult to make distinctions between Tejanos and Mexicans—especially as this book argues that there were a great number of Mexican nationals moving in and out of the state during this period. Many Tejanos simply wanted to steer clear of the conflicts on both sides, and their national affiliation was not always clear to Anglo Texans. (This was especially true when they sought refuge on the other side of the border.) In order to clarify my usage, when I refer to people as "Mexican" (*mexicano/a*) I mean either nationals of that country or people who mostly resided on that side of the border. "Texan" is a category that today is inclusive of both class and race, but the Texans I refer to in this book were white, and generally they lived on the eastern side of the Colorado River before the 1850s. Alternatively, I may follow a widely used convention in Texas history and refer to them as Anglos.[19] There were Anglo Texans who felt differently from the ones I discuss in this book, who were not nearly so monolithic in their racism or vitriol. Their voices are somewhat lost to the larger story, unfortunately, as they did not drive political discourse or violence along the border.

"Native American" is an equally problematic category. I try to be as specific as possible when referring to the ethnic or tribal identities of Indians, but I cannot always call Native Americans by the names they would have preferred due to a scarcity of evidence. I use the terms "Native Americans" and "Indians" interchangeably, but I avoid the term "American Indians" for the sake of clarity. Many in Latin America would have considered themselves "Americans" in the nineteenth century (and beyond). Labeling Indians with a national identity that has come to be associated solely with the United States obfuscates the transnational aspect of their lives. The Native Americans in this work whom I refer to most often were the highly mobile tribes of South Texas, chiefly the Lipan Apaches and groups affiliated with them. I divide them into the groups that anthropologists and ethnohistorians have deployed to discuss different branches of the Lipan people. I also write about a more highly organized migration of Indians into Mexico whom I refer to as immigrant tribes, following the Spanish term for them (*tribus emigradas*). These tribes were ethnically mixed, and in fact they consisted of several distinct migrations—something that becomes clear in chapters 2 and 5. Included among these tribes were Nadaco Caddos, Seminoles, Western Cherokees, Black Seminoles, Southern Kickapoos, and a few others.

I also try to use the term "enslaved people" rather than "slaves" where I can to acknowledge the failure of slavery to reduce the humanity of

African Americans to terms defined by their captors. There are a few places where the use of the adjective "enslaved" is awkward, however, and I have used the term "slave" for clarity. In addition, I use the term "runaway slave" throughout since I find the contradiction in this phrasing both productive and interesting. A "runaway" by definition resists his or her enslavement.

There are a number of words and place-names that will not be familiar to U.S. American historians. At first use of a Spanish term, it is in italics followed by the English translation in parenthesis; subsequent uses are not italicized. I have also chosen place-names to reflect the transnational theme of the book, keeping the Spanish term when it is relevant, but I refer to the Río Bravo by its English equivalent, Rio Grande. This seems to be the most common convention in English-speaking academia, and my preferred terminology—Río Grande/Bravo—is simply too unwieldy to use consistently. Other geographic locations that need some explanation are regional. "Mexican North," in this book, refers to the northernmost stretches of the states of Coahuila, Nuevo León, and Tamaulipas (which, if one wants to be precise, is really the Mexican Northeast). People who lived in the Northeast were either mexicano/as or norteños. Most documents refer to the gentile non-Indian citizens in this region as *vecinos* (literally, "neighbors") and I follow this convention. My geographic designations on the other side of the border need some explanation as well. "South Texas" refers to the primarily Tejano region south of Austin. "West Texas" refers to the plains in the western half of the state, generally dominated by Indians of different types. Again, these geographic designators are anachronistic; any area on the other side of the Colorado River was considered West Texas in the early nineteenth century. In the interest of resonating with a modern readership, however, I have chosen not to reproduce the terms used then.

The Early History of Migrancy in the Rio Grande Borderlands

Decades before the international boundary arrived at its present-day location in 1848, the territory on either side of the Rio Grande was already a borderland. Over the course of the preceding century and a half, a great number of cultures had come into contact with one another in the coastal plains of present-day Texas, Tamaulipas, and Coahuila. They had created an entirely new world there. Originally Karankawa, Tonkawa, Coahuiltecan, Caddo, Carrizo, Pinto, and other Indians dominated the plains, constituting a Gulf Coast Indian culture that shared a few similarities but also contained a great many linguistic and cultural differences. Newcomers would disrupt this group in the 1700s—although their diseases heralded their coming long before they actually arrived.[20]

The influx of new migrants in the 1700s began to transform the Rio Grande frontier from a grand *despoblada*—or sparsely populated zone— into a borderland characterized by a significant degree of intercultural contact and exchange. Comanches and Lipan Apaches were among the first to disrupt the ancient aboriginal world of the coastal plains when they began migrating into West and then South Texas in the early 1700s. By the 1730s, a pioneering group of Canary Islanders joined these newly arrived horseback Indians in Texas, settling in the municipality of Béxar. By the late 1700s these Canary Islanders were joined by other migrants, mostly settlers from Central Mexico who spread out along the San Antonio River and swelled the populations of both Béxar and La Bahía. On the other side of the Rio Grande, José de Escándon founded a colony of Spanish Creoles in 1747 in an area that would one day become northeastern Tamaulipas. All of these migrant groups dreamed that geographic mobility would somehow translate into economic mobility, social mobility, or greater liberty. When they migrated they hoped to find the opportunity and resources that had eluded them in their homelands. They shared this vision with the many, many mobile people who would follow their tracks into the borderlands of the eastern Rio Grande. In the meantime, the arrival of all these new groups to the Rio Grade borderlands created an entirely new demography in Texas and the Mexican North— one riven by multiple ethnic boundaries.[21]

It did not take long for newly arrived peoples to begin interacting with the earlier residents. Over time some of their cultures blended but rarely on equal terms. Along the Rio Grande, the families descended from the earliest colonists defended their Spanish ancestry and sharply contrasted their identities with those of the native *indios* (Indians) of *el norte* (northern Mexico). Some local Carrizo Indians integrated into Hispanic society through enslavement or the institution of servitude, becoming *criados* (bonded youths) whom paternalistic Spaniards intended to tutor in the ways of civilization and Christianity. The large number of debt peons who populated the Mexican North in the nineteenth century descended from these former servants, but in the intervening years they shed their original ethnic identity. By 1800, *mestizaje* (ethnic or cultural mixing) had occurred on a large scale in the Villas del Norte, incorporating the descendants of formerly independent Indians into norteño society as subordinates. By the 1830s, the category "indio" disappeared from the census roles altogether along the Rio Grande. Around the same time, a similar ethnic rebirth occurred in San Antonio de Béxar among the Indians who had integrated into Hispanic society.[22]

But there were also the Lipans and Comanches, fairly new arrivals themselves, who interacted quite differently with Latino/as. They were enticed by the new, fuzzy borders separating Euro-American and Native American communities, and they saw great opportunity in these boundaries. Horseback Native Americans, including Lipans, Comanches, and a few others, dipped in and out of settlements, exercising a type of situational mobility that allowed them to visit Tejano and norteño villages and ranches for much-needed food, horses, and captives.[23] The social geography of the eastern Rio Grande borderlands encouraged this practice. A great space of Indian refuge existed outside of the small islands of Euro-American settlement, sustained by extensive raiding and trading networks.[24] The Spanish settlers in the North of Mexico acknowledged their precarious situation, and their insecurity registered in the layout of the landscape itself. Spaniards built ranches north of the towns that dotted the southern bank of the Rio Grande that they intended as a last line of defense against hostile Indians who raided them from the safety of the nearby despoblada. Time and time again, ranchers instead had to flee their properties and retreat to the nearby municipal centers. They only returned when the threat had subsided—and the Indians had already driven off their horses and cattle.[25]

Missions and presidios served a similarly unintended function as the Tejano ranches in that they too supplied the largely nomadic Indians who dipped in and out of Hispanic settlements. They were institutions established in the vast despoblada that looked south, toward the center of the empire and the seat of ecclesiastical and military authority. But in reality they were isolated islands in a vast Indian sea. In Coahuila and South Texas, Comanches, Lipans, Karankawas, and others gleaned resources from the lonely missions before retreating back into the vast Indian Territory that surrounded them. The Lipans soon became notorious for pressing their advantage. They were brazen in their demand for gifts and supplies from the missions and refused to stay in those places and receive religious instruction. Not only did this raise the ire of the people in charge of these institutions, the way Lipans treated the missions as a sort of all-you-can-eat buffet irritated those few Indians who remained at the missions in the early 1800s. Nor did the settlers much like the expensive policy of placating with gifts Native Americans who had no intention of incorporating with them.[26]

They would not have to worry about the missions much longer. After Mexican independence, the missions underwent full secularization in 1823, destroying one of the few lifelines that connected el norte to the center. In addition to separating Texas and Coahuila from the center of the new country, secularization contributed to a budding sense of autonomy among many people in the Mexican North, particularly in Béxar.[27] In the following years most former "Mission" Indians stayed in barrios near the old missions, but they registered as mestizajes rather than Indians on census roles so as to distinguish themselves from the "indios bárbaros."[28] The presidios underwent significant changes after independence too. In fact, presidio soldiers had always been too immobile and short on resources to deal effectively with nomadic raiders. Already by the end of the eighteenth-century, *pobladores* (settlers) took it upon themselves to defend their homes from raiders without the help of the presidios, and they pressed their own horses and arms into service against the enemy, forming flying volunteer companies (*companías volantes*).[29] They recognized that highly mobile Indian raiders could not be countered with immobile, static, and poorly staffed presidios. With the establishment of Mexican Liberal control briefly in the 1820s, responsibility for frontier defense passed almost entirely to the citizens of the territory. The local militias prided themselves on their mobility, which would "give chase to and defeat" Indian enemies while the declining presidios were garrisoned with national troops, drawn from the population of "vagrants and disorderly" persons who lived nearby. These troops were used sparingly, only to supplement the national army.[30]

By the 1820s, the Mexican settlers and Indian migrants who added to the population of the great northern borderlands were joined by two new groups. Stephen Austin, along with three hundred families and a legion of squatters, crossed the U.S.-Mexico border into East Texas in the early 1820s to establish a colony. Other empresarios soon followed, establishing new Anglo, Mexican, and even Irish colonies in Texas.[31] Like those who preceded them, these new arrivals hoped to achieve riches, prosperity, and an opportunity to start again in Texas. Not coincidentally, many of the immigrants who moved into Texas during this decade had problems with debt or the law, and Texas promised a new start. Many also sought out cheaper lands in Texas to embark on new agricultural enterprises, usually with the labor of enslaved people. Tejanos found themselves outnumbered in the mid- to late 1820s, but they became important cultural brokers between Anglo immigrants and the Mexican state.[32]

Less well known is a group of "Americans" who crossed the border from Louisiana around the same time. Sixty Cherokee families went into

Mexican Texas in 1820 under the leadership of Chief Bowles, who had recently quarreled with American land surveyors in Arkansas. He initiated what became sustained diplomacy between the Cherokees and the Mexican government, and he brought a significant number of kinsmen with him when he crossed the Sabine River from American Louisiana into Mexican Texas.[33] More Native Americans soon joined him, immigrating from the United States into Texas in the 1820s to escape grasping U.S. Indian policy. This fact greatly surprised the famous visitor General Manuel de Mier y Terán when he made his reconnaissance of the Mexican North—including Texas—in the late 1820s. He found that many Kickapoos, Shawnees, Dealwares, Choctaws, Chicaksaws, and Cosushattas had arrived over the course of the previous decade, numbering more than ten thousand all told.[34]

Organization

Even before the temporal scope of this book (roughly 1821–61), the coastal plains along the banks of the Rio Grande had a long history of immigration and cultural interchange. These borderlands became more cosmopolitan in the decades surrounding the establishment of the international border. This book is organized into nine chapters that follow a rough chronological trajectory.

Chapter 1 begins with an overview of the Lipan Apaches and a few other affiliated Indian groups who arrived in the borderlands in the early eighteenth century. It focuses on the era that followed Mexican independence in 1821 to tell the story of how the new state sought to forge alliances and loyalties with the eastern Rio Grande borderlands' most troublesome Indian inhabitants. Mexican officials dreamed of using the Native Americans in the area as a sort of buffer zone, but this dream all too often foundered upon the rocky shores of Indian independence. Chapter 2 continues to trace the effect of Indians on the rise of Mexico in the North but shifts its focus to a different group, immigrant tribes. Again we see attempts by the Mexican state to embrace and incorporate the native peoples set afoot by white supremacist government policies in the United States.

Chapter 3 discusses an entirely different group of border crossers. It traces the origins of the borderlands between Mexico and the United States as a "line of liberty" between a slaveholding country and a non-slaveholding country. It queries the many meanings of liberty devised in the age of the Texan Revolution by retelling the story of secession from the vantage of runaway slaves. Chapter 4, meanwhile, traces the history of different mobile people but ones who used the border in a similarly emancipatory way. It focuses on runaway debt peons from Mexico who crossed the border and found freer working conditions in Texas. This chapter ends by demonstrating that runaway debt peons lent significant meaning to the new border and even promoted a political agenda for Texas that, oddly enough, focused on more liberal working conditions for migrant workers.

Chapters 5 and 6 continue the story of international migration, tracing the effect that the the the border—newly reified by the Treaty of Guadalupe Hidalgo—had on immigrant tribesmen and women as well as runaway slaves after 1848. Chapter 5 tells the tragic story of the Mexican failure to incorporate Seminoles, Kickapoos, and others in the Mexican North due to a lack of resources and mutual understanding. Chapter 6 details the many ways that runaways from slavery turned the new border into a line of liberty and continually taxed the resources and political will of the Mexican North.

Beginning in chapter 7, the narrative focus zooms out to examine the ways that mobile people contributed to the souring of relations between Mexico and Texas by crossing and recrossing the border and playing both sides off against each other. Chapter 7 concentrates on the violence of both the vigilante and state-sponsored varieties that de facto expanded the slaveholders' regime into the Mexican North. Chapter 8, meanwhile, looks into the way that Lipan Apaches continued to cross from one side to the other and affect relations between the United States and Mexico. Chapter 9 concludes the narrative by tracing the evolution of a new Liberal regime in the Mexican North that was more willing to work alongside Texans to wrest the border (and its many meanings) from border crossers. This chapter tells the story of a Mexican campaign led by newly ascendant Liberal officers and manned enthusiastically by vecinos who at last saw things the same way as their commanders. They fought against the Lipan Apaches, dealing them a blow that ultimately proved disastrous for them. The norteños' military response to the Lipans also augured a greater degree of cooperation across the border between Mexican and American officials, often brokered by interrelated Tejano and norteño families. That cooperation would only grow stronger in the decades that followed.

Chapter 9 suggests that Mexican and Texan officials pioneered new ways of working together in the mid- to late 1850s, but it does not go so far as to say that they erased the old transnational routes laid down by the Indians in the eighteenth century and then traveled by so many others in the centuries to come. It is my contention that these old routes have never disappeared. Throughout the book many different and long-forgotten maps, or territorialities, come into view as I trace the paths of long-forgotten mobile people. People and the environment—usually in conjunction—have the power to transform abstract spaces on maps into particular social places.[35] There were, for instance, any number of Native geographies, territorialities, or social spaces that crisscrossed zones claimed by the Anglos, Mexicans, and powerful Indian empires. Sociospatial practices had a tendency to endure and shape even the most concerted efforts of states to bend particular places into conformity with their maps. Alternative routes and geographic epistemologies survived, despite the attempts of some governments and their local deputies to lend the border meaning as a line that hermetically sealed one nation off from the other. Alternative routes endured and encompassed a whole history of transborderland social practices that intercepted the new, sup-posedly evacuated space mapped out by the new boundary.

These new geographies intersected older ones, sometimes adding power to the conceptions of both—sometimes reinforcing the new national dividing line and sometimes undermining it. Lipan Apache territory, for instance, included large swaths of the map claimed by Mexico and Texas, from the Bolsón de Mapimí up through the Nueces Strip. African America had its own borderlands as well, reaching from the empresario grant of Austin's colony down to Nacimiento de los Negros, just outside of Músquiz in present-day Coahuila. When North American expansion pushed a human wave ahead of it, refugees responded creatively, claiming their own space in advance of the shock troops of empire who followed closely on their heels, turning frontiers into newly colonized U.S. American places. They reimagined the zones just beyond the edges of Anglo expansion to fit their own needs. When the Caddos and their friends arrived in Monclova, moving from eastern Texas to Coahuila to escape grasping Texans, they pioneered routes and laid down roots across a newly expanded Caddo map that transcended the narrow confines of the American and Mexican nation-states. Many more mobile people would follow in the wake of the Caddos, expanding the map of an alternative Native America, refining it, and adding way stations and anchor points along the way. These routes have long been paved over by the stuff of more recent memory, but it behooves us to remember that the highway that takes us from San Antonio past dusty Texas outposts and into Piedras Negras is the same route traveled by runaway slaves and refuge-seeking Indians over 150 years ago.

1 / La Frontera del Norte: Lipan Apaches and the Troubled Rise of Mexico in the Borderlands

In July 1829, the Mexican officers in charge of the old presidio at La Bahía ran out of gifts for their Indian allies. Unfortunately for them, they ran low on supplies just as an envoy of Indians arrived. Which tribe, ethnicity, language group, or "nation" these Indians belonged to is unclear. Mexicans often recorded this information when they encountered Indians but did not do so this time. Probably they were Lower Lipans since La Bahía was located within their territory and had long served as a point of contact between their people and the Spanish. These Indian visitors might also have come from the Tonkawa, a people who were closely affiliated with the Lipans. The commander of La Bahía only noted that some "peaceful" Indians from the surrounding area approached the presidio in search of the gifts they considered their due. Whoever they were, the Indians found disappointment rather than the supplies they had hoped to receive. The commander of the presidio informed them that he had nothing for them and that the Supreme Government in Mexico City had not even been able to pay his own salary. Everybody, he told the Indians, had to make sacrifices. The Indians responded angrily to the commander's refusal. They abused him bitterly, calling him "captain cochino" (captain pig), "mezquino" (skinflint), and other things that were "even more indecorous." The Indians must have wondered what good these people were. They showed up in small numbers, claimed territory they clearly did not control, and then failed to keep their promises.[1]

The officers were there because the founders of the new nation of Mexico had dreams for the far North, just as their colonial forebears did. Immediately following the war for Mexico's independence, the Mexican government picked up the old Bourbon (or late colonial) custom of handing out gifts to loyal and steadfast Indian allies in the borderlands in exchange for promoting Mexico's national interests. The gifts that the Indians received were a form of tribute, but getting the Indians on the Mexican military's side would pay off in the end. In exchange for giving out resources, Mexican officers charged the independent Indians with protecting the interests of Mexico in Texas. They were supposed to fight invaders, develop the territory, and transform themselves into *buenos mexicanos* (good citizens).[2] This practice of gift-giving was born out of necessity since it resulted from the chronic problem that Mexicans, and the Spanish before them, had populating their vast, far-flung northern frontiers. This diplomatic strategy never really worked. For one thing, the frontier was a low priority in the troubled and newly independent Mexican Republic. For another, the officers in charge of pacifying the frontier never had the resources on hand to placate their Indian friends, who were stronger than their allies in the Mexican government.

Chronically short of cash, Mexicans rarely delivered the promised goods to their Indian allies, which had consequences. Rather than security through alliances and friendships, the broken promises of the Mexican government created enemies instead. If the promised resources were not forthcoming, Lipan Apaches had little compunction about taking them without permission—which alienated them from many Mexicans, who brutalized both the Lipans and the vecino populations, leading to long-standing hatreds.[3] In addition, sustained contact born out of decades of attempted diplomacy and exchange had made the Lipans familiar with the locations of Mexican peoples, resources, and pastures on the distant frontier. As a result, vecinos trembled before the independent Indians who all too often rode off toward the horizon with their animals and children in tow. The considerable familiarity that Lipans had with their borderlands milieu made them frightening enemies indeed to the vecinos on the Mexican side of the border. Their alliance was a gift to the Texans, and by joining up with them they would not have to come to terms with Mexico for decades.

Independent Indians in the borderlands have warranted a good deal of scholarly attention in recent years, and we now know that they managed to stymie Mexico's attempts to bring its borderlands under control. Whether part of a vast "Comanche Empire" that ruled over the West

Texas plains and beyond until the middle of the nineteenth century or as the antagonists in an undeclared war that turned northern Mexico into a "thousand deserts," independent Indians held sway over the hinterlands of the North American continent. U.S. Americans and Mexicans alike had difficulty recognizing the military strength of independent Indians in the borderlands, and they preferred to look through them and blame each other for the violence endemic to their frontier societies. Each country assumed that the other was behind the Indian raids, either by arming them or somehow putting them up to it.[4] Scholars now know that Indians often acted alone, and if they acted in concert with other powers it was most often to pursue their own interests. This recent scholarship on independent borderlands Indians is very compelling, and it manages to recenter the perspective of western U.S. history squarely on the role played by Native Americans. In most cases these histories focus more on contact or interaction with Euro-Americans than on Indian autonomy. Nevertheless they have established the fact that Indians were primary players in the stories of western borderlands. If there is any shortcoming in this scholarship, it is that it puts so much emphasis on the military aspect of Indian independence, which is a function of the concentration on the Comanches. Lipan strength did not stem from military power but from subversive knowledge and mobility. They knew the land and cultures of the people who inhabited the borderlands well enough to dip in and out of Mexican "civilization" and their own reserve in South Texas. Geographic savvy, familiarity with vecino culture, and a willingness to play different populations off against one another in the borderlands allowed them to remain independent.

Lipans' skill at playing off major powers against one another is well known. Thomas Britten, who has written the most comprehensive history of the Lipan Apaches, argues that they maintained their independence through military struggle, theft, forming fleeting alliances, and harvesting the wild herds of buffalo in Texas. Through self-reliance and strategic alliances, they avoided domination by the many more powerful groups who encroached upon their South Texas domain from the nineteenth century on.[5] But while Britten looks at a number of different strategies employed by the Lipans to ensure their survival despite worsening odds, I consider one in depth here. I argue that it was territorial knowledge and familiarity with the borderlands that made it possible for the Lipan Apaches to maintain their treasured independence. Like Britten, I argue that the struggle to maintain independence exposed the Lipans to many dangers, but, unlike him, I do not emphasize how

historical changes brought crisis to the Lipan Apaches. I am more interested in how shifts in the South Texan/northern Mexican borderlands
brought opportunities. In this respect, my analysis is more in line with
Nancy McGown Minor's concentration on the "survivance" (to borrow
Gerald Vizenor's provocative term) of the Lipan Apaches.[6] As the Mexicans, Tejanos, Comanches, and Anglos closed in on Lipan ranges from
all sides, the tribe might have been doomed. Instead, they found new
powers to play off against one another to maintain their independence.

Lipans and the Nascent Mexican State

The Lipan Apaches began to move into Texas in the early eighteenth
century in advance of the powerful Comanches. During this period,
Texas was (nominally) a part of the Spanish Empire, but for a while
the Lipans dominated parts of that territory, living off of the buffalo
herds and engaging in some trade with the Spanish. The Lipans were, in
Minor's term, "the men in the middle," between the Spanish to the south
and the Comanches to the north and west. Their enemies were "at their
backs," and the Spaniards were "on the horizons." By 1750, some bands
of Lipans reached the Medina River and a few others had set up camp
on the Rio Grande. Largely migratory, the "Forest Lipans"—as the Spanish referred to the Lipan tribes in South Texas—pursued buffalo from
the Texas Hill Country and made their winter camps along the Pecos
River. Some even crossed into northern Coahuila, perhaps to avoid the
smallpox that Spaniards brought to their populations. They also became
greatly skilled at domesticating the wild *mesteños* (mustangs) of South
Texas and taught some of the earliest vaqueros, who spoke admiringly
of Lipan technique. Slowly, as they found themselves in sustained contact with Spaniards, theft began to replace bronco busting among the
Lipans as the preferred way to grow their horse wealth. Lipans found it
much easier to integrate domesticated horses, and norteño herds simply
represented too tempting a target to resist. By the late 1700s, domesticated horses greatly outnumbered mustangs in Lipan herds.[7] Even before
an actual border existed, Lipans were adept at taking what they needed
from vecino populations and then disappearing into the wilds of South
Texas. This did not make for good relations between neighbors.

Sometimes the Spanish sought to incorporate and befriend the plains
Indians that advanced into Texas during the eighteenth century, turning
them into allies and plying them with goods. But when the carrot did not
work, they turned to the stick. Presidio soldiers and military colonists

FIGURE 1. Lipan Apache's arrived in the lower Rio Grande in the eighteenth century and continued to cross the Trans-Nueces frontier with impunity up to the late 1800s. LC-USZC 4–5368 (color film copy transparency); Library of Congress Prints and Photographs Division, Washington, D.C. 20540 USA.

chased down refractory Indians, especially from the 1780s on. Lipan Apaches, in particular, were targets of Spanish colonial violence because of their reputation for theft. This dual-pronged approach to pacifying independent Indians bore some fruit—although the great borderlands historian David J. Weber has insisted that sporadic episodes of peace along New Spain's far northern frontier owed more to deft diplomacy and a desire for peaceful trade than violent reduction undertaken by the Spanish colonial state. Nevertheless, through a combination of arming some Indians, fighting others (the Lipan Apaches were actually slated for extermination by the Spaniards), and paying off a few more, New Spain's farthest northern inhabited frontiers knew some peace in the last two decades of the eighteenth century. It was an expensive policy, and some groups like the Comanches clearly valued their independence more than their alliance with Spain, but all things considered, the colonial-era peace was better than the alternative.[8]

Unfortunately, the comparative tranquillity of the late Bourbon era—which lasted from the mid-eighteenth to the early nineteenth century—collapsed as soon as fighting broke out between the colonists of New Spain and the mother country. Mexico, like other Latin American colonies, demanded the restoration of Fernando VII after Napoleon removed the Bourbons from the Spanish throne in 1808. Then, in 1810, a parish priest in a small country town in the Bajío ascended a church tower, called together his parishioners, and cried out for the return of the king from Bonaparte's captivity. Mayhem ensued. The padre's flock grew into an enormous army, and New Spain began its long, bloody course toward independence. This war reached the North as well, and Indians took advantage of the chaos, especially when republican Tejanos overthrew the royal government in 1811–13. Lipans made peace with the royal authorities briefly, then broke it quickly thereafter, raiding for supplies alongside the Tonkawa. Then, in 1816, when the Comanches made peace with a band of Lipans led by El Cojo, these unlikely allies gained access to the vast trans-Nueces borderlands, its horse wealth, and its potential captives. For the final years of the revolution, the Latino/a population of Texas and Tamaulipas found themselves the targets of Lipan Apaches who coveted both their horses and their children. The Indians rustled animals in great numbers and kidnapped many Spanish-speaking children, bringing them into their bands to replenish their own dwindling numbers. The Comanches harvested the Mexicans in a similar fashion but a bit farther to the west—effectively dividing the spoils of the war-torn borderlands with the Lipans. The alliance between Comanches and

Lipans did not last long, but in the meanwhile the population of Texas diminished as many *fronterizos* (frontier colonists) moved toward the interior of Mexico and remade their lives farther south in safer environs, abandoning the potential wealth of South Texas and Tamaulipas to the Indians.[9]

The Mexican war for independence produced a violent, tumultuous train of events throughout the old viceroyalty of New Spain, and when the new nation of Mexico ultimately emerged from the ashes of the colonial order eleven years later, the revolution had lost much of its original meaning. A newly independent Mexico entered the world stage as an empire ruled by a privileged Creole turned revolutionary—and then emperor. Augustín Iturbide I ruled over the empire of Mexico for about one year. His overthrow in early 1823 owed to the divide between Mexicans who wanted to continue colonial traditions and those who wanted to emulate the liberal democracies emerging along the Atlantic, especially the United States.[10] This division between Centralists and Federalists, as these two camps named themselves, would not go away anytime soon. In the North, vecinos tended toward federalism and its doctrine of decentralized power since they felt distant from the center of authority in Mexico City. Unfortunately for them, they were most often saddled with officials of a Centralist persuasion until the 1850s.

During Iturbide's brief tenure, another growing problem in the North emerged. This was the arrival of masses of displaced Native Americans at Mexico's border with the United States along the Sabine River in the 1820s. (The Adams-Onís Treaty of 1819 established the eastern border between Texas and Louisiana at this river.) The introduction of entire new groups of ethnic, linguistic, religious, and cultural aliens to the western Louisiana frontier beginning in 1817 destabilized an already volatile situation. Kickapoos, Delawares, and Caddos began to arrive in far western Louisiana to take advantage of the fertile hunting grounds in the Lost Prairie near the Red River. They also enjoyed being beyond the reach of either nation-state, in an area considered by both the Spanish and U.S. Americans as a neutral zone. This borderland, distant as it was from centers of Euro-American settlement, had a drawing power that would only increase once the Sabine became the eastern Mexican border. By 1817, two hundred or so Cherokees had joined the other displaced Indians on the eastern side of the Sabine River, in the contested area between Spain and the United States. They soon began to press deeper into disputed territory west of the river as more and more American Anglos began to arrive in Louisiana after the conclusion of the War of

1812.[11] The Indians pressing into Texas from Louisiana, in turn, began to push the Lipans and other Indian groups of Texas who predated them deeper into the region and closer to the major Mexican settlements at Béxar and Goliad.

Another root cause for instability in Texas was competition over a basic resource of the North American plains. The Anglo Americans who poured into western Louisiana once they cleared the Great Raft on the Red River, needed more horses. Their demand for horses soon destabilized relations between Comanches and Tejanos. The Comanches, who were the great horsemen of the plains, fulfilled the Americans' demand for horses beginning in the 1820s through raiding and then selling their plunder to various intermediary Indians like the Pawnee. Many of the horses that ended up in Louisiana began their lives in Tejano herds.[12] The Comanches were not alone in taking advantage of the opportunities opened up by these new Anglo populations, however. Lipans also stole horses from Tejano herds and then sold them to Americans. Even worse, they did so in exchange for the guns that the Spanish had long refused to provide them.[13]

The solution to this problem for the new Mexican nation was to make alliances with the Native peoples of Texas and turn them against the American threat and the most hostile Indians. Indians held the balance of power in the borderlands that lay between Mexican Texas and Louisiana, and although they were not united politically, they outnumbered Tejanos by fifteen or twenty to one.[14] In 1822, cognizant of their precarious hold on the frontier, representatives of the Mexican "empire" approached the major Indian groups of Texas with new terms.

The Lipans had been especially troublesome to Spanish colonial officials, who had long sought to isolate them from other Indian groups like the Comanches by making constant war on them. After independence, Iturbide sought to change course and bring the Lipans into the nation, so imperial agents led by Anastasio Bustamente approached the Lipan chiefs Cuelga de Castro and Yolcha Pocaropa from the Nutria del Sol (Tche Shä) band that lived outside of San Antonio, inviting them to Mexico City to sign a treaty. His agents subsequently asked the Lipans to secure their homelands against Mexico's enemies and to unite with the imperial troops when they fought against intruders who approached the Frontera del Norte. They planned to turn the Lipans into buffer Indians—allies nominally subject to the Mexican government—who would protect the area from outside threats in exchange for land, munitions, and the right to round up mustangs.[15]

Merely forming an alliance was never enough for Mexican officers, however. Officials expected Indians to recognize Mexican sovereignty, and they pushed them to assimilate to "civilization," the hallmarks of which were the Spanish language, Catholicism, sedentary agrarianism, European clothing, and adoption of the basic tenets of European culture—however strange and foreign these practices seemed to them. "Civilization" had its roots in the old world, but it was the standard by which Europeans measured all other cultures. At best, non-European societies were on their way to becoming civilized, although most indigenous cultures that Europeans observed fell woefully far from the mark.[16]

When they made treaties with Indians, Mexicans invariably included measures intended to tutor them in the ways of civilized society. In the treaty with the Lipan chiefs, Mexican officials promised to send a priest and a Spanish-speaking official to the Lipans. Becoming Catholic was especially important to their incorporation into Mexican society and treaties with both Lipans and Comanches in Texas as well as Coahuila and Nuevo León often hinged on this condition. (Even whites had to convert to Catholicism, a condition that the historian José Ángel Hernández believes discouraged European immigration.) The Lipans were also supposed to turn captives and prisoners of war over to the Mexicans rather than exchange or exploit them or adopt them into their tribe. It was hoped that this agreement would end the ad hoc, unsupervised, violent, and chaotic system of intercultural exchange that dated back centuries.[17] It could also expand Mexico's control over the frontier.

The most important request that the Mexicans made of the Lipans in exchange for gifts was that they cease their roaming. The power of the Lipans flowed from their willingness to move across space and boundaries to seek out resources and new opportunities.[18] At the dawn of Mexican independence, the vast northern frontier was a semi-anarchic reserve and a place of refuge to which independent Indians could retreat and carve out autonomous spaces for themselves. Through deploying play-off diplomacy and practicing the well-rehearsed art of the retreat, mobile Lipans managed to hold on to their liberty. It was this power that Mexicans had the most difficulty reconciling. When Indians did not stay where they were supposed to they called the authority of the national government into question. Civilized people stayed in one place—where the state could extract services from them and where they could plant corn and make deserts bloom.[19]

As much as they hoped to dictate terms, Mexicans recognized that arrangements had to be reciprocal since they simply did not have the ability to enforce their fiats through force. Thus, in exchange for their service and peace, Lipans were promised water rights and titles to lands not yet claimed by Mexicans (*terrenos baldíos*)—although they likely never received them.[20] Other favors were granted to them as well. For example, they could continue rounding up the mustangs that wintered in the Nueces Strip. Of course, they had to return any strays they found. The way the Mexicans saw it, as soon as a vecino put his brand on a horse, the animal was transformed from a resource available to the Indians into a commodity protected by the law. Land worked in a similar way. In addition to land, water, and mustangs, the Lipans received gifts and resources, doled out to them at the old presidio of La Bahía.[21] Lipans also expected entertainment when they visited the Mexican villages in Texas. Typically money for their entertainment was drawn from the Fondo de Indios, and in 1824, Ramón Músquiz, *jefe político* of Béxar, and Felipe Enrique Neri, Baron de Bastrop, requested sixty-six pesos for the "urgent necessity" of amusing Lipan visitors.[22]

The peace process appeared to be on track as both Lipans and Comanches sent delegates to Mexico City to celebrate their respective treaties in 1822–23. Then, in 1824, a rising star in the Mexican government introduced an energetic new policy in the North. General Bustamente established a military canton in the borderlands of Texas and northeastern Mexico with three hundred presidial soldiers, which was an attempt to flex the new nation's military muscle in the distant frontier. Unfortunately, the soldiers of the presidios never received the pay, uniforms, or rations they needed. As a result they were constantly demoralized, and discipline was lax. The authorities, when they were honest with themselves, realized that these soldiers could not hold back the many Indians and Americans advancing toward them from the plains of Texas.[23] In addition to professional soldiers and military colonies, vecinos in Texas, Nuevo León, Coahuila, and Tamaulipas were expected to serve in loosely organized volunteer militias and push back Indian or foreign raiders, especially after the foundation of the Civil Militia in 1823. When Indians attacked, sometimes a vecino would "se puso sobre las armas" (arm himself quickly) alongside his comrades and go after the attackers. Violence was of central importance to the manhood of at least some norteños—long before the late nineteenth century, when most historians have identified the origins of revolutionary masculinity in the North.[24] The Civil Militia went a long way toward building community, but it was fairly autonomous and did not owe loyalty to the nation.

Despite the supposed peace, warfare continued unabated throughout the 1820s between mexicanos and Native Americans as all people on the frontier had to vie for the scarce resources. This led the great historian of the Mexican North, Isidro Viscaya Canales, to deny that there ever was a peace after 1822—despite the fact that all of the Indian tribes of Texas were supposedly pacified following Iturbide's diplomatic overtures. Most likely the Indians did not think that the terms of peace covered all the Mexican vecinos who inhabited the frontier. As Pekka Hämäläinen writes, "Mexicans assumed that the treaties covered all their communities; Comanches did not."[25] This was true for the Lipans as well. The failure of the Mexican state to live up to its side of the bargain also played a role in renewed warfare and the consequent insecurity on the frontier.

In the ensuing years, Lipan and Comanche raids continued unabated despite the signing of treaties, flummoxing Mexican officers who thought they were at peace. Valecillo, in northern Nuevo León, for example, suffered raids led by the Lipan *capitancillo* Morongo during the halting peace of the 1820s. Capitán Andrés de Mendiola, in charge of a northeastern frontier region, complained bitterly about the perfidious Lipans and their hostile presence in the neighborhood. He registered a typically fiery complaint about the raiding Indians and their effect on the frontier. Indian raids had forced ranchers to flee farther inland, he said, leaving their lands abandoned and useless. Mendiola told his superiors that the ranchers and hacendados who dared to stay in the area found that their shepherds and cowboys were afraid to venture too far out. Mexicans had good reason; these agricultural laborers were most often the victims of Indian violence since they so often went into the countryside alone and without weapons, "despite repeated orders" to the contrary. The Comanches (and probably Lipans too) often killed adults on the spot, but if the *criadores* (herders) were young enough, they were taken captive and incorporated into their bands. The Comanches often used young boys taken captive to do "squaw work," tasks that included the care of horse herds.[26] Lipans could be equally destructive. Jean-Louis Berlandier, a French naturalist who toured Ciudad Guerrero in the late 1820s, claimed that Lipan theft and war destroyed any Mexican attempts to pasture animals or grow corn in the neighborhood.[27] Perhaps, had the Lipans received the promised land and resources, things might have turned out differently. Broken promises and weakness on the part of the Mexican government instead resulted in continued mobility and independence on the part of the Lipan Apaches as they procured for themselves the resources they needed, ranging widely across the borderlands.

Adding yet another wrinkle to this problem, Lipan mobility turned out to be infectious. Lipan raids and theft caused mexicanos to migrate and abandon the North, effectively setting an entire landscape in motion. Efforts to make peace with the Lipans had resulted in neither stability nor security in the far North.

As a result of Indian violence, the Mexican Congress sent Bustamente, in charge of the internal provinces, north to Palafox in 1826 to take control of the eastern states. Ironically, when he arrived at his post in Palafox he found it destroyed by Indians and relocated to Laredo. Lampazos and Candela likewise suffered attacks during these years. In 1827, raids reached even farther east, to Mier, Tamaulipas, where the Indians killed three people, carried several more into captivity, and stole a large number of horses and mules. But this time the vecinos had prepared themselves. A small militia drawn from the population of Lampazos caught up to the Indians, killed two of them, recaptured the stolen animals, and freed the three young captives.[28]

Other vecinos played a role in the ongoing war with Native Americans in a very different way. Some vecinos eagerly bought horses stolen from Texas and points farther east, even though they were plundered from their own countrymen. This illicit trade was a serious problem since it put vecinos in search of cheap animals and soldiers and militias looking to pacify the Indians at odds with one another. Some officers took steps to curb this problematic trade. As early as 1828, the *alcalde* (mayor) of San Fernando de Rosas warned Cuelgas de Castro—an important Lipan chief ever since the Mexican War of Independence—that he no longer allowed the sale of any animals "whose brands had been scraped off with a knife, burned off with fire, or in any other way disfigured." In addition, Bustamente recommended to the state governors that they forbid the sale of animals with other types of suspicious brands. He hoped that by putting an end to the black market he could end the Indians' nomadic ways. Without traffic in contraband beef, starvation would force the Lipans to establish themselves "in fixed towns and to live under the rules of a civilized society." Of course, if this did not happen, said Bustamente, they would have to be destroyed with force.[29] Civilization or extermination were the options Mexicans considered for the "barbarous" Indians. Of course, they could not actually enforce either of them, and Lipans maintained their independence. Quick raids and stolen horses were the bedrock of Lipan mobility as they continued to expand their routes across the borderlands, to interact with many different populations, and to remain outside the grasp of the Mexican state.

Despite efforts at peace in the early 1820s, by the end of the decade it was clear that a war was raging with the Lipans over scarce frontier resources. Rather than try to incorporate the Indians, Bustamente now bowed to local pressure from the vecinos and their captains to cut off the problem. He devised a military solution that increased violence on the frontier and sought to reduce Native American power. Bustamente must have felt tremendous pressure. Local officials and citizen soldiers more familiar with the situation on the frontier disagreed with edicts handed down from Mexico City to incorporate the Indians into the Mexican "family" and turn them into allies. Bowing to the desires of the vecinos, Bustamente improved the presidial companies and secured arms, horses, and uniforms for the soldiers. The soldiers even began to receive their salaries on time.[30]

No less a figure than Manuel de Mier y Terán praised this military response. Mier y Terán was a prominent Mexican general who played an important role in the Mexican War of Independence and then, in the late 1820s, was put in charge of reconnoitering the Mexican North for the central government. He found much to write about during his journey to Texas. Most of the evils to be found on the northern frontier, he said, came from the fact that vecinos had never been allowed to use and carry arms in their personal defense under the Spanish government. The Texans, he claimed, had the healthy habit of uniting in armed posses to defend their property, and this had resulted in the extermination of the "worst" tribes. But Mier y Terán got it wrong. In fact, the northern vecinos had carried arms during the colonial period as well, sometimes under force of law. They also had a tradition of mustering into volunteer militias that predated the arrival of the Texans. It must have been something else that led to their failure to reduce the Indians. Most likely it was Indian military power in the case of the Comanches and the fact that the Lipans knew Mexico much better.[31]

By 1830 or so, peace with the Comanches had evaporated. Alliance and friendship with the Lipans likewise remained elusive. The Lipans were supposed to stay in the Nueces Strip on the northern side of the Rio Grande under the 1824 treaty, but they were simply too free to move about and Mexicans had tremendous difficulty making them stay put above the old line of presidios that ran along the riverbank. When opportunities beckoned on the other side of the Rio Grande, Lipans took them. By the end of the 1820s, friendly Apaches—Mescaleros and Lipans alike—were already crossing the river and trading with vecinos in the Santa Rosa Valley, with whom they would carry on an illicit trade and troubled relations for decades to come. This area, in the foothills of the Sierra Madre, was home to a fairly dense (by frontier standards) population of Mexican vecinos. Predictably, peaceful relations with the vecinos of northern Coahuila did not last long. In May 1829, not long after their visits began, the vecinos accused the Lipan Apaches of rustling.[32] A couple of years later, *alférez* (lieutenant) Gregorio Pérez and twenty-five men from the state militia were joined by the civil militia and volunteers from Lampazos to try to force the Lipans out of neighboring Nuevo León, where they pastured stolen horses around the Laguna de la Leche.[33] Relations between vecinos and Indians were contentious, and Mexican officials did their best to separate the two populations. But Mexican pueblos in northern Coahuila and along the banks of the Rio Grande simply offered too many tempting resources for the Lipans to ignore. Unfortunately, their unhampered movement across the river, away from La Bahía where they did not receive supplies, guns, or powder from the Mexican government, and through the Nueces Strip brought Mexico's mastery over the borderlands into question. It also greatly soured their relationship with local vecinos.

In the end, failed efforts by the Mexican government to come to terms with or control mobile Indians resulted in bad feelings on the part of both the Lipans and the vecinos. Lipans, in fact, came up with their own arrangements to gather the necessary resources in the absence of assistance from the Mexican state. Martha Rodríguez writes that the truces Lipans made with the nearby villages were a "trick of war" and that they served a practical purpose in the scarcely populated and resource-poor northern frontier. During the halting peace that followed a season of raiding, both sides understood that they could rebuild and prepare for the next round of attacks that inevitably followed the disruption of peace. This method of alternating war and peace allowed both sides to make perpetual war over scarce resources. It also had the effect of allowing both sides in this sparsely inhabited country to avoid demographic collapse. The Lipans, after all, needed Mexican captives to replenish their dwindling numbers, and they needed their horses and cattle to carry and feed them.[34]

Hence, Indian power remained unbroken in the borderlands of the lower Rio Grande despite the best efforts of Iturbide and his successors to make peace and turn the Indians into friendly allies. Rather than military power, the Lipans had the power of mobility, geographic familiarity, and cultural knowledge. There was no advantage to joining with the Mexican government. The federal government—or rather, the many authorities and officials who represented it in the borderlands—failed to bring about improvements, leaving the vecinos resentful of its presence and meddling. Mexican villages, presidios, and colonies remained tiny islands in a vast sea controlled by Indians. Given the state's invisibility in the borderlands and the troubling state of Mexico's government in the decades following independence, villagers and Indians in the North were usually left to their own devices—despite the best efforts of such earnest military figures as Anastacio Bustamente. By 1835, for instance, the "cruel and devastating war of the barbarous Indians" had left Coahuila and Texas in shambles. The presidial companies were incapable of chasing the Indians into the deserts of northern Coahuila because they had no supplies.[35] Men and munitions were yet other resources the government could not spare for the North.

Adding to their woes was the "capriciousness" of the military commanders. They often left the frontier on a moment's notice to pursue other national problems. National politics and civil wars offered more glory to ambitious military men than fighting "indios bárbaros" and securing the North from its enemies. Officers and the conscripted soldiers they led faced off against enemy armies during the endless civil wars that raged across Mexico in the early to mid-nineteenth century. Caudillos (military chieftains) and their retainers constantly schemed to fill the power vacuum left by the collapse of the colonial state from 1821 on— even as the frontier languished. Career-driven officers proclaimed lofty plans and hatched military escapades that operated on a regional and sometimes national level. Meanwhile, local militias and military colonists were left with the task of fighting Indians, reflecting a great divide between the interests and goals of governing elites who represented the central government and local elites. Federal officers who thought first of their own careers in the national army "sacrificed the lives and haciendas of the citizens" to go off and fight in Mexico's many wars, according to one regional newspaper editor writing from Matamoros.[36]

In the absence of state power or successful diplomatic efforts, the terms of war and peace as laid out by the Indians stood in for more regular negotiation. Mexicans had done little to bring an end to the Lipans' migrancy in search of horses, cattle, and other sources of wealth on the frontier. Face-to-face negotiations constituted the bulk of communication, and the sovereign government was a distant authority that little understood the compromises that made life in the borderlands manageable. In reality, granting the peace on regular, seasonal intervals revealed the powerlessness of northern Mexicans in the face of borderlands

Indians who knew the land better and could traverse it easily. Truces allowed for a degree of coexistence and association, but treaties never resulted in the reduction and assimilation of indigenous people into northern vecino society.[37] The Lipans simply knew the frontier too well and gained too little by entering into any sort of alliance with the Mexican government. Nor did military incursions do much to discourage them. The Lipans had managed to hijack all the resources they needed to sustain themselves and had little use for the Mexican government that all too often failed to live up to its promises and provide for them. As a result, Lipans were reluctant to enter into a long-lasting alliance with them and they continued retreating into the frontier to maintain their independence. After 1836, they would have a new border to cross, and the transborderlands mobility that they had long practiced would become even more dangerous to Mexican vecinos.

Lipans and Texans

The Mexican government experimented with other potential buffer zones in the borderlands besides those formed by allied Indians. The most calamitous of these experiments involved transplanted whites and enslaved blacks from the United States. In what must be one of the greatest miscalculations in Mexican history, Iturbide's government allowed Stephen F. Austin, whose father had applied while the Spanish were still in charge, to set up an empresario grant in Texas. Anglos in Texas (the so-called Texians) were supposed to provide a buffer against further U.S. expansion into the heartland of the continent. Since southern Anglos were moving westward anyway, the Mexican authorities tried to direct them into a territory that desperately needed settlement. As a result, hundreds and then thousands of immigrants from the United States poured into Texas in search of cheap land.

The Texans soon revolted against Mexican governance.[38] Like Zacatecas and Coahuila to the south, Anglos and some Tejanos chafed under the ascendancy of General Santa Anna's Centralist government in Mexico City, especially once he abolished the 1824 Federalist constitution in 1835. The Centralists suspended home guard militias and began passing laws augmenting the national government's power at the expense of the states. They also threatened to end slavery in Texas. The violence that ultimately resulted in the Texans' revolt was not just another Federalist uprising by citizen soldiers, however. In 1836, white Texans and a handful of Tejanos—who were now outnumbered by Anglos by at least four to one in Texas—elected to secede and form their own republic. They were successful, but the boundary between the newly independent Republic of Texas and Mexico remained contested long after the end of hostilities. Mexicans claimed that the Nueces River separated the two countries, while the victors of the Texan revolution claimed the Rio Grande. In reality, neither Mexico nor Texas could exercise sovereign authority over the Nueces Strip that lay between the Nueces River and the Rio Grande in the decade 1836 to 1846. The historian Octavio Herrera Pérez has fittingly dubbed this era "la década de la frontera indefinida" (the decade of the undefined frontier), when this arid strip became ground zero in the conflicts between Texas and Mexico.[39] A running war continued long after Santa Anna surrendered to the Texans at the battle of San Jacinto.

Texas had not only failed as a buffer zone against foreign threats and "indios bárbaros." The whole disastrous train of events involving Anglo empresarios had made the borderlands even more insecure, and it created new boundaries that mobile people like the Lipans could manipulate to their advantage.[40] With opposing states now facing each other on either side of the Nueces River, the Indians gained the option of playing them off against each other. The Lipans, whose territory stretched across the yawning gap that opened up in the Nueces Strip, pressed the hostility between the two countries to their own advantage. In 1836, there were nine hundred Lipans in territory claimed by Texas, mostly in the Nueces Strip, but there were even more in Mexico living near their old mission of San Lorenzo outside of San Fernando. Geographically, they were in a unique position to play newly independent Texas and Mexico against each another. Emboldened by the rebels' example and eager to curry the favor of the Republic of Texas, many Lipans saw the Texans as potential new allies and courted them.

Officially, Lipans declared neutrality in the ongoing war between Mexico and Texas that characterized the decade following Texan independence, but Anglo Texans represented a new source of gifts, manufactures, and supplies.[41] The Lipans were likely impressed with the superior equipment that the Anglos brought with them to Texas. Ever since Anglo Americans began appearing in Louisiana, more guns had flowed into the Mexican North. Many Indians quickly turned these guns on their poorly armed Mexican neighbors, who sometimes fought with lances and bows and arrows.[42] The Lipans mastered the art of moving in-between, raiding on one side and building black markets on the other, using mobility and geographic knowledge to remain independent.

Fundamentally this total war between independent Indians and their neighbors was driven by access to scarce goods.[43] Then, after 1836, the new, undefined border became instrumental in the way that mobile Indians like the Lipans waged war and redistributed resources across the borderlands. Lipans, at least those in Texas, made alliances with the Texan Anglos because they had more to gain from them, and they regularly provided them with horses stolen from Mexico in exchange for goods. Consecrating this new friendship in 1838, Chief Cuelgas de Castro chose a side and signed the first of many treaties with Texas. He accompanied it with loud declarations of friendship.[44]

It is doubtful that Castro was as enamored of the Texans as he professed. Much more likely, his band was interested in employment as scouts and receiving the goods that Texans could offer them. This treachery on the part of this band of Lipans represented a brutal realpolitik that promised plunder on one side if they joined up with the other. Thus did the Lipans lend the embryonic border a new meaning: it separated a people with resources from a people without.[45] The Lipans immediately pressed this contradiction to their advantage since they had the know-how to move between the two peoples. The Texans recognized the benefits they gained from their new allies as well, although they would try to push them westward and away from their settlements in the years to come.

Samuel Truett writes that outsiders often imagine what frontiers can become, and they gloss over local conditions to see what they want to see.[46] Mexicans were hard-pressed to settle the borderlands, and they imagined that the Native people and Anglos there could ultimately be turned into friends, assimilated, and civilized. This would solve two problems: it would provide Mexico with citizens in a scarcely settled territory, and it would make allies of former enemies. But the Mexicans were ignoring reality, and ultimately their plan backfired. Native peoples pressed their new familiarity with mexicanos to their advantage. Lipans raided between frontiers, farming the borderlands for the resources that the Mexican government promised them but could never deliver. The quest for supplies—horses, cattle, guns—drove an undeclared war, and the Indians' familiarity with the territory lent them a marked advantage and guaranteed their independence.

Before 1836, Indians mostly raided between municipal boundaries—making peace with one village and war with another. Or they retreated into the vast, anarchic plains of Texas after a raid. This changed after the Texas Revolution. If borders have lifetimes, then the one between Texas and Mexico was in its infancy. Nevertheless, even at this early stage it still offered Indians a refuge they could never have imagined. This nebulous boundary line—located somewhere south of the Colorado and increasingly separating Anglo and Latino people—conducted all sorts of movement across it. Texans succeeded in courting many Indians where Mexicans failed, inviting them to cross over and join their side. Indians recognized the white peoples' borders when they wanted to—and across this border they saw a line that separated a people with resources from a people without. Lipans then turned their attacks against the very people who had sought sporadically to incorporate them, crossing the border yet again in their own interests.

Buffer zones were not necessarily a bad idea. The Lipans and Comanches were just not the right people for the job. Attempts to reach out to Indians merely familiarized them with Mexican places and people and created greater insecurity. Under the guidance of Mariano Arista, who became general of the Army of the North in 1839, the Mexicans realized that other types of Indians and immigrants might become better buffers than the Natives who predated them in the borderlands. Lipans were simply too familiar with this territory, and the government had far too weak a handle on them. But if immigrants unfamiliar with this territory could be transplanted there, they would be more dependent and less mobile. They might then represent a better prospect. We turn to this story in the next chapter.

If Mexico remained frustrated that buffer zones rarely worked, Indians like the Lipans perfected the art of borderlands perfidy in the meantime, crossing over to play off one side against the other. And the more significant the international border became, the more emblazoned the line became in the minds of the denizens of the borderlands, and the more Indians crossed it and helped turn the newly ascendant states on either side against one another. Independent Indians—like the other mobile people who followed in their wake—sought the best possibilities for themselves, and they saw opportunities and distinct meanings in borders. Settling down meant that Indians could no longer pursue new situations by means of crossing cultural frontiers. So many chose not to do this. In mobility they had independence, and borders between peoples helped ensure their liberty.

2 / Racial Fault Lines: Immigrant Indians in Mexico

Simultaneous with the largely failed policy of making alliances with Indians in the Mexican North, the authorities devised another strategy. They began to entice Indian populations of a very different sort to immigrate to the frontier in the hope that they would become loyal citizens. They invited disaffected tribes from the American Southeast to cross the Sabine River into Mexican Texas. The state was not overly concerned with the ethnicity of potential Mexican citizens, which clearly differentiated Mexico's policies from those of the United States. Hence, many displaced Indians from the southeastern United States and a small number of African Americans began to cross the Sabine River (the border between Louisiana and Texas after 1819) into Mexican territory in the 1820s and 1830s. Mexican frontier officials, like their contemporaries on other Latin American frontiers, believed that "gobernar es poblar" (to govern is to populate).[1] Perhaps the government could attract people dispossessed by Jacksonian American society and put them to their own national ends, settling a frontier in desperate need of citizens in the trade.

Mexico's recruitment of displaced Indians from the United States signified the way that the international border represented a racial fault line. The Cherokees, one of the most important group of immigrant Indians, arrived in Mexico beginning in 1819. Their agreement, signed with the governor of Texas, Félix Trespalacios, in 1822, established that the Cherokees "shall be considered Hispano Americans, and entitled to all the rights and privileges granted to such." They founded between three and seven towns near Nacagdoches, with nearly five hundred Cherokee people inhabiting them alongside Kickapoos, Miamis, and other migrant Indians. There they raised cattle, hunted, and grew corn, establishing themselves just on the Mexican side of the divide with the United States.[2] They also took on another tenet of Mexican frontier culture when they agreed to fight the enemies of civilization, the "barbarous" Lipans and Comanches.[3]

Chief Bowles (aka Duwali), a Cherokee, and one of the most famous early immigrants to Mexican Texas, became the de facto leader of the immigrant Indian towns. A few years after his migration, in the aftermath of a rebellion against central authority in Texas—the Fredonian Rebellion, which involved a handful of Cherokees—Bowles wanted to express his loyalty and gratitude to Mexico for welcoming him and his people. He was well aware that the main goal of frontier officials was to "civilize" the Indians who immigrated to Mexican Texas in the 1820s. Thus, he decided to give one of his sons to the Mexican government to be educated. This, he hoped, would "tighten their [the Cherokees'] relations with Mexico." Removed from the frontier and immersed in national institutions, Bowles's young son was educated as a Mexican.[4] Mexicans could be quite flexible on the ethnicity of potential immigrants, but they did demand assimilation. Nevertheless, such exchanges underscored the principles behind Mexico's "frontier of inclusion" and threw into sharp relief the contrasting policies of the United States on the absorption of ethnic outsiders in the Jacksonian era.[5]

Unfortunately for the immigrant tribes, their journeys did not end with their arrival in Texas. When Texas seceded in 1836, Indian immigrants found themselves beached in a hostile land deep within the Texas republic. All these peoples had suffered an irreversible decline in the American Southeast as King Cotton spread across their old homelands. Then, just a few short years later, southern Americans transplanted to Texas caught up with the immigrant Indians there and soon outnumbered them once again. Immigrant Indians were forced by circumstances to move a second time. They crossed to the other side of the Nueces, sometimes even across the Rio Grande to reach secure Mexican territory. The Mexican town of Matamoros on the Rio Grande attracted a good number of immigrant tribespeople from the newly independent Republic of Texas, Indians who had arrived along the Sabine River just a few years before.

Nor were Texans the only problem that immigrant Indians faced in Texas. Indians may have been willing to immigrate, but the Mexican government did not have the resources to absorb them. Often starving, many immigrant Indians found that they had exchanged one type of insecurity for another. Despite the best intentions, the Mexican government did not offer them a workable alternative. Nor did most Tejanos or norteños appreciate the presence of Indians living so close to them, especially ones hostile to the United States. They brought on increased conflict with the Americans, who were moving toward the western Louisiana frontier in ever larger numbers in the aftermath of the War of 1812. General Felipe de la Garza, commandant general of the Eastern Internal Provinces at Saltillo, registered his distaste for the project of encouraging immigrant tribes by suggesting that the Cherokees be moved to the interior and that no further immigration from that tribe occur.[6] This migration had another disastrous effect as well. As one astute Texas newspaper editor put it, competition for resources pushed the older Indian groups of Texas—particularly the Comanches and Apaches—farther toward the hinterlands of Texas and northern Mexico. This was bad news for frontier people. The displaced Comanches and Apaches began raiding south of the Rio Grande, along a geographic line that stretched from Matamoros through La Punta de Lampazos, and ultimately they reached Santa Rosa in Coahuila far to the west. They raided along this line with impunity, as they did not want to compete with the growing camps of immigrant tribes in eastern Texas for resources.[7] Given the problems they faced, not many Cherokees ended up staying in Mexico. Their last colony in Coahuila floundered, and many went hungry before it ultimately disappeared in the early twentieth century.[8]

Despite the ultimate failure of Mexico to absorb this first wave of immigrant Indians, they worked in conjunction with the national government to lend the border an important meaning. The immigration of Indians to Mexico underscored the way that the boundary between Mexico and the United States, and later Texas, transformed into a racial borderline. The international border ossified distinct racial ideologies.

Racial Borderlines and Mexican Cherokees

Few immigrant tribes ended up staying in Mexico, but by crossing the line to find refuge they left an important imprint on the newly emergent international borderline, one that would be taken up by later migrants described in subsequent chapters. In essence, they lent meaning to the border as an international line that separated two countries that had very different ideas about race. In the years after independence, Mexico refused to implement categories of race in any official capacity—including immigration policy—and they abolished the caste system. And while Mexico may have preferred European immigrants, few arrived. The United States, and then Brazil and Argentina, simply represented better options for émigré Europeans. Further, as was the case with most Latin American independence movements, there was a social element involved in Mexico's revolt against Spain. The many mestizos, pardos, mulattos, and others who made up the great armies commanded by Fr. Miguel Hidalgo y Costilla and his successors pressed for emancipation, the abolition of tribute, the end of the caste system, and social justice. When the ashes settled from the independence movement, and after Mexican Creoles had appropriated the revolution, the promise of social and racial equality remained.[9]

Yet if Mexicans did not subscribe to the hardening racism current in Jacksonian America, they did evince a sort of "soft racism."[10] Mexicans still expected immigrants to adapt to their host society even if they did not explicitly call on them to "whiten." Many nineteenth-century thinkers believed that cultures existed along a spectrum from barbarity to civilization, and Mexican officials (like their Bourbon forebears) may not have necessarily wanted white colonists, but they wanted "civilized" ones. They anticipated that the Indians who they collected under the category "immigrant tribes" would transform themselves into Christian, Hispanic, and sedentary—that is, "civilized"—citizens. Referred to as the "civilized tribes" in the United States since they had adopted many Euro-American agricultural practices, Cherokees, Seminoles, and Creeks made especially good candidates for immigration. In a sense, the commanders of the new Mexican government took up again the old Spanish friars' mission in the North. They hoped to civilize and catechize the Indians and make them over into what were, by their reckoning, "buenos mexicanos." Children held out the best hopes for civilization and incorporation into the "Mexican family," and the government sought them out in particular. Accordingly, Mexicans could actively recruit Indians as immigrants in the 1820s and hold out the promise that they would eventually integrate into the nation and gain all attendant rights. Indians could become citizens in Mexico, unlike in the United States.[11]

In search of refuge, the Cherokees quickly became dominant among the thousands of immigrant Indians who arrived in Mexican Texas (joined with its neighboring state as Tejas y Coahuila in 1824) to escape the southern plantation belt. They received land near Nacogdoches in 1822 and became the inhabitants of the territory between the Sabine and Angelina Rivers, claiming nearly three thousand square miles in the years that followed. They never did receive title to these lands, and they soon found that the empresarios Frost Thorn and Haden Edwards claimed their land as part of their grant. Manuel de Mier y Terán, after his visit of the early 1830s, recommended that the government rectify this situation and that the Cherokees, Shawnees, Delawares, and Kickapoos receive official title to the lands they inhabited since they were loyal to the Mexican government and good citizens. Mier y Terán feared for the future of Texas, and he vested some hope in these immigrant tribes since they were generally hostile to the Anglos pouring into the state. But this transfer of land never occurred. In 1832, Mier y Terán was so desperate about the future of Texas that he fell upon his own sword, ending his life. That same year, the sympathetic governor of Tejas y Coahuila, who supported Mier y Terán's request, José María Letona, died of yellow fever. The next governor, Vicente Filisola, felt differently about the situation—especially since he personally claimed parts of the Thorn empresarial grant, where the Cherokees lived. Then, when the troubles with Mexico began, Anglo Texans refused to recognize Cherokee claims to land as legitimate, despite Samuel Houston's urging. When war broke out, none of the immigrant tribes had been brought into the Texas fold, again despite Houston's efforts to make alliances. The aloofness of the immigrant Indians during the Texas Revolution made the rebels deeply suspicious of them, and soldiers feared a fifth column made up of immigrant tribesmen. (Eslaved blacks were equally problematic, a topic I address in chapter 3).[12]

The Texans had good reason to fear the immigrant tribes. When war came in 1836, some fifteen Cherokee warriors crossed the Rio Grande and sought out the Mexican general José de Urrea. The Cherokees probably offered to open up a second front against the Texans far to the northeast, along the Sabine River. Indeed, when the Texas Indian agent Michael Menard sent a woman disguised as a Mexican officer to meet with Duwali, the chief boldly stated, while holding a sword given to him by Colonel Matteo Ahumada a decade before, "This shall pass through my heart, before I prove false to my former friends, the Mexicans."[13] The Texans soon learned of the Cherokees' negotiations with Urrea, which added to their resentment, since they knew that Duwali met with representatives of General López de Santa Anna earlier—even as Sam Houston tried to persuade the Texans to recognize the immigrant Indians' land grants.[14] Relations only worsened at the end of the Texas Revolution. In 1837, the Texans learned that a group of Cherokees helped the Mexican army recover some Texan prisoners who had escaped from a Matamoros jail.[15] That same year, the Texas senate's Standing Committee on Indian Affairs rejected a treaty that would have recognized Cherokee titles to land in Texas.[16] As an undeclared war raged between Texas and Mexico in the ensuing years over the undefined boundary, the more militant Cherokees found themselves moving closer to the Mexican side.

As Mexicans continued to fight the war against the Anglo Texans and their diminishing number of Tejano friends, Cherokees allied with pro-Mexico forces. Vicente Córdova, a Tejano revolutionary with close ties to the Mexican army, tried to rouse the immigrant tribes in East Texas to join his forces to defend the original Tejano inhabitants of Nacagodoches. Texans only learned of this plot when Córdova's lieutenant, Manuel Flores, died in an ambush and an expeditionary force discovered papers on his corpse. "The Cherokees were about to form a combination with all the eastern [Texan] tribes, and under a promise of protection from the Mexican government, they were about to commence hostilities upon our whole frontier" warned the *Texas Sentinel*. Indeed, a small branch of militant pro-Mexico Cherokees were thick as thieves with Córdova, and it was with him that some Cherokees made trips to Matamoros in search of arms and ammunition to fight the Texans.[17] Texan officials also learned that there were Cherokees in Matamoros negotiating with Mexican army officers to take an even more active part in the war against the Texans.[18] Mirabeau Buonaparte Lamar soon succeeded Samuel Houston as president of Texas and inherited the deteriorated situation. He had much less tolerance for Indians in Texas than Houston did, however. In 1839, all efforts to make peace with the Cherokees were abandoned. Nor did Lamar have much difficulty turning his countrymen against the Indians in their midst.

Since the Cherokees were no longer citizens of the United States or the Republic of Texas because they had sided with Mexico, they were not entitled to their country's protection, and many considered them traitors. Anticipating trouble, Duwali moved his settlement to the Neches River in 1836. In 1839 the newly emboldened Texan congress forcibly ejected the entire tribe from the republic after claiming victory against the Cherokees and their Delaware, Shawnee, and Kickapoo allies at the battle at the Neches River on July 16. In the aftermath of the battle, the Republic of Texas confiscated once and for all the lands that the "tyrant" Iturbide had supposedly allocated to the immigrant tribes in 1822.[19] Many Cherokees went back to eastern Texas only to find their ranches burned and their cattle run off. They never received the compensation promised to them. Others went back to the Cherokee reservation in

Indian Territory and felt both shock and disbelief when they witnessed how acculturated their kinsmen had become in the interim.[20]

The most militant Cherokees inevitably gravitated to Mexico. Many members of Duwali's confederacy of Cherokees and Kickapoos—who had long enjoyed close ties with the Mexican government—migrated south to Matamoros after the Battle of the Neches River. The eighty-three-year-old Duwali himself died at the hands of Texan soldiers at the Neches, but his followers pushed on. They eventually made it to safety in Mexico after enduring yet another run-in with the Texas Rangers when they met a detachment of Edward Burleson's troops on Christmas Day. The survivors of this ambush went on to straggle across the Rio Grande to safety. For the second time in under twenty years a pan-Indian confederacy headed by Cherokees crossed an international border to seek refuge with the Mexicans. All in all, this migrant band included many Cherokees, about eighty southern Kickapoos, and a number of other Indians from Texas. Like most of the immigrant tribes who had come to Mexican Texas the decade before, they were ethnically diverse but shared a similar conviction. They were virulently opposed to the settler empire of the Anglo Americans on the other side of the Colorado River.[21]

Indians continued to trickle into Mexico south of the Rio Grande in the aftermath of the Texas Revolt. In 1839, the U.S. consul in Matamoros observed "various small parties" of Indians arriving in town to seek out General Urrea. These groups of migrants consisted of Cherokees, Kickapoos, Delawares, and Caddos, and they received rations, arms, ammunition, and clothing from the Mexican officers. The Mexican government recognized that they had a right to consular protection as they had been citizens of that country prior to the Revolution of 1836. Even more alarming for the Texans, the Indians in Matamoros were still in communication with other immigrant Indians along the Sabine River. In effect, a network of pro-Mexican Indians and warriors stretched across the heart of Texas, connecting the Mexican army's nerve center at Matamoros to the Indians' old home grounds west of the Sabine. Fighting broke out almost immediately given this volatile situation; eight of the Indians who had gone to Matamoros mustered into service on the side of Mexico. They set out against a party of Texans (or perhaps Tejanos) and *sirvientes* (Mexican debt peons) who Mexican agents had discovered in the Nueces Strip traveling on the road that ran from San Antonio to Mier. The Indians killed all of the Texans, but spared the lives of the servants, merely imprisoning them and returning them to Matamoros.[22] The message could not have been clearer: this disputed territory was deadly to the rebellious Texans, and the Indians were helping to make it so.

The next year, in 1840, dissident Indians stationed around Matamoros crossed back over the river to once again join the rebel Vicente Córdova, who had now relocated to the environs of the Rio Grande after his aborted rebellion along the Sabine River. Camped on the Brazos Santiago pass near Padre Island, Córdova soon moved against the Texans along with as many as sixty Cherokees, "half as many runaway negroes," and a hundred counterrevolutionary Mexicans. The *Texas Sentinel* called on the republic's government to move troops to that region to meet the threat.[23] At least for the time being, the Nueces Strip remained contested and the Cherokees were key allies there against the Texas Republic. Cut loose from their homelands by the informal empire of Anglo immigrants in Texas, these confederated Indians had become the shock troops Mexican officials hoped would resist further Texan expansion and defend their claim to the disputed Nueces Strip. They were better potential allies than the Comanches and Lipans who Iturbide's agents had tried to settle a decade and a half earlier. They helped hold the Nueces Strip for Mexico during the turbulent (and bankrupt) years of the early Texas Republic.[24]

In the aftermath of the Texan Revolt, Mexican military officers kept a simmering war going along the contested frontier between Mexico and Texas. This only added to the woes of the Texas Republic during the years of deflated demand for cotton following the Panic of 1837. The Mexican government wanted to build a buffer against Texan expansion in the Nueces Strip, and the new general in charge of the frontier, Mariano Arista, was allegedly instrumental in implementing this plan. Texans kept a wary eye on the general's maneuvers, and many believed that the Mexicans beyond the Nueces under his command were "constantly threatening . . . with invasion."[25] Hundreds of miles to the north, Mexicans allegedly schemed along the Sabine River as well. As late as 1842, a Chickasaw Indian communicated to Thomas Farrow Smith (a member of the Texas Congress) that Mexican emissaries moved "among the Wild Indians, for the purpose of enlisting them in behalf of Mexico to wage a war of extermination against Northern Texas." If these rumors were not true, then they at least indicated intense anxiety on the part of white Texans about pro-Mexican Indian saboteurs. And there were many Indians who were likely to hear out Mexican plans.[26] If the new, ill-defined, international border separated two racial regimes from one another, then a race war simmered along it during the decade of the Texas Republic.

Some Mexicans recognized just how incendiary it was for the Mexican government to set immigrant Indians upon the Texans. There was always a disconnect between what officials planned for the frontier and what local vecinos thought was the best course to follow. The majority of local vecinos in el norte hoped to maintain good relations with Texas and not antagonize them further so that peace might reign along the frontier. Some had kin among the Tejano population. And many others saw white Texans as agents of progress.[27] In addition, many vecinos did not see the Indians as guarantors of greater security on the frontier. Rather, they saw in them yet another threat. An editor for Ciudad Victoria's *Atalya* put it bluntly during the war with Texas. The Creeks, Seminoles, and Cherokees who were pushed off their land had only one place they could go. The editor was certain they would head toward the Mexican frontier, which had a "vast infinity of wood, and whose plains, forests, mountains and prairies," along with the many "buffalo, deer, and other animals" found in the region, would provide them with sustenance. Maybe he exaggerated about the bounty of the northern frontier, but in his opinion these were resources best reserved for Mexicans. The Mexican government, insisted the *Atalya*, "must prevent these tribes from coming to devour us."[28]

Certainly Mexico was more capable of absorbing ethnic outsiders than the United States. But not all Mexicans were as magnanimous as Mariano Arista in their estimation of the immigrant tribes' ability to assimilate and promote Mexican national interests. A writer for *Atalaya* revealed that some vecinos feared that rather than protecting Mexicans, these Indians would consume them and that the federal army's plans to beget greater security just might result in greater insecurity. At the end of 1836, *Atalya* published the rumor that Indians from Texas had met with Mexican officials to coordinate attacks against the Texans. The editor could not believe this was the truth since it was, in his opinion, such an unwise course. He feared the wrath of not just these Indian allies. He worried that the Texans who lived north of the Colorado River would take out their vengeance on peace-loving northern Mexican vecinos and their Tejano friends.[29] Many vecinos feared and distrusted Indians—whether "civilized," immigrant, or otherwise. Distrust between vecinos, long accustomed to seeing all Indians as enemies, and immigrant Indians continually undermined attempts by Mexican officers who represented the central government to bring dissident tribes from the United States in as protectors of the frontier. Contrasting attitudes resulted in significant tensions between Centralist policies and frontier vecinos.

Immigrant Tribes in Coahuila

Texans were not mistaken when they quipped, as the *Texas Sentinel* did, that "the Indians were prefered [*sic*] in many instances to the white man, and privileges were granted them which were reserved from us."[30] Endemic frontier warfare between Texans in the eastern part of the state and Mexican troops stationed along the Rio Grande continued into the late 1830s and beyond. Despite some misgivings on the part of locals, the national government continued to deputize Mexican officers to enlist the immigrant tribes in this fight.

In 1840, Indian immigrants began to arrive in Coahuila. In January, Capt. Juan José Galán, military commander of the canton of the Rio Grande far to the west and near the Coahuiltecan desert, welcomed a large group of Indians. The Cherokee, Savano, and Coushatta refugees who showed up there had come a long way to see the land promised to them by the Mexican government. They would decide, based upon what they saw, if they would migrate there and take up arms in defense of the Mexican frontier. If they found conditions favorable, they would also bring their families and many more compatriots later. Isolated and terrorized by Comanches and (sometimes) Lipans, Coahuila needed friendly colonists and military protection even more desperately than Tamaulipas. When the Cherokees and associated Indians arrived, the officers in charge of Rio Grande sized up these Indians who had immigrated to Texas while it was still under Mexican control a decade earlier and now showed up in the military canton of Rio Grande. They decided that help had at last arrived. Galán was certain that the Mexicans "could count on them in case Texan adventurers intended to invade these lands." He also said that these Indians had proven themselves good "Mexican Indians," since they were the most "grateful and loyal" colonists in Texas. Welcoming them to Mexico would surely have repercussions, but Galán's superior, Mariano Arista, was convinced that the Texans would fear their armies and Indian allies as they prepared to renew warfare. He also figured that the most useful of the Texans, the merchants, had already emigrated anyway as a result of ongoing war. There was not much to lose by inviting the Texans' enemies to settle in Coahuila.[31]

The trip across the frontier was difficult for these Indian refugees. Many of them were in bad shape upon their arrival at the canton of Rio Grande because of the attacks the Texans had recently made on them. Quite a few wore only rags, and many were starving; without gunpowder, they had difficulty hunting during their trip. Some of the starving

Indians fainted when the Mexican army fed them, and others remained infirm for days. Such "misery" aroused a good bit of compassion on the part of everyone who saw them—soldiers, officers, and even some vecinos. They were good Mexicans, even if they were immigrant Indians, and they could count on the "protection of the government," the frontier commanders insisted. Galán collected the rents from the nearby town and reached into his own purse to support the new arrivals. He then implored the president of Mexico to send them the tools and other implements they needed to make their harvest that year. They deserved the help, he said. "It would be very unjust not to alleviate the suffering of these unhappy indigenes who suffered in the trip with their families as they traveled over 200 leagues of unpopulated territory and came here to live under the protection of the Mexican government." They soon received rations, munitions, and clothing in exchange for a promise to serve in the military.[32]

Mariano Arista, recently appointed general of the Army of the North, agreed wholeheartedly with Galán's assessment of the Cherokees. Earlier, he had written that the Cherokees "and other civilized tribes" would be very useful as a buffer, and they could settle along the banks of the Rio Grande just as they had along the Sabine a couple of decades earlier. They could become "honorable citizens" who prevented the Comanches and other "barbarous tribes" from invading and "decapitating [*degollar*] thousands of victims," which he added was something that occurred all too frequently of late. Further, they were all "white men, humans, they worked the land and the Texans and barbarous tribes alike knew and feared them."[33]

To Arista, whiteness was not a reference to these Indians' phenotype alone, although centuries of intermixing with Europeans did make them lighter-skinned than the Comanches and Apaches. More important, Arista believed that the Indians had the potential to transform themselves into sedentary, Christian, Spanish-speaking civilizados. The immigrant Cherokees could be assimilated into the fabric of Mexican national life, transforming from *gandules* (unreduced Indians) to civilizados in quick order. The very Indian-ness of the Comanches and Lipans brought the putative "whiteness" of the Cherokees into focus. The plains raider emerged as the ideal "other," barbarous tribes who were not offered citizenship, and they were the foil against which Mexicans could measure the whiteness of the immigrant tribes. In Arista's mind, the Cherokees and their friends were already well on their way toward civilization on Hispanic terms. Maybe this had to do with their long history of

living alongside Anglos, but in any case these Indians were clearly different. Of course they were also "humans." This meant something to Arista
and the other officers who watched over the frontier. They were not like
the "bárbaros"—fiends in human shape (to borrow a nineteenth-century
insult) who razed the countryside, lived savage lives, and did not figure
among the rational creatures to be found upon the earth. It is important
to note, of course, that it is doubtful that most vecinos saw the distinction between the Cherokees and other Indians.

Adding to their desirable racial qualities, at least according to Arista,
were the martial virtues the immigrant tribes extolled. Their willingness to serve as warriors was an important resource in the Mexican
North, and something very dear in the war-ravaged frontier Coahuila
shared with Comanchería, Apachería, and Texas. Although it may seem
ironic to us in the twenty-first century, norteños had long considered
the willingness to shed the blood of unassimilated Indians a hallmark
of civilization and whiteness. Manly violence in the borderlands turned
the tide of war against the enemies and foils of civilized mexicanos—the
"savages." They also made the territory safe for God-fearing ranchers,
peons, and peasants. Hence organized warfare against barbarous others
was not only a step on the stage to civilization; it was an important aspect
of frontier civilization itself. Many of the principal men of the frontier
from Chihuahua east had earned their reputations doling out pain and
violence to plains raiders. Accordingly, when Arista quipped that "the
bárbaros and Texans have infinite fear of the immigrant tribes" he was
in fact singling them out for praise and marking their progress toward
civilization on frontier terms.[34]

The Conservative Mexican president, Anastasio Bustamente, agreed to
these Cherokees' entrance and the government granted them land alongside the Rio Grande. Since they had lost the land originally assigned to
them in Texas in 1824, Arista ordered Galán to find vacant land (terreno
baldío) for the anticipated two hundred Cherokee families. The establishment of the Cherokees, Arista insisted, would help save the frontier
since the chain of presidios no longer functioned. The frontier was in sad
shape "because of the expeditions of colonists and revolutionaries" who
brought "torrents of blood to thousands of Mexicans under the savage
knife of the barbarians, Comanches, Lipans, and other nations." At the
same time, added Arista, they could earn their keep by cultivating the
fertile land along the banks of the river.[35] Sedentariness was yet another
norm of civilization, one that all immigrants needed to adopt. The Mexican officers in charge of the project knew that most immigrant tribes

had extensive experience with farming, as many had adopted European practices of agriculture and animal husbandry in previous generations. They could help develop the agricultural resources of the frontier, which had long laid fallow as a result of Indian raiders, warfare, and scarce population. The commanders pinned great hopes on these Indian immigrants as both the defenders and the developers of the northern frontier.

The Cherokees who arrived in Mexico once again joined their old comrade Vicente Córdova in battle at the Salado Creek in 1842, where both the colonel and ten or eleven of his Cherokee companions died.[36] But despite their assistance to the Mexicans in the continuing border war with the Anglo Texans, the Cherokees of Coahuila quickly lost access to whatever scarce supplies might have facilitated their settlement. Nor could they attract the promised number of kinsmen and women to the colony; they therefore failed to gain a permanent land grant. When the Cherokee Ujiya visited the Mexican Cherokees around 1842 at the behest of Sequoya, he eventually located them just beyond a Maroon colony established at San Cranto. The Cherokee colony established in Coahuila under Galán remained impoverished and underdeveloped. Ujiya even had to borrow a horse from the neighboring Mexican military colony just to make the trip back to Texas. The Cherokees and the affiliated tribes had failed to bring more settlers and live up to their side of the agreement. As a result, Cherokees remained only a minor presence in northern Mexico alongside the Kickapoos until the early twentieth century.[37] Lack of food and implements ultimately resulted in yet another failed attempt to control the frontier with loyal, armed allies. The country on the other side of the dividing line promised more resources. The Cherokees were moderately successful in U.S. Indian Territory, and surely this fact lured many back from Mexico in ensuing years.

But Cherokees were not the only North American emigrant Indians sounding out possibilities in Mexico south of the Nueces to escape the Texans. Caddos, the longest inhabitants of eastern Texas, also endured increasing tension with the Texans after siding with Mexico during the War of Independence. By early 1835, the Kadohadachos—who had once been great allies to the Americans in Louisiana—had been ravaged by alcohol and lost their chief. They could no longer stand up to the intense pressure that American settlers and the Indian agent Jehiel Brooks put on them to sell their land. In the end they traded their land for a one-time payment and an annuity. They then joined the Hasinai and Nadacos Caddo factions in Texas.[38] Enduring the increasing Indian hatred endemic to Texas following the ascension of President

Lamar, they soon began to look for other options. In 1839, alongside Kickapoos, Cherokees, and Delawares, some Caddos began arriving in Matamoros to offer their services to General Urrea, receiving ammunition and rations from the Mexican officers in exchange.[39] The Texans, long suspicious that Mexican officers operated among their Indian enemies, found the evidence for this accusation later that year, when a party of Texans defeated a confederated band of Indians and Mexicans in the eastern part of their new republic. At the end of the battle, they discovered that at least one Caddo chief was involved in the conspiracy.[40] Just as the Cherokees could not long endure living alongside the Texans once Lamar assumed the presidency, neither could the Caddos. Soon after the battle described above, in the late spring of 1841, a group of 330 Caddos, including 130 warriors, set out for Coahuila.[41] More soon joined them. In 1842, supposedly as many as 1,200 warriors from the Adai and Nadaco factions camped along the confluence of the Sabinas and Canete Rivers in Coahuila, potential immigrants to protect Mexico's frontier with Texas.

This site in northern Coahuila continued to attract Indians and potential Mexican citizens, becoming a sort of pan-Indian refugee camp. Then, in 1843, an enigmatic figure named Dalgi Imaya arrived. Soon, he approached the governor of the state of Coahuila, Francisco Mejía, with an ambitious plan. Dalgi Imaya was likely the scion of the "Mascogue" chief Espopogne Imaya, in whose name he bargained with the Mexican governor. Imaya was not a Caddo but a Muskogee-speaking Seminole or Creek, maybe of mixed African heritage, and he was hopeful for his camp of Indian asylum seekers. He thought that it could grow larger still, maybe even transforming into a real basis for a pan-Indian colony. (His would not be the last pan-Indian dream that played out against a Mexican background). He negotiated the transfer of a large population of Native Americans in Indian Territory and Texas—over 129,000 individuals in all—to Coahuila. In one respect, such a project was immensely promising to the officers who manned the frontier and fretted endlessly over its security. Such a massive immigration of allied Indians may have defeated the Comanches once and for all, settled the frontier with useful citizens, and protected vecinos in the trade. A large immigration of Indians friendly to Mexico might also give Texans pause before invading their territory. The plan had one major drawback. The arrival of thousands of foreign Indians to the frontier of Coahuila would surely alarm the vecinos who inhabited the region and irritate white Texans and Tejanos alike across the border.

In any case, the migration never occurred, and Mejía did not believe that Imaya had authorization to speak for the many different tribes he purported to represent. Their bargain is interesting nonetheless, and the hopes and dreams of both Imaya and Mejía can be seen in the treaty they worked out together. In exchange for making war (*hacer la guerra*) against the Comanches, Mejía promised to give the immigrant tribes the lands on which they were squatting in perpetuity. As was typical in such arrangements, the Indians could not remain independent and autonomous. Rather, they were to "live under the subjection of the government" and—aware of the difficulties they might cause with the local population—remain at peace with the local people and "toda la nación" (the whole country).[42] This proposed massive emigration from Indian Territory would have resulted in the fullest culmination of an Indian buffer zone carefully monitored by the watchful Mexican government, but Imaya's proposal never worked out. Nevertheless, this area of far northern Coahuila continued to attract immigrant Indians across the racial frontier and inspire similar schemes among a new generation of Centralist-leaning Mexican frontier officers. A little less than a decade later, Mexican authorities at the frontier would try again to attract immigrant Indians, ultimately resulting in the grand experiment that involved Seminoles, Kickapoos, and Black Seminoles.

As we have seen, all of these plans to settle and secure Mexican territory with Indian immigrants had several major drawbacks for security on the frontier. Yet another serious threat was that the Indians who sounded out possibilities in Mexico sometimes associated with runaway slaves from Texas and Indian Territory. Runaway slaves joined groups of immigrant tribes passing through Texas. Coyote, for example, brought a runaway slave with him when he came to Mexico.[43] The immigration of 1850 would include many more African Americans and black Indians (see chap. 5). The presence of renegade Indians and runaway blacks in northern Mexico was extremely offensive to Texans. And since a number of runaways joined Indian caravans traveling across the state in the coming years to reach Mexico, Texans never managed to disentangle the issues of runaway blacks and immigrant tribes. Thus, in the wake of the immigrant Indians' arrival in Mexico, the vecinos would have to deal with their own fears of Indians, regardless of tribe. But they would also have to deal with yet another terror: Texan raiders, filibusterers, and slave hunters. Just as was the case in the buffer zones composed of Lipan Apaches who could never become the immigrants and citizens the

Mexican government wanted them to be, the immigrant tribes likewise threatened the security of the frontier.

Despite the hackles they raised among vecinos, immigrant tribes set a precedent that a generation of border crossers would follow as they crossed a racial frontier. Immigrants to Mexico found that, whatever their ethnicity, they were often welcome to populate the frontier as long as they accepted the government's terms. This contributed to a stark difference in racial thinking along the frontier between the Texans and Mexicans. This was, in part, because of the desperation of the Mexican government to people its frontier. The revolutionary commitments of the independence movement to social equality regardless of color also played its part. But immigrant tribes needed to take on the trappings of norteño civilization, become Christian, and, most important, defend their newly adopted home from outside threats if they wanted to become citizens. Unlike the buffers that the Mexicans tried to build with Lipans and Anglos, buffers composed of immigrant Indians sometimes succeeded—at least for a while. The Mexican military and its Indian allies managed to keep the Nueces Strip in a state of turmoil for years, until at least 1846. They also stalled further Texan expansion to the south, which was precisely what the Mexican government wanted them to do. In this case, the interests of the Mexican government and the immigrant tribes converged.

It is easy to see why the projects of immigrant tribes met with some success: when plans worked out properly, everyone got something in the trade. In the sparsely populated and resource-poor areas of the Nueces Strip and western Coahuila, the promise of land and independence away from racist Anglos could entice many Indians to cross the border. North American democracy may have amazed and amused European observers, but the most astute among them—Alexis de Tocqueville for instance—saw that equality and political enfranchisement eluded many racial others who had the misfortune of living in the United States.[44] Indians and blacks had little hope for inclusion in American society, so they looked for alternatives on the other side of the border. Mexicans, meanwhile, had their own dreams of governing an elusive and vast frontier by populating it with loyal and soldierly citizens. Citizenship in exchange for service to the government—these were the ties that bound the Mexican government and immigrants together. If only the Mexican officers who dreamed of a developed frontier had the resources to establish aliens and the support of local citizens for their plans, they could have properly managed and overseen a mass migration of immigrant tribes in the 1830s and 1840s, migrants who would have used force to protect Mexican national interests. Instead, none of their projects met long-term success. The reasons for this were fairly simple. The Indians never assimilated, the vecinos remained suspicious, and immigrants did not receive the resources that would have made their lives secure.

But we should not write this project off as a complete failure. It was tremendously successful in one way. The Mexican government worked with immigrant tribes to lend the nascent border meaning as a line of refuge for victims of U.S. American apartheid and racism. Mexican authorities continued in this course—insisting upon offering racial refuge and protection under the law in their country—even as relations with the Republic of Texas, and later the United States, deteriorated and then collapsed. Nevertheless, escapees from the United States learned an important lesson during the years surrounding the Texas revolt: borders between different peoples could be gateways to opportunities and alternatives. Nobody knew this better than runaway slaves.

3 / "Impatient for the Promised Freedom": Runaway Slaves in the Age of the Texan Revolution

In 1829 President Vicente Guerrero officially emancipated slaves everywhere in Mexico. By this point, one could only find a handful of enslaved people in any part of the country, with one major exception. Anglo Americans continued to pour into Texas alongside the enslaved people they brought with them to that territory. As a result, Guerrero felt immense pressure to make an exemption for Texas from a vocal group of congressmen in Saltillo (the capital of the conjoined states of Coahuila y Tejas) who supported the white immigration to Texas, their enterprise, and the slavery that helped make their dreams made out of cotton and Texas dirt a reality. Two months later, Guerrero made the concession to Texas.[1] Nevertheless, potential immigrants to Texas, still under Mexico's control, watched warily as the national government deepened its commitment to emancipation. Nor did it take long for Texans to notice a correlation between Mexican liberality on questions of race and freedom and how difficult it was for them to keep their slaves from running away.

Noah Smithwick, for instance, undertook to record his memories of Texas in his old age. He recalled the anxiety that slaveholders felt in the days of Mexican Texas. Smithwick is candid in his recollections about the difficulty slaveholders had forcing the enslaved to stay in place during the 1820s and 1830s. It was "probably owing to their ignorance of the language and country [in Mexico] that more of them did not leave," he wrote. Blacks knew that when they went toward Mexico they were going into a foreign and unknown land. But they also knew they were on their way to a country that had emancipated slaves. Despite the perilous journey and the unfamiliarity of the country, many enslaved people were—again, according to Smithwick—"impatient for the promised freedom" and took their chances.[2] Enslaved blacks ran away to Texas outside of the areas controlled by Anglo empresarios, where they could often find freedom. Béxar and Goliad, both of which were dominated by Tejanos, drew a few runaways. Other enslaved blacks went to the Mexican villages that dotted the banks of the Rio Grande to claim their freedom. Matamoros, Tamaulipas, often served as a final destination, but a smattering of runaways resided in all of the towns that lay along that river.

There were instances of Mexicans returning enslaved people to Americans according to the principles of comity in the years prior to the Texan Revolution.[3] After that conflict, however, feelings hardened, and Mexican officials were less likely to hand over runaways. As a result, a new line of liberty emerged in the Texas-Mexico borderlands. This line of liberty was a moving target before 1848. After the 1836 Texas Revolution, the southwesternmost border of slave country moved to the Nueces River. Ten years later, after the U.S.-Mexico War, the Rio Grande, the present-day international border, became the line between slavery and freedom.

This chapter picks up on the scholarship pioneered by Rosalie Schwartz, Sean Kelley, Karl Jacoby, and Alice Baumgartner detailing the border's role in the history of slavery in the era before the U.S. Civil War.[4] I emphasize one aspect of this history in particular: the role of officers, officials, and authorities who represented the interests of the Mexican Supreme Government in the borderlands in transforming the international line into a limit of liberty. Some locally situated Mexican officials served as key allies for runaways. There was a reason for this, one that resonated with the officials' nationalist feelings. It had to do with the pressure that Texans, and later Americans, put on Mexican officials to work with them to recover runaway slaves. This stance was not necessarily for humanitarian reasons but rather to assert the independence of the Mexican government in the face of North American pressure.[5]

Runaway Slaves in Mexican Texas

By the 1820s, although there were some black enslaved people (and Maroon colonies) in Veracruz and along the Costa Chica—the spit of land that runs along the elbow-shaped coast of Guerrero and Oaxaca—slavery had ceased to exist on any meaningful scale in Mexico. Every September 16, Independence Day, the Mexican president traditionally bought and freed a handful of the few enslaved blacks who remained. In 1829, Vicente Guerrero, who was an Afro-mestizo, like several heroes of Mexican independence, finished the job. The congress in Coahuila y Tejas hesitated to publish his national emancipation decree, fearful of the commotion it would surely cause in Austin's grant and around Nacogdoches, another slaveholding area in Texas. (Indeed, it did cause quite a stir around Nacogdoches when the Anglos there caught wind of it, even though Guerrero excepted Texas from the decree in December 1830.) They had good reason to be fearful.[6]

Runaways quickly took advantage of Mexico's deepening commitment to emancipation. The decree of April 6, 1830, outlawed further American immigration, of blacks or whites, to Texas and expressly forbade the entrance of new slaves to Mexican territory. Nor did Mexico explicitly promise to grant refuge to any African Americans who crossed over into Mexican Texas. Nevertheless, runaways began immediately to take advantage of the contradictory nature of the laws, fleeing into Mexican Texas from Louisiana. Like the Cherokees and other immigrant tribes, they crossed at Nacogdoches near the Sabine River and at other points along the eastern border, hopeful that they would find freedom in Texas outside of the empresario grants.[7] It might seem counterintuitive that some runaways initially went into Texas. But outside of the Anglo empresario colonies slavery was virtually unknown, and Mexican officials often protected the freedom of black runaways. In a very real sense African American runaways from slavery began driving Mexico and Anglo Texas toward a conflict on this issue.

The Tejanos who lived in Béxar and Goliad and the white Texans who lived above the Colorado River often found themselves in difficult situations vis-à-vis runaway slaves because of the many complicated and contradictory attitudes and laws regarding them in Tejas y Coahuila. As Raúl Ramos has demonstrated, Tejanos—even those in San Antonio—held slaves on occasion.[8] Tejano settlements were hardly slave societies, however, and some runaways went toward them. One runaway, known only as José, ran away from a plantation that lay along the Brazos River within Stephen Austin's colony in 1831. Taking along his son, Tom, and another black man named Peter, they made it to the department of Béxar (modern-day San Antonio), far to the west of the white empresario settlements, before a gang of kidnappers led by Henry Brown caught up to them. Brown had written Austin a couple of years earlier to let him know that Mexico's liberality on the issue of slavery was discouraging immigration to Texas. Apparently Brown had now decided to take

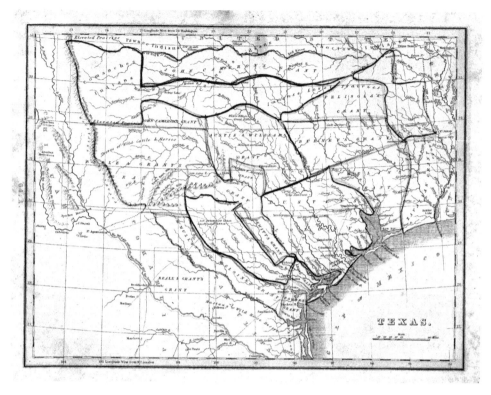

FIGURE 2. Empresario grants of Texas. Notice the presence of San Antonio de Béxar, just south of Austin's colony. From Comprehensive Atlas, Geographical, Historical and Commercial by Thomas Gamaliel Bradford, 1835. First issue of the first separate map of Texas to appear in an atlas. Courtesy Dorothy Sloan-Rare Books, Austin, Texas. Courtesy of the University of Texas Libraries, The University of Texas at Austin.

matters into his own hands. He led a posse made up of several men from Stephen Austin's colony, Green DeWitt's colony, and a couple who came all the way from Arkansas. They eventually caught up to the runaways and overpowered them, removing them from Tejano custody. Ramón Músquiz, jefe político of Béxar, sent a captain of the civil militia on their trail. Músquiz even authorized an agent to pay $800 for the men's freedom, in recognition of the property rights of the black men's former enslavers. Like most other elite Tejanos, Músquiz recognized that white Texans and their enslaved workers had done much to help develop Texas economically, and he did not want to alienate them. Most elite

Tejanos, supported by an important coalition of representatives in the Tejas y Coahuila congress in Saltillo, did not criticize slavery because they believed that the Texans who lived to the northeast of them had done much to improve their state.[9]

The extent of his efforts are not known, but, Músquiz was not able to recover the captives. When the Mexican captain in charge of the civil guard arrived at DeWitt's grant, he was too late, and the trail of the kidnappers had turned cold. Eventually the law caught up with Brown, but by then other members of his posse had taken possession of the kidnapped blacks and smuggled them out of Austin's grant to points unknown.[10] By offering to pay for the men's freedom, the jefe político recognized the legal foundation of slavery in Texas. Músquiz, like José Antonio Navarro and José Miguel de Arciniega, looked to slaveholders to bring progress to Mexican Texas.[11] But his offer to pay for the men's freedom also signaled ambivalence, if not confusion, on the part of Músquiz regarding Mexico's policies on runaway slaves.

Despite the ambiguity expressed by the Tejano allies of the Texan planters, runaway blacks who entered the more ethnically Latino/a areas of Texas and steered clear of the empresario grants could reasonably expect to find freedom and even sympathetic government officers. Juan (originally John) Davis Bradburn, for instance, a Mexican official in Texas, enforced the law against introducing new slaves into the territory passed in 1830. Bradburn did not seem a likely enemy of Texas slaveholders. He generally supported planter and mercantile interests in Mexican Texas and had even trafficked in slaves himself as a young man in Natchez, Mississippi.[12] As the commander at Anahuac, Bradburn, like some other officers in Mexican Texas, expressed ambivalence toward slavery. Still, he found himself on the payroll of the Mexican government in the early 1830s, and when forced to choose between his duties and the desires of local Texans he followed the letter of Mexican law.

In 1832 he faced trial by fire. Bradburn granted two runaways from Louisiana asylum in Texas. He could have turned them back—no American immigrants or slaves were supposed to enter Texas from the United States after April 1830—but he did not follow this course. Predictably, this move angered slaveholders in Austin's colony, and Bradburn soon caught wind of a rumor that one hundred armed men were at the ready on the Louisiana frontier, prepared to cross the Sabine River into Mexican Texas to reclaim the runaways. The rumor was a ruse. But while Bradburn prepared to fight off the invaders, William B. Travis—a failed lawyer from Alabama who had recently moved his practice to

Anahuac—took advantage of the commander's divided attention. He tried to kidnap the two runaways who had found shelter with Bradburn. Travis did not time his subterfuge well, and he failed to recover the runaways. Instead he landed in prison for a short time. His imprisonment outraged fellow Texans who could see the writing on the wall. So long as Texas remained a patchwork of confusing laws and practices regarding freedom and slavery, liberty outside the Anglo pale of settlement would not only attract Louisiana runaways, but it would also siphon off enslaved laborers from the plantations in Austin's colony.[13]

In contrast to the Anglos and their Tejano friends, some Mexican officials in Texas saw slavery's days as numbered. From Goliad, for instance, the clerk of the civil court wrote to Ramón Músquiz, listing the names of black children born of enslaved parents. The clerk even referred to the black children in his district as "*hijos* [children] *Coahuiltejanos*" rather than slaves.[14] Many officials, like this clerk, who represented the Mexican government in the North, promoted an antislavery agenda for Texas. Others, Tejano elites in particular, saw the interests of slaveholders and Mexican Texas as united. This resulted in two competing factions in Saltillo on the slavery question, but surely white immigrants to Texas were not used to having their institution threatened. This is what made Texas a borderland of slavery and freedom.[15]

Transplants from the U.S. South tried to adapt to Mexican attitudes toward blacks in Texas, which were not always in line with their own, but they were not about to give up their servile laborers. If they could no longer bring enslaved blacks into Texas, they instead brought in black laborers as indentured servants. In one instance, a kidnapper named Patrick Henry Herndon took a black woman named Sarah from her erstwhile master in New Orleans and trafficked her to Texas. He forced her to sign a ninety-year indenture contract before crossing the border. This effectively transformed her into a debt peon, which was a legally recognized form of servile labor in Mexican Texas.[16] General Manuel de Mier y Terán, investigating Texas for the supreme government, learned of this kidnapping from the aggrieved former master, who wrote to him from New Orleans. He had reason to object to Herndon's entrance into Texas. According to the Law of April 6, 1830, no new white—or for that matter, black—Americans could legally enter Texas. Thus both Herndon and his victim were in Texas illegally. They were sent back to Louisiana, despite the fact that Sarah was not technically a slave.[17] Soon thereafter the Mexican government closed this debt peonage loophole. In April 1832, the government of Tejas y Coahuila—under intense pressure from the antislavery faction—issued a law limiting the term of indenture in Mexico to not more than ten years.[18]

A Mexican diplomat in New Orleans, Francisco Pizarro Martínez, too, was chagrined by the "clandestine" nature of the "traffic of so many slaves into Texas, which was not approved by our [Mexico's] laws," under the name of indentured servitude.[19] Unlike officials stationed in the borderlands, Pizarro Martínez did not have to worry about harmonious relations with neighbors, so he unabashedly promoted the interests of freedom in Texas. Mier y Terán represented another Centralist voice in the Mexican government opposed to Texas slavery. He famously wrote the following after visiting Texas:

> Most of them [Anglos who came into Mexico illegally after 1830]
> have slaves, and these slaves are beginning to learn the favorable
> intent of the Mexican law towards their unfortunate conditions
> and are becoming restless under their yoke, and the masters, in
> the effort to retain them, are making that yoke even heavier; they
> extract their teeth, set on the dogs to tear them to pieces, the most
> lenient being he who but flogs his slaves until they are flayed.[20]

Clearly, Mexicans' distaste for slavery in Texas was grounded in real anxieties. They had good reason to fear large-scale social upheaval on the northern frontier led by dissatisfied, abused, and terrorized blacks seeking revenge on their masters. Mexicans already had enough problems in their troubled young nation without having to worry about becoming another Haiti.[21]

Other officials in the government promoted freedom because they reckoned that emancipated African Americans would owe Mexico their loyalty. Pizarro Martínez shared his disappointment about the confusing laws surrounding slavery in Texas with the strongly antislavery Mexican secretary of war, José María Tornel. Free blacks were not supposed to immigrate to Texas. But "If there were one species of inhabitants who would show repugnance in joining the [North] American confederation," he wrote, "it would be the free blacks since they are deprived of such a large part of their political rights." Further, "they would have a motive in staying under the Mexican government, which recognizes no distinctions of color."[22] Pizarro Martínez continued to promote the immigration of free blacks wherever he could despite the 1830 law. In 1831, for instance, when the schooner *María* was scheduled to leave New Orleans for Brazoria carrying several "industrious" free blacks who hoped to settle in Texas, Pizarro Martínez petitioned the central government vigorously in their support.[23] This would be far from the last scheme to introduce free African American immigrants to balance the power of Anglos in Texas and create a buffer against their further expansion.

Freedom South of the Rio Grande

Whereas the central Mexican government and even some members of the legislature of Tejas y Coahuila in Saltillo may have promoted freedom in Texas to balance the power held by the growing Anglo population, most runaways knew that it was much safer to cross the Rio Grande and head into territory where no whites lived. One pioneering runaway, Andrés Dortola (as he called himself after he left), moved far into the interior of Mexico in 1825 to escape the United States. Only when he reached Guadalajara, in the western state of Jalisco, did Dortola petition the Mexican government for citizenship, claiming that he had adopted Catholicism and met all of the requirements. Nestled deep within Mexico, Dortola had little risk of capture and reenslavement, but becoming a citizen in a country that demanded cultural assimilation of its immigrants was a daunting task. Like the other enslaved blacks who ran away to Mexico and petitioned for citizenship, he faced difficulty becoming a vecino.[24] Runaways were at the whim of Mexican officials who could easily turn them over to their former masters, although there is little indication of this happening very frequently. Nor did runaways find much in the way of economic opportunity in postcolonial Mexico, and as noncitizens Mexican authorities could jail them, and they had no legal recourse. But at least Dortola was free.

Dortola arrived in an area where slavery was virtually unknown. Most runaways, however, did not travel quite so far. A few hundred miles south of Austin's colony, the towns that dotted the Rio Grande—Las Villas del Norte, as Mexicans knew them—drew runaways in larger numbers than anywhere else. In the early 1830s, the great British abolitionist Benjamin Lundy arrived in the largest of these towns, Matamoros, to seek a land grant for a black colony in Tamaulipas. While visiting the town, he encountered a small community composed of free blacks as well as runaways from Texas, New Orleans, and the Caribbean already living there. He also observed that the state of Tamaulipas, which reached to the Río Nueces, offered a congenial home to people of color. He wrote appreciatively of the racial diversity of the region. While touring Tamaulipas he pronounced that the Mexicans there were "descended from European,

African, and original American ancestors, their *color* varies from the Castilian white to the darkest shades of the torrid climes."[25]

Lundy was right about the significant population of blacks in Tamaulipas. Africans and black creoles had indeed been a presence in northeastern Mexico for many years before Anglos pushed into Texas. The viceroyalty of New Spain began importing them to Nuevo Santander (as the Spanish referred to Mexico's Northeast) in the 1770s to work the new mines established in the region around San Carlos, which lay at the foot of the Sierra Madre Oriental.[26] Runaway slaves and refugee blacks from Texas, Louisiana, and other places added to this older black Mexican population in Tamaulipas by the 1830s at the latest. During this decade Lundy discovered the small but growing black expatriate community in Matamoros. He wrote that they enjoyed success and that they did "quite well in pecuniary matters."[27] Among the members of this small black community were two blacks from San Domingo who worked as tailors, a man named Guillermo Parent and another who was probably his son.[28] Lundy also encountered another black man—recorded as Antonio Dody in the Mexican archives—from Louisiana who worked as a carriage maker. Dody, in turn, had two friends—one a fellow carriage maker and the other a carpenter—who also hailed from Louisiana. Lundy befriended yet another black man, a brick mason named Henry Powell, who had also immigrated to Matamoros from Louisiana, with whom he boarded. The blacks from this small community encouraged Lundy in his project to establish a colony of free blacks, even giving him personal loans when he ran out of money.[29] Given their newfound freedom and reputed financial independence, the experience of blacks in Tamaulipas differed greatly from that of blacks in the southern United States. Whether or not all of these African Americans had begun their lives enslaved, they were now free on Mexican soil.

Given the relative liberality of Matamoros, it may not come as a surprise that Lundy's was not the only plan to settle blacks in sparsely populated northern Tamaulipas. Just as Pizarro Martínez saw the potential for free blacks as a buffer against aggressive Texans, some colonization officials already had a plan under way to settle loyal black citizens in the contested Nueces Strip before Lundy arrived. This strip lay just south of the border claimed by Mexico between Tamaulipas and Texas, along the south bank of the Nueces River. The colonization scheme involved the most well known and respected among the blacks who lived in Matamoros, a mulatto named Nicolas Drouet. He had already received an empresario grant from the state of Tamaulipas to bring a number of blacks from Louisiana, perhaps the ones aboard the schooner *María*.[30]

But despite their similar goals, Lundy and Drouet found themselves working at cross purposes. For one thing, Drouet was not as anxious as Lundy to overcome the bureaucratic hurdles that stood between him and his plans. Lundy wanted to leave right away for Ciudad Victoria to meet the governor of Tamaulipas, and he contemplated whether he should go on ahead without the dawdling Drouet. Lundy fell miserably sick while he waited for Drouet to make the necessary preparations for the journey. Then, while fighting off dysentery with laudanum, Lundy heard rumors that Texas and Mexico were about to go to war—a development that would certainly throw a wrench into his plans. Since war with Mexico would require Drouet's services as a soldier, Lundy decided to strike out alone for Ciudad Victoria. Drouet joined him at the last moment, and they had many disagreements along the way and once almost came to blows.[31]

Although the two men had similar aims, they had very different ideas about the sort of colonization project that would work best. Lundy hoped to emulate the British model of postemancipation society, imagining a type of black colony that produced staple crops. He was intensely interested in visiting sugar plantations while in Mexico, and he thought that the best model for a colony would be to set up a free labor experiment that produced this staple for global demand. Drouet, on the other hand, who lovingly attended to his own radishes and cabbages, probably imagined a military colony comprising free blacks with their own plots of land. This was the model that later Mexican colonization efforts followed. Military colonies in the Mexican North were comprised of peasants who tended their own *ejidos* (communal gardens) when they were not otherwise engaged protecting the country from raiders and rebels. Drouet likely envisioned something along these lines, and this came closer to what many former slaves actually wanted. If other examples from around the postemancipation Atlantic tell us anything, self-subsistence and truck farming most often meant independence to African Americans. They preferred growing food on a small scale over producing staples as enslaved people did.[32]

As far as we know, neither Drouet's nor Lundy's colony ever left the planning stages. Tamaulipas, however, continued to attract black runaways. Word of Mexican freedom spread among the enslaved. In the years following Mexican independence, the border cities along the Gulf of Mexico and the lower Rio Grande began to attract all sorts of visitors and new residents. Trade restriction along the Gulf of Mexico relaxed (for a time) following Mexican independence, and Americans quickly moved into this virgin market. They took their enslaved servants along with them to do the heavy lifting. Many enslaved blacks who traveled back and forth with their masters to the cotton emporium of Matamoros realized that Mexico was a very different country—especially when compared to the white supremacist colonies established by Anglos. Masters unwittingly exposed blacks to the more liberal climes of Mexico when they brought them along on trips to the lower Rio Grande. In turn, the most well traveled slaves undoubtedly spread the word about Mexico, greatly expanding the geographic knowledge of enslaved people in Texas.[33]

Still, no hard-and-fast rule guaranteed the freedom of African American runaways in Mexico from extradition. This began to change in 1833, when the U.S. consul in New Orleans asked his Mexican counterpart for a reciprocal treaty that returned runaways who had escaped from Louisiana to Mexico. Pizarro Martínez flatly refused.[34] The young republic's faith in liberty for all peoples stemmed from ideals promulgated by revolutionary leaders as diverse as Miguel Hidalgo y Costilla, José Morelos, and Vicente Guerrero. In addition, the majority of the Mexican population was composed of people whom North Americans referred to as mixed race—though in significantly less polite terms. Most important, North American attempts to influence Mexican policy felt like bullying. Mexicans had not just stained their patria with ten years' worth of blood and fire to trade one colonial overlord for another. Further, Pizarro Martínez belonged to a faction especially dedicated to the antislavery cause.

Finally, Mexicans had another reason for granting the African Americans who showed up at their borders freedom and refuge. This act demonstrated a magnanimity that sharply contrasted with policies on the Texan side of the border. In order to express the sovereign law of their territory—and to demonstrate the differences that marked Mexican space from Texan (and later American) space—the Mexican government protected the freedom of runaways. This was especially true once a new border separated the nascent Texas Republic from Mexico and feelings between the two sides soured accordingly.

Runaway Slaves and Texas Independence

The year 1836, when Texas achieved independence from Mexico, is seminal in the history of slaves escaping to Mexico. Before the events of that tumultuous year, the status of slavery in Mexico remained far from settled. As long as slavery could legally exist in the empresario colonies, it was not clear where the boundaries of slave country lay. After Texas seceded from Mexico, however, conditions changed. Mexican officials in the borderlands no longer had to walk a fine line between emancipation decrees issued in Mexico City and planter interests in Texas. Then, after Texas claimed victory at San Jacinto in April 1836, relations between Mexico and Texas worsened, and African Americans took advantage. The alliance between runaway blacks and free African Americans and Mexicans caused tremendous consternation among whites who claimed mastery over both Texas and African Americans. Violent encounters between Mexicans and Texans continued up through the North American invasion of 1846, and Texans fumed when they saw runaways on the other side.

As soon as the Texas Revolution began, enslaved people realized that they might have an ally in the Mexican army. Joining the so-called enemy in exchange for freedom was not an uncommon experience in the history of the African diaspora. From the American Revolution through the Haitian Revolution through subsequent revolutions in Latin America, many of the enslaved ran to the side that promised them freedom. Texans were not slow to see the precariousness of their situation vis-à-vis slaves. Some of them feared that blacks might comprise a fifth column as the Mexican army approached. Some Texan rebels alleged at one point that the president of Mexico and general of the punitive military expedition, López de Santa Anna himself, entertained a plan of reconquest that involved inciting a slave revolt.[35] The specter of Haiti, Hidalgo, and every other racially charged social revolution in the Americas haunted the events in Texas as enthusiastic volunteers from throughout the U.S. South sought to avenge the Mexican massacres of Texans at the Alamo and Goliad.

Revolt and flight among the enslaved greatly troubled the proceedings of Texan independence.[36] Mexican officers in revolutionary Texas deployed African Americans to serve as spies and report on their masters. Juan Almonte, a high-ranking Centralist officer and companion to Santa Anna during the years of warfare against Texans, hired African American valets and generally took advantage of their familiarity with Texas for reconnaissance. In 1836, Texans near Galveston captured one of Almonte's African American servants, who escaped with the help of "Santa Anna's personal secretary." He reached General Pedro Ampudia to report on the number of "yanqui" soldiers gathering in that city and to inform him that the majority of Texan volunteers in Galveston were in fact adventurers from New Orleans.[37] This confirmed the suspicion of the Mexican government that the majority of insurgents in Texas were southern pro-slavery filibusterers and fire-eaters, recent arrivals radicalizing the Texan rebels.

The war ended in April 1836, and some runaways took advantage of the confusion that ensued to make good their escape to Mexico and join officers there. As the lines of Mexican soldiers slowly retreated south, many runaway slaves joined them. Mexican officers generally accepted the runaways into their lines. José de Urrea, who served in Texas during the war, reported that fourteen runaways came to him with their families seeking asylum at the conclusion of the war with Texas. He sent them on to live in Ciudad Victoria in Tamaulipas. But Urrea's course of action was not the only one that Mexican commanders took. Although the central government outlawed slavery and granted asylum to all runaways who made it to Mexico, officers in the borderlands sometimes hesitated to grant asylum. Interested in maintaining some sort of peace with their neighbors to the north in Texas, Mexican commanders sometimes acted against the wishes of their superiors and sent runaways back to slavery in Texas. Urrea registered his disgust when the commander in chief of the Mexican army in Texas, Vicente Filisola, agreed to return the slaves who had run away to his lines during the conflict to the Texan peace commissioners. Filisola, who owned land outside of Nacogdoches, had a vested interest in maintaining some semblance of peace with the Texans.[38] This discrepancy in the behavior of Mexican commanders vis-à-vis runaways demonstrates a central paradox in the borderlands. Enforcing edicts handed down by a distant central government was not always a top priority among officials saddled with the day-to-day burden of maintaining peace along a highly contested frontier. Mexican officials, and the governments they represented, came and went with alarming frequency. Local vecinos and Tejanos were the ones who had to actually eke out a living in the north alongside hostile neighbors.

Nevertheless, if Tejanos rarely involved themselves in the conflict, there are some instances of vecinos in the Mexican North on the other side of the Rio Grande rallying in defense of runaways. Archival sources provide insight into the relationship between blacks who ran away from slavery and Mexican officers in the borderlands, but on occasion the desire to protect African Americans had popular origins. After the war, for instance, when a party of Texans arrived in Matamoros to retrieve a group of runaways, several vecinos colluded with the town's authorities to hide them. When found out, instead of turning over the runaways, the

Mexican authorities arrested the Texas peace commissioners. They eventually returned to Texas empty-handed.[39] In another instance involving the peace commissioners, the people of Matamoros collected $80 to buy one of the Texans' slaves who wished to stay behind.[40] Thus some people who lived in the villages of the lower Rio Grande sympathized with the blacks seeking refuge there.

The war concluded with Texas winning its independence but losing a good number of slaves. As late as 1840, Texan slaveholders and bounty hunters still crossed into Mexico searching for the runaways who had joined the retreating Mexican armies four years earlier.[41] Thus the years of the Texan conflict with Mexico mark an especially important period in the history of runaway slaves. The mobility of the enslaved blacks from Texas who took advantage of the confusion caused by the war translated directly into expanded knowledge of where the limits of liberty lay. It was also during these years that, at least in Texas, running away became the focal point of slave resistance. The presence of so many Mexican soldiers and officers who represented a hostile foreign government that lay just south of them and the experience that so many runaways had during the war were communicated via underground networks, translating into increasing numbers of blacks sojourning across the borderlands to liberty. Runaway flights produced a subterranean geography among the enslaved, composed of routes produced by hundreds of individual journeys to freedom.[42]

With independence won, Texan slaveholders had still failed to remove the threat posed by pro-emancipation Mexico. In fact, independence may have made the situation worse. The proximity of a free country and a hostile army had destabilizing effects on slavery in Texas. The routes laid down by mobile African Americans in the borderlands remained outside the control of Texas authorities. Pedro Ampudia and Mariano Arista, for instance, encountered blacks far to the south of the Anglo settlements in the Nueces Strip, which they considered free Mexican territory. In 1840, both officers wrote to the Mexican minister of war on different occasions after receiving intelligence about the Texans from English blacks that wandered into their camps near the Rio Grande. Confident in their new knowledge of the state's geography, at least some blacks began to roam the contested Nueces Strip, the borderland between the Republic of Texas and Mexico—and, not coincidentally, the borderland of slavery and freedom.[43]

Runaways and Mexican Abolitionism
after the Battle of San Jacinto

After the secession of Texas Mexicans had another reason to grant asylum to runaway slaves: politics. Mexican nationalists had swallowed an especially bitter pill when the Texan rebels captured Santa Anna at San Jacinto and made him sign papers recognizing the independence of the Republic of Texas. The Texans—and, implicitly, Santa Anna—recognized the border at the Rio Grande, but their area of effective control did not extend beyond the Nueces. Henceforth, ideological differences regarding race and freedom ossified along the fault line that separated Mexico from the newly independent Texas. When Mexicans proclaimed themselves a country of liberty for all, they drew a sharp contrast between themselves and the repressive Texans to the north. The ties between popular sovereignty, anti-gringoism, and emancipation tightened for Mexicans and runaway slaves alike in this heated political atmosphere.

Abolitionist sentiment flowered in Mexico after the Texas revolt, as many Mexicans expressed disgust not just with Texas but with slavery as well. Declarations of human equality and condemnations of Yankee aggression streamed from the pens and presses of patriotic Mexicans located in various parts of the country. Humiliated by their recent defeat, Mexicans began to celebrate their republic's dedication to color equality. As the editor of Mexico City's *El Universal* put it, Mexico afforded all people greater life opportunities regardless of color: "In the United States neither the most moral nor the richest descendant of Africans is free to enjoy the benefits of other men who have no advantage except for the color of their skin." From a conservative corner in Mexico City came a similar condemnation of racism. According to *El Monitor Republicano*, "the Catholic laity does not now see distinctions of blood or color amongst Mexicans. They protect with equal benevolence all of the sons of this country, whether they are white, black, pardo, or *cobrizo* (copper colored). They give charity to men of all origins, and prepare for the fusion of all human races, something that is coming to pass more and more every day."[44] Universal equality and the celebration of human intermixture in an intensely Catholic country clearly had precedents that predated the cult of *la raza cósmica* (the cosmic race) in the twentieth century. Nearly a hundred years before José Vasconcelos's famous tract, Mexicans had already begun to define their racial identity in opposition to the colossus to the north, adding antiracist meaning to the border.[45]

Some Mexicans wondered out loud how a country that claimed to be democratic could practice racial slavery. In response to the *Herrenvolk* democracy of the Jacksonian era—where white male equality was predicated on slavery and black subjugation—some Mexican writers pointed out the obvious racism. They did not see why some groups were repressed in order to ensure the greater liberty of others in the United States. According to an article in *El Universal,* written in the aftermath of the U.S.-Mexico War:

> Why is it that, in the [United States] despite the Federal system
> they profess, and notwithstanding the principal of equality estab-
> lished there, and not withstanding their jealousy of the natural
> rights of man, are slaves, Indians, all people of color, and all other
> rational beings and individuals making up a large part of society
> excluded from elections, the military and from public office? The
> answer is simple: they do not know their natural rights because . . .
> they are kept in a state of frightening misery and sad intellectual
> degradation.[46]

Mexicans who sought to downplay North Americans' putative dedication to liberty needed only to point out the wretched situation of noncitizens in the United States—which newspapers did frequently. As *El Monitor Republicano* put it during the heat of the U.S.-Mexican War, "In the [American] patria, there is neither liberty nor political rights except for the dominant race."[47]

Runaways, and the issue of racism generally, played an important role in the ongoing conflict between Mexico and the United States as ammunition in an ideological war fought between the two countries. They helped connect the issues of anti–North Americanism and antislavery in Mexico. These two issues could at last not be separated, and it is not coincidental that two of the strongest colonization laws that Mexicans passed explicitly prohibiting slavery in the northern Mexican frontier dated from 1837 and 1846. The first date corresponds with the end of the war against Texas; the second, with the outbreak of the U.S.-Mexico War. In both cases, Mexico lost large portions of its territory.[48] Having lost the actual physical ground of northern New Spain itself, the Mexican government sought to hold the moral high ground.

As a result of contrasting polices regarding slavery and freedom on either side of the border, African Americans fought alongside Mexicans in the years of the embattled and debt-ridden Texas Republic (1836–46). Fighting did not cease after San Jacinto. In April 1839, for instance,

Mexican troops faced off against a force of Texas Rangers serving under Ed Burleson and Ben McCulloch in Texas. One of the captives the Texans took after a battle near Seguin was a large Francophone black man named Raphael. Despite his protests that he had never been a slave, he was executed at dawn the next day by the Texas Rangers. The Rangers celebrated the execution of this unfortunate man; the Texan James O. Rice even paid a soldier assigned to the firing squad five dollars to take his place. Unfortunately for Rice, his gun failed upon firing, leaving him "crestfallen."[49] The Texans considered it a privilege to execute a black man who fought for Mexico. When the firing squad finished its work, a dead man who represented not only the threat of Mexico but also the threat of black freedom lay before them.

Nothing represented national difference on ideas of race and slavery better than black men fighting alongside Mexicans. The Tejano caudillo Vicente Córdova occasionally recruited runaway slaves as well as immigrant Indians to fight Texans and to defend the original settlers of Nacagdoches.[50] In March 1841, Burleson met Córdova's "motley crew of Mexicans, runaway negroes and Bilouxie Indians" near Seguin. During the battle, Burleson's Texas Rangers captured an elderly black man and another African American serving the Mexicans and prepared to sell them into slavery. The old man violently protested, claiming that he had run away from slavery years ago to work with the Mexicans in a silver mine just south of Seguin. He refused to be sold back into slavery and said to Burleson, "You had better kill us now, for we will fight till we die before we will be slaves again." While he was enslaved, he claimed, he had killed many others: "I kilt my master and his whole family, nine in number, to get freedom and I won't be a slave long at a time no more." The Texans executed both the elderly African American and his companion.[51] Although this account may have been exaggerated, it betrayed a real anxiety on the part of the Texans. African Americans fighting alongside the Mexicans during this undeclared war risked everything to throw the whites' mastery of Texas into question.

Black friendships with high-ranking Mexican military officers particularly ruffled Texans' feathers. After his victory over the Texan filibusterers at Mier in 1842, Pedro Ampudia took a number of combatants prisoner and forced them to march under armed escort to Matamoros. As they made their way, the villagers who lived along the river turned out to celebrate the victorious general. He was warmly received in each of the towns where the military convoy stopped—confirming at least some popular anti-Texas sentiment along the Rio Grande. Among the friends and "principal men" who turned out to greet Ampudia in the tiny village of Guadalupe were two black runaways named Esau and Thomas. They were General Samuel Houston's former slaves, and the most famous runaways in Texas history. As Esau and General Ampudia embraced, Ampudia's Texan prisoners looked on, wishing they could make a "carcas" of the man. Esau, who more than likely ran away while hired out from Houston's Cedar Point plantation in 1840, undoubtedly received their meaning and stayed far away from the Texan prisoners. Thomas, however, had no fear of venturing among them and represented himself as Houston's former secretary and a man of importance in Ampudia's entourage.[52]

Soon, the convoy left Tom and Esau behind to continue its journey to Matamoros, where the prisoners discovered that still more runaway slaves had mixed with popular Mexican society. In Matamoros, the army paraded the Texan prisoners along the streets, and the townsfolk turned out en masse to witness the spectacle and celebrate the Mexican victory over the Texan volunteers. The Mier prisoners had become unwilling participants in an important ritual of the political culture of the nineteenth-century Mexican North. In the *zócalos* (central plazas) of these dusty frontier towns, patriotic spectacles inculcated a largely illiterate frontier society with a sense of belonging to the newly independent nation of Mexico.[53] For the very special events that celebrated the capture of the Mier prisoners in 1842, the display of the prisoners' living but broken bodies was the centerpiece of the patriotic festivities. The capture of the Texan raiders had been quite a fête for the Mexican army, and the display of the prisoners was meant to inculcate in the norteños a sense of *mexicanidad*—Mexican national identity—that set them apart from the Texans. The vecinos of Matamoros shunned the Texan prisoners in an affirmation of their own Mexican identity. In the federalist North, the army brass turned this festivity into a far from trivial event. Here there was a decidedly national (or at least regional) celebration put on by such Centralist officers as Ampudia and Almonte in an area known for its Federalist predilections that included many from Matamoros's popular classes, including blacks.[54]

The spectacle attracted a cross section of the vecinos and inhabitants of Matamoros, including African Americans who had found freedom on this side of the Rio Grande. One of the prisoners, William Stapp, even as he endured the agony of the exhibition, spotted the "ebony-vissages" of some Texan runaways among other lower-class spectators milling about in the streets. He made the rather far-fetched claim that he recognized several of them, saying that they had once belonged to friends at home in Texas. In an uncanny reversal of roles, feeling like historical justice, formerly enslaved black people could gawk at the captive white bodies on display. But African Americans were just part of the great crowd staring at the Americans, reversing the order of things, and "othering" the unfree white Texans.[55] Beneath the terraces occupied by Matamoros's genteel set, Stapp wrote, the crowds "positively hived with the lower orders of the population" and "ill-vissaged beggars," who "hissed at us as we passed, with a venomous malice and hate." With the exception of some elites in Matamoros who avoided the spectacle, anti-gringoism appeared to be on the rise among the popular classes along the Rio Grande. This is not surprising, given the Texans' willingness to invade the frontier and hold the borderlands captive in pursuit of their own expansionist, slaveholding goals, and at the expense of Mexican sovereignty.[56]

The encounter between blacks who were free—because they had moved to a country that promised liberty—and captive white men was remarkable. One incident in particular reflects the menace with which Texans viewed the African Americans who lived free in Mexico. A captured Texas volunteer named Andrew Neill at last learned from an African American in Matamoros what had happened to a certain Mr. Stinnett who disappeared from Texas two years before. It turns out that Stinnett had run across a camp of African American runaways en route to Mexico and hailed them cheerfully in the dark, mistaking them for fellow hunters. The runaways immediately relieved the white man of his horses, provisions, money, and life. The African American who related this information to Colonel Neill also told him where he should look for the body so it could be "found and interred."[57] Another runaway in Matamoros named Sawney evinced a "professed devotion" to the Texan prisoners and even an "attachment to their interest," visiting them regularly in the jail. But when the Texans hatched a daring plan of escape, Sawney alerted the Mexican authorities, who quickly put an end to their schemes.[58]

When the war with the United States came, runaway slaves continued in their pattern of finding freedom behind enemy lines alongside Mexican friends and allies. In 1846, the decade of undeclared warfare across the Nueces Strip reached a climax when Zachary Taylor campaigned along the Rio Grande as part of a larger North American invasion of Mexico. Many officers in Taylor's army had brought their enslaved bondsmen with them since the army paid them an extra stipend of up to $10 a month to defray the cost of keeping servants. These slaveholding officers did not

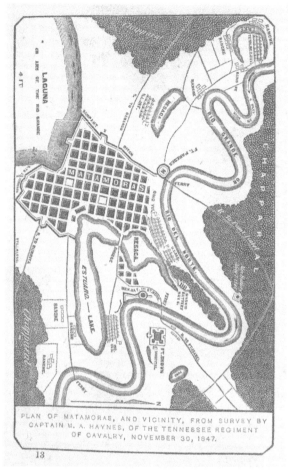

FIGURE 3. Matamoros during the U.S. occupation. Plan Of Matamoras [*sic*], And Vicinity, From Survey By Captain M. A. Haynes, Of The Tennessee Regiment Of Cavalry, November 30, 1847. 1847. From Rice University. http://hdl.handle.net/1911/35712.

know, however, that the Rio Grande was now the line of liberty. Blacks began to desert as soon as Taylor's army arrived at the river in May. In Matamoros, at least one group of the invading Americans' enslaved servants took advantage of the proximity of freedom and ran away to join the black community there, leaving behind three very disappointed officers who would have to do without the comforts of home.[59]

African Americans and Mexican Statecraft

The freedom that blacks found in Mexico came at a cost. When blacks exited Texas for the country to the south, which formally granted them freedom in 1849, they did not step into a vacuum.[60] Mexican officials expected to tie the interests of African American immigrants to the attempts of the government to exert control over its territory, and thus incorporate them in Centralist politics. As early as the 1830s, Mexican officials decided that Lundy's colony of free blacks should be located in the Lipan-dominated and highly contested Nueces Strip. Known on contemporary maps as the Wild Horse Desert, this area was a borderland long before either Texans or Mexicans started moving toward the Rio Grande Valley. The proposed black colony would serve as a buffer zone between the Mexican settlements along the river and the Anglo settlements filling up Austin's empresario grant and bounded by the Lavaca River to the south. The blacks' residency in Mexico depended on dutifully accepting roles assigned them by the Mexican state or face extradition. In a sense, they were hostages of the federal government.[61]

The U.S.-Mexico War made any plans to set up a black colony in the Nueces Strip irrelevant, but fugitives from slavery could be useful in other parts of the country. In Tampico, Tamaulipas, for instance, when a "multitude" of mulattos from New Orleans showed up in the late 1830s seeking refuge, they were allowed to stay contingent on their serving as artillery men in the national militia.[62] Hence, the myriad pronouncements made by Centralist Mexican officials on color equality must be taken with a grain of salt; they expected to gain something from the black migrants. Mariano Arista served Santa Anna dutifully during the U.S.-Mexico War (although he would later become a leading Liberal). When he became secretary of war after the U.S.-Mexico War he expressed intense interest in defending Mexican territory. Early on, he recognized the key role that African Americans—as well as other North American dissidents—could play in the insecure North. When invaders threatened Tampico in the immediate aftermath of the war, the events that followed foreshadowed the borderlands projects that involved using black immigrants in the state-building efforts that characterized the 1850s.

Although the port city of Tampico did not belong to the Mexican North, the deployment of loyal African American auxiliaries there hinted at new policies that commanders would soon undertake along the international frontier. Threatened by invasion from abroad in 1849,

Arista looked for soldiers to come to the aid of the republic who would be free from "the seduction of our enemies." The commander of the plaza in Tampico nominated the black immigrants in Tampico, saying they would "decisively defend the country in which they had found liberty and protection under the laws." To prepare for the invasion, he suggested that they drill frequently with a Howitzer captured from the North Americans.[63] The commander continued, saying of the black emigrants from New Orleans who had come to Tampico, "Although they are a small number, [they] are the natural enemies of the Americans, they have always been prompt to lend their services to the Mexican Republic, and they have never, despite having been invited, mixed in any disturbance of any class."[64] Just as he predicted, in 1849, the "mulattos" of New Orleans helped the Centralist officers recapture the plaza of Tampico from Federalist revolutionaries—earning the scorn of some vecinos. The townsfolk felt that the commanders could "easily bribe" the African Americans who relied on their largesse to guarantee their freedom.[65] In the 1850s, similar dynamics operated along the Rio Grande frontier, where African Americans beholden to the central government for their freedom did not always act in the interests of vecinos or federalist officials. But regardless of local tensions, African Americans found that Mexico guaranteed their freedom—especially during the years of Centralist (and later, Conservative) domination of Mexican politics. The U.S.-Mexico War only further committed the government to the cause of emancipation and international refuge for African Americans.

This chapter has told two related stories. The first story is of African Americans' imagining the border between Mexico and the United States as a line of liberty. Runaway slaves left the United States for Mexico as early as the 1820s and never stopped coming—at least until the end of the Civil War. As I discuss in subsequent chapters, their history was more complicated. The growing menace of Texan slave hunters and filibusterers constantly imperiled the runaways' liberty. Nor did all runaway slaves always find the economic security that Lundy insisted they did. Finally, not all northern vecinos were happy to have runaways in their midst. But blacks did find freedom in Mexico, an important fact that we should not underestimate. Just as the borderland became less nebulous in the period 1836–48, when the Rio Grande became the international border, so too did the border between freedom and slavery firmly take hold in the aftermath of the Texan Revolt and, especially, the U.S.-Mexico War. This was due in no small part to the political agency of runaway slaves, who brought on conflict between Mexico and Texas and pushed the government on the south side of the Rio Grande toward embracing abolitionism wholeheartedly.

The second story takes place at a higher political level, even if it is still a history driven by runaways from slavery. The Mexican government's deepening commitment to emancipation from 1829 on was not only a result of runaways coming across their border; it was also a result of growing Anglo bellicosity in Texas. Some (but not all) Mexican officials recognized the threat represented by the Anglo presence in Texas, and they realized that a contrasting policy on slavery might prevent further immigration by Americans. Once runaways entered the picture, some Mexican officials, especially Centralists opposed to the pro-Texas and pro-slavery bloc of Tejanos and norteños in Saltillo, began trying to insert them into their own efforts at nation building. This was an act intended both to express sovereignty and to defend their frontiers. Suffice it to say here, protecting runaway slaves continued to be a strategy on the part of the Mexican state to assert different ideals from those of the Texans. Runaway slaves were a political football punted back and forth between Mexican and American government. But the explosiveness of the situation did not make for a secure situation for the runaways who merely wanted to live a life of freedom away from United States.

4 / A "Great System of Roaming": Runaway Debt Peons and the Making of the International Border

In 1834, a debt peon named Magdaleno Treviño ran away from his *amo* (master), Rafael Vidaurri of Laredo, whom he owed a sum of forty-six and a half pesos. Up until the day he decided to remove himself from his master's service, Treviño had served as Vidaurri's sirviente, or debt peon. Treviño most likely labored in the fields, and he was supposed to continue doing so until he paid back the money he had borrowed from Vidaurri—something that would likely take a lifetime, if not longer, to accomplish. Treviño lived on Vidaurri's property and went further into debt, taking room and board and buying articles at the hacienda store (*tienda de raya*). At some point, he simply left all this debt behind. Vidaurri waited a while after noticing Trevino's disappearance before he reported him, probably hoping that Treviño would return of his own accord. When he did not, Vidaurri contacted the nearby municipal authorities, expecting them to search for Treviño in the surrounding area and return the fugitive servant to Laredo.[1]

Sirvientes were not slaves, but Vidaurri could count on the help of the municipal authorities to bring his debt peon back. Indentured servitude for debt was a legal labor arrangement throughout Mexico, and Vidaurri's message intended to put potential captors on guard. It contained only a bare minimum of information about the runaway, however. He merely recounted the amount of money his servant owed him. But it was this sum, about a year's wages, that formed the crux of the servant's identity, at least as far as the debt holder and the municipal authorities were concerned. It was after all not Treviño himself who Vidaurri owned but the debt, held in perpetuity until the day Treviño died or paid him back. In some places, children became responsible for the debts of deceased parents. This was how debt peonage differed from slavery, even if it did not always appear so different.

There were debt peons all over Mexico, but the proximity of alien peoples and cultures nearby made Treviño's situation somewhat different from that of his cohort farther south. For one thing, he had been gone for two months when Vidaurri alerted the authorities, perhaps delaying notification because he thought Treviño had taken an unauthorized, temporary leave. It was not unusual for sirvientes to take leave from their amos in this region. In fact, some ranchers and hacienda owners blamed the latitude allowed the peon workforce for the borderlands' lack of development. One farmer found that "nothing advances in agriculture because some agricultural servants hide, others fake being sick, others don't obey, and others leave service with no intention of returning." In the sparsely populated frontier there was a dearth of laborers, so the bosses did not always get to call the shots. Runaway peons were also problematic because, like deserting soldiers, they allegedly joined gangs of highwaymen that roamed the borderlands, making travel on the roads perilous.[2] But it was the ever-growing economic opportunities on the other side of the border that most attracted runaway laborers from northern Mexican haciendas and ranchos.

This chapter argues that the mobility of sirvientes in the Texas-Mexico borderlands—their penchant for absconding from their erstwhile masters—made them different from debtors farther into the interior of Mexico. And it was the promise of refuge among the growing Anglo population in Texas that made runaway servants, or better, *siriventes prófugos* (fugitive peons), so important to the history of the borderlands. The many individual journeys (*jornadas*) such as Treviño's from servitude to freedom affected the history of this region greatly, for these journeys did not just result in the liberation of individuals. They also had an economic effect on the development of the borderlands. Flights such as Treviño's resulted in the transfer of scarce resources (labor and horses in particular) from Mexico to Texas. The sheer volume of runaway peons also forced many Northern Mexican elites to take stock of the situation and rethink peonage, their own native form of servile labor, if they wanted to see agriculture in the Mexican North advance.

This unauthorized mobility, the flight of debt peons from one side to the other—from the south to the north side of the Rio Grande—has deep roots, reaching back to the 1830s if not earlier. By 1834, when Treviño fled, there were other opportunities to the north where Tejanos lived. Even farther north, Anglos and enslaved blacks were filling up the river valleys of Texas. Peonage also existed on Tejano ranches, but once runaways reached more distant foreign populations, they could work for wages, contract new debts, or cart goods for Anglos and Tejanos. Especially after 1848, when the Treaty of Guadalupe Hidalgo drew a hard political line between Texas and Mexico, debt peons recognized the flexibility of their situation. They believed this border fiction, this new invisible line between Texas and Mexico, and invested it with significant meaning. They turned the line into a limit of liberty. Unlike runaway slaves, however, the course they plotted ran from south to north.

Debt Peonage

Debt peonage is a relatively unexplored topic by historians, and there is some disagreement regarding where debt peons originated. The earliest debt peons probably began as enslaved Indians, and it is likely that those in the U.S.-Mexico borderlands descended from Indians captured and sold to the earliest vecinos of the Río Bravo.[3] As such, when Texans disparagingly referred to the runaway peons who moved into their state in the 1850s as "Indians," there may have been something to their claims. They looked different from the light-skinned vecinos who dominated Mexican society in the North. Omar S. Valerio-Jiménez, in his impressive work on the lower Rio Grande Valley, writes that peons were enslaved Indians who became de-ethnicized criados or *mozos* (servants) over succeeding generations. Unfortunately for them, the lack of Indian identity stripped indebted laborers of any sort of refuge that an Indian community or village might have offered (though few of these existed in el norte). And by the time Anglos and runaway peons began to encounter one another, captive Indians and their descendants had surely adopted Spanish as their primary language and acclimated to the norms of their Hispanic host society. Farther west, in New Mexico and California, Latino/as still practiced Indian enslavement alongside debt peonage. Most likely the peons in Texas and northeastern Mexico discussed here were a discrete category of servile labor, separate from Indian captives. But this topic requires further research.[4]

More and more impoverished Mexicans and Indians who needed credit contracted with masters and worked until they paid off their debt (if they ever did), becoming indentured servants or debt peons in the trade. This situation was not entirely disadvantageous in theory. In

Mexico's central valley some debt peons considered credit an honor and a guarantee of future work. In the far North, however, generalizations about the benignity of debt peonage—the sort that Alan Knight or Harry Cross make about central and near northern Mexico—do not hold true.[5] Conditions on the northern Mexican frontier were miserable (although probably not as wretched as in the far south of Mexico).

There were a number of reasons for the northern debt peons' unending misery. The haciendas in the North encompassed vast territory since the frontier was so sparsely settled and the extensive development of large semiarid ranges was necessary to make them productive. As a result, only a handful of haciendas, such as the Sánchez-Navarros' holdings in present-day Coahuila and the Hacienda de La Sauteña in Tamaulipas, came to dominate vast regions. This land monopoly by a handful of borderlands elites put potential debtors near northern haciendas at a disadvantage. If peasants or free vecinos needed credit in the North, they only had one source: the local elites and landowners who were often related by blood. There were few other lenders or employers and, as a result, little room for negotiation. Freeholders and villagers existed in the North only in small numbers. Permanent peon, vaquero, and *peon acasillado* (resident) workers provided the sprawling haciendas with the bulk of their labor needs in a region dominated by large-scale agriculture. [6]

Aboriginal plains raiders acted alongside landholders to keep servants chained to the land. "Bárbaros" and hacendados may have made strange bedfellows, but their interests converged to reduce peons to dependency. The walled hacienda complexes often offered the only protection from the near-constant depredations of Comanche and Apache peoples in the 1830s and 1840s, and peons might have chosen virtual imprisonment on the hacienda rather than death on the open plains. The fortresslike center of the hacienda could provide the only protection for miles around against an Indian attack—and even so the peons, especially shepherds who worked far out in the fields, were still quite vulnerable. Hence, the plains raiders were a push factor, causing peons to congregate into the relative safety of the hacendados' complexes.[7]

Another coercive factor was the legal framework that gave amos complete control over their indebted servants. Even if a peon ran away and managed to escape harm, all nearby municipal authorities had legal authorization to return fleeing debtors to their masters. Given the scarcity of labor, the authorities in the borderlands made the return of fleeing debtors a priority. If a peon somehow managed to make it across Indian Country intact, he or she would likely be spotted in one of the dusty, scarcely populated, and endogenous town centers that dotted the frontier. Only through the courts could peons redress particular grievances, and they typically found the odds stacked against them.[8] Even without the presence of plains raiders or unfair justice systems, it should not surprise us that debt peonage may been especially brutal in the frontier North. The historian Howard Lamar discovered long ago that in labor-starved areas where employers and masters compete to hold onto working men and women, they often employ intense coercion to keep their workers in place.[9]

With few options and walled in by plains raiders on all sides, peons often lived desperate lives. To use one oft-cited example, the peons who lived on the latifundia of the Sánchez-Navarro clan, which at its height encompassed most of the present-day state of Coahuila, suffered terribly. One outside observer wrote that the walled compound he discovered on one hacienda held many indebted vecinos from the villages of northern Coahuila. The peasants had no choice but to move to the hacienda and reside in the "little huts made of corn stalks" and labor alongside "200 lousy peons [who] lived in misery while working off their debt." Peons were not often able to put their entire wages toward their debts either. They typically had to buy their effects at company stores with hacienda tokens. Without their own ejidos, dependent peons on northern haciendas were at the mercy of the hacendado and his clerk's price gouging.[10]

In the state of Nuevo León, according to the historian Juan Mora-Torres, labor conditions may have been the worst of all on the Mexican frontier during the immediate postindependence period. The relative poverty of the landlords in this largely undeveloped state compounded the difficulties for peons who sought shelter on the haciendas. Hacendados in that state did not have the wealth of landowners in central Mexico or the Sánchez-Navarros and, as a result, could not pay the higher wages or provide the services that debt peons in other parts of the country demanded. Central Mexican hacendados, and probably the Sánchez-Navarro latifundia as well, typically offered some medical services and schooling to resident laborers and their families. In Nuevo León, however, the only perk the resident debt peons received was some respite from the near-constant war Comanches made on that state during the 1830s and 1840s. Amos in Nuevo León were also notorious for physically abusing their peons. Further, debts often passed from parent to child—either legally or through other means.[11]

Peonage had its defenders in Mexico, however. Indebted workers on Mexican haciendas had far greater legal recourse than did enslaved people on Texan plantations. Mexican amos were subject to a number of laws that protected the rights of debt peons. In the early 1850s, in a well-publicized case from San Fernando, Coahuila, a peon successfully sued his master for back wages.[12] Another compelling example comes from Nuevo León and involved a remarkably unfortunate debt peon named José María Botello. In early 1856, a band of Lipan Apaches approached Botello as he labored in the countryside and took him captive. He was freed when the Mexican Army of the North massacred the Lipan band in March that year. After his redemption, however, an officer named Antonio Zapata claimed Botello as his own servant. Botello contested this new captivity and pressed his case with the *juzgado* (magistrate) in Guerrero, claiming that his amo had died shortly before his capture by the Lipans.[13] Botello's ultimate fate did not make it into the historical record, but unlike recaptured runaway slaves from Texas, his case demonstrates that peons did have at least some legal recourse against the arbitrary abuse of power.

Mexicans were quick to point to cases such as these to prove that peons had legal protection and to disrupt the burgeoning image in the American mind of the Mexican debt holder as a sadist. Their servants' recourse to tribunals made the "custom" of peonage much more "noble and human" than slavery, according to a writer for Mexico City's *La Sociedad*.[14] But the bureaucratic cogs of the Mexican state turned slowly in the Mexican North if they turned at all. Mexico's northern frontier had never followed the pattern of state incorporation in the colonial or early national epochs. Thus, the legal protection that a peon may have had in central Mexico did not have as much purchase in the north of the country. In practice, frontier peons could be treated just as poorly as enslaved blacks in Texas, and it was precisely the arbitrariness of the relationship between peon and master that lay at the heart of the problem. As the case of Botello illustrates, neither peon nor peasant was immune to erratic treatment by powerful men.

Defenders of peonage also pointed out that peons could sell their debt. Theoretically, debt peons could trade an abusive master for a kinder one. This had a downside, however; the alienability of peon debt could also break the bonds of reciprocity between masters and debtors. This ability to separate the person from the debt lay at the root of many observations that hacendados seldom felt personally responsible for the well-being of peons, especially once debtors grew too old to work. One Pennsylvania volunteer serving in the U.S.-Mexico War wrote that masters could transfer debt peons on a whim and treat debts like chattel, sending old men away from their families once they were no longer productive and required care. He had witnessed the transfer of one peon to a new master and referred to it as a sale worse than any made by Southern slaveholders.[15]

Mexican defenders of peonage also argued that debt could not supersede the lifetime of the peon, whereas enslaved children followed the condition of the mother. Amos had to keep very clear accounts of the exact sum their peons owed them, and they had to show these *libros de cuentas* (account books) when the (usually illiterate) peon asked to see them. The libro de cuentas sometimes expired with the debt holder's life—although neither North American nor Mexican commentators were much impressed with the commitment of Mexican amos to this principle.[16] In fact, debts regularly passed from one generation to the next through last rites fees. And in some places, the passage of debt from one generation to the next was legal. John S. Ford, noted Texas Ranger and South Texas newspaperman, reported that indebted shepherds, herders, and laborers earned about twenty-five cents a day, a rate he suggested was not enough to sustain life. At the end of the month workers found themselves deeper in debt. Given the growing debt that fathers incurred over a lifetime, their wives and children often followed into service for the same amo, who could force them to honor the deceased father's debt.[17] As one high-ranking U.S. diplomat put it, a peon "is not only a slave for life, but his children after him [are as well], unless the employer chooses to release [them] from his service."[18] These examples betray how easily the cycle of debt could pass from generation to generation—even if laws existed outlawing hereditary debt.

Mexican elites argued that slavery was much worse than debt peonage. Debt peons were not enslaved alien outsiders, as were blacks in America, they insisted. Rather, sirvientes were countrymen enmeshed in what was supposed to be a mutually beneficial relationship in a country that valued social hierarchies. If amos treated servants arbitrarily or abusively, that was a miscarriage of justice. Thus, a writer for *La Sociedad* claimed that Mexican sirvientes' recourse to tribunals made the "custom" of peonage much more "noble and human" than slavery, where African Americans were denied all judicial rights. He added that peonage was an ancient system of servitude held over from Iberian custom, and unlike American chattel slavery, it was not based on the arbitrary distinction of skin color—although it should be noted that most peons almost certainly descended from Indians.[19]

Debt peonage did indeed have a long pedigree in the Spanish-speaking world. Many interlocking systems of vassalage and hierarchy had existed since the conquest of Mexico (if not even longer, dating back to the great tributary indigenous Mesoamerican empires). Servitude did not carry the same stigma for Mexicans as it did for fiercely independent Americans who would only enslave Africans and not their own countrymen. Mexicans did not possess the same cult of republican individualism and liberty that viewed any countryman who served another with suspicion. The quasi-feudal bonds of loyalty and honor held over from Iberian seigniorial culture, which many Mexicans believed sustained the system of peonage, contrasted sharply with the individualistic and capitalist system of the United States.[20] Accordingly, Mexican critics did not fault peonage but rather pointed to its corruption by amos motivated more by profit than by patronage as the problem.[21] Rather than condemn the system in its ideal form, a critic for *El Universal* drew attention to the arbitrariness of amos who emulated American slaveholders. This newspaper claimed that some amos were "hardhearted" toward their servants and that peons were supposed to be treated as loyal dependents, not "natural enemies."[22]

All of these defenses of peonage must be entered into the record with caution. Debt peonage was clearly not a favorable situation for many Mexicans in the North. As soon as new opportunities on the other side of the border emerged, debt peons seized them and left their masters. When new people and new demands for labor encroached on distant northern Mexican enclaves, servile frontier people left whatever bonds of debt and loyalty kept them in place, and they escaped across the frontier to radically changed conditions.

"Escaping from This Species of Bondage"

Just as was the case with runaway slaves at roughly the same time, the proximity of foreign peoples nearby served as an enticement to abandon wretched conditions for peons. Once Texas began to fill up with new populations, northern Mexican debt peons broke out of their geographic isolation. From the 1820s on, some Mexican laborers went toward the Anglo colonies or Tejano ranches—even before the Battle of San Jacinto left the old Texas-Mexico borderlands riven in two. Then, after the U.S.-Mexico War, runaway sirvientes truly transformed the new border into a line between misery and opportunity. Exemplary people-in-between, they pioneered a durable tradition of renegotiating the terms of their labor through mobility.[23] After 1848, they moved frequently across the border, playing one people off against the other and procuring for themselves better wages in the trade. In Coahuila, peons received between three and five pesos monthly (a bit farther south, in Zacatecas, they received between four and six pesos). In Texas, meanwhile, they received fifty cents per day. This wage was about three times higher.[24] Why work in Mexico for such low wages when employers located nearby paid so much more?

The arrival of Anglos in the borderlands encouraged the out-migration of debt peons from the very start. In 1846, shortly after Zachary Taylor's forces arrived at the river, runaway peons began seeking refuge in his army's encampments near Matamoros. As Miguel Ángel González Quiroga writes, they drifted toward Taylor's forces once the Americans burned and sacked the haciendas they labored on. Still more of them left to take advantage of the opportunities offered by the new American presence. It did not take long for Mexican hacendados and ranchers to notice that their agricultural servants fled in increasing numbers to the North American lines, and the flight of these peons had immediate consequences. According to various reports, a cluster of cotton plantations had existed along the lower Rio Grande outside of Matamoros before the U.S. intervention in Mexico. These plantations relied on a large, pliant workforce, but cotton cultivation along the river came to an abrupt end. According to one observer, its demise owed entirely to the crossing of Mexican laborers to the U.S. side during the war. As soon as indebted workers saw the U.S. Army arrive on the Rio Grande, they began to leave the Mexican cotton plantations in droves. A few amos wrote to General Taylor personally, in the hope that he would oversee the return of their sirvientes, but he refused to turn them over and even employed a good number of them in his own camp.[25]

Taylor was not the only one pleased with this turn of events. This new limit of liberty for the indebted laborers, triggered by the expansion of the U.S. military frontier to the Rio Grande, occasioned favorable responses from U.S. volunteers stationed near Matamoros. One soldier from Illinois took heart in the fact that if the U.S. forces stayed camped in one spot for any length of time, runaway peons eventually found their way into the army's lines. Such volunteers saw themselves as the liberators of abused and indebted Mexicans. The obvious irony that some volunteers' and officers' enslaved African American servants deserted to Mexico seems to have been lost on these memoirists.[26]

No matter where the North American soldier or sojourner at the military frontier came from, he or she cheered on the liberty that peons found when they escaped to the American camp. Helen Chapman, who traveled to Matamoros in 1848 as an army officer's wife, was a progressive New Englander who applauded the escape of peons from their masters and their new employment by the U.S. forces.[27] The occupying soldiers and their attendants could feel good about a war that most Whigs saw as a slaveholder land grab. Some of the fleeing laborers found work with the army quartermaster, who reportedly paid them thirty dollars per month—significantly more than an average peon's wages in Mexico.[28]

Then, after the war, Mexicans began to flood into the state of Texas in even greater numbers, initiating what must be one of the largest and most durable migratory patterns in human history. The Mexico City newspaper *Siglo xix* estimated that between 1840 and 1851, nearly 3,000 people abandoned the state of Coahuila. By 1852, another 4,000 had left. The writer of this alarming news reasoned that the flight of indebted laborers to Texas alone accounted for this staggering loss of people from the Mexican North. The peons of the North "found themselves in a state of slavery worse than that of beasts; they suffer every type of terrible treatment and they never receive the money that is the fruit of their work." They were stuck in a cycle of debt, they received articles of poor quality rather than wages, and they could never hope to escape indebted bondage. Their only option was to flee "in bands" to Texas, and to this end *Siglo xix* claimed that, in 1856, 11,000 Mexicans had migrated from Coahuila to San Antonio. (This number exceeds the number of Mexicans and Tejanos living in San Antonio that year.) There were, the same newspaper claimed, another 40,000 Mexicans to be found in other parts of the state.[29] These numbers are likely exaggerated, but they still represented a tremendous loss of workers from the Mexican North, and peons did make up the majority of the non-Indian population in Coahuila. Like other autonomous people who were independent of larger state projects, mobile laborers frustrated their erstwhile masters and debt holders by running to the other side in search of liberty and security.

The sparse evidence that exists about runaway peons in the wake of the U.S.-Mexico War suggests that in the years following the outbreak of the war and the subsequent drawing up of the border the incidents of peon flight increased dramatically. For example, 321 peons ran away from their amos between 1842 and 1868 from Ciudad Ciénegas, San Buenaventura, Nadadores, and Monclova in northern Coahuila's Región centro de desierto. The years 1850, 1855, and 1856 witnessed the greatest number of flights to the other side. The runaways from the towns listed above owed a varied amount of money to their former masters. Inocencio García of Monclova, for instance, owed his master, León Villareal, the paltry sum of ten pesos—probably about two or three months' wages. Runaldo Trinidad of Nadadores, on the other hand, owed his amo, Ignacio Sertuche Ramires, the astounding sum of 360 pesos. Perhaps Trinidad served his master dutifully, earning his trust, and wanting for little. But he absconded anyway, and we can speculate that his flight left his master particularly crestfallen.[30] In any case, many others followed in Trinidad's wake. Rather than seeing a wall, laborers stuck in cycles of debt and the violent repression on either side of the boundary saw *el lindero* (the line) as a gateway to freedom and opportunity. For Mexican nationalists hoping to populate the desolate frontier, this out-migration was a major blow.

Runaway peons were not the only Mexicans abandoning the country after 1848, of course. Even as the ink on the Treaty of Guadalupe Hidalgo dried, Texan newspapers began reporting on a wide variety of migrants from Mexico arriving in their state. The regional origins of these migrants varied widely. Some came from the upper Rio Grande to settle in San Antonio to escape the Indian wars. Others, "very wealthy Mexicans" from Tamaulipas, visited Corpus Christi with an eye to settling there. In addition, some less well-off Mexicans from Matamoros crossed the river and set up "temporary jacales" (huts) on the Texas side. There were still other Mexicans who began to claim the land granted to them long ago in the Nueces Strip, more confident now in American protection from the Indians—even if, as the historian Brian Delay has effectively argued, this trust was misplaced. "Our country," opined the *Corpus Christi Star,* "has been and is now the asylum of the misgoverned of every land, and the children of our near neighbor can never be an exception." It was hard for Texans not to get inflated egos when they saw so many migrants moving into their state.[31]

But among these migrants making their way across this new divide, runaway peons were probably the most sizable group—and they drew extensive commentary. Among those seeking protection in the United States, said the editor of the *Corpus Christi Star,* were "many of those, who being in debt, are held in slavery under the Mexican laws. The opportunity of escaping from this species of bondage is being availed by many." At first, Texans welcomed fleeing peons into their state, as it demonstrated the superiority of Texas, its laws and institutions. And maybe slavery did not look so bad when oppressed laborers were flooding out of Mexico and into Texas.[32]

When the issue of peonage entered wider public discourse around the time of the Treaty of Guadalupe Hidalgo, Texan slaveholders became some of the fiercest enemies of peonage. In newspaper editorials, advocates of slavery pointed to the tide of Mexican laborers crossing the border to work in Texas, sure that these people were escaping from far worse conditions. They defended their own system, asking why peons would run north if liberty lay to the south as enslaved people believed. The *Texas Gazette*, for example, expected its readers (and potential runaway slaves, by word of mouth) to see slavery as a more benign option than Mexican penury.

> The inducement for a negro to run off to Mexico, is the idea that he will be there on a footing with the peon Mexican whom he sees here, and with whom he associates on a perfect equality. He little considers . . . that the very peons around him in Texas, were starved out in Mexico, and came here to be able to obtain a living. When the negro gets to Mexico, he makes the discovery, and finds nothing but the most squalid wretchedness, poverty, and starvation for his lot.[33]

John Ford was particularly sanguine about the hypocrisy of Mexicans. In relation to many Centralist Mexican officials' stark opposition to slavery, he wrote that Mexicans "seemed to forget that they made their own countrymen slaves—*peons*—for the inability to pay a debt." (In the American republic, meanwhile, only African and Irish outsiders were servants).[34] He also referred to the criticism of Indian and black slavery in the northern U.S. press as a vast "humbug" and wondered why Mexican peonage came in for so little scrutiny by these same authors. Cora Montgomery (Jane Cazneau), a contemporary of Ford's, also wrote extensively of her experiences in the borderlands from her home in Eagle Pass. An ardent supporter of Anglo expansion, she simply referred to peonage as Mexican slavery and criticized the antislavery Free Soilers for taking on only one form of human bondage in their platform.[35] To make the comparison explicit, Montgomery noted a conversation she had with a Mascogo (Black Seminole) woman who accompanied Wild Cat's band to Nacimiento, Coahuila. "The only difference she ever found between being a slave and a peon," Montgomery reported, "was in the hard way they had of grinding corn in Mexico, and that meat seemed scarcer."[36]

There was one notable exception to this general trend of defending slavery when compared to Mexican peonage. It was Frederick Law Olmsted, who spent part of the 1850s traveling through the South and writing widely on slavery, who offered a dissenting opinion on peonage. In his *Journey through Texas*, Olmsted wrote that he was "amused at the horror with which this Mexican Peon Law is viewed," adding, "I have been asked, many times, if I did not think it worse than negro slavery," which he did not. Olmsted wrote his book over the course of the early 1850s with a mind to promote the Free Soil agenda over the expansion of slavery. He chose to write about Texas as an example of what happened to free territory when slaveholders seized the land. Accordingly, his criticism of slavery ended up tacitly defending peonage. He found peonage, while not an "enlightened" labor system, far less damaging to the soil and society than slavery.[37]

Olmsted wrote against the grain of public opinion in an effort to point out the hypocrisy of slaveholders. While in Texas, Olmsted learned that some resolute slaveholders were also vehement critics of peonage. In 1852, around the same time he passed through Texas, the authors of the Sierra Madre Republic movement assaulted the tiny village of Cerralvo in northern Tamaulipas. The group hoped to break off part of Mexico as an independent republic, basically repeating the revolt that had occurred in Texas fifteen years earlier. They referred specifically to Mexican peonage in their founding doctrine, declaring that the signers were "tired of the National Declaration that Slavery shall not exist in our Land when Peonage, a system hideous and cruel, exists, unrestricted and unnoticed."[38] The Sierra Madre Republic movement, which Ford thought of as the greatest opportunity for Texans to safeguard slavery in their state, sought to spread slavery into northern Mexico on the principle that it was more benign than peonage.[39]

Nevertheless, some criticisms of peonage were valid. Observers were correct when they wrote that peonage drew many free plebian norteños into its web since landholders were the only source of loans in an area that suffered from a dearth of resources, credit, and opportunities. Another American volunteer offered up an observation that laboring Mexican "mechanics" (a term that implied the very essence of artisanal independence in the United States) could fall into debt and find themselves at the mercy of the master's whims. The mechanic borrowed money from a local landholder to pay the priest's fees for the sacred rites performed at his wedding; he then became "as much a slave as the negro of the south, and in far worse condition," until, and if, he could repay the debt. This source confirms what the historian Charles H. Harris finds in his study of the Sánchez-Navarro landholdings in Coahuila: the marriage ceremony and its related fees very often began the cycle of debt for peasants, who then fell into long, if not permanent, tenures as peons on neighboring haciendas.[40]

Despite the milieu in which North Americans made these remarks against debt peonage, they were not that far off the mark. Even before the U.S.-Mexico War, some amos who complained about the "immorality" of mozos had to acknowledge that there were some abusive hacendados. A particularly harsh law passed in Tamaulipas in 1844 was considered, by at least one Mexican newspaper editor, as a "law worthy of Texas where slavery abounds."[41] Never mind the anger many Mexicans felt toward their aggressive neighbors, some agreed with the observations that North Americans made about debt peonage. The commander of the frontier of Coahuila, Emilio Langberg, seconded criticisms of debt peonage emanating from North America. He witnessed the abuse of hacienda peons firsthand and commented on the system's physical violence. He tersely summed up his feelings in a letter to frontier caudillo Santiago Vidaurri when he stated that Texas slaves "were treated with more consideration [by their masters] than we treat our own peons." His concerns echoed those of another peon who complained to the authorities about being beaten by his master, who treated his peons more like "beasts than men."[42]

On a final note, it is important to say that debt peonage did in fact exist in Texas, despite the many protests voiced against it there. Texans were not unfamiliar with the practice; laws protecting peonage allowed them to bring enslaved African Americans into Texas during the Mexican period. Tejanos who were friends to the Anglos and the Texas Revolution also practiced peonage regularly in Texas. Even after the war, many migrant laborers surely ended up contracting new debts once they arrived in the state of Texas. Some may have wanted to go into debt anew once they got there. Owing a patron money meant that the laborer's employment might very well outlast the planting or shearing season and guarantee future work. They did want steady employment after all. Cattle and sheep ranching particularly attracted migrant Mexican laborers for this reason, since these workers toiled year-round.[43] In the final analysis, Texas was a land free from neither slavery nor debt peonage. But crossing the border at least guaranteed a fresh start.

The Transfer of Wealth

The loss of so many workingmen from Mexico's sparsely populated frontier zone resulted in a significant transfer of labor to Texas. The effects of this loss did not go unnoticed for long. In Nuevo León, near Montemorelos, an authority complained of the "constant and frightening" flight of servants. In Coahuila the flight of servants "paralyzed" agriculture.[44] Farther east, in Tamaulipas, the ranchers and planters who lived near Matamoros also complained about the loss of their laborers. As noted above, their flight caused the demise of cotton cultivation along the Rio Grande.

A second economic problem caused by the loss of laborers was even more significant. It led to an upswing in crime on the frontier and resulted in the transfer of animal wealth from the Mexican to the Texan side of the border. Indeed, migrant Mexican laborers have always found themselves accused of criminality, but interestingly enough in the earliest days of the border it was Mexicans, not Americans, who made this accusation. From the very beginning, runaway peons who followed the U.S. Army likely associated with the North American criminals and smugglers who deserted from or followed Taylor's forces in Mexico. Hacendados watched helplessly as their former servants moved about freely among the baser elements of the occupying army and its hangers-on. In fact, some of the first recorded joint Anglo-Mexican criminal ventures along the border occurred around Matamoros during its occupation by North Americans.[45]

Before delving into the transfer of animal wealth from Mexico to Texas, and its resultant effect on the international disparity of wealth, I must acknowledge the fact that plenty of cattle and horses went missing from Texas too. The Anglos and Tejanos alike who occupied the Nueces Strip had suffered greatly from the loss and theft of their cattle since at least the War of Texan Independence. The greatest loss from the Texas side seems to have occurred from the 1860s on, however, culminating in the "Cattle War" of the 1870s.[46] The history of cattle and horse rustling along the border still awaits its historian, but the evidence thus far points to a far greater quantity of animals stolen from the Mexican than the Texan side—at least up until the Civil War era.

As a result, Mexican authorities began to conflate the issues of migrancy and criminal delinquency. In newspapers and circulars, they published a few broad pronouncements against runaway servants and their North American accomplices. One Mexican alleged that once peons arrived in Texas they threw in their lot with rustlers and criminals and led cattle and horse raids back into Mexico.[47] Mexican peons who ran away to Texas knew the exact location of Mexican *agostaderos* (pastures) and the size of the herds and could easily lead forays back to them. Some norteño employers knew that peons possessed this geographic knowledge, and they claimed that escaped Mexicans on the Texan side of the river were too lazy or unable to find work. They alleged that runaways sustained themselves by raiding the herds of their former employers.[48] In addition to the problems that runaway peons presented to agriculture along the Rio Grande, their presence was a grave threat to the property of ranchers along the border.

The norteños' problems only intensified after 1848. Once the United States secured the Nueces Strip, Texan merchants and ranchers expanded into the borderlands, opening up still more opportunities for Mexican migrant laborers to sell stolen animals. The Anglo-Texans Charles Stillman, Richard King, and John Salmon "Rip" Ford all founded towns along the river shortly after the Treaty of Guadalupe Hidalgo and became important men in the borderlands. The ranches that immediately bordered the Rio Grande remained in Tejano hands, but soon after the treaty was made, white farmers began to move into the region. They expanded their ranges into the Nueces Strip and beyond beginning in the 1850s as well. The new ranches that dotted this territory both increased the competition for labor and provided a market for horses stolen from ranchers on both sides of the Rio Grande. In addition, the absence of an extradition treaty for criminals and runaways helped plug the labor and ill-gotten gains of runaway peons directly into the Texas economy. Once peons crossed the river they usually found safety, protected by Anglo authorities who wanted to meet the demands of ranchers for both laborers and horses.[49]

When Anglos established North American authority on the left bank of the Rio Grande in 1848, the new bosses immediately took advantage of their power to the detriment of Mexican and Tejano ranchers. One Tejano rancher remembered that in the years following the drawing of the boundary there had been instances of extreme impropriety on the part of the Texan officials. He alleged that the sheriff of Roma, on the Texas side, assisted runaway peons in stealing horses.[50] Other witnesses also attested to the assistance of Texan officials in the illegal traffic, explicitly implicating the sheriffs of Eagle Pass, Edinburg, and Roma. Vecinos and rancheros on the Mexican side of the border insisted that the runaway servants had established routes and contacts with not just Texan Anglos but also Tejanos and transient Mexicans to facilitate the crossing of stolen animals.[51] The majority of Mexican vecinos did not know whether it was Latino/as from the Texas side or from their own side who committed the majority of the crimes. Most witnesses assumed they acted in tandem and pointed to a vast transnational underground network of cattle and horse thieves with contacts all over the border region and far into the interior of Texas. Julian Donet, to name just one successful rancher of the period, owned a ranch located due north of Eagle Pass that reputedly owed its existence to the trade in stolen animals carried out by runaway servants and their companions.[52]

Rustlers needed to be particularly wary of Anglos, however. When Juan Chapa Guerra, an itinerant mexicano, was captured by a posse for stealing horses from Charles Stillman, the gang lynched him immediately. The authorities in Mexico might have put up with some extradition attempts and violence against Mexican cattle rustlers among the Texans, but not in this case. It turns out that Guerra was innocent, and Mariano Arista himself voiced outrage to the American consulate.[53] The Cortina Revolt of 1859 had at least some of these major violations of Mexican life and liberty at its root.

Nevertheless, when they found their causes connected, Anglos could be great allies to fleeing peons. Migrant laborers especially found that Anglo Texan authorities along the river protected them when they took animals from the Mexican side. Clemente Zapata, who owned and managed the Clareño ranch on the Texas side with his brother Octaviano during the 1850s, testified about the immense traffic in stolen animals that runaway peons conducted with Anglo Texans. He watched from his ranch as Mexican laborers crossed over to Texas with stolen animals; they would take still more from Tejano ranchers as they traveled into the interior of Texas. For his part, Zapata knew they were stolen because of the low prices for which they sold. He fumed over the protection authorities offered to these criminals. Mexican ranchers crossed over to the Texas side to try to reclaim stolen animals from the Anglo authorities who dominated the towns founded after the U.S.-Mexico War. But Zapata did not recall many instances when ranchers had met with success. Mexicans failed to recover the stolen animals because of the onerous requirements that Texan authorities placed on them to prove ownership. If Mexican ranchers could meet the burden of proof on Texan terms, the court costs theys incurred were prohibitive. There were cases in which the court costs exceeded the price of the stolen livestock.

The geographic boundaries between the borderlands of the Rio Grande—where so many horses originated—and the interior of the state mattered too. Zapata testified that he had also been a victim of horse theft by runaway debtors passing close to his ranch. He once found his stolen animals as far away as San Antonio and attempted to reclaim them. He approached the authorities and showed that the stolen horses bore his brand, but he

Roma, Texas.

FIGURE 4. View of Roma, Texas, engraved during the U.S. Boundary Commission of 1849–1857. Roma, Texas. 1857. From Rice University. http://hdl.handle.net/1911/35382.

recognized that the odds were stacked against him. A "North American" (Anglo) with no proof of ownership except for some corroborating witnesses "proved" that Zapata's horses were his own property and took them away. This problem was systematic according to Zapata; he insisted that no Texan rancher could resist the urge to buy animals at the cheap prices that runaway peons asked for them. Texans were acting in conjunction with the runaway peons to transfer the great horse herds from Mexico to Texas. Texans refused to condemn this theft and ultimately sanctioned the growth of a tremendous trade in stolen goods.[54]

An additional factor aiding the runaways' transfer of horse wealth across the Rio Grande was that Texans were not legally required to recognize the papers that certified Mexican ranchers' brands.[55] As a result, Texans bought the animals from runaway servants at very low risk and for very low prices, sometimes paying as little as five pesos per animal—less than half the market value.[56] Once horses were on their way to San Antonio, it proved impossible to recover the stolen property.[57]

Finally, the Mexicans accused of rustling neither owned property nor stayed in one place for long, which made it exceedingly difficult for ranchers on either side of the river to locate the criminals and their associates.[58] The Texas side not only offered opportunity; it also offered anonymity. The flight of peons and their trade in stolen animals could continue unabated precisely because the ranches on the Texas side were so spread out. Texas ranches sprawled over vast spaces, whereas in Mexico one could "almost see the houses from one ranch to the others." In Texas people could not recognize the "vagrants" and *gente perdida* (lost souls) who passed through their towns and found employment on their ranches.[59] North American development patterns encouraged the sort of itinerancy and anonymity that allowed laborers to escape oppressive and overly intimate environments in the Mexican North. Open space bred the conditions for free labor. Migrant Mexican laborers were transformed into units of production that Anglos and Tejanos could incorporate into the expanding ranching and agricultural economy on the other side of the river. Runaway peons faced challenges in mobilizing new routes and reaching the free labor market in Texas. They had to escape the vigilance of horseback overseers, travel through Indian territory, and pass through villages where they could be easily spotted and turned in by Mexican authorities. But once peons escaped the oversight of norteños and their cousins on the other side of the river, they reached a vast transnational labor market.

Mexicans rancheros and hacendados watched worriedly as their workers absconded to Texas with their animals, and they responded to the problem through the means of repression, reform, and diplomacy. In terms of repression, since they could find no justice on the Texan side, Mexican hacendados and ranchers clamped down hard on their laborers in an effort to stem the flow of labor and animals northward. After 1848, in an effort to keep debt peons in place, the state governments began to allow amos to employ especially heavy-handed punitive measures. The North might have even witnessed a resurgence in corporal punishment due to the new pressures on the labor market caused by the international border. Foreign Minister Luis de la Rosa noted in 1851 that a law passed in the northern Mexican states allowed amos to whip their peons.[60] The Mexican authorities also tried other approaches to contain the problem. In Tamaulipas they passed a measure that made amos responsible for thefts committed by their laborers. The purpose of this measure was to make somebody accountable for the thieves who had crossed to the Texan side.[61] It also may have led to amos stepping up their brutal treatment of their laborers, lest they be punished themselves for the crimes their servants committed.

There were other procedures put in place as well. As early as July 1848, the government of Matamoros passed a law that required every Mexican crossing the river into Texas to carry a passport and show it to the authorities so that "evildoers, animal thieves, and runaway servants" could not cross to safety in the United States. Military colonies were another option tested by Mexican authorities. They intended these colonies primarily to combat against Comanche and Apache raids into Mexico. But, the governor of Tamaulipas insisted that it would also be the job of the colonists to pursue evildoers, rustlers, and runaway servants seeking "impunity" in the United States.[62] Given the increasing number of complaints from ranchers along the lower Rio Grande about runaway servants, it is doubtful that these top-down measures met with much success. The most effective measure employed by Mexicans to recover their runaway peons were individual efforts made by Mexican ranchers. On occasion, Mexicans crossed into Texas to violently extract debtors in flagrant violation of Texan law—just as Texans did in Mexico to recover runaway slaves.[63]

When the stick failed, some Mexicans turned to the carrot, pressing for reforms that would ultimately address the worst abuses of debt peonage. In March 1851, for example, the government of Nuevo León took up the cause of indebted peons, likely in an attempt to stem the tide of runaways. The state legislature explicitly outlawed the practice of passing onto children the debts of their deceased fathers. The measure was probably an attempt to bring amos to heel and to ameliorate the condition of indebted laborers who were abandoning Mexico to work in Texas after 1848.[64] Another reform targeted the practice of making peons buy articles at the hacienda's tienda de raya. Again, in a top-down effort meant to curb flight to Texas, the legislature of Nuevo León passed a law that required the tiendas to price their commodities at market value. Legislators may also have made some progress toward ending the corporal punishment of hacienda and rancho peons.[65] When the Liberals came to power in 1855, they too sought to reform the institution of debt peonage as part of their platform against slavery in all its forms.[66]

Finally, Mexican ranchers and hacendados began to pressure their officials to seek diplomatic solutions to the runaway problem. They called for an extradition treaty with Texas, putting special pressure on Mexican diplomats to come to some sort of arrangement.[67] It fell upon Luis de la Rosa, Mexican minister plenipotentiary in Washington, to do something about this problem. He drafted a treaty containing an article that called for the return of servants from Coahuila and other parts of Mexico who had fled to Texas and owed their masters large debts. But for this measure to be put into effect, the U.S. minister insisted that Mexico would have to agree to return African Americans living in Mexico—a trade-off de la Rosa found "odious." The final treaty included neither a provision for the return of Texan slaves nor a provision for the return of runaway peons, and it pleased nobody. De la Rosa's failure to find a diplomatic solution to the problem of runaway peons enraged norteños. To them, it suggested that the central government did not have their interests at heart. The loss of servants and "the impunity of thieves"—according to one provincial newspaper editor—was costing the frontier its "scarce fortune."[68] Some norteño elites resorted to local and informal solutions in the absence of a diplomatic one. This sentiment grew throughout the decade. In 1857, one Texan wrote, "Get out of the way presidents and senates," after learning that a local treaty had been signed in Rio Grande City to return runaway peons.[69]

Despite a few limited successes, the border continued to hemorrhage productive laborers and horses from the northern frontier of Mexico into Texas. After having failed to work out a diplomatic solution to the runaway peon problem, Mexican employers found themselves at a disadvantage when dealing with potential laborers. They had to begin reconsidering the terms with which they contracted peones acasillados, giving workers entering into short and long-term contracts an advance on their wages. This practice persisted into the Porfiriato (1876–1910) but was not entirely satisfactory to the amos, who complained that many debtors fled to "asylum" in Texas after receiving an advance payment.[70] These reforms were small steps toward the liberalization of labor in the north of Mexico. Eventually, the border brought so much pressure to bear on northern employers that norteño laborers enjoyed the most favorable working conditions in the country. The dearth of labor, in addition to the proximity of a foreign labor market, meant that cowboys and other workers in the North had to be well remunerated in comparison to their peers in other parts of the country.[71]

In the final analysis, the runaway peon problem resulted in disaster for agriculture in the Mexican North after the U.S.-Mexico War. Hacendados and ranchers lost both their laborers and their horses, compounding the problems mobile horseback Indians already presented to their enterprise. The state of Coahuila reportedly lost the most peons and property to Texas. With the Comanches on the retreat toward the Panhandle in the 1850s, runaway peons could pass with impunity from Coahuila to San Antonio and other South Texas towns. So great did the volume of migrants to Texas become that the old military colony of Guerrero turned into something of a way station for laborers en route to Texas. So many families and single men arrived there in the early months of 1852 that the commander of the frontier took special note of it, saying that the new arrivals in town came almost entirely from "the class of sirvientes prófugos—murderers and thieves—who were looking for refuge and to liberate themselves from the knife of the law."[72] Guerrero was connected to San Antonio by a road through the state, and many migrants who left Coahuila used this road en route to Texas. Eventually, many of the runaway peons from Coahuila ended up far in the interior, swelling the population of San Antonio and contributing to the herds and labor needs of its citizens and neighbors. Millions upon millions more would follow them in the years to come, crossing the border to reach el norte.

An unforeseen result of the establishment of the border at the Rio Grande was the tremendous loss of laborers and capital from the Mexican to the Texan side. The border between the United States and Mexico represented an opportunity for runaway peons from Mexico just as it did for runaway slaves from Texas. Runaway peons lent an extraordinary meaning to the post-1848 boundary, turning it into a border between free labor and servitude. North Americans were happy to receive this influx of laborers from Mexican haciendas and ranches. Runaway peons justified the U.S. military's endeavors in Mexico and cast doubt on the Mexican republic's dedication to the principles of emancipation and liberty. In addition, mobile workers inserted their labor and their former master's animals directly into the ranching revolution then transforming the borderlands north of the Rio Grande. Thus, not only did fleeing peons represent a vindication of Anglo Republican, free-market values—and ironically, slavery, at least for Texans—but it also resulted in the transfer of resources from the Mexican to the Texan side of the border. The Mexican side, meanwhile, suffered economic underdevelopment due to a lack of resources, the loss of horse wealth, and a dearth of labor.

Yet the flight of peons from northern Mexico to Texas had other effects besides impoverishment on the Mexican frontier. The creation of routes between the Mexican North and Texas labor markets eventually had a profound effect on labor practices in the borderlands of the Rio Grande. Runaway peons' peers and families who remained behind on Mexican haciendas in the North forced wages there to rise and working conditions to improve to counter opportunities on the other side. This was the long-term effect of the border on labor conditions on the northern Mexican frontier—an effect thoroughly studied by Friedrich Katz.[73] The argument above merely suggests that the effect of the border on labor mobility has roots going back even further than the Porfiriato.

The flight of peons and other debtors into Texas continued unabated for the next twenty-five years. In 1873, the Mexican boundary commission again attempted to quantify its effects. They found that 2,812 servants had fled from Nuevo León and Coahuila since 1848, often with their families (the women and children made up an additional loss of 2,582 people). The commissioners also calculated that runaway peons were responsible for the loss of about 250,000 pesos from the state of Nuevo León and 125,000 pesos from Coahuila in debts and stolen animals. This drain of capital, the commissioners maintained, was entirely to Texas's gain.[74] Thus, in 1873, norteños still clamored for an extradition treaty with Texas. They believed it would go a long way toward recovering labor and capital lost to this "great system of roaming . . . indulged in by the people of the States of Nuevo Leon, Coahuila, and Tamaulipas, towards the frontier of Texas."[75] It must be noted that these numbers could be greatly exaggerated. They were prepared in the context of the Cattle War of the 1870s, and Mexicans wanted to show that they too had lost great amounts of animal wealth to the other side. Nevertheless, the numbers were significant, and Mexico would never recover these resources or workers. The transfer of wealth and labor across the frontier by runaway peons in the wake of the U.S.-Mexico War was permanent.

5 / Warriors in Want: Immigrant Tribes and Borderlands Insecurity

In 1848, wary of Indians and of losing more territory, Mexico began building military colonies along its newly established northern border. Secretary of War Mariano Arista sent soldiers to man them, complementing the new National Guard units, which were volunteer forces composed of vecinos defending their homes against outside invaders. Fifty-nine colonists from the Sierra Gorda in San Luis Potosí also joined them, bringing along some prisoners taken in a recent rebellion. By 1851, nearly half of the proposed number of military colonists had arrived. All of these new forces joined the recently energized presidial companies.[1]

The final stroke in Mexico's militarization of the border involved bringing in Indians from the U.S. South as allies against Texan expansion and Comanche and Apache aggression in the borderlands of the Rio Grande. The idea of bringing in Indians as allies and citizens and investing them with the mission of protecting the borderlands from outside marauders was not new. Yet, in the wake of the Treaty of Guadalupe Hidalgo and alongside other efforts to militarize the borderlands, inviting them to Mexico's frontier represented a new concerted effort. The project involved the migration of hundreds of dissident Indians in search of a new home and willing to take up arms for Mexico in exchange for refuge. This new wave of immigrant Indians would sometimes fight "barbarians" alongside other vecinos; sometimes they would fight alongside soldiers drawn from the presidios and the new military colonies; and sometimes they would go after enemy Indians alone. This chapter, unlike the many book-length histories of these groups that already exist, considers the immigrant tribes of the 1850s together to analyze their overall effect on the making of the international border.[2]

The Seminole Coacoochee (known as Wild Cat to Americans and Gato del Monte to Mexicans) led the group of Indians invited to settle along the Mexican side of the new border and take up arms. He arrived in June 1850 with a broad cross section of peoples from Indian Territory. His migration was the end result of an impressive pan-Indian project he had dreamed up during the previous decade. Traveling widely through the Llano Estacado and Creek Territory in the late 1840s, Coacoochee practiced an adroit plains diplomacy and gathered a large number of potential immigrants to Mexico. Many knew of his plans in Indian Territory, and he probably intended the project as a power play to take over leadership of the Seminole tribe. In the end, his bands were ethnically diverse, but they all shared opposition to Creek hegemony in Indian Territory as well as distrust of Anglo Americans and their government. Together these tribes constituted a community similar to that of the disaffected Indians who had migrated to Mexico with Chief Bowles ten years earlier. Included among this group were some Southern Kickapoo, Seminoles, Black Seminoles, and Tonkawas and a few runaway slaves from Creek Territory.

Las Tribus Emigradas (the immigrant tribes—capitalized in the original documents) came to Mexico in the summer of 1850. Once there, they met several Mexican officers along the frontier and waited around the new military colonies at Guerrero and Monclova Viejo to receive their commissions. They also began to eat their way through the Mexican commanders' supplies. The first contingent of Indian colonists who had arrived at Piedras Negras in July 1850 numbered as many as seven hundred, and they were hungry and in pitiful shape due to the hardships of the monthlong journey to the frontier.[3] Not only their raggedness but also their sheer numbers had caught the Mexican commander at Piedras Negras, Sub-Inspector Manuel Maldonado, unprepared. He quickly fired off a missive to his superior in Monterrey, Antonio Juáregui, asking him to forward a request to the central government for tools, oxen, and plows so that the immigrants could plant their corn. He assured his superior that they just needed to get established and that they would not be a permanent drain on state coffers. Just as Arista had argued ten years before in relation to the immigration of the late Chief Bowles's band, Maldonado said that these immigrants were already "semicivilized" and would soon be able to sustain themselves.[4]

But once these Indians arrived en masse, the project met with opposition. Juáregui and Maldonado understood that they represented only the initial migration to Mexico and that many more Indians were on their way. Coacoochee promised that up to 1,800 more of his people would arrive shortly, and the great chief also believed that he could convince the balance of Seminoles to migrate from Indian Territory to Mexico.[5] A few months later, in October 1850, when the central government of Mexico at last formalized a treaty with the immigrant tribes, Coacoochee promised that he would bring 4,000 more Indians from Arkansas, mostly Kickapoos.[6] Then, in November 1850, another large group of immigrant Indians presented themselves to Maldonado. They swore allegiance to Mexico, and Maldonado admitted them into the territory "as Mexicans."[7] The following month, the rest of the Southern Kickapoos belonging to captaincillos Marcua's and Pecan's tribes arrived, adding over 500 more people to the growing camp of Indian asylum seekers stationed outside of Monclova Viejo. In late December, Coacoochee returned to Coahuila from Indian Territory with more than one hundred additional Seminoles, Black Seminoles, and runaway slaves from the Creeks.[8] This was many more immigrants than the impoverished Mexican North could absorb.

Reportedly, 1,500 immigrant tribesmen and tribeswomen sat outside the presidio of Monclova Viejo and El Remolino in the winter of 1850–51, waiting for directions and in desperate need of food and supplies. When Arista made another plea in favor of these Indians, he mentioned the growing concerns of nearby vecinos and politicians in the state capital who did not believe Mexico could afford to meet the needs of the immigrants. Still, Arista remained hopeful. He wrote glowingly of the immigrants, seeing in them the key to stabilizing the frontier. Just as he had said of the Cherokees, he maintained that the new immigrants differed greatly from the "bárbaros . . . [who were] used to spilling human blood and razing the countryside."[9] The immigrant tribes were hardworking warriors (*guerreros*); if they were stripped of their customs, they could become ideal colonists—especially in the North, because they were the "masters of the desert, close to nature," and, most important considering what followed, "greatly used to suffering."[10] Immigrant tribes would indeed find privation in Mexico, and their poverty undermined Arista's efforts to secure the frontier. Further, with so few resources made available to them, squabbles with vecinos inevitably broke out.

This chapter recounts the experience of the immigrant tribes loosely confederated under the Seminole Coacoochee, the Black Seminole John Horse (John Cowaya), and the various Kickapoo captains in the borderlands of Texas and Coahuila. The immigrant Indians hoped to trade their labor to the state as warriors and military colonists in exchange for refuge, land, and a steady supply of resources. Ultimately—or so Arista and his subordinates thought—this plan would lead to greater security in the borderlands for all since the Indian colonists would hold off Comanche and Apache raiders. Arista expected the Indian warriors to protect their own families as well as those of nearby vecinos and to integrate into Mexican society, becoming good citizens in the trade. This plan did not work out the way he hoped because of the lack of resources on the frontier. As a result, even greater insecurity became the lot of both immigrant Indians—who never received the promised resources—and vecinos, who trembled when the immigrant tribes, their supposed allies, turned on them and pressed their villages for supplies. Then, when Indians crossed the river to raid in Texas in their search for horses and food, they brought raiders in their wake who threatened Mexico's sovereignty over its frontier. In the end, an elaborately planned effort to increase security on the frontier actually produced greater insecurity.

Starvation and Misery

The immigrant Indians more or less fulfilled the commanders' expectations as warriors, especially in the initial years of the project. They went on over forty campaigns against the Comanches and Lipan Apaches.[11] But their transformation into sedentary farmers demanded resources that the Mexican commanders did not have at their disposal. It turns out they were not quite "the masters of the desert" that Arista thought they were. The governor of Coahuila's desk groaned under the weight of the many unanswered requests made by the Mexican commanders for plows, oxen, seeds, and arms for the immigrant tribes and military colonists. Various officials' appeals to the governor and to Juáregui, commander of the frontier, often struck an emotional note, betraying their utter bewilderment at the array of forces set against them and their fears of the consequences if they did not act. In one remarkable letter dating from 1852, the alcalde of Músquiz informed the governor that the women of the immigrant tribes approached him while the warriors were campaigning in the Comanche redoubt of the Laguna de Jaco. They complained that they were in a state of great misery; their husbands were not there to help when they planted, and they had not received their monthly sum from the government. They asked for corn, oxen and plows, which on this occasion they received.[12] The derelict state of the women served as a sobering reminder of the government's broken promises. These women, wasting away from hunger, did not resemble the wives of healthy and independent civilized frontier vecinos.[13]

Coacoochee, who entertained high hopes for the project, also realized that the Mexican government did not have the ability to keep the promises it had made. In 1852 he traveled to Mexico City against the wishes of the local commanders to negotiate for the transfer of the Hacienda of Nacimiento to the immigrant tribes. He at last received this land grant after the victory that fourteen of his Seminoles, four of Papicua's Kickapoos, and a few Black Seminoles achieved alongside the presidial soldiers of Monclova Viejo against the Tejano and Anglo attack on Cerralvo, Tamaulipas.[14] The land grant did not immediately ease the poverty in which the growing population of Indians lived, nor—as they discovered later—was the transfer of the hacienda entirely legal.[15]

In 1853, Coacoochee again stepped outside the chain of command to forward his concerns about the poverty of the colony directly to the governor of Coahuila. He wrote that of the hundred muskets—along with gunpowder and balls—promised to the colony none had arrived. Nor could the colony feed itself, and it recently endured a smallpox outbreak. Coacoochee played on the sympathies of the governor, pointing out that the colony now contained a number of widows who had recently lost their husbands to the war against the Comanches. These women suffered greatly and could not clothe themselves. Coacoochee simply asked that these widows be allowed to cover their shame—especially given the fact that his people had just won an engagement against the Comanches, capturing three captives and returning three horses to Santa Rosa.[16] The great chief was clever to refer to the women of his tribe. The Indians had done their part to meet the terms of the project to "civilize" them, but a profound lack of supplies challenged the officials' best efforts—and ultimately undermined the Indians' good faith as well.

Coacoochee's letter also engaged in a remarkable bit of borderlands diplomacy. Aware that Mexicans distrusted dealings between Indians and Anglos, he alleged that Texans paid other Indians to make war against the Mexicans—manipulating the long-standing fears of the Mexican officers. He also said that a representative of the U.S. government visited the colonists at Nacimiento the previous year to request that the Seminoles return to the Creek Reservation. His surrogates had heard the representative out, but Coacoochee declined the offer. He informed the North American agent that he still planned to transport two thousand Seminoles remaining in Creek Territory to Coahuila.[17] Despite his faithfulness, he complained to the governor that the Mexicans had done very little to help him bring the rest of his people to Mexico—another promise they had failed to fulfill.[18] The hardships faced by the immigrant Indians discouraged further immigration from Indian Territory and frustrated Coacoochee's bid to take command of the Seminoles.

Coacoochee wrote a second letter to the governor of Nuevo León that contained an even longer litany of complaints against Mexico for not issuing the immigrant tribes the promised resources. First, the president of Mexico himself had promised Coacoochee a bull and a cow for each family, in addition to supplies and corn, but had failed to deliver them. Then he complained that the authorities made unfair demands on the Seminoles, taking away the scarce resources they had. The governor of Coahuila had recently asked for two of the Seminoles who were most useful to Coacoochee to come to Saltillo to serve him. The first was one of the few literate Seminoles who, alongside the black man Julian, served as Coacoochee's interpreter. The second was a blacksmith, an essential role in the Indians' military colony since they needed to keep the few rifles they brought with them in working order. Using the government-issued flintlock muskets to hunt and fight Comanches was not a good option.[19]

The immigrant tribes also found themselves constantly relieved of the booty they captured from the Comanches and Lipan Apaches. The vecinos of Santa Rosa laid claim to the recaptured horses they brought back from their engagements, and the governor demanded the recaptured captives. Coacoochee would have liked to assimilate the redeemed captives into his colony but instead had to forfeit them to the governor for public works.[20] Immigrant Indians competed with the government for resources. They competed even more fiercely with neighboring vecinos.

Distrust

Many vecinos were distrustful of all Indians, and they did not all support the efforts of Centralist-leaning officers to antagonize Texans and bring foreign populations into their midst. Accordingly, in his letter to the governor of Coahuila, Coacoochee also spoke of the bad faith that existed between the immigrant tribes and the Mexicans on the frontier. It was the vecinos of Santa Rosa (Músquiz) with whom Coacoochee found himself most at odds. The vecinos, he claimed, were "bad people" and "treat us very poorly, running them [the Seminoles] off instead of allowing them to buy the things they need for the pueblo and even threatening them with arms despite the fact that they did nothing to the vecinos."[21] The townspeople generally did not appreciate the presence of the immigrant tribes. Decades of warfare had made them unfamiliar with the concept of friendly Indians, or "buenos indios."[22] Scarce resources almost certainly led to a revival of raiding among the immigrant Indians into neighboring towns and Texas, causing further deterioration of the situation.

The commanders had in fact anticipated the conflicts between the immigrant tribes and the locals. Try though they might to differentiate the immigrant tribes from the "bárbaros" who ravaged the western frontiers, norteño identity was in no small part predicated on violence against nomadic, raiding Indians. And despite Arista's description of the "whiteness" of the immigrant Indians (see chap. 2) and Manuel Maldonado's affirmation of their move toward becoming civilized, the vecinos who inhabited the dusty pueblos of the frontier remained skeptical of the project. They had manned military colonies and presidios for decades. The failure of either immigrant Indians or vecinos to form meaningful bonds across ethnic lines resulted in a lack of empathy and understanding. Renewed raiding on the part of the immigrant Indians only added to this misunderstanding.

As early as December 1850, just six months after the initial group arrived in Mexico, the tribes already found themselves in a "critical state." They lacked the plows, oxen, and seeds promised by the Mexican commanders. Juáregui admitted candidly in a letter to his superior that the Indians were in dire straits. Short of the promised resources, the immigrant tribes might resort to retribution. Their poverty could have real consequences, he said, and the commanders feared that the tribes might begin to commit depredations if the government did not start living up to its word.[23] Even Juáregui—an early champion of the project— worried about the very large congregation of immigrant Indians on the outskirts of Monclova Viejo in early 1851. He asked for an additional 2,000 pesos from Arista to tend to them, certain that without aid they would begin to attack and cause considerable damage to the frontier.[24]

The commanders were right to fear acrimony between the two groups. The vecinos of northern Coahuila manifested their suspicions of the project from the moment the tribes arrived. In an area where civilized manhood stemmed from doling out pain to "barbarous" outsiders, fronterizos had come to regard Indians of all stripes with suspicion. An unfavorable appraisal of the immigrant tribes sent from the ayuntamiento of Cuatro Ciénegas, Coahuila, in August 1850 reflects the distrust that the vecinos had of all Indians. The ayuntamiento declared that Indian

FIGURE 5. View of Monclova Viejo, a military colony founded shortly after the U.S.-Mexico War as part of a renewed effort by Mexico to secure the border. It was located at a short remove from Piedras Negras, Coahuila. Military Colony opposite Fort Duncan-Texas. 1857. From Rice University. http://hdl.handle.net/1911/35543.

troubles would not diminish with the arrival of the immigrant tribes but instead would "grow alongside the benevolent shelter that has been given to the tribes." The ayuntamiento's report continued, stating that the immigrant tribes "pretend to be tame, and offer to us what they are incapable of complying with . . . in order to learn . . . . about our weaknesses and take possession of isolated lands." They alleged that their "dress and arms have been seen many times" among the Comanches. Further, their familiarity with the Comanche language betrayed the many years they had spent on the plains among them. It was also jealousy that led to the vecinos' distaste for the project. The ayuntamiento bristled because it felt that Juáregui did not esteem the "Mexican Warriors" in the western colonies and hired immigrant tribesmen warriors instead.[25] (In fact, Maldonado had earlier encountered extreme difficulty finding any Mexican willing to go near Comanche territory.)[26] Not only would they have to compete with the new arrivals for the scarce resources that the commanders distributed; they would also have to compete with them for the military's respect.

As far as the vecinos were concerned, they saw very little of the promised assimilation of the immigrant tribes. Most damning in this regard was the fact that they simply looked different from "civilized" Mexicans—something commented on by many. The Seminoles retained most of their customs in Mexico; they continued to carry rifles, wear bangles and bracelets, sport brightly colored and boldly patterned frocks, and wear turbans adorned with turkey feathers.[27] Coacoochee's interest lay primarily in founding a colony that would provide refuge to dissident Indians and other potential allies. Whether he was a pan-Indianist or a caudillo in the making is not clear. But his plans for weaving his people into the social fabric of Mexican life on the frontier did not include hispanicization or intermarriage. When the commanders appointed the chief *juez de paz* (magistrate) of the immigrant tribes, they allowed him a latitude that resulted in greater isolation. Coacoochee issued laws that differed from neighboring courts (juzgados). In an effort to promote group cohesion, he decreed the death penalty for any Indian in his colony who sold lands from the colony without permission, committed adultery, or murdered a fellow immigrant Indian. Although he enjoined his fellow immigrants to observe Mexican laws so that peace would reign between "our various tribes and with the inhabitants of our adopted country," his intentions were clearly not assimilative.[28] That he forbade Mexican men from visiting the colony when the warriors were out on campaign confirmed the chief's desire to protect the tribe's women from outsiders, indicating a desire for biological and cultural isolation.[29]

They also remained aloof from the larger agricultural enterprises of the frontier. The Seminoles and Kickapoos continued to live from scavenging, farming, hunting, gathering, and limited trade in the absence of meaningful assistance from the government. They supplemented their meager corn with deer, turkey, and bears killed in the foothills of the Santa Rosa Mountains.[30] The women of the tribes, meanwhile, gathered fruits from the countryside and brought them to Músquiz to sell or exchange for basic foodstuffs they needed to feed their families.[31] Despite the fact that the commanders hoped the immigrant Indians would work on the neighboring haciendas and ranchos to supplement their village life, this does not seem to have happened in any meaningful way.[32] Many of the immigrants were inexperienced agriculturalists (with the exception of the Black Seminoles), and they did not often lend their labor to neighboring landowners. There were exceptions, of course: Tiger, a high-ranking Seminole, worked alongside two others from his tribe at the ranch of Rafael Aldape in 1854.[33] But overall, the Seminoles and Kickapoos were much more likely to supplement their corn with hunting than wage labor. Foraging in the countryside allowed them to maintain, to borrow Sarah Deutsch's term, their "separate refuge." It did not, however, integrate them into the larger frontier economy.[34]

Segregation was not only the Indians' choice. Well aware of the bias against Indians in the North, Maldonado had thought it best to keep the vecinos and Indians separated from the beginning—even if this policy contradicted the authorities' stated effort to assimilate the Indians. Shortly after their arrival, several of the Black Seminoles and Kickapoos presented themselves to the captain of Monclova Viejo and asked him for a passport to go on to San Fernando, assuming that they would settle there, near where the old Cherokee colony had been and close to the most populated pueblo on the frontier. The captain balked at this request. He was afraid of allowing a population of armed Indians from the United States, known for being "bellicose," in the midst of a Mexican population. [35] The governor of Coahuila cringed when he saw the number of Indians entering the territory and realized that they could now muster more warriors than any of the towns. He declared that any future immigrants must be preapproved by the "Supreme [Central] Government." He reflected the concerns of the vecinos when he asserted that the immigrant Indians must settle far away from the main population centers and the best lands of Coahuila.[36] On the one hand, the norteños wanted the Indians close by for purposes of surveillance; on the other, they wanted them far away so that they would not have easy access to the towns. As a result, they located the burgeoning camps at a distance from the towns but still under their military jurisdiction—demonstrating in physical space the ambivalence of the project.

Over time, given their military prowess, the immigrant tribes gained some praise from frontier officials. The officials also delighted at efforts made by the Indians to "civilize" themselves. When the Indians began to clamor for a primary school, the Mexicans saw a golden opportunity to educate them.[37] Within a few years, all Black Seminole and Seminole youth began to receive a parochial education, underwent the rite of baptism, and received catechism in Músquiz.[38] They also chose Spanish names and godparents (*padrinos*) to administer to their spiritual needs.[39] Juan Vidaurri served as schoolmaster and godparent of many of the Seminoles and blacks. As a tribute to his role in ministering to the spiritual and educational needs of the children, some of the Indians adopted Vidaurri as a surname.[40] Likewise, the sub-inspector of the frontier who had welcomed the immigrant tribes to Coahuila, Manuel Maldonado, served as padrino on occasion. While Papicua lay on his deathbed in December 1852, Maldonado granted the Kickapoo chief his last request, serving as godfather while a priest administered the rites of baptism.[41] Very important personal ties connected the immigrant tribes to the administrators of the frontier. Unfortunately, these connections did not seem to have extended to the wider neighborhood.

Instead, among the vecinos of the frontier, distrust abounded from the very beginning. In January 1851, vecinos noticed the very large population of Kickapoos from various bands congregated outside of Monclova Viejo and Remolino.[42] They were especially suspicious of the the Indians' sizable horse herds. At least one vecino won a horse from the Kickapoos' herd after complaining that he had lost it years ago to the Comanches. For his part, the Indian who formerly owned the horse claimed he had bought it from the Comanches, and, since it was the only horse he owned, "he loved him very much." But he handed the animal over anyway. Unfortunately, more vecinos came forward to claim Kickapoo horses after Maldonado resolved to return the animal to the vecino and compensate the Kickapoo with ten pesos.[43]

After the fiasco with the horses, the Kickapoos must have realized that they had not entered a rich country.[44] In March 1851, several Kickapoo men approached Commander Ignacio Galán with tears in their eyes, insisting that they needed food for their families while they waited for the meager corn to grow in the creek bed of Tulillo. Upon hearing this request, Sub-Inspector Maldonado was quite moved: these were "men with children, who are very poor [and] in a strange land." But he could do little to soothe their pain.[45] Many Kickapoos soon looked to harvesting resources from their new neighbors as a solution.

Squabbles between the Kickapoos and the vecinos over scarce foodstuffs, gunpowder, and horses intensified in the coming months. Also in March 1851, the Kickapoos visited several pueblos on the frontier to try to sell a number of antique flintlock muskets—one of the few things the Mexican government had been able to provide them. During these visits to the pueblos, they also allegedly began to demand "presents" from the townspeople.[46] Starving and ravaged by a smallpox outbreak, a group of Kickapoos approached the town of Guerrero where Maldonado reported that they ordered the townspeople to give them corn, meat, flour, and other items. The Kickapoos demanded the exact amount of thirty-two pesos to buy these things for themselves if the townspeople could not provide the goods. For their part, the vecinos feared an attack if they did not comply with the Kickapoos' demands, and they again complained loudly to their flustered officials. Maldonado ultimately acquiesced to the Kickapoos' blackmail and scrounged up the money to buy food for them.[47] Maldonado's superior, Juáregui, also grumbled about the Kickapoos' behavior, but he somehow found nine hundred pesos to buy tools for them from Texas, since the implements could not be found on the Mexican side of the border.[48] Relations between the Kickapoos and vecinos continued to deteriorate as they argued over scarce frontier resources. Sometimes, of course, the vecinos were the guilty parties. In May 1851 the authorities caught the norteño Teodor Treviño trafficking horses stolen from the Kickapoos.[49]

Most Kickapoos soon decided to leave, but first they took out some of their frustrations on their neighbors. In June 1851, a U.S. Indian Bureau agent deputized the Kickapoo Seslvot [sic] to negotiate with Pecan, another Kickapoo chief, for his band's return to the Arkansas River. Seslvot caught up to the chief while his Kickapoos were out on a campaign against the Lipans. Seslvot conferred with Pecan in English, leaving the Mexican commanders who knew none of that language to puzzle over the meaning of his visit. The U.S. Indian Bureau was trying to entice the Kickapoos to return to the other side of the border, even promising them 7,000 pesos payable immediately upon their return.[50] The U.S. government recognized that mobile Indians were at the root of many troubles along the new border and sought to bring them back under its control. As a result, the Kickapoos soon deserted the campaign, leaving their fellow immigrant tribesmen and presidial soldiers in the lurch.[51] When they deserted the Kickapoos took with them the pay, gunpowder, flour, tobacco, and arms they had received as provisions for the campaign. In addition, they took twenty-six of the horses that the campaign had recovered in a brief initial encounter with Indian raiders.[52] Most Kickapoos then headed toward the border, but they had several encounters with vecinos along the way. One Kickapoo warrior killed a vecino in Guerrero after an altercation.[53] Soon, the Kickapoos, with the exception of Chief Papicua and about twenty of his followers, exited Mexico for Texas. Papicua admitted, when questioned by the authorities, that the Kickapoos who had deserted the campaign were predisposed to hurting the vecinos after their bitter experience.[54] Put on alert, Maldonado wrote to Colonel Wilson at Fort Duncan to try to apprehend the Kickapoos once they crossed over the Rio Grande into Texas, but nothing came of his request.[55]

In the end, the Kickapoo debacle resulted in the norteños gaining more enemies. A couple of years later, Juan Zuazua, who took over as commander of the frontier in 1853, reported that the Kickapoos had begun to raid in the far western frontier in Coahuila, and they quickly earned a reputation for staging a kind of war with no quarter against the Mexicans. When Zuazua made an expedition with a force of 120 men toward the Laguna de Leche, he reported on the cruelty of the Kickapoos who were camped at the headwaters of the Sabinas. The raiders had allegedly murdered all the Mexicans in their path rather than taking captives, and they had not spared the children they encountered. In addition, they killed all of the wild horses they found, transporting only the tame ones that they could use immediately, leaving a trail of butchered animals in their wake. Zuazua, privy to the rumors of Kickapoo cruelty that had circulated since their desertion, was certain of the identity of the raiders. He accused them of crossing back and forth from Texas to Coahuila to make their *correrías* (raids).[56]

Zuazua's reports need to be taken with a grain of salt. Nuevo León had suffered unduly from the loss of blood and treasure to Comanche raiders over the previous forty years. By the 1850s, the vecinos of the small towns in northern Nuevo León became the most Indian-hating of the vecinos who populated a frontier that was far from enamored with Native Americans.[57] But more than likely Zuazua knew his enemies. For the Kickapoos who deserted, raiding turned out to be much more lucrative and secure than waiting on the broken promises of the Mexican government and dealing with jealous vecinos. For the Mexican government, failure to live up to its side of the bargain had disastrous consequences and destabilized the frontier further. As long as reverting to old raiding patterns remained an option, the frontier would not be secure if the immigrant tribes remained impoverished.

It was not only the Kickapoos who terrorized the vecinos. In October 1852, a party of Indians attacked twenty vecinos from Abasolo, Nuevo León, who were returning from gathering mustangs near the Sabinas River. The attackers ambushed them near the point known as Santa Cruz, killed one of the vecinos, stole all of the horses and saddles, and then ran the terrified men off, scattering them in all directions. In response, the alcalde of Abasolo wrote to his counterpart in Santa Rosa, copying the governor, with an accusation against the immigrant tribes. He was convinced that either the Seminoles or Papicua's Kickapoos—or as he called them, the state's "newest enemies"—had perpetrated the attack and then "thrown themselves out into the desert." His evidence was damning. The attackers traveled in a group of twenty, whereas Comanche raiding parties usually consisted of no more than a handful of warriors. In addition, the attackers had light skin, wore hats, and carried carbines instead of bows and arrows. All these things pointed to evidence of mixed heritage among the raiders. The alcalde did not have sufficient evidence to support the claim, but he was sure that the Seminoles raided in "certain points of the state." (In fact, the alcalde was probably wrong in accusing the Seminoles in this instance. At least two women had accompanied the war party, and Seminole women remained at home.)[58] Whether or not it was the Seminoles, the mayor's letter shows the general suspicion among vecinos in Nuevo León of all Indians, immigrant or otherwise.

Meanwhile, the alcalde of nearby Músquiz had seen a tremendous drop in Comanche raids into his war-torn village ever since the immigrant tribes had arrived. He hoped to defend the Seminoles against the charges from Nuevo León. He said that, in general, the immigrant tribes have "good intentions" and make war against the Comanches, but it was inescapable that, "motivated by booty" and the poverty in which they live, they make "raids which cause notorious damage to the lives and property of the citizens."[59] Nevertheless, he agreed to watch over them, even though he repudiated the allegations made from Nuevo León—a state where they were hostile to Indians of any sort given their long history with Comanche raids.[60]

But the alcalde of Músquiz was much more candid in a private letter he wrote to General Doroteo Nava. He said that the impoverished immigrant Indians felt a great temptation to plunder in the neighboring towns due to the poverty in which they lived. Further, they could easily overpower the vecinos and then ride out into the western deserts where the vecinos would be very unlikely to follow them. Nor could he keep tabs on them at all times as they often failed to request a passport when they went out to hunt deer around the Sabinas River. Finally, they had recently stolen several fat cows from the vecinos to "attend to their own personal conservation, the supreme law of society."[61] Even the alcalde of Músquiz, whose besieged frontier town sat near the foothills of the Santa Rosa Mountains and who had benefited the most from the arrival of the immigrant tribes, could not entirely endorse them.

If they were innocent of the attack made in Abasolo, the immigrant tribes were certainly guilty of some of the raids that followed in Nuevo León. In April 1853, a party of Indians killed four men at the Puerto de los Pedernales near Mina, Nuevo León, in a manner that appalled the officials of that state. One of the men killed, a peon of Santiago Villareal, had suffered terribly; the Indians "reduced his head to nothing from the force of blows." After investigating, the juzgado of Mina wrote that it must have been Coacoochee's Indians who perpetrated the attacks; the men were well armed, wore blue frocks and *levas* (short jackets with long tails), and carried pistols in their belts.[62]

The immigrant tribes did not get along with the vecinos closer to their home base at Nacimiento either, although they refrained from large-scale raiding in Coahuila. Near Músquiz, the incidents that involved the Seminoles had a character more closely resembling squabbles between fractious neighbors than depredations. In late 1853, for example, a couple of Seminoles whom the Mexicans generally regarded as drunks tried to steal two horses from the pastures of Músquiz when the townsfolk captured them. They then beat them on the head with rocks and knifed them in the back. Remarkably, the Indians survived. The alcalde had tried to keep the Indians out of the village before this incident, but they had begun to enter and demand sweet corn and money from the vecinos anyway.[63] The alcalde of Músquiz was aware that the immigrant tribes were at the root of a reduction in Comanche violence visited upon the town. Nevertheless, he could do little to soothe the troubled relationship between the Indians of Nacimiento and the vecinos.

The alcalde of San Fernando made several efforts to keep the Indian men out of his town as well, but also to little effect. Frederick Olmsted, when he passed through in the early 1850s, observed the ongoing conflict between immigrant tribes and vecinos. He said that the Indians congregated on street corners in mixed groups comprising Lipans, Mescaleros, Tonkawas, and Seminoles and molested any strangers who passed through the town. They were especially interested in handling the strangers' rifles. During his visit, he also witnessed a group of Indians in town acting riotously. They were, according to the writer, entering and exiting the vecinos' houses without knocking, laying about in the streets, imbibing spirits, "patting women on the cheek," and generally "carrying themselves everywhere with such an air as indicated they were masters of the town." The townspeople, for their part, were quite used to the Indians and commented little on their presence.[64]

The immigrant tribes never gained much in the vecinos' estimation. When smallpox carried off Coacoochee, Coyote, and fifteen other renowned warriors from the tribe in 1857, Vidaurri hoped to replenish their numbers, bringing in more immigrant tribesmen, but this proposal did not sit well with the norteños. In October the Tamaulipas newspaper, *El Prisma,* expressed a common sentiment in the Mexican North and warned against colonizing the frontier with yet more "savages." The newspaper called on the government to stop experimenting with Indian colonization. It referred to their arrival as "a terribly disastrous plague" and said that the Seminoles were far from civilized. According to *El Prisma*, the vecinos and military colonists could finish the war against the "savage," and immigrant tribesmen and women were an irrelevant and dangerous distraction. It insisted that the frontier would be better "colonized with honorable, industrious, and enlightened men from Europe who will make our society progress."[65]

Such colonists were unavailable in the borderlands, of course, but the newspaper absolutely refused to draw a distinction between the Seminoles and plains raiders. In the years that followed, complaints against the Seminoles persisted, many of which were unjustified. A tirade by Santos Benavides of Laredo against the Seminoles to Santiago Vidaurri, governor of Nuevo León, demonstrated that the anti-Indian attitude crossed the border, drawing Tejanos and norteños together in common cause.[66] Bad faith continued to characterize the relationship between the immigrant tribes, the Mexican vecinos, the Tejanos on the right bank of the river, and, of course, the white Texans deeper within the state. Finally, a brief drop in Comanche violence in the Mexican North, a result of the U.S. military's pressure against the plains raiders as well as the concerted efforts of the Mexican military colonies, likely contributed to the vecinos' conviction that the immigrant tribes were no longer needed at the Coahuiltecan frontier—if they had ever been needed.

The Mascogos—as the Mexicans called them—were also a major problem. Mascogos were Black Seminoles who had lived alongside Coacoochee's tribe for years and accompanied him into Mexico, even though they lived apart after they arrived. Their numbers had grown with the more recent arrival of black runaways. They were equally objectionable to the vecinos but for different reasons. The alcalde of Músquiz sounded a common complaint against them, lamenting that, in contrast to the Seminoles, they "did not leave on campaign willingly." Further, they indiscriminately slaughtered their neighbors' cattle, and they committed other crimes—the result of which had landed not a few blacks (perhaps Mascogos) in jail in Monclova and at other places on the frontier. The addition of many runaway slaves to their colony over the course of the 1850s may have introduced a criminal element into their ranks. Whatever the case, the alcalde recommended a judicious solution, suggesting that the authorities move them someplace else where they would not cause so much trouble with the vecinos, the immigrant tribes, and the Texans. He justified his proposition by writing that while the blacks did indeed occupy themselves with working the earth dutifully, they disliked abandoning their farms and families to go out on campaign. Nor did they obey the authorities, causing all sorts of trouble with the neighboring villagers. Worse yet, some of the blacks believed—according to the alcalde, at least—that they had "immigrated to a country where their liberty was absolute."[67] Mexico may have offered freedom to African Americans when they crossed the line, but they expected them to contribute to their projects on the frontier, immerse themselves in civil society, and live by Mexican law. Most problematic, however, the black colony at Nacimiento de Negros attracted especially resentful glances from the Texans on the other side of the river.

Nacimiento de los Negros

Black Indians and the runaway slaves who joined their community represented a particularly dangerous threat to the security of the northern Mexican frontier. Slave hunters routinely violated the border for profit, and the Mascogo colony was an especially tempting target. John Horse—known as Juan Caballo to the Mexicans—was chief of the Black Seminoles, and he began to look for a new home removed from the other migrants, the border, and slave hunters almost immediately after arrival. He never lost sight of the immense danger posed by living close to the border at Monclova Viejo and Moral. Thus he lobbied for a piece of land deep in the interior of Nuevo León, far removed from the border and its dangers, and eventually won a meeting with several of the authorities in Monterrey to discuss his plans. Horse received a small allotment and a military escort to travel to Monterrey to speak with the sympathetic inspector of the frontier, Antonio María Juáregui, but nothing came of his efforts.[68]

Horse himself would fall victim to the insecurity of living too close to the border. The slave hunter Warren Adams kidnapped him and the black Indian Hongo de Agosto in September 1851 in Eagle Pass. He was able to return home to Mexico only after his fellow black Indians collected two hundred allegedly blood-stained pesos to hand over to Adams to obtain his release. The blacks who paid his ransom had, in fact, threatened to invade Texas to free him if Maldonado did not succeed in negotiating his release. Maldonado, fearing the ramifications of a black invasion on the United States, could not convince the authorities in Texas to release John Horse. He even forwarded the authorities proof that Horse and his companion were free men. With negotiations stalled, an open war almost broke out. In the end cooler heads prevailed, and a major international confrontation between angry blacks in Mexico and Anglo Texans was avoided. After his ransom, however, Horse still feared for his safety. A year later, an accomplice of the mail carrier from Béxar attempted to kidnap Horse at a dance in Piedras Negras. This time the authorities immediately put the kidnapper in irons upon discovering the plot. The kidnapper nevertheless managed to escape his captors and swim across the river to Texas and safety.[69]

Even Coacoochee was not above working with slave hunters on some occasions. One of the free blacks who immigrated to Coahuila alongside Coacoochee made an egregious complaint against the chief in 1853. The African American man, known simply as Cofé (Cuffy), left his family behind in Santa Rosa to travel with Coacoochee as his interpreter in 1852 when he went to Texas. Once the men crossed over to Eagle Pass, however, the Seminole chief sold the black man to a white man for eighty pesos. After paying Coacoochee, Cofé's captor bound him and carried him off to San Antonio. Fortunately for Cofé, a few months later he managed to escape slavery in San Antonio and rejoin his family in Santa Rosa. Once back to safety, he made a formal complaint to the military juzgado against Coacoochee and said that he had seen another black man in San Antonio whom the chief had sold to the whites.[70] Such indiscretions by Coacoochee became part of Black Seminole folklore. Years later they still told stories about Coacoochee trying to trade the blacks who traveled with him to Texas for whiskey.[71]

Because of Texan complicity with slave hunters and the filibusterers' refusal to respect the new border, the authorities in Mexico acquiesced to the blacks' demands to move them farther inland, away from Monclova Viejo. The immigrant tribes and blacks received Nacimiento in 1852 after their assistance in defeating a Texan and Tejano filibuster at Cerralvo. Hacienda de Nacimiento, which was located close to Santa Rosa and a couple of leagues removed from the border, was unimproved land that had once belonged to the Sánchez Navarro latifundia in Coahuila. John Horse helped secure the transfer of the property from eminent domain, picking out two "sitios de ganado mayor" (10,000 acres of pasture) four miles from the main settlement of the Seminoles at the headwaters of the Río Sabinas to settle Black Seminoles and other blacks who might join the group.[72] Nacimiento de los Negros—as the black settlement would be known—sat at a remove from the border. But the residents were still not safe. Just a few months earlier, Warren Adams had stolen an entire family of blacks under cover of night from Santa Rosa, which was located even farther into the interior. And despite his distance from the border, Adams still managed to escape with a National Guard unit of thirty-five men drawn from the citizens of that town close on his heels.[73]

Mexican authorities hoped that by "internalizing" the Black Seminoles and other blacks at Nacimiento they would ease pressure on the border. Mexico did experience a brief reprieve from attacks by Texan filibusterers following the move to Nacimiento, but this had more to do with the resolution of the wars involving the caudillo Carvajal than the removal of the blacks and black Indians. The halting peace that ensued at the end of these disturbances did not last long. In 1854, another rumor surfaced that five hundred Texans were preparing to raid Coahuila to abduct all the blacks outside of San Fernando and the surrounding ranches that employed the runaways.[74] The attack never materialized, but others would.

It turns out that the military commanders in Coahuila had also threatened to sell the blacks to the Texans on at least one occasion. During an underfunded military campaign in early 1856, the black Indian force wound up in a tight spot once they reached the western Coahuilte-can desert under the captains José María Chisman and Tomás Santa Cruz. Separated from the main force under Francisco Treviño, the captains complained that Treviño had failed to provision them adequately and initiated a revolt against him. The Black Seminoles refused to follow Captain Chisman in his revolt, standing by their principle to fight only Indians and not other Mexicans. John Horse informed Chisman—rather calmly it would seem—that his fate was tied to Treviño's, and he would remain loyal to the command. Chisman then made the ultimate threat against John Horse. He threatened to expel the blacks who did not second his mutiny from Mexican territory and turn them over to the authorities in Texas if they continued to support the "tyrannical government."[75]

In the end, the twenty-two Mexicans serving under Chisman and Santa Cruz left the Black Seminoles in the desert to fend for themselves. The captains' revolt was not ultimately successful, but neither did anyone punish them. The tribunal that investigated the revolt acquitted the insurgents of all charges. Santiago Vidaurri, then serving as commander in chief of the northern presidial colonies and the army, found that Treviño had been very poorly provisioned for such a long expedition into the desert and the insubordination of the officers was justified on these grounds. Their threats against the blacks, although investigated by the tribunal, did not ultimately warrant any punishment.[76] There was no need to grandstand for the rights of blacks and their promised liberty when there were no Texans watching. In any case, this was the last expedition the Black Seminoles undertook willingly for some time. Consequently, Vidaurri showed a marked preference for Seminole and Caddo immigrants over blacks in the years to come.[77]

For the Black Seminoles, insecurity did not result just from the threat of slave hunters and extradition to Texas. Like the Seminoles, they too had to deal with the state's galling lack of resources. During campaigns, for instance, their wives and families left behind at Nacimiento suffered keenly. They were unable to complete the farm work on their own, and often they faced terrible delays in collecting their sons' and husbands' salaries. In one instance, the mother of a black Indian soldier named Juan Garza took it upon herself to make a complaint. She traveled to Parras to seek out General Francisco Treviño and inquire about the military assignment that had taken her son away. She asked for her son's release, stating that he was not capable of carrying arms because of his youth. Treviño agreed with the young soldier's mother, and he commenced a review of the rest of the blacks under arms. Ultimately, Treviño decided to release the other thirteen blacks from the campaign and pay them their full salaries, minus the cost of the food they had consumed while on duty. None of the blacks had yet received their entire payment, he realized, and what they had received had been given to them in very small parts. Treviño admitted that the paltry sum contributed little to the maintenance of their families.[78]

Despite the worsening alcoholism of John Horse, the black Indians had done well on a campaign against the Comanches—a campaign during which, it might be noted, the Mexican companies in the expedition mutinied. But even their small salaries could be paid only after Treviño had made a special entreaty to his superior recommending full compensation for the black Indians.[79] They may indeed have found liberty, legal protection, and refuge on the Mexican side of the border. But like the other immigrant Indians, they also found painful insecurity. Nor had they managed to make the vecinos who lived around them more secure in their lives.

The racial fault line of the Rio Grande resulted in the migration of many ethnic outsiders from the United States to Mexico. The idea of inviting disaffected tribes from the United States to settle in Mexico fired the imagination of frontier officials who dreamed of settling and securing the vast, sparsely populated borderland. But there were just too many problems with this proposition. First, and most important, the immigrant tribes never received the resources they needed to establish themselves in Mexico. Second, the arrival of some two thousand or more Indian immigrants in 1850 and 1851 intensified the competition for already scarce gunpowder, weapons, foodstuffs, and horses. Third, most vecinos, who knew only "bárbaros," watched the arrival of waves of immigrant tribes with great apprehension. Nor were they dedicated to transforming the border into a racial fault line by inviting and then living alongside so many dangerous foreigners. And fourth, because they lacked resources, the immigrant tribes ended up raiding their neighbors on the Mexican frontier and in Texas as well. This brought on the threat of a disastrous counterstrike led by Texas Rangers and volunteers that would imperil the lives and property of the Mexican vecinos. Rather than greater security along the frontier, the immigrant tribes had produced greater insecurity for the vecinos.

Nor did the immigrant tribes feel secure. Despite the many services they had rendered, they felt unappreciated. Combined with the fact that the old problem of dearth still dogged them at every turn, the Indians at last had enough and decided to leave. The Seminoles and their friends had made great sacrifices to fight the Comanches and Lipans over the previous decade, and because they felt unappreciated, American officials easily convinced the Seminoles to return to the United States. When U.S. Indian Bureau agents invited the Seminoles to return to the Creek Reservation in Indian Territory in 1858, many of the Indians slowly began making the journey out of Mexico. Then, when the Sánchez-Navarro clan claimed that the government had not reimbursed them for the hacienda of Nacimiento, even more Seminoles left. A vecino of Músquiz who encountered twenty-five of the Seminoles camped at Remolino with their families en route to Texas reported back on the Indians' feelings. He said that they were going back to their lands in the United States because the "Mexican government did not give them justice." They had never received the promised resources, and their land grant was in jeopardy. Unable to find a viable solution, the Seminoles returned to the other side of the border the following year, devastated by the loss of their chief and the lack of resources in Mexico. By 1861, none remained in Mexico.[80]

As people-in-between, many Indians historically kept their options open. In Mexico, the Indians had been free to maintain their identity, liberty, and mobility in exchange for taking the war to the Comanches. The Seminoles, Kickapoos, and Black Seminoles did find a degree of independence and liberty in Mexico. Of course, the Indians were much more independent than the authorities on the Mexican frontier had anticipated, and they never properly integrated into Mexican society. But from the point of view of the immigrant tribes, what good was independence if it also meant poverty and insecurity? The Kickapoos were the first to leave, and by 1870 all of the groups comprising the immigrant tribes—including Black Seminoles—had struck a deal to return to the United States. Interestingly, however, some would also maintain land in Mexico. For these Indians, liberty meant crossing the border—not once but many times—in search of the best opportunities for themselves.

6 / The Line of Liberty: Runaway Slaves after the Treaty of Guadalupe Hidalgo

In the early 1850s, Frederick Law Olmsted went on an extensive visit to Texas. Upon his return to New York, he published his impressions in a travelogue called *A Journey through Texas,* hoping to acquaint his readers with one of America's newest states. Olmsted's book was not, however, politically neutral. A Free Soiler and dedicated "scientific farmer" from Staten Island, Olmsted wrote at length and with great consternation about the agricultural enterprises of Texas. He thoroughly disapproved of slave labor, especially its implementation in Texas, arguing that it was particularly brutal there, hearkening back to the "original moment of captivity." In Texas, enslaved blacks had not adopted the docility that he observed in other southern states; the violence that underscored the reduction of human beings to commodities had not lessened or ameliorated in Texas despite the passage of time and generations. An inevitable result of the brutality with which Texan slaveholders treated black slaves—at least according to Olmsted—was a large number of runaways. Olmsted does not say so explicitly, but it may have been the proximity of Mexico that transformed the institution of slavery in that state, turning it into something Olmsted referred to as "slavery with a will."[1]

It would be hard to imagine a labor system further removed from the free labor that Olmsted and his proto-Republican contemporaries idealized than slavery in Texas. The same cultural and ideological movement that gave birth to the national political career of Abraham Lincoln highly valued the ethic of working hard to get ahead in life. Living on other's work was not only lazy, but it was morally wrong. Of course, Texans balked at Olmsted's descriptions of the conditions in their beloved state and his demonization of the slavery he found there. His condemnations were part of "a large proportion of the Northern papers [that] have taken every opportunity to vilify and abuse that part of the citizens from the United States living South of the line known as Mason's and Dixon's, and sought in all ways to interfere with them in the peaceable enjoyment of that peculiar institution, which is so absolutely necessary to their prosperity and full development," according to the *San Antonio Daily Herald*.[2] But there was no clearer indication that Texans were not in control of the situation than the abundance of runaways from slavery. Just as runaway peons indicted that system of labor in northern Mexico for many Texans, so too did runaways impugn the so-called peculiar institution for outside observers like Olmsted.

Olmsted also encountered a number of runaways when he crossed into Mexico briefly. In Piedras Negras across the river from Eagle Pass, Olmsted learned that runaway slaves were "constantly arriving." At least forty runaways had crossed the river in the past three months, according to one black man with whom he talked. Olmsted describes the encounter he and a companion had with one runaway slave in detail:

> As we turned the corner near the bank, we came suddenly upon two negroes, as they were crossing the street. One of them was startled, and looking ashamed and confounded, turned hesitatingly back and walked away from us; whereat some Mexican children laughed, and the other negro, looking at us grinned impudently—expressing plainly enough—"I am not afraid of you."

Olmsted and the black man then nodded at each other, and the latter politely touched his hat before walking away whistling. Olmsted, his curiosity piqued, followed the man. He caught up to him, and they entered into friendly conversation. The black man was born in Virginia, but he got caught in the interstate slave trade—the trafficking that transferred so many African Americans from the East to the bourgeoning cotton dominion of the new Southwest. He ended up in Texas and soon afterward ran away to Mexico. Upon crossing into Mexico he went to Piedras Negras, where he worked as a mechanic and earned a reasonable wage. He spoke Spanish, adopted Catholicism, and traveled widely in Mexico, describing himself as "very well satisfied with the country." Not unlike the runaways discussed in chapter 3, this man found his circumstances much improved by the mere fact of crossing the border. He adapted to the demands made by the Mexican government to become a citizen—conversion to Catholicism and immersion in Spanish—and in exchange he found a new home.[3] But his friend, the one who ran off to the sound of giggling Mexican children, showed that this newfound freedom could be fleeting. It was a precious thing that slave hunters could easily steal.

These runaways were part of a large human wave lapping the shores of northern Mexico in the 1850s. The new border that separated Mexico and Texas after 1848 resulted in a marked increase in the number of blacks seeking freedom on the other side. In addition, the practice of granting freedom to runaway slaves who crossed into Mexican territory, which began in earnest during the years of the Texan Revolt, was enshrined in Mexican law, eventually becoming part of the 1857 Constitution.[4] Texas slaveholders had hoped to turn the new border into a fence, a definite limit to slave country that contained all of that institution's misery and injustice within a demarcated geographic territory. But if this was what they hoped for, Texans would only find disappointment. By 1851, Mexicans estimated that "upwards of two thousand fugitive slaves" were to be found in their country east of the Sierra Madre. A former Texas Ranger who hoped to form a hunting party to recover runaways put the number closer to three thousand runaways from Texas alone, nearly 5 percent of the enslaved population in Texas.[5] Surely these figures represented slaveholder anxiety as much as they did reality, but the number must have been considerable to provoke such worry on the part of Texan slaveholders.

The most obvious cause for the increase in runaways was that there were more enslaved African Americans in Texas after 1848. The 1850s witnessed a tremendous transfer of southerners and their human chattel westward to Texas. But there was another reason for the number of runaways to Mexico. The new international border was a line between slavery and freedom—a line of liberty. In this chapter, I discuss just how much blacks thought about the border and how freedom in Mexico captured the imagination of enslaved people in Texas.[6]

"The Insecurity of Slave Property"

As the number of slaveholders in Texas increased, so too did the number of runaway slaves to Mexico. The 1850s witnessed intense population growth in the newly annexed state of Texas as Anglos and their enslaved laborers poured into the area after the U.S.-Mexico War. Transplanted white southerners most likely believed that with the boundary issues

settled and the U.S. government taking over the old Spanish borderlands Texas was at last safe for slavery. From 1848 to 1860, the total population of Texas nearly quadrupled, from around 150,000 to just over 600,000. Included in this general population increase were many slaves—some migrating with their former masters and others sold through the interstate slave trade. The number of slaves in Texas increased in both absolute and relative terms. Their population grew at an even greater rate than whites, from 58,161 in 1850 to 182,566 in 1860.[7]

Not only did the number of slaves grow during this decade but the geographic expanse of slaveholder power increased as well. Slaveholders grew their territory, moving not only to the Brazos but also into the Matagorda Bay area and along the Colorado River. These two areas, broadly considered, constituted the slaveholder's frontier in Texas. Central Texas was the farthest south and west that slave country extended in the antebellum United States. But despite the growth in the slave population in the areas surrounding the old land grants, the region south of the Colorado River never really evolved into a society with slaves. No county on the other side of that river contained more than a thousand enslaved people in 1860. In most cases, the number of slaves resident in any county in South Texas never amounted to a majority. They always made up under 50 percent of the total population, and most of these counties remained overwhelmingly populated by Tejanos and mexicanos. South Texas, broadly considered, was a borderland in a variety of ways. It was a borderland between Texas and Mexico and between mobile Native American raiders and sedentary settlers. But it was also a borderland of slavery and freedom.[8]

As slavery grew in Texas, the possibility of slave flight gravely affected the practice and halted it from expanding significantly beyond the Colorado River. As the *New Orleans Crescent* correspondent W. P. Reyburn wrote, the frequency of runaways to Mexico "has been one of the excitants of bad feeling between the citizens of Mexico and those on the frontier; consequently, all the household drudgery and menial services

FIGURE 6 (opposite page). Felix Haywood elegantly explained what Mexico meant to the enslaved in Texas to the Works Project Administration in the 1930s: "In Mexico you could be free, they didn't care what color you were, black, white, yellow, or blue. Hundreds of slaves did go to Mexico and got on all right." (Tyler, The Slave Narratives of Texas, 69–70). LC-USZ62–125235 (b&w film copy neg.); Library of Congress Prints and Photographs Division, Washington, D.C. 20540 USA.

are performed by Mexican servants."[9] Following Reyburn's lead, we should not attribute the paucity of slaves in frontier Texas to the aridity of that zone. Peonage may have been the customary institution, but Texans and Tejanos alike could have employed slavery profitably in agricultural enterprises other than cotton production in the region south of the Colorado. There were plenty of black cowboys throughout the history of nineteenth-century Texas after all. And mine owners had employed slavery profitably throughout the western hemisphere in the preceding centuries. Furthermore, other American frontier zones—the Colombian llanos east of the Andes or the Argentine pampas, for instance—had large numbers of African American workers and cattlemen.[10]

It was the "insecurity" of South Texas that forestalled the further expansion of slavery. Texas slaveholders complained tirelessly about the difficulties they faced in South Texas brought on by the proximity of Mexico and Mexicans. They insisted that they wanted—needed—a secure border. As the editor of the Clarksville Northern Standard agonized, "If slavery should be abolished by force of circumstances in Western [i.e., southern] Texas, how much longer will it continue in the East?"[11] Slavery was on particularly unsure footing in the settlements near the Colorado River. Perhaps the largest number of runaways to Mexico came from the area immediately adjacent to Austin's grant, the region around Austin, Béxar, and Bastrop. Slaveholders quickly recognized the "insecurity of slave property" in this area. Citizens of Bexar County said so explicitly when they asked the governor of Texas for additional protection after capturing a Mexican preparing a runaway slave for his getaway.[12]

Texans' complaints about runaway slaves did not always fall upon receptive ears—at least not at the federal level. To some American policy makers the problem of black runaways to Mexico was not really a problem at all. These runaway slaves fulfilled a vision Jefferson had publicized a generation before: slavery would diffuse through space and eventually drain off beyond the frontier through westward expansion. Even in the 1840s, some Americans still hoped that Mexico would absorb African Americans from the United States, tidily taking care of their race problem for them. John L. O'Sullivan himself, who coined the phrase "Manifest Destiny" (although that is now debated),[13] joined this debate. He insisted that Latin America would do in a pinch to solve America's race problem. After making the customary slurs on Latin American peoples, he went on to suggest that Mexico would "afford the only receptacle capable of absorbing that race [blacks] whenever we shall be prepared to slough it off." Of course, the exact point at which American slaveholders would be "prepared to slough it off" was also a matter of intense debate. The safety valve or, better yet, "drain," thesis proposed by O'Sullivan was a convenient one. It justified the land grab we know as "Manifest Destiny" and, at the same time, attempted to satisfy critics of slavery by means of a clever redeployment of racism. Maybe moving westward would get rid of black people once and for all, some proponents of expansion argued.[14]

We should not think that this argument was a sincere one, at least not as far as slaveholders were concerned. Once enslaved people actually started "sloughing off" to Mexico, slaveholders in Texas and Louisiana howled at their representatives to do something. In an attempt to stave off the insecurity of slave "property," federal diplomats took the pleas of Texan planters seriously. Minister to Mexico James Gadsden called on Mexico to do something.[15] He also took the additional step of forbidding all American diplomats serving in Mexico from issuing cartas de seguridades (visas) to African Americans. With the stroke of a pen, Gadsden decreed that the categories of blackness and citizenship were mutually exclusive worldwide, and he implored Mexicans to bar them from their country since they were not American citizens. No matter where African Americans stepped, even outside the territorial boundaries of the United States, American lawmakers and officials were not supposed to consider them citizens or afford them civil rights.[16]

But Mexicans had already demonstrated their willingness to vouch for African American immigrants. In San Buenaventura, the "African" Alexander Ardí applied for a carta de seguridad in 1853 and received it in the absence of an American consular official in that remote town. He was a laborer, married, and wanted to live in Mexico where he and his family would be protected "under the ample protection of the law." Whether he had come as a refugee from slavery or as a freeman or how he had arrived in America from Africa (and whether it was his generation that had made the voyage) did not figure into the paperwork.[17] That same year, farther west, in the dusty Coahuiltecan pueblo of Nadadores, the alcalde municipal recorded the presence of three fugitive "negroes."[18] Officials could fill out the paperwork in ways that did not offend the Americans and still protected runaways. Nor is their much evidence that these new requirements from Gadsden would do much to discourage black immigration to Mexico—especially in remote places.

Gadsden's circular was important nonetheless. It was a dress rehearsal for a rethinking of blackness and belonging in U.S. jurisprudence, but the reality of granting "amparo" to fugitive blacks in Mexico contrasted sharply with Gadsden's outlawing of black citizenship. Americans eventually enshrined the impossibility of black citizenship in law in the Dred Scott decision of 1857, and Mexicans noticed. Interestingly, this was the same year that their new constitution once and for all granted blacks freedom when they crossed the border.[19] Nevertheless, Mexicans as well as their American counterparts could be quite confused about all of this. The Mexican officer, Juan Nepumuceno Almonte, was aware of this new direction in American racism, and he feared for the safety and freedom of his black valets when he traveled to the United States. Before Gadsden banned visas, Almonte wrote to the secretary of state, William S. Marcy, to request special passports for Augustine Watts and Turley Burke, "two men of color," to accompany him while he traveled to the United States. Marcy gladly issued the two men the necessary documents. But a year later, after Gadsden's circular, when Almonte again asked Marcy for a passport for Watts to accompany him and his family on a visit to Charleston, Marcy demurred. Instead, he suggested that Almonte issue Watts a passport himself, which "would, under the law of the United States, be ample for his protection."[20] The United States could no longer guarantee the freedom of a man of color, but Mexico could. Efforts to limit the citizenship of African Americans internationally were an early step toward conflating the categories of blackness and servility on the part of U.S. American policy makers. But as Marcy implicitly acknowledged, Americans could not restrict citizenship guaranteed by other, sovereign governments—at least not legally.

Despite the fact that blacks were "citizens of nowhere," as Sarah Cornell has argued, it was difficult to enforce Gadsden's circular in areas like Matamoros that continued to draw black immigration. It is also doubtful that blacks had an overriding concern with obtaining citizenship. The circular applied only to African Americans and runaway slaves who did the paperwork to obtain a carta de seguridad. (It is difficult to know how many blacks actually obtained cartas de seguridad, as few records exist of blacks in the Mexican North holding them, either before or after 1854.) In addition, the North American consul who served in Matamoros, Thomas Hirgan, found it inconsistent with earlier practices that allowed blacks consular protection if they produced evidence of their freedom, and he may not have implemented the new policy. The restrictions were rather "obscure," he said, and he did not understand why blacks could no longer be citizens abroad or at home.[21]

Like Gadsden, many Texans did not feel bound to respect Mexico's difference on the subjects of race and slavery and hoped to foist their

THE WAR IN TEXAS—BROWNSVILLE, NOW OCCUPIED BY THE ARMY UNDER MAJOR-

THE WAR IN TEXAS—THE CITY OF MATAMORAS, MEXICO, OPPOSITE BROWNSVILLE.—FROM A SKETCH BY L. AVERY.

FIGURE 7. Matamoros, perhaps more than any other town along the river, drew runaway slaves. It also attracted Indian immigrants in the 1820s and 1830s. This illustration of the town is from the Civil War era. Illus. in AP2. L52 1863 Case Y [P&P], Library of Congress Prints and Photographs Division, Washington, D.C. 20540 USA.

racist policies on Mexico. Slave raids were a much more direct way than consular circulars to conflate blackness and servility outside of the United States. Illegal abductions of black people by Texans could abjure Mexican legal protection through force. In 1851, white Texans allied with the Tejano caudillo José María de Jesús Carvajal who filibustered in Tamaulipas in the fall, hopeful of capturing runaway slaves. Carvajal's revolution aimed, for the most part, to liberalize trade across the new frontier. Anglo Texans, in conjunction with Carvajal's forces, attacked Cerralvo in their effort to break off an independent "Republic of the Sierra Madre" from Mexico. Carvajal intended his revolt to overthrow the Centralist policies of the Mexican government. Most important, he wanted free trade across the border, unrestricted by the central government's tariffs and other protectionist policies. Most likely he allied with the Texans because he needed help, but the Anglos and Tejanos who made up the movement shared many of the same political and economic convictions. Their liberal economic views have led some historians to dub the Carvajal conflicts the "merchant wars." But if the revolution had been successful, Carvajal would also have allowed Texans unimpeded access to Tamaulipas in order to recapture runaways.[22] (Filibustering and slave hunting often converged.) Ultimately, the revolt failed, and the Mexican authorities labeled Carvajal a traitor for bringing Texas Rangers into his army.[23] The plot also captured the attention of an anonymous former senator (possibly Daniel Webster) who implored foreign minister plenipotentiary Luis de la Rosa to do something about the situation lest northern Mexico become an extension of slave country.[24]

Despite the Texans' best efforts, blackness and slavery remained unlinked on the other side of the border. No one person better represented this geographic and racial contradiction than the commander of Matamoros, Francisco Avalos, an Afro-mestizo. Avalos's National Guard brigade of volunteers helped defeat Carvajal's forces in fall 1851 when Carvajal attempted, with a number of unruly Texans, to take the plaza of Matamoros. Avalos was hailed by the people of Matamoros as having been heroic in his efforts on their behalf.[25] The opposition to Avalos did not stop there, however, as he remained a figure who represented Mexican intransigence and liberality on issues of race and slavery. That a mixed-race man could be seen as an important figure just over the border seemed incongruous to Texans. One commissioner assigned to settle land claims on the Rio Grande after the Treaty of Guadalupe Hidalgo informed Avalos "that if he were caught east of the Colorado, he would readily sell for a prim negro, and be put to work in a cotton field."[26] This statement perfectly demonstrated the point that runaway slaves were trying to make in the 1850s: geography as much as race determined free or unfree status.

Texans could never inextricably link servility and race as long as geography worked against them. Gadsden tried to make blackness and slavery one and the same through his circulars. Filibusterers tried to do the same thing through force. Individual slave hunters—like Warren Adams—tried to undo freedom by crossing the border and violently disrupting the sovereignty of Mexican laws. But none of these methods worked to undo the damage that so many blacks had done to slavery in Texas. When runaways crossed the border, they undermined the best efforts of Texans to make slavery essential to black character. The newly reimagined border denaturalized the institution of slavery and the racism upon which it was predicated from just beyond its most distant edges.

The Journey to Freedom

Despite the mightiest efforts of slavery's champions, when African Americans ran away they were refusing Texan attempts to transform them into chattel. Texan newspapers, unfortunately, are our best source on these runaways, and they are of course heavily biased. In Mexico, blacks could testify in court, but they could not do so in the United States, so we must read against the grain in publications put out by their enemies. Nevertheless, a sketchy outline emerges when one considers the hundreds of ads placed in Texas newspapers. Runaways were something of a self-selected set. They were rebels who made a mockery of their masters' pretensions to control them. They were pioneers who shared their knowledge and experiences with their enslaved peers. They seized opportunities, boldly contesting the will of the slaveholders and exploiting the limits of slave country.[27] They were also enterprising self-starters who took advantage of the circuits opened up by the new border. They were paragons to their enslaved peers as well.

They were an especially inventive lot. They employed the articles of everyday life to their own ends, investing the quotidian with subversive meaning. For one thing, runaways pressed their masters' horses into rebellion against them. To make the trip from South Texas or points farther east, runaways needed horses, lest they be stranded on the sterile plains. Horses were valuable to runaways since they were useful as both conduits to freedom and starter capital in Mexico. In a scrape, they could be eaten. Blacks in the Texas borderlands became famous for riding and dealing in stolen horses. Walter Johnson has argued that horses gave white slaveholders—or to use his terms, the jailers of the American South's "carceral landscape"—the technology of surveillance to use against the enslaved. Stealing horses turned that technology back on the supposed master class.[28]

African American runaways were notorious horse thieves. One black man—perhaps a runaway slave himself at one point—known as Francisco to border Mexicans was an especially well-known horse rustler. Francisco (whose name Mexican officials probably Latinized from English) operated in the Texas borderlands and raised hackles on both sides of the border. The authorities in Texas informed their counterparts in Mexico that they wanted him for horse thievery alongside his son and a group of "others of the same color" with whom he worked. Almost certainly this gang had swollen with the addition of runaway slaves, who most likely added even more horses to the herd. In August 1851, the authorities spotted Francisco with some accomplices in the barren plains just west of the San Antonio–Eagle Pass line driving a herd of stolen animals.[29] The Mexican military authorities apprehended this band of thieves and the animals they transported at Guerrero, the terminus of their route. The horse, mare, mule, and two colts that they drove came all the way from the Colorado River and bore Texas brands. Eager to avoid conflict with the Texans, the Mexicans sought to punish these thieves and return the animals to their owners. But as long as Mexicans were willing to buy stolen animals from Texas the traffic continued, and runaway slaves undoubtedly played a role in it.[30]

Runaway slaves pressed their own skin into service as well. Runaways attempting to pass stand out boldly against the blotchy, ink-spilled columns of the many runaway advertisements that made their way into the Texas weeklies. Some Texan whites had particular difficulty with runaways like George Smith, from near Corpus Christi, who attempted to pass as a "Mexican Greaser" (which was the preferred Texan slur for mestizos and lower-class Mexicans).[31] Another runaway, a mulatto with "small hands and feet," likewise attempted to pass. He had two horses at his command and carried twenty-five pounds of bacon and a gallon or two of corn meal to feed himself as he traveled west. More mysteriously, he carried pens, pencils, paper, and some sort of math textbook. He also packed good clothing, including two extra white shirts, before he ran away to Mexico. He was well prepared for the trip, and we can only speculate as to what he hoped to do when he arrived in Mexico. Unfortunately for him, a Mr. Hays in Blanco City mistook him for an Indian and shot and killed him.[32] In this case, the mulatto fell victim to the risks of fair skin. Texas pioneers, who were used to dealing with Comanche and Lipan horse thieves, had little compunction about murdering Indians. But runaways were too valuable for such treatment. In this case, Hays's failure to correctly read the race of the runaway not only resulted in the murder of a fellow human being; it cost him a considerable reward.

Another item that runaways used to make their getaway were the firearms their masters lent them or lost to them. A shotgun "stolen" from a master (how could enslaved "property" steal after all?) likewise turned the technology of the master class against itself.[33] A shotgun could be transformed into a murder weapon through the alchemy of slave subversion. Or it could help a runaway feed himself or herself on the barren plains.

Guns were crucially important items that slaves carried if they intended to go west into Mexico and hunt for themselves and pass—either literally or figuratively—among the plains raiders and Texan slave hunters. It was so common for runaway slaves to take firearms with them that their former masters often advertised the weapons their former slaves stole to help identify them. When a man named John ran away near Fort Worth, he armed himself to the teeth, taking not only a silver-mounted Colt five-shooter but also a double-barreled shotgun.[34] Another group of at least four runaways that headed west from Wilbarger's Creek near Bastrop were likewise heavily armed, carrying a gun each and a cache of extra weapons.[35] A different runaway, Lewis, was not so well equipped as other runaways. He fled from Washington on the Brazos in the company of six or seven other runaways and carried an "antiquated single-barrel English shotgun."[36] This gun might have killed prairie chickens or other wild game; it would not help in a fight with hostile Indians or Texas slave hunters.

There was nothing unusual about traveling armed through the plains of Texas. Guns were common articles of frontier life. Nor was it unusual for slaves to use shotguns to hunt game or take on tasks for their master. But the firearm started to have quite a different meaning once enslaved people elected to head to freedom in Mexico. When runaways stole weapons from their former masters, they pressed their property into rebellion against them, putting everyday frontier items to their own subversive use and transforming the supposed mastery of the slaveholders into the stuff of myth. Erstwhile masters watched as groups of armed runaway slaves left the plantations for freedom in Mexico. One Texan spotted a runaway outside of San Antonio and attempted to arrest him. In order to avoid arrest the runaway beat his would-be captor over the head with a pistol and severely hurt him. Another runaway near Washington on the Brazos opened fire on a "Mr. Yerby" who sought to reenslave him but missed his mark, losing his freedom when Yerby returned fire and "empt[ied] the contents of his shotgun" to cripple him.[37] Yet another runaway from somewhere near Bastrop used the barrel of his gun to beat his would-be captor, a Mr. Layman, senseless.[38] The news items and advertisements that circulated in Texas newspapers usually listed the firearms the runaways were carrying. The newspapers published this information not only to help identify the runaways. They published it as a fair warning to bounty hunters.

The most subversive tool that the Texas runaways had at their disposal was the expanded geographic knowledge that they possessed. The most troublesome runaways shared their geographic knowledge with others in the slave community when they returned from Mexico. Sometimes they guided others of their enslaved brethren to freedom. This is just what happened in LaGrange, Texas, in January 1851. A runaway named Philander spent an evening visiting a campground on the outskirts of town. He stayed behind at night, after the din of the revival held there during the day had died down, and waited until everybody left. As night fell, Philander stole some horses that answered his purpose and rode off on one of them. He did not make it far. The authorities quickly apprehended him with the stolen horses and another African American named Talbot, who, it turned out, had made the journey to Mexico before. Talbot more than likely planned to guide Philander to Mexico, and they needed mounts to make the trip. Probably Talbot charged Philander with the duty of obtaining horses from the campgrounds. Instead of reaching freedom both men undoubtedly returned to slavery.[39]

Talbot was not the only runaway who returned to Texas to spread underground geographic knowledge and tell of his experiences. During his journey through Texas, Olmsted heard of another runaway, a "powerful and manly-looking mulatto," who Texan filibusterers recaptured from Mexico. Before the capture, slave hunters had already kidnapped him from Mexico twice. And after his most recent capture, his captors set him to work near the Leona River. Undoubtedly he shared his experiences with his enslaved peers.[40] On another occasion, a wildly unkempt stranger materialized from the wilderness in the town of LaGrange to report that he had seen three runaways armed with rifles and mounted on two mules near Brenham. Even more alarmingly, they were in the company of a recently reenslaved African American who a man named McIntyre claimed as his property. The year before, McIntyre had forcibly brought him back from Mexico. The recaptured runaway undoubtedly shared his geographic expertise with McIntyre's other slaves, several of whom decided to join him when he attempted another escape.[41] Such examples show that there were indeed mobile African Americans who traveled back and forth between Mexico and Texas—sometimes voluntarily and sometimes against their will—spreading the word along an underground information network that prepared and encouraged runaways in their trip to Mexico. Another group that helped runaways learn about the route were the Mexican runaway peons who went to Texas (see chap. 7).

Runaway slaves built a conduit of sorts into Mexico, and advertisements seeking their return highlight a number of nodes in their network.

These were places where newspapers reported runaways' presence. The town of Bastrop figured prominently among these places. The Bastrop Road drew runaways west and was the initial stage of many flights to Mexico. Due west of the main plantation settlements of East Texas, Bastrop was a convenient stopover on the way to Indian Country to the west or to the largely Tejano settlements to the south. A great number of the runaway slaves advertised in papers hailed from Bastrop, nearby Austin, and the region just east of the Colorado River. Many started their journey to Mexico by wading across that river.[42]

Way stations were places where mobile blacks could gather, glean information, and look for assistance from migrant Mexicans. Right after the United States annexed the Republic of Texas in 1845 and war between the United States and Mexico loomed large on the horizon, twenty-five blacks ran away together from the town of Bastrop, supposedly induced by the Mexicans of the area. A posse later caught up with seventeen of them near Seguin, directly to the west, but seven or eight likely escaped to the Mexican towns on the Rio Grande. Ten years later, Bastrop continued to have the same problem, long after the Treaty of Guadalupe Hidalgo settled the border with Mexico. In 1857, four or five runaways "piloted" to Mexico by two Mexican "peons" had made good their getaway, even though slave hunters eventually recaptured two of them.[43] So great was the traffic of runaway slaves through Bastrop that one man there with a "No. 1 pack of hounds well trained for catching negroes" sought to turn others' misfortune to his pecuniary advantage, and he placed an advertisement for his dogs in the newspaper.[44]

Once they left Bastrop, the runaways could go either south or west. Those who went west might end up near Nacimiento de los Negros, the black Indian colony founded by John Horse. For those who continued south, on the path to the border towns on the lower Rio Grande, the road passed through Texan towns that contained a vast majority of Tejanos and mexicanos over whites. In these towns individuals and groups of runaway slaves might find Mexican guides. These towns were especially attractive way stations for runaways, and their arrival put local whites on alert. In 1852, a runaway named Alfred, a mulatto with a "bold and impudent appearance," ran away from Colorado County and passed through Goliad in southeastern Texas.[45] A year later, three blacks who escaped from the area around Gonzales passed through the same town en route to the border.[46] Just to the east of Goliad, in Victoria, an eighteen-year-old runaway named Frank from Lavaca County passed through on his way to freedom.[47] All of these men probably made good their escape, and certainly more followed, passing through overwhelmingly Tejano towns like Goliad and Victoria en route to the border.[48]

More dangers lay ahead, one of which was crossing the Nueces Strip. Olmsted summarizes the danger in that region: "A good many [runaways] got lost and starved to death, or were killed on the way, between the settlements and the river."[49] The Nueces Strip was not just a no-man's land that separated the United States from Mexico; it was also a barren and dangerous place. One group of runaways traveling in the far western reaches of the Nueces Strip, perhaps in an attempt to reach Nacimiento in Coahuila, met a grisly end. Near the Devil's River—which was farther west than any runaway would want to travel—a group of blacks got lost. One traveler found the only evidence of their passing much later. It added up to the remains of a camp littered with one man's bones, who the traveler surmised the runaways had eaten. If starvation and getting lost were not bad enough, the Comanches were on the retreat at this time, and they did not spare African Americans captured in the west from cruel treatment.[50]

After runaways moved beyond the Texas towns, crossed the Nueces Strip, and reached the banks of the Rio Grande they still had not reached safety. The most immediate danger involved crossing the river whose notoriously treacherous currents claimed their share of lives indiscriminate of color.[51] But if the runaways made it through Texas safely, they could reasonably expect to find freedom. Matamoros emerged as an important destination for runaways particularly early on. Ben Kinchelow, a formerly enslaved man interviewed by the Works Project Administration in the 1930s, gives us a hint as to why Matamoros attracted so many runaway slaves. He said that many blacks tasked with accompanying their masters taking cotton to Brownsville were then "persuaded to go across the border by Meskins," and many African Americans would "never return to their master." Kinchelow's description generally

FIGURE 8. Ben Kinchelow joined the black community in Matamoros, where his mother worked as a washerwoman, allowing young Kinchelow to grow up with greater opportunities. He remembered the community warmly; his family lived in a log cabin with a grass roof just outside of town, not unlike the ones inhabited by their neighbors with whom they shared the game they killed and the corn dodgers they cooked in a Dutch oven. (WPA, Slave Narratives, 267–269). LOT 13262–7, no. 101 [P&P], Library of Congress Prints and Photographs Division, Washington, D.C. 20540 USA.

confirms a newspaper account that bemoaned how "trustworthy, now insolent" blacks often abandoned their masters near the mouth of the Rio Grande to go to Matamoros—a place where Reyburn said it was common "to meet your own property" on the street. Despite these strange encounters, Reyburn continued, any attempt at recapture was "folly."[52]

The free black community in Matamoros was the same one that Benjamin Lundy encountered in the 1830s and that later nurtured Kinchelow and his mother in the early 1850s. It had continued to grow on the outskirts of that town in the wake of the Treaty of Guadalupe Hidalgo. In 1853, official reports from Matamoros counted the number of foreigners living in that city of roughly 11,000 people, among them 50 "negro" heads of household. [53] This number seems somewhat low, but we need to keep in mind a couple of facts. First, African Americans did not only fit into the racial category "negro" in Mexico, where centuries of intermixture taught people early on that "white," "red," and "black" were not always useful categories. Humanity came in many hues and shades. While the Matamoros census for 1853 only counted a total of 201 "negros" in Matamoros, it also counted 250 mulattos; together, they made up about about 4.5 percent of the town's population. There were other runaway slaves who fell into different categories in the colorful, if also derogatory, Mexican racial classification system. Mexicans abolished racial categories after independence, but racial language still crept into government documents. When officials issued cartas de seguridad they described the physical characteristics of the applicants. Runaway slaves could be "negro," *mulato, trigueño* (wheat colored), or *moreno* (dark). In any case, Tamaulipas, the Mexican state where Matamoros was located, had a significant population of African descent. The entire state, which included 180,514 souls in 1853, had some 10,541 people, or about 5.8 percent of the population, who were of African ancestry. Outside of Tampico, Matamoros had the highest concentrations of African descendants in the state, but all of the Villas del Norte registered some African descendants. These inhabitants were runaway slaves from Texas, black fugitives from the United States and the Caribbean, or descendants of Tamaulipas's colonial-era population of African transplants.[54]

Matamoros continued to swell with black freedom seekers as the United States teetered on the edge of civil war. In 1861, *El Rifle de Tamaulipas,* ever vigilant of American hypocrisy, made a judicious observation. "This port city," the editor wrote in reference to Matamoros, had recently attracted a multitude of "free families of the race enslaved by the liberty of the United States."[55] He was pointing out the ugly truth behind the U.S. promise of freedom—that it was predicated on enslaving blacks and disenfranchising racial minorities. In any case, the newspaper found the new arrivals a good addition to the city. They worked hard, they were sober, and they were thrifty, which was exactly how Mexicans wanted immigrants to be. They had begun to build houses on the outskirts, facing toward the most charming part of the old port city, between the estuaries and the river. The writer further surmised that more would come soon, given the conditions in the United States and the oncoming war.[56]

Hence there was a northern "Black Mexico," one that grew as as the Civil War loomed in the United States.[57] Of course, African Americans found very real limits to their liberty on the Mexican side of the border. First and foremost was the issue of slave hunters. In addition, Mexico was not a rich country offering significant economic opportunities. Some runaways were undoubtedly on a "footing with the peon" in Mexico and encountered only the most "squalid wretchedness, poverty, and starvation." Some surely committed crimes just to survive.[58] As noncitizens, they could be jailed and stripped of any civil rights they may have had. But insecurity—both personal and financial—did not haunt the lives of all runaways. Olmsted reported conditions quite to the contrary, saying that runaway slaves were "almost invariably doing passably well."[59] A formerly enslaved man who made it to faraway El Paso married a Mexican woman and was "in a fair way to do well." Sadly, his former master heard about his good fortune, and, after having a "little brush with his father-in-law and others of his new relatives," reenslaved him with the help of officers from Fort Duncan.[60]

Despite poverty and the constant threat that Texan slave hunters might cross the border and turn them into white property once again, many former slaves evinced great pride in their newfound freedom. Maybe it was this fact that most bothered Texans and fired their resolve to turn the border into an absolute limit to slave country. In fact, many newly free runaways developed a certain conceit in their freedom. One has to read closely to discern their dignity amid the scorn heaped on them, but their pride stands out against the grain. In a dispatch from Monterrey, a Tejano correspondent for the *San Antonio Ledger* wrote that the African Americans in that city who had found some measure of success "carr[ied] their heads high as monkies [*sic*]."[61] In another instance drawn from Monterrey, a runaway known simply as Dan in Texas chose to adopt his Mexican father-in-law's name when he married. He became Don Dioniso de Echavaría and claimed that his old name was only fit for a "plantation nigger." Indeed, this Don Dionisio even went so far as to complain about "lazy Mexicans," which was certainly a sign that he had adopted some of the elitist habits of his host country.[62]

The pride evinced by runaway slaves who found freedom in Mexico underscores their immense accomplishment. They would not be reduced to property, and they would not bow before the "white man's will"; if any enslaved people had "agency," they did.[63] They rejected Anglo Americans' attempted transformation of the black race into noncitizens and enlisted Mexican diplomats, Mexican migrants, and masters' former property in their cause. Maybe they faced challenges becoming citizens in Mexico. And maybe the Americans did not respect their rights abroad—just as they did not feel bound to respect any of their rights at home. But once they got to the other side of the border, they were free. Then the porous border suddenly hardened, and they could count on at least a degree of protection from the Mexicans deputized by the state to enforce its laws regarding runaways. Olmsted was right that Texas slavery was "slavery with a will." There were just too many African Americans who refused to be reduced to mere chattel when freedom beckoned from the other side.

The border represented a limit to liberty in the sense that it delineated the farthest extent of the slaveholders' domain. Limit has another meaning, however; while the border represented freedom to African Americans, it was not absolute. Liberty was something precious and difficult to win, and many African Americans found that they had to continue to fight for it, long after they had arrived in Mexico. Slaveholders actively contested their meaning of the border, violating it to superimpose white supremacy arbitrarily, and mooting Mexico's claims to sovereignty in the process.

The example of the Henderson family, who found freedom on the Mexican side of the border, amply illustrates just how precious and limited freedom could be for African Americans who traversed the line. In 1859, a black woman named "Merlley" crossed from Edinburg, Texas, and visited the alcalde of Reynosa, Tamaulipas, to tell him that something terrible had happened to the Hendersons. Someone had abducted them all from near Reynosa and returned them to their old master. This family—a black man, his wife, Anna, and four children—had come to Mexico "to liberate themselves" from slavery and found employment and shelter at the ranch of Juan Longoria Tijerina. Not long after, a suspicious group of North Americans visited northern Tamaulipas, allegedly seeking cattle and horses for Texas buyers. They were, in fact, reconnoitering the area for runaway slaves. After learning the whereabouts of the Hendersons from an acquaintance of the family named Manuel Muñoz, the Texans waited one night until after dark and then smuggled the black family back across the river. The Texans paid Muñoz for his guidance and likely also remunerated the vecino Salvador Cavazos, who owned the boat that the men used to take the captive family across the river. Many officials might have stood on the side of liberty for runaways, but everyday vecinos were a different story, and their loyalties and motivations varied widely. With the help of a few Mexican auxiliaries, Texans had returned a black family to captivity. The next month, at least one of the Henderson girls was found in domestic service in Brownsville, but the consul in that town was powerless to do anything for the family.[64] If runaway slaves found the border porous, so too did those international criminals who wanted to cross over illegally and arbitrarily enforce foreign laws on fugitives who thought they had found safety beyond the line. It would be the job of the Mexican state to enforce the border against these unwanted border crossers and prosecute treacherous vecinos in defense of the blacks who found protection under the Mexican law. We turn to that story in the next chapter.

From 1848 on, enslaved African Americans ran to Mexico in significant numbers and found freedom there. The border invited transgression almost immediately, and runaways invested in a meaningful line between Texas and Mexico. The freedom they found on the other side was not the same for everyone. Many blacks were impoverished, but there were also those—like the ones encountered by Lundy and Olmsted—who did well. Some scraped by in urban economies; others worked on ranches. A few obtained pieces of land near Nacimiento de los Negros; others undoubtedly contracted debts and became peons. Still, they were free, and this fact contradicted the assumptions about race on which American slave codes were based. Mexican legal territory disentangled blackness and servility, proving to Texans that an entire race of human beings could not be reduced to slavery and white property by mere fiat.

Some newly Mexicanized blacks, like the eminently respectable Don Dionisio, took great pride in their subversion of slavery at the border. Why wouldn't African Americans be proud of the freedom they found in Mexico? Runaways transformed a line meant only to separate one geopolitical entity from another into a line that meant something else, something even greater. They transformed it into a line between freedom and slavery. More abstractly, they frustrated attempts by North Americans to strip blacks of personhood both at home and abroad. This was a bold affront to the United States in the age of the Dred Scott decision, which stripped black people of any claims to citizenship within American territorial bounds. International movement on the part of blacks—and the help of foreign allies—underscored the parochialism of ideas about an essential black servility.

However, there were very real limits to the liberty that African Americans found in Mexico. I continue with this strand in the next chapter. The frequency of slave hunters going into northern Mexico made it abundantly clear that African Americans' understanding of the border as a line between slavery and freedom was highly contested. A violent battle over meanings between runaway slaves and Texans ensued. Mexicans, in order to protect their own national dignity from Texan predators, found themselves thrown into the fray. They tried to hold off Texan raiders and slave hunters. They were not always successful—as the tragedy that befell the Henderson family illustrates. But when Mexicans mustered into service to fight Anglo Texan filibusterers, they ended up reinforcing the meaning of the border as a line between slavery and freedom. This line could harden once runaways made it to the other side, depending on how rigorously Mexicans enforced the law on their side of the border. In the trade, when Mexicans fought slave hunters-cum-filibusterers they also fought for black liberty—even if this was an unintended consequence of defending their sovereignty.

7 / Bordering on the Illicit: Violence and the Making of the International Line

One horrifying August night in 1850, a black woman nearly lost her freedom in Matamoros. The evening began innocently enough, when several "North Americans" (probably Anglos) staying at a rooming house in Matamoros approached the owner, Luis del Fierro, and invited him to accompany them to a concert. Del Fierro did not even know the foreigners' names, however, and this seeming act of bonhomie aroused his suspicion. He declined their invitation and began preparing for bed, taking care to remain aware of any unusual activity. Meanwhile, just north of town, a Texan named William Cheney and an accomplice crossed the river and began heading to the del Fierro house. A short while later, del Fierro heard a terrible shriek coming from downstairs. Matilda Haynes (or perhaps Hanna; the document is difficult to read), an African American woman living in the house, let out a terrible cry. What she had just witnessed terrified her. Cheney and his accomplice had broken into the house through a back door and fallen upon her. The men carried firearms and intended to kidnap her, as well as "a small creature of color" also present at the scene, likely her child.

Her scream immediately captured del Fierro's attention. He quickly descended to the main room with a weapon in his hand and confronted the men, demanding that they tell him their names and purpose for being in his house. Meanwhile, del Fierro's wife went out on the balcony upstairs and called for the police. Del Fierro's interrogation of the men netted little information, and just as the police arrived on the scene Cheney's accomplice grabbed the black child and ran out the back door.

The police gave chase, and the Texan kidnapper, losing ground to his pursuers, abandoned the child. He probably did not stop running until he reached safety on the other side of the river.[1]

Cheney was not as lucky as his accomplice. The police took him into custody. Under interrogation, he maintained his innocence, claiming that he had simply sought Haynes out so that the two might come to an arrangement. He said that he had hoped to deal with her rationally and calmly and that he had simply implored her to pay for her *rescate* (emancipation) or else return to him after finishing her work in Matamoros. Cheney felt that she still owed him service as she had possibly come to Matamoros in Cheney's custody and refused to return to Texas, taking advantage of the freedom offered by Mexican law. None of the other witnesses corroborated Cheney's version of events. Others described a terrifying attempt to abduct mother and child at gunpoint. Even worse, Cheney had prepared himself for probable conflict. He made efforts to recruit people in Matamoros as auxiliaries in his attempt to enslave Haynes and the child. A foreigner named Enrique Fority (probably Richard Ford) testified that Cheney offered him a hundred pesos to help abduct the woman, a sum that he had refused. As a result of the botched kidnapping, Haynes remained free as Cheney languished in a Matamoros calaboose. A month later, when he petitioned the local judge for his release owing to his "grave internal injuries" and the infirmity of his wife in Texas, he was still imprisoned.[2]

The would-be captor became the captive. In the grander scheme of things, the skirmish between Haynes and her former master went beyond the simple struggle between a hunter and his quarry, between an enslaver and his human prey. Since the incident involved sovereign Mexican space and Mexican people, theirs was also a violent struggle over the meaning of the border and what it meant to be African American outside of U.S. territory. The Mexican border underscored the obvious: slavery was a national institution, not a natural one. In order to undo the damage that runaway slaves did to the system of slavery, Texans illegally crossed the border and trafficked runaways and fugitives back to their side of the river. Inevitably this drew additional people into the conflict.

This chapter illuminates how the contradictory laws and attitudes on either side of the border resulted in violence. It also goes one step further in its analysis, to not only offer up the root causes of border violence, but to argue that Mexicans used conflict to build loyalty and to draw out sharp contrasts across the border. When violence resulted from the contradictions brought out by the border—the line between freedom and slavery, for instance—it effectively set Mexico and Texas off from one another. Violence polarized government officials and military commanders alike across the line. But episodes of violence drew vecinos and other third parties into the fray as well, essentially politicizing them and sometimes forcing them to take sides. The fracas caused by Cheney's slave hunt involved several people who were not part of the original conflict between the slaveholder and the formerly enslaved woman: the foreigner Richard Ford, for example, but also the boarders at the rooming house, the Matamoros militia, and the municipal authorities who investigated the crime. In the 1850s, not only vecinos but also Tejano/as, norteño/as, Anglo Texans, and others found themselves drawn into similar quarrels resulting from the inherent contradictions between Mexico and the United States. Everyday people were either unwilling or unable to stand by as all sorts of violence began to reach across the troubled border and spill over into their communities.[3]

With compromise on several key issues out of reach, violence and ad hoc solutions surfaced to solve the problems caused by unauthorized mobility across the poorly policed border. Bloodletting resolved some of the issues associated with transborder troublemakers in the absence of federal assistance, especially since national authorities too often remained distant, unresponsive, and not well versed in the local realities of trying to maintain order in the borderlands. In the national government's stead, local solutions and local deputies emerged to try to take control of the border. Violence inevitably resulted.

Transnational Abductions

Try though they might to keep their enslaved laborers in place, Texans could not disabuse African Americans of the notion that the new border represented a line of liberty. Texans could expect little help from their federal government—at not least through the normal channels of diplomacy. "The utter helplessness of expecting the federal government to effect an arrangement to protect slave property," reported one newspaper, reflected "the great injustice done to Texas by the treaty with Mexico, which in no single instance guarantees to us our property."[4]

The absence of meaningful diplomatic progress on the issue of runaways was not due to a lack of trying. In the aftermath of the failed Carvajal revolts of 1851, the American minister to Mexico, James Gadsden, fired off a letter to his counterpart in the Mexican office of foreign affairs, the Conservative Juan Almonte. He must have caught wind of a failed extradition arrangement proposed in 1850, which the Mexicans had refused because of its twelfth article, enjoining Mexicans to return runaway slaves. As a response to the Texans' dashed hopes, Gadsden wrote a remarkably tetchy and racist letter on the subject to the Mexican foreign minister:

> Don't permit the two neighboring Republics to get into a war of . . . abstraction, on the relations of the Mexican Government to her Indian Peons and those of the United States to the Affrican [sic] Race entailed in their protection. Beware how you decline the opportunity, as one of the statesmen who Mexico looks to for instruction and protection, of excluding the serpent from your Eden if permitted or encouraged to get a foothold in your land. They [African Americans] cannot amalgamate and will, as they have done in our Southern Country and States, lead to the expulsion and final extermination of the Asteck Race from their Inheritances. Don't encourage, but rather exclude the Affrican from intruding on your land of promise [unless] you wish to [add] it to your own inferior caste.[5]

But little resulted from such insulting diplomatic injunctions, and Texans felt ignored, overlooked, and too often left to their own devices by the U.S. government. Not all people in the borderlands appreciated the anarchy endemic to their area; some Texans would have liked more national government oversight.[6]

If Texan slaveholders found their own federal government unresponsive to their plight, the Mexican government was even worse. A particularly bellicose set of newspaper editors in Texas rattled their sabers in the general direction of Mexico, railing against its laws regarding slavery and freedom. John Ford, now editor of the *Southwestern American*, was especially determined to fan the flames. Ford was an influential South Texan. He was a well-respected newspaper editor, a much-celebrated veteran of the Texan Rangers, and something of an expert on Mexico—or at least his readers thought so. In his newspaper columns he often cited Mexico's weak hold on the frontier as a justification for illegal raids, saying that Mexico was not "in possession of the real attributes of a sovereignty."[7] At other times, he vindicated filibustering and raiding since Mexicans would not return Texan slaves and had "so little respect for themselves or any other country."[8] Slave raids reflected the failure of both states—the United States and Mexico—to respond to the demands of Texas planters to secure their "property." In the absence of legitimate federal authority or meaningful national oversight, vigilantes stepped in to bring justice and order as they saw fit.[9] The state government of Texas usually supported them in this effort.

Violence in the service of the slaveocracy met with general approval on the Texas side. Deputized by aggravated slaveholders to bring their bondsmen and women back, slave hunters ranged throughout the borderlands during the 1840s and 1850s. They acted in accordance with the Texan slaveholders' moral economy and even with the support of the state government. As early as 1839, the Texas congress passed a law fining anyone who abetted a runaway from $500 to $1,000, a tremendous sum of money. This was clearly an attempt by the state to institute racial apartheid from the top down—and likely a shot across the bow at the Germans, Tejanos, and mexicanos living in Texas who were long suspected of harboring abolitionist sentiments. The congress also offered rewards to slave hunters, even acknowledging that their jobs became more difficult as they approached the border. As early as 1844, the Texas congress authorized a reward of $50 to anyone who captured and returned a runaway taken up west of the San Antonio River. If someone claimed the runaway slave, he or she would be expected to pay the slave hunter. If not, the state government would foot the bill and take possession of the captive.[10]

Into the 1850s, Texan slaveholders could continue to count on the support of state and municipal officials. Both Texas governor Peter Bell and the sheriff of Bexar County deputized all citizens in South Texas to lend help to slave hunters (in particular, Warren Adams) along the border in fall 1851.[11] Some slave hunters crossed over the border in their pursuit as well. John Crawford, deputized by the sheriff of Bexar County, forded the river and then captured and imprisoned two blacks who were citizens of Mexico in order to reduce them to slavery. (One of these men was likely John Horse.) Juan Manuel Maldonado, sub-inspector of the eastern military colonies, soon learned of this kidnapping and ordered the president of the ayuntamiento of Guerrero to detain Crawford, ask for his passport, and inquire into his reasons for being in the country. The slave hunter seems to have gotten away, however, because he committed his crime in the isolated countryside surrounding Eagle Pass and was able to cross the river again undetected. Even more troubling, this attack was only the first in a series. Maldonado had recently heard rumors that a large force of Texans from Bexar intended to invade the frontier and remove "by force" the blacks who lived there. Maldonado called upon his subordinates not to dally. He also wrote to the governor of Texas, asking him to free the two African Americans captured from Mexico and to keep his men in check if he wanted to maintain "friendly relations."[12] Clearly slave hunting faced little censure in Texas, and the authorities surely knew that slave hunters often crossed the line. In sharp contrast to these attitudes, Maldonado reiterated that the vecinos, the colonists, and the commanders on his side would resist any "attack on our laws, and the cause of liberty which they protect."[13] Maldonado, who represented his central government and its antislavery tenets, hoped to draw a sharp contrast along the line and involve local Mexican citizens in the cause.

Despite the full-throated protests of Maldonado, individual masters continued to deputize slave hunters. Some even advertised a scaled reward for the capture of their runaways, offering a larger sum the closer to Mexico the runaway was taken up. One master, for instance, offered a bigger reward if the runaway, Gib, was recovered in the largely Tejano/ mexicano towns that lay beyond the Colorado. He offered a greater sum still if the slave hunter illegally went into Mexico to reclaim the slave. The reward for stripping Gib of his freedom was $200 if captured west of the San Antonio River. If captured in Mexico, Gib netted his captor a $300 reward—a huge portion of an average annual salary.[14] Masters continued to deputize private citizens to go into Mexico to kidnap slaves, even after Texas seceded from the Union. At the late date of June 1861, the *Nueces Valley Weekly* carried an advertisement from a Major S. Peters from Padre Island who wanted a man, a woman, and four children who ran away from slavery to Mexico recovered. "Boys on the Rio Grande," he wrote, "times are hard, and now you have a chance to get a large reward."[15] Thus even in public forum of Texas weeklies, slaveholders openly encouraged traffickers to go into Mexico.

Sometimes local federal officials and soldiers also encouraged slave hunting in Mexico. In February 1850, four soldiers left Fort Duncan to speculate in runaway slaves. These enlisted men learned about a runaway who took shelter on a local ranch named Sanguijuela, just outside of Guerrero, and they left their posts to cross the river and find him. Once they reached their destination, with the help of a couple of Mexican guides, they held the inhabitants of the ranch hostage and demanded that they turn over the African American who worked there. Fearful for their lives and unable to resist, the vecinos stood by as the soldiers abducted the black man. But the violence did not stop after they had achieved this end. The soldiers then turned against the vecinos themselves. They badly beat Ramón Gonzales, the elderly man who owned the ranch. Gonzales's son and wife came in for similar treatment. These soldiers implicated local federal officials, and they would have surely aroused howls of protest in the American North—had anyone ever learned about it.[16]

Instead, it was left to the Mexicans to do something about this international crime. Juan Manuel Maldonado, again, protested this illegal enslavement of an African American who had "fled from slavery in search of the liberty that the Mexican laws offered." As was so often case, raiders from the other side of the river failed to respect Mexican law. Eventually, the authorities identified the two vecinos who had assisted the invaders, José María Nuncio and Marcos Mariscal, demonstrating that official attitudes and policies did not always align with those of the locals.[17] The Mexican authorities could only investigate the conspiracy on their side of the river. They exercised the right to punish their own citizens, however, and they imprisoned one of the Mexicans who had led the soldiers to the ranch for violating the antislavery laws of 1837 and 1846.[18] If nothing else, Maldonado's frustration indicated the contrasting attitude of federal officials on the other side of the river. In addition, his arrest of the vecinos who assisted the slave hunter pointed to a desire on the part of the local officials to instill dedication to the principles of emancipation in the local population. This arrest was not so different in practice from the way Texans detained and fined those who assisted runaways. Both were attempts to impart moral principles from the top down, drawing locals into the violence wrought by the contradictions of the international border.

The example above is the only known instance when federal soldiers hunted for runaway slaves in Mexico, but other federal deputies situated close to the borderlands acceded to the demands of aggravated slaveholders as well. Marcellus DuVal, the Seminole Indian subagent, lent assistance to slave hunters like Warren Adams during Coacoochee's disruptive travels through Texas. In summer 1850, Coacoochee transported around sixty blacks into Coahuila from Indian Territory. Then, in September and October, another 150 to 200 blacks left Indian Territory with him. In December, he conducted still more African Americans and black Indians to Mexico, probably taking a group of blacks enslaved by the Creeks when he left for Coahuila that month.[19] Soon thereafter large parties of Creek men, reported to number up to five hundred, attacked Coacoochee's convoy on its way to Mexico to capture the blacks who accompanied him.[20]

DuVal, fully aware of the problems that a porous border presented for slaveholders in Texas and Indian Territory, condoned these Creek slave hunters. So great had the number of blacks crossing into Mexico become that DuVal also deputized the commander at Fort Duncan to detain forcibly all people of African descent who approached this corner of the frontier. He recognized that if they made it across, the border would seal up behind them. He offered a reward of fifty dollars per head for any black man or woman (free or not) that bounty hunters captured on the Texas side. Among the blacks DuVal hoped to capture was one man who had once belonged to his Creek brother-in-law. DuVal's actions deeply implicated the federal government in bounty hunting—especially since his order resulted in the capture of around sixty African Americans by Texans and Creeks.[21] His directive also clearly revealed the widespread approval that slave hunters met with on the Texas side of the borderlands, even among some government agents.

In a striking contrast to their counterparts in Mexico, federal and state authorities in Texas and Indian Territory acted in accordance with their own different laws and energetically aided slave hunters. Their attitudes complemented those of many Texan private citizens, who were ready to resort to any means necessary to keep enslaved laborers in place. Some anecdotal evidence of the support private citizens lent slave hunters comes from Olmsted's account of antebellum Texas. He writes of encountering a Texan in pursuit of an escaped slave who had run off with a stolen shotgun. The slaveholder grew impatient as he realized that the bounty hunter he hired to track down the runaway was not going to appear at the agreed-upon time and place. Demonstrating some degree of humility, the slaveholder asked for help from other men gathered around him at the tavern, receiving an earful of useful and not so useful advice from these would-be masters of slaves. They all offered to help the disgruntled master, and one even had a clever ruse in mind. He said he could "induce him [the runaway] to let me take the gun by pretending I wanted to look at it . . . I'd talk to him simple make as if I was a stranger, and ask him about the road and so on, and finally ask him what he had got for the gun, and to let me look at it." The slave hunter decided it was a bad idea. He did not believe the runaway would let go of the gun, as he was, after all a "nigger of sense—as much sense as a white man." The slaveholder eventually decided to give up the pursuit as he assumed that every African American and Mexican the runaway encountered along the way would help him escape to Mexico.[22]

There may have been no treaty between Mexico and the United States in regard to border-crossing runaways, but government agents and locals in the borderlands often lent slave hunters help. In Texas, moral and legal codes sanctioned slave hunters. Slaveholders and slave hunters found their mightiest opponents on the other side of the border, when they crossed the legal frontier. Over there, in Mexico, slave hunters, who were the guardians of "property" in Texas, transformed into international pirates. Many norteños, especially in Coahuila, took matters into their own hands to protect their patria from international raiders, pirates, and slave hunters in the name of Mexican liberty and Mexican law. In the end, everyday vecinos became entangled in the web of violence brought on by the attempts of one state to enforce the line as a limit of liberty and the other state's efforts to undermine these attempts.

Slave Hunters, Officials, and Vecinos

Once they crossed the border to pursue runaways, slave hunters crossed a legal border and ran afoul of the Mexican authorities. This was largely because—like any sort of filibusterer—slave hunters spoiled that country's pretended sovereignty over its frontier. Illegal slave hunts and filibusters in Mexico became a major sore spot between Mexico and the United States in the immediate aftermath of the U.S.-Mexico War. Volunteer soldiers who stayed behind in Nuevo León after the cease-fire became the first filibusterers to outrage Mexican authorities. They attacked the villages of Sabinas Hidalgo, Aldama, and Bustamente in July 1848 in search of loot. And at least in Sabinas Hidalgo, the filibus-terers' reported mission was to recapture a runaway slave.[23] The violence experienced by the vecinos of Sabinas, even as the dust settled from the recent war, augured more terrible things to come. Most towns along the new border suffered at least one attack from a slave hunter in pursuit of a runaway in the years following the Treaty of Guadalupe Hidalgo. Runaways drove a number of explosive confrontations between Texans and the Mexican authorities since their flights—and the inevitable slave hunts that followed in their wake—tested the resolve of Mexican officials to protect their territorial integrity and enforce the law of liberty against human traffickers.

Mexican authorities became very wary when they spied large groups of heavily armed Texans setting up camp near the Rio Grande. In late 1851, during the height of the Carvajal disturbances, a large group of Texans camped out near the river sent alarms all the way up the chain of command. Emilio Langberg, then acting commander of Guerrero, reported that four hundred Texans had parked themselves across the river alongside Warren Adams. They hoped to join Carvajal's revolu-tion, but Langberg figured that they also intended to kidnap African

Americans from Monclova Viejo; of a population of 440, they made up the majority at that moment. Fortunately the Texans went home when Carvajal's revolution proved unsuccessful.[24] In the dusty border towns that dotted the south side of the line between Mexico and Texas, the defense of African Americans took on a nationalist cast since norteños often found that protecting runaway slaves under Mexican law and fending off Texan filibusters added up to the same thing.

Mexicans did not always get advance warning when slave hunters threatened their territory. And when raiders succeeded, Mexican national pride faltered. Near Nuevo Laredo, three runaway slaves who were well aware that just on the other side of the new border they could be free, crossed the Rio Grande to Mexico. Once there, they went to the alcalde to seek out the refuge that Mexico offered to runaways. The alcalde granted them the protection they requested, but soon afterward several Anglos appeared before him to claim that the African Americans were their property. The alcalde cited Mexican law and refused to turn the black men over to them, saying that slaves were free once they set foot on Mexican territory. The alcalde could not, however, stop the Texans from crossing over, "scorning Mexican laws," and kidnapping one of the runaways.[25] Protecting national sovereignty and legal integrity hinged on keeping filibusters and slave hunters out of Mexican territory. But despite the nationalism of officials along the line, force could upend even the loftiest principles proclaimed by Mexican authorities in the absence of a monopoly on violence.

Another bloody episode occurred at Mier, Tamaulipas. A free African American named Melchor Valenzuela lived and worked in Mier, employed by Bernardo Baker, a shipbuilder. In many ways, Valenzuela lived a typical life for an African American in the borderlands, scraping to get by in both the formal and informal economies. Many knew Valenzuela as the fiddler who performed at fandangos thrown by merchants and officers in the borderlands. He also may have dabbled in cattle rustling and even stolen a Mexican barge on one occasion, putting it up for sale on the Texas side in Roma. Wanted for crimes in Texas, Valenzuela ultimately lost his freedom to the arbitrary power of slave hunters in Mexico. One night, while performing at a fandango, two Texans—a Captain Jack and a man known as "Dickson" (Dixon)—approached him, shoved a gun into his chest, and forced him into a boat that carried him to the Texas side. [26]

The raiders justified the kidnapping by saying that Valenzuela's employer owed a debt to a merchant in Roma. Thus, even after he found freedom in Mexico, an African American could be transformed at the point of a gun into chattel. No black was secure from this illegitimate use of violence, and even in Mexico African Americans could not completely escape the reduction of blackness to servility. Texas outlawed the very presence of free blacks in the state on joining the Union (and manumissions were exceedingly rare before that).[27] Now, through violent confrontations with African Americans in Mexico, Texans looked to expand their racial regime beyond their legal borders. When the kidnappers secured Valenzuela as payment on a debt they stripped him of his personhood and transformed him into a commodity, flaunting the laws of Mexico and reducing him to slavery with no greater justification than their own might. They removed him from his social milieu and tore him from his Mexican wife and employer in Mier. Undoubtedly the Texans sold him into slavery to repay the Roma merchant's debt.[28] Such were the dangers of living in a legal borderland of freedom and slavery.

No matter how illegitimate the Texan traffickers' use of violence and enslavement of Valenzuela, nothing could undo what they had done. Baker tried to recover Valenzuela and consulted a lawyer in Starr County, but he had no success. The jefe político of Mier had the final word on the episode, and the damage these slave hunters had caused to his national pride colored the terms he used to describe it. Texan "pirates" had not only abducted an African American, but they had also "violate[d] Mexican territory" and cast indignity on Mexico's "national honor"—yet again.[29] Diplomatic pressures and measured responses could not ensure the freedom of African Americans, even on the Mexican side of the border. If they were serious about protecting the freedom of runaway African Americans—and, perhaps more important, their national honor and legal integrity—Mexicans would have to meet Texan pirates on their own terms.

Mexicans sometimes mustered into military service to protect the frontier from the incursions of human traffickers, especially in Coahuila. As we saw above, there was one attack made by federal soldiers against a ranch in the northern part of that state, the attack on Rancho Sanguijuela where four U.S. soldiers badly beat the owner of the ranch, his wife, and his son. This attack did not catch the Mexicans completely off guard. A small force of vecinos and a handful of military colonists drawn from the frontier towns pursued the slave raiders as they withdrew towards the river. Even though this force failed to reach the kidnappers, the alcalde of Guerrero expressed his hope that the next time such a raid occurred, they would repel "violence with force."[30] Volunteer militias in Coahuila and Nuevo León became, by coincidence, the guarantors of liberty and the law in the borderlands since the authorities often called on them to banish Texan filibusters and slave hunters. Over the course of the 1850s, slave hunts (and other types of filibusters) brought the volunteers out time and time again. Whether formally mustered into National Guard units or simply gathered into ad hoc volunteer forces, Mexican vecinos and officers alike responded to the menace of slave hunters by resolving to meet force with force.

A raid that took place outside of Guerrero in 1851 served as a warning to would-be slave hunters about the growing Mexican resolve to halt illegal and illicit kidnappings. The incident began when a Mexican man approached an African American to ask him if the ranch that employed him had any meat for sale. The African American replied in the affirmative, but on returning with the goods, a hidden white man set upon him, tied him up, and began to fasten him to a horse. The black man struggled mightily, even managing to grab the American's pistol and shoot his Mexican accomplice in the wrist. But he still lost his freedom. As the men carried him away, the African American protested loudly that he would rather be dead than captured in this way.[31]

Luckily for the captive, a Mexican youth soon spotted the traffickers and their captive en route back to the border. The boy alerted the officer Manuel Flores, who set off with three other vecinos in pursuit of the slave hunter and his accomplice. Picking up the trail, they soon discovered the African American's hat on the ground. They then happened upon the camp that the kidnappers had made. Flores and his deputies quietly approached the kidnapper, surprising him. The commander then demanded that the slave hunter surrender. Instead, the Texan looked up with "swiftness and resolve" and reached for his holster. Before he could reach his pistol, however, Flores and the vecinos who accompanied him fired, and he fell from his horse. The Texan raider, lying on the ground, shot in the lung and the arm and bleeding to death, still managed to draw his weapon "with his last breath," but Flores knocked it out of his hand. Shortly thereafter, an American doctor living nearby came to the scene and pronounced him dead. (According to his report, the raider was neither breathing nor responding to his questions—and he evinced other "señales cadavéricas," or corpselike signs.)[32] A small military party in Coahuila comprising three vecinos and a captain had done what nobody in neighboring Tamaulipas had previously been able to accomplish. They arrested and executed a Texan slave hunter filibustering in Mexico.

Quick to learn their lesson, a subsequent attempt to loot and traffick runaways by Texan volunteers involved a large and loosely organized party of volunteers recently mustered out of the Texas Rangers. Despite the Mexicans' success in overpowering this particular would-be slave hunter outside of Guerrero, the attempt clearly spooked Manuel Flores. He watched the border closely and soon reported to his superiors that he had heard a rumor that slave hunters were gathering in a massive party, this time at the Paso de Pacuache, to cross the river, perhaps to avenge their fallen comrade.[33] Fortunately for the cause of peace along the border, they never did.

Nevertheless, every few months a new rumor arose about large gangs of slave hunters stationed on the Texas side of the border, threatening the security of Mexican fronterizos. Since slave hunters had learned that they would meet resistance when they filibustered in the highly militarized society of northern Coahuila, they organized themselves into large parties that were easier to spot camping around the Leona River in far western Texas. Rumors that arose from dubious eyewitness accounts came to function as the main source of disseminating information on the frontier about potential attacks. And even if the attack never materialized, as was the case in November 1851, the rumors served as a pretext to gather vecinos into their militias. Hence in Coahuila vecinos found themselves drawn to the causes of both the state and abolitionism by obeying officials and mustering to protect the line against filibusterers. In Tamaulipas, this was not so common—and, indeed, most instances of slave hunting there involved assistance from Mexicans.[34]

Beyond gathering vecinos into the civil militias organized under the National Guard program, there was another way the Mexican authorities sought to enforce the legal and moral line against Texan slave hunters among their populations. They sought out and punished those who assisted Texan kidnappers. The Mexican authorities were seldom remiss in discovering and punishing the traitors in their midst who supplied the Texans with information.[35] Certainly there were those Mexicans who helped the Texans, motivated more by profit than principle. Those who assisted the Texans pointed to a disconnect between nationalist policies and the local desires of vecinos who may well have wished to cooperate with their neighbors on the other side of the line in the name of peace and harmony. They could also make a profit from doing so. But in seeking out the Mexicans who worked alongside the Texans in their abductions and punishing them, the officers in charge of the frontier imparted a top-down policy intended to instill the defense of liberty, national pride, and a respect for law and order in the breasts of the norteño vecinos— although not always with success.

The best example of violence perpetrated with the help of vecinos occurred in Matamoros. In 1859, Luis Cabos and his brother Timoteo lent assistance to Texan slave hunters. Cabos and another accomplice, Manuel Hernández, surprised the African American Anastacio Aguado (or Elua) while he labored at his brother-in-law's ranch outside of the city. After abducting him, Luis and his accomplice met a man named Francisco Camargo (perhaps Frank Cameron), who helped them pass Aguado over the river in a ferry owned and operated by Timoteo. Once safely on the other side, the Cabos brothers delivered Aguado to two men awaiting them at the river. The Texans immediately stripped off Agaudo's clothing, tied him to a stake they had pounded into the ground for the purpose, and proceeded to whip him while accusing him of rustling. They then carried him off to Brownsville and deposited him in prison.[36]

The following day, Aguado's brother-in-law, Juan Cos, reported the kidnapping to the regional magistrate. An investigation followed, and the Mexican consulate in Brownsville discovered that Camargo had recently offered a reward to any Mexican who would help him recover runaway slaves. The Cabos brothers had decided to capitalize on this proposition, kidnapping Aguado—who may not have even been a runaway from slavery. The Mexican consul in Brownsville, made aware of this indiscretion on the part of the Cabos family, discovered Aguado languishing in a Cameron County jail. The consul, after some wrangling, managed to return Aguado to his wife and brother-in-law at the nearby Mexican ranch from which the Cabos brothers had abducted him. Upon returning to Mexico, Aguado himself testified before the regional magistrate, a testament to the legal personhood of this black man on the other side of the border. He exculpated himself from the charges of cattle rustling (a charge that was a much worse offense than running away from a master and subject to lynch law on the Texas side). He also condemned the Cabos brothers for their role in his terrifying abduction. In the end, the judge found Luis Cabos and Timoteo Cabos guilty of kidnapping and condemned them to four-year sentences. Their accomplice, Manuel Hernández, could not be found, having escaped to Texas.[37]

In the final analysis, slave hunting may well have been licit on the Texas side, encouraged by local authorities, celebrated from the bottom up, and something that drew whites together in a common defense of their racial prerogative. Capturing runaways was not human trafficking in Texas; it was maintaining law and order and protecting property. But things were very different in Mexico. On this side of the river, slave hunting was illegal and illicit, and slave hunters faced condemnation as pirates and kidnappers. But Texans had problems with human traffickers as well. They, too, would come up with creative and equally violent solutions in an effort to secure the line against those who sought to illegally move people across it.

Slavery and Mexicans in Texas

Cora Montgomery (Jane Cazneau), in her remarkable *Eagle Pass; or Life on the Border*, relates the heart-wrenching story of a Mexican laborer named Severo, his wife, Josefina, and their son. At the conclusion of the U.S.-Mexico War, Severo, who was a vaquero and former peon, sought to buy the freedom of his wife and son from their amo. Owner of a fine horse and having a few dollars to his name, Severo approached Josefina's master (also his former master) in an attempt to liberate his family. He offered to give up the horse and his cash and to work alongside his wife and son for one or two years more in exchange for the whole family's freedom. Instead, he found himself ensnared in peonage once again. His former master took his horse—claiming it was a neighbor's stray—and seized Severo, returning him to debt peonage alongside his wife and son.[38]

Back at work on the rancho with his family, Severo endeavored to escape to freedom. At last, when his master put them to work on a cattle ranch near Mier, the family took the opportunity to escape. They crossed the river and made their way toward Brownsville but were soon put upon by men in the employ of their former master. Bound and tied, all three were taken back to the ranch in Mexico, because—according to Montgomery— of the "weakness or obscurity of our [Texas] laws!" Returned to Mexico, the couple's young boy died. Severo soon escaped again and did not stop running until he reached San Antonio, where he endeavored to send money to his former master until he could buy Josefina's freedom.[39]

The story of the hapless Severo and the tragedy that befell his family in debt bondage has clear parallels with the story of runaway Texas slaves, recaptured in Mexico despite that country's laws. Severo realized that if he wanted to escape the cycles of violence and debt that underscored Mexican peonage he would have to extricate himself entirely from his borderlands milieu. He escaped to San Antonio and new opportunities. As Mexican amos haunted the Texas side of the border, the lax enforcement of the law on that side could do little to protect Severo and his ilk from illegal, transnational violence from Mexico. Caring souls, like Cora

Montgomery, waxed melancholy over the treatment of peons—although she was also a major proponent of Manifest Destiny and sought to condemn Mexican practices wherever she could.[40] Nevertheless, she recognized the futility of the law when it came to the issue of border crossers and transnational violence.

If Severo's experiences in San Antonio were at all like those of other runaway peons in that city, he would not find safety or security there either. It was not because he and other peons were the prey of human traffickers in San Antonio. Rather, it was because runaway peons often found themselves accused of trafficking African Americans into Mexico. For the crimes of associating too closely with enslaved peoples, of not subscribing to the tenets of white supremacy, and of occasionally helping runaways reach Mexico, Mexican laborers in South Texas found themselves in the crosshairs of the white power structure. The violence generated by a contradictory border separating slave Texas from free Mexico caught up to runaway peons in the hinterlands of Texas. Helping runaways escape slavery ran afoul of the moral economy of the Texan slaveocracy in this part of the state. Despite the fact that some Texans had been great champions of the cause of runaway peons in the wake of the U.S.-Mexico War, the violence necessary to maintain slavery near a frontier of freedom soon changed that.

Runaway debt peons underwent a racial transformation in Texan discourse during the 1850s once they began illicitly associating with enslaved blacks. Texans differentiated migrant Mexican laborers through the language of racial stereotypes during this decade, creating images of lower-class Mexicans that would remain deeply entrenched as tropes in the minds of Anglo Texans for generations to come. Newspaper editors and other observers began to discuss at great length the racial shortcomings of the mobile laborers flooding into the state, conflating the categories of race and class in an effort to assign racial degradation and criminal delinquency to Mexican workers. This was a practical solution to a nettlesome problem. Many influential Texans racialized and "othered" peons both to condemn their illicit association with African Americans and to deny them any claim they might have had on the promises of republican liberty.[41] In a sense, they began to see what the Mexican defenders of peonage had been saying all along.

With things calming down after the recent war, white Texans looked anew at all the debt peons who had recently come into their state. They began to feel that they were surrounded by aliens who had no interest in upholding their laws and who all too often engaged in illicit activities.

Thousands of Mexicans arrived in Texas during the 1850s to take the place of many of the Tejano elite who had departed during the years of uncertainty between the Texan secession and the U.S.-Mexico War. Some found work on farms and ranches for low wages that were still superior to the money they earned in Mexico. Migrant Mexican laborers in Texas earned a rate of six to eight dollars a month and a ration of corn and beans. Basically they worked out the same arrangement as peons de *sueldo y ración* (salary and ration) in Mexico, except they were better remunerated. Another continuation of their career from Mexico was that they worked as sheep and cattle herders.[42] Mexican laborers also managed to corner the carting trade. As early as 1850, San Antonio employers were visiting the border towns to contract Mexican laborers as carters in Texas—despite the Mexican authorities' fears that they would run off from their debts while they were in Texas. Undoubtedly, some migrant Mexicans contracted new debts, but at least life in Texas represented a fresh start.[43]

But as Texas began to fill up with lower-class Mexican laborers, Texan nativists took note. Interestingly enough, a few commentators recognized that theirs was a problem of class rather than race. Lower-class Mexicans were, according to one newspaper editor, "greasers," a class that included "peons, pelados, picaros, sin verguenzas, [and] putas, . . . in short, the whole tribe of low flung Mexicans." These Mexicans alone made up the greatest threat to slave "property" and livestock in Texas. This editor argued that the only solution to their laziness and thieving was to force them all to become "sheep and stock" peons.[44] Another observer did not mince words, naming which Mexicans were guilty of robbery, meddling with slaves, and other such activities: it was the migrant laborers, or the "lower class of 'Peon' Mexicans . . . [who] have no fixed domicile . . . [and] hang around the plantation, taking the likeliest negro girls for wives . . . and endeavor to run them to Mexico."[45] Some Texans were drawing a line between the elite Tejanos, who they occasionally considered friends, and the great tide of lower-class migrant laborers working its way into the state of Texas. Even some old guard Tejanos piled on, singling out lower-class Mexicans for special abuse. The Spanish-language *Bejareño*, for instance, wrote disparagingly of the gambling and raucousness endemic to the migrants' working-class culture—especially fandangos—which was surely an opinion shared by Anglo moralizers in San Antonio.[46] It should be noted that the vast majority of white Texans could probably not tell the difference between Mexicans and Tejanos. Elite Tejanos surely also suffered from the racism of newcomers and the proliferating expulsion decrees.[47]

The key element in the racialization of lower-class Mexicans resulted from their illegal behavior and, for lack of a better term, racial promiscuity. They failed to adopt the racial norms and abide by the laws of the Texans when they met illicitly with African Americans. Accusations soon abounded that these Mexicans were trafficking runaways out of the state. Olmsted, for one, noticed the tremendous strife that runaway peons who associated with Africans caused between Anglos and Latino/as in Texas. Texans found the "intimate terms" on which migrant Mexicans associated with enslaved blacks troubling. Associating with blacks indicted the whiteness of lower-class Mexicans, refuted their claims on (white) republican liberty, and made them into criminals.[48] And in exchange for this perceived racial treachery, they became "greasers" in the minds of Texans. Undoubtedly, the term "peon" implied lower-class status as well, and it did not always refer specifically to indebted Mexicans. Nevertheless, runaway debt peons and other migrant Mexicans in Texas found themselves subject to violence and expulsion. Associating with blacks may have been accepted in Mexico, but in Texas most whites considered it highly suspicious.

Runaway debtors who entered the plantation districts that lay north of the Colorado River found themselves in a society under siege, where the violence necessary to maintain slavery threatened to spill over from the master-slave relationship and affect them directly. In Gonzales, Bastrop, Austin, San Antonio, Refugio, and Goliad, migrant laborers were soon seen as a threat to Anglo property and slavery. [49] And the slaveholders' anxiety about the new mexicanos in their neighborhood deepened when they discovered that, for a small fee, a few were willing to help African Americans reach the Rio Grande. Trafficking runaways into Mexico was an odd job that migrant Mexicans in Texas took on at tremendous personal risk, but the evidence overwhelmingly indicates that some did just this. Their involvement with this activity was probably overblown, however, since the slightest offense drew wide comment and infuriated Texans. Not only was abetting runaway slaves illegal, but it was an activity largely condemned in Texas.

The first great outrage involving Mexicans and blacks occurred in 1851 when Charles Couple, a citizen of San Antonio, overheard a Mexican man offer to take an enslaved black man to the Rio Grande. The Mexican offered to supply him with a horse and to show him the way to the border for a fixed price. Couple alerted the authorities, who arrested the Mexican the next morning and brought him before a judge. Much to the chagrin of local slaveholders, however, the judge found that there was no law that punished the attempted robbery of a slave; attempted robbery was a misdemeanor. Seriously offended by the shortcomings of the law, forty-eight citizens of San Antonio wrote to the governor asking for a law that would make "tampering" with the slave population punishable. They wrote that Mexicans in San Antonio especially concerned them, given the great "insecurity of slave property" in Bexar County.[50]

Afraid that they would lose their human property, Texans overreacted to the perceived threat posed by runaway debt peons and began to propose a new solution—decrees that sought to expel all Mexicans and Tejanos from the area. The aggravated slaveholders of Bexar County were the first to propose expulsion. Their attempt was not ultimately successful since whites were greatly outnumbered in that city by Tejanos and mexicanos, but some nearby towns succeeded where San Antonio had failed. The towns of Seguin, Bastrop, and Austin—as well as the counties of Uvalde, Matagorda, and Colorado—passed measures during the 1850s that expelled Mexican laborers as a class from the city or county limits. Bastrop attempted one as late 1857, although the residents expressed more concerned about the "peons" who were "prowling about our streets" than those who were tampering with the slave population.[51]

Closer to the Gulf Coast, in areas where slavery was more established, reprisals for illegally trafficking runaways to Mexico were harsh. Local vigilance committees doled out exemplary punishments to those who came into their communities and violated their laws and standards. In 1852, for instance, the authorities in Wharton caught a group of Mexicans stealing horses and running three slaves off to Mexico.[52] In Matagorda, a committee expelled the entire population of Mexicans from the town. One editor justified their expulsion by saying that it was a much milder course than the other option for dealing with rustlers and traffickers—lynching.[53] A couple of years later, in nearby La Grange, every Mexican in the county faced the accusation of trying to help runaway slaves escape to Mexico. The La Grange vigilance committee arrested the principal leaders of the alleged conspiracy and expelled the rest of the migrant population, telling them that their return would be punishable by death. The *Texas State Time*, reflecting on the banishment, explained that it was "satisfied that the lower class of Mexican population are incendiaries in any country where slave are held and should be dealt with accordingly."[54] This was not just a racial indictment of Mexicans; there was a class element here as well.

Despite the threats and expulsions, some mexicanos formed intimate bonds with enslaved people, and their relationships went beyond the mere trading of goods or services. In the fall of 1854, a large number of working-class Mexican migrants began to arrive in Austin—and almost immediately the racial situation deteriorated. Hysterical slaveholders blamed the "peons" for the loss of enslaved laborers.[55] Many Mexican laborers who worked for various Austin employers camped in the suburbs of the city, where they met with the local slaves in the evening and formed personal and recreational connections. A traveler from Bastrop in 1854 said that near Austin he encountered an encampment where there were "a large number of Peons, Mexican women and slaves." The Mexican and black men gambled together, playing at *monte*, smoking, and drinking. Even more scandalously, "he noticed one slave with his arms around a señora and another señora lay her shawl over a slave while he was reclining on the ground." The *Texas State Gazette* reported on this gathering, opining, "It is not surprising that our citizens should feel disposed to rid themselves of this low and dangerous class of Mexican Peones, when scenes like these are transpiring around us." A week later, the local vigilance committee rode to the outskirts of the city and instructed the migrant Mexicans they found camped there to leave the county. Patrols were appointed soon afterward, and they forcibly ejected the Mexicans who remained.[56]

A year later the Mexican migrants returned. They did odd jobs for Austin residents during the day and spent the nights in a camp outside the city. Another newspaper alleged that while socializing illicitly low-class Mexicans and African Americans sometimes struck deals:

> There is no doubt but they are, and have been, abetting negroes to escape from their owners. On last Saturday night Mr. Butts visited the camp and found two negroes in it. He caught one and called to his wife to bring a rope to tie him [but] before she could reach him, the negro tore loose from him. Mr. Novell went to camp on another occasion, and found the Mexicans dealing *monte* and the negroes betting. Something must be done to prevent the negroes and Mexicans from associating.[57]

A week later, the citizens held another meeting. This time they elected to resort to the same expulsion measure that had recently passed in other Texan towns. They expelled all "transient Mexicans" in order to "relieve the community from the pernicious and growing influence of the Mexican peon population now in our midst." This expulsion order was the second decreed in Austin within a span of three years.[58] Enforcing white supremacy would henceforth rely on the crude method of deportation.

This did little, however, to disabuse runaway slaves of the information they already possessed. Further, Mexicans continued to stream into Texas in even larger numbers than African Americans crossed into Mexico. Thus blacks and Mexican laborers met in the middle and undoubtedly conspired together. Blacks had a number of routes into Mexico figured out by the 1850s, thanks in no small part to the knowledge they gathered from other runaways and their Mexican friends.

But expulsion was just one of the local solutions proposed to deal with the problems posed by Mexicans in South Texas who trafficked runaways into Mexico. Another solution was vigilante terror. Although an expulsion decree failed to pass in San Antonio, some evidence suggests that Texan Anglos resorted to extralegal means to rid themselves of the Mexican population. In 1851, a ragged bunch of Tejanos arrived in Laredo at the terminus of one of the routes to Mexico from San Antonio. The refugees declared that vigilantes had recently assassinated seventy-five Latino/as from Bexar County and robbed many more. Clearly, the Anglos of Bexar County had begun to take out their frustration on the entire Mexican-descended population, causing a considerable number to flee. The commander at Laredo noted that the bexareños had left in such a hurry that they had brought neither their property nor the fruits of their harvest.[59] In nearby Gonzales, meanwhile, a white mob also resorted to violence to deal with the perceived treachery of migrant Mexicans. In 1854, some men there caught a "peon" who had helped an enslaved black man escape, and local whites demanded a fitting punishment for him. They soon hit upon the punishment. A number of white men held him tight while a companion with a branding iron burned the letter "T," for thief, into his forehead. The mob then administered 150 lashes to his bare back for having betrayed the white power structure.[60] Unlike the aggrieved citizens of San Antonio who could find no redress from the town council for a Mexican helping an enslaved man escape, these men turned to their own local solution—and one likely approved by the larger community—that went unpunished by the local authorities.

The trouble did not soon let up. In 1858, two Mexicans had arranged to help a "lot of negroes" escape Gonzales and cross the border. But they were discovered before the flight could take place. The *Bastrop Advertiser* commented on what happened in a way that might have been chortle-worthy in white supremacist antebellum Texas but that—from a contemporary vantage—can only mortify. According to a witness, the two Mexicans involved in the plot "became *entangled* in the brushy bottoms of the Guadalupe, and . . . it is not probable they will give further annoyance to slave owners." The *Advertiser* warned its readers to keep a sharp eye out "for similar schemes of negro stealing." Just as in Mexico, those who were caught moving people illegally through the state faced exemplary punishment. The only difference was that in Mexico traffickers moved people back to slavery and in Texas they moved them to freedom. Whether it was the movement to freedom or slavery that locals and officials deemed illicit depended on which side of the border one was standing.[61]

The presence of so many new migrants from the southeast in Texas only added to the estrangement between lower-class Mexicans and Anglos during this decade. As long as Mexican migrants engaged in illicit activities, Texans felt perfectly justified in protecting their territory and "property." Just as was the case in Mexico, Texans responded to illicit outsiders in their midst who threatened law and order with ad hoc, violent solutions—not always legal, but condoned by the larger moral economy. In the absence of meaningful national oversight or an international treaty, violence solved issues on local terms in this legal borderlands. It also engulfed entire populations and spread the violence inherent to slavery to third parties who did not hold slaves or subscribe to the institution. In Mexico, it was officials and militias meting out justice, enlisting local vecinos to help them in their cause. Meanwhile in Texas it was most often vigilantes who doled out pain and punishment to international transgressors. In each case, ad hoc violent solutions found moral and legal sanction in the absence of a international arrangement. And in both cases it was everyday Mexicanos, vecinos, and Tejanos along the border and in the hinterlands of Texas who were ensnared in the violence wrought by a highly contradictory border between freedom and slavery.

Slavery was a tremendous source of tension and strife between the Mexicans and Texans who inhabited either side of the border. Texans who crossed the line to enforce the dictates of slavery in a country that did not recognize people as property ran afoul of the law and the moral code of Mexican authorities. Slavery also entangled the many runaway peons making their way into Texas in the 1850s. Human traffickers—whether slave hunters in Mexico or migrants who befriended and helped African Americans escape slavery—outraged their surrounding communities. As a result, all sorts of people in the borderlands found themselves subject to local, violent solutions that sought to resolve the issue of outsiders behaving badly in the absence of national oversight or treaties. In Mexico, vecino militias and local police hunted down traffickers and the Mexicans who helped them. In Texas, vigilance committees passed expulsion decrees and lynched offenders who moved black people illegally. These were local solutions that solved some of the problems wrought by the contradictory border.

Thus, a swinging body hanging from a tree, eyes bulging and tongue twisted and swollen, served as a warning to potential wrongdoers against violating communal norms and laws. So too did the body of a fallen comrade, gasping for his last breath of air, shot through the lung, his blood pouring out into the dry sands of the northern Mexican desert. Violence was particularly rife along the border because local officials and peoples on either side sought to impart laws, moral codes, norms, and customs that contrasted sharply with those on the other side of the border. As a result, an artificial line drawn across the sand (or in this case, along the channel of a river) became very real. When actions and attitudes that received praise on one side of the river met with imprisonment, expulsion, or even death on the other, great discord resulted. The grim specter of death and violence—in the form of local people taking action—stepped in where the violence of state power failed to achieve monopoly and legal codes greatly contradicted one another. This confusion resulted in spectacular bloodletting.[62]

Unless authorities on either side of the border came up with a common code or a treaty that allowed one side to extricate their enemies from the other side, violence would remain at epidemic levels. Only when Texan and Mexican officials found that they had common cause might they begin to work together against common enemies. Nevertheless, the border most often served to polarize the authorities on either side who drew sharp contrasts between their laws and customs and tried to draw local populations into the fray—often against their better judgment. Mobile people drove this history of confrontation between neighboring governments, peoples, and policies. And no one mobile group of border crossers pushed neighbors farther apart than the Lipan Apaches.

8 /   "Not Even Seeming Friendship": Lipan Apaches and the Promises and Perils of Play-Off Diplomacy

Many different bands of the Lipan Apaches, whose home ranges cut across the Nueces Strip and west to Coahuila's Santa Rosa Mountains, invested heavily in the border drawn between the United States and Mexico in 1848. They were old hands at play-off diplomacy, and the new border offered up new opportunities. As discussed previously, raised borders result in new opportunities for some people, and the Lipan Apaches were masters at "turning adversity to advantage." They seized upon the disorder and the new border created in the wake of the seismic events of 1848 to pursue new opportunities across the line. No longer content to raid on just one side, they expanded their "shadow economy" into northern Mexico, and trade in ill-gotten Texan horses and cattle helped to subsidize their independence. The new border remained at their backs as they rode off to the hinterlands of northern Coahuila, leaving enraged Texan ranchers behind.[1]

As long as Native Americans could freely pass back and forth across the border and profit from an illicit trade network they remained at liberty. But this freedom required that they constantly remain in motion. They did not practice cross-border mobility in the same way as migrants or immigrants. The tactic adopted by Lipan Apaches to hold on to their independence, indeed their liberty, was to cross the border constantly in search of resources and to play one side off against the other. This tactic made them quite different from the Comanches, who relied on their military might to expand an empire into the vast hinterlands of the American continent from its western margins. Lipans were not the military threat to Mexicans and Texans that the Comanches were, but they were nuisances and continual irritants that refused to go away. The Lipans knew their neighbors well, and in many cases they were the most intimate of enemies. They had inhabited the borderlands for at least a century, many spoke Spanish, and they were very familiar with their Texan and Mexican neighbors—where they lived and where they pastured their horses. Knowledge made them dangerous in an entirely different way from the Comanches. If independence for the Comanches rested on a foundation of military power, a veritable horse-breeding industry, a robust trade in captives, and stable territoriality, then the independence that the Lipans pursued rested on geographic and cultural savvy. In traversing and mastering the borderlands of Coahuila and Texas, the Lipans eventually established a network of routes, paths, and roads that was finite and geographically bounded.[2]

In the years immediately following the secession of Texas in 1836, Lipans generally took advantage of the new border to raid into Mexico. Yet in the 1840s the political winds began to shift and some Lipans reconsidered their loyalties. Then, in the aftermath of the Treaty of Guadalupe Hidalgo, different Lipan bands stepped up their cross-border raids, this time alienating the Texans. In pursuing their own independent course by moving between many different polities and expanding their raiding network across a transnational space, they sustained a reputation for fickleness. This did little to endear Lipans to villagers in neighboring Mexican towns, with the exception of a few friendly towns like Santa Rosa and San Fernando that always bought the plundered booty Lipans supplied.[3] Fortunately for the Lipans, bad feelings between Texans and Mexicans hampered efforts to come to terms with their common problem. Instead, they blamed each other for harboring the Indians.[4] As a result, the Indians could continue to cross the border as they watched feelings between international neighbors freeze over time and time again. In fact, they helped make relations between these two neighbors worse. This in turn raised the border and made the Lipans' refuge on the other side of the border more secure. It would take some time for either side to realize that these Indians were playing them off against one another and that hostility between them benefited Lipan mobility.

New Borders in Old Borderlands

Cuelgas de Castro's alliance with Texas began to crumble in advance of the U.S.-Mexico War. A seminal event that led to the unraveling of their alliance occurred in 1843, when a couple of Texas brigands murdered the son of the Lower Lipan chief Flacco. During the Texas revolt, most Lipans had remained neutral, but some had used the chaos as an opportunity to plunder from both sides. But Flacco's group (the High-Beaked Moccasin Band) established themselves as steadfast allies to the Texans early on. This triggered a widening gulf between the Lower Lipans who lived along the Nueces River and allied with the Texans and the Upper Lipans farther west who maintained better relations with Mexico.[5] Now, with the chief's son dead, Flacco's group retreated to Mexico just as the Upper Lipans had already done. Other friendly Lipans departed as well, going east and west, escaping the environs of San Antonio.[6] The decade of Texan independence had not been kind to the Lipans. As a result of warfare and disease, the population of Lipans in Texas dipped from one thousand to five hundred. Texans also began to restrict their presence in their towns. Further, Comanches and Towakanis alike continued to attack the Lipans in retaliation for their assistance to the Texans. The historian Thomas A. Britten tells us that the already leaderless Lipans led a scattered and even "nomadic" existence from the mid-1840s on. Comanches and Texans alike began to demand that the Lipans be removed from South Texas and placed in Comanche territory, under their "watchful eyes," in the San Gabriel Valley.[7] By the late 1840s and early 1850s, Texans had expanded with settlements along the Gaudalupe River, including Boerne, Kerrville, and Comfort. Thus, beginning in 1847, the Texans actively also sought to drive out the Lipans.[8]

By the end of the U.S.-Mexico War, plenty of Texans had caught on to the fact that the Lipans' alliances were built on expediency and self-interest as much as loyalty and friendship. Pressure mounted to remove them from the state. Some Texans lamented the Lipans' fickleness. On the one hand, wrote the editor of the *Corpus Christi Star* in 1848, the Lipan Apaches "professed so much friendship for the Texans." Many of them had long served as scouts for Texas militias, and the Castro family in particular had close ties with certain fabled Texas Ranger captains. On the other hand, this editor continued, "[the Lipans] have killed more [Texans] in Western Texas, and stole more horses than any other tribe." This was surely an exaggerated claim, if still an indictment of deteriorating relations. Nor were the Lipans limiting their raids to the Texas side. Bands of Lipans began committing depredations around Lampazos, Nuevo León in the months immediately after the U.S.-Mexico War from safety in the sparsely inhabited Texan frontier. "To the Mexicans they have not even seeming friendship," wrote the same editor as he pondered the violence this tribe visited on both sides of the new border.[9]

The Lipans continued to harass people on both sides of the new border in the aftermath of the war. In 1848, for instance, a band of Lower Lipans allegedly committed a number of murders in the Brownsville area. The following year, these "Apaches" targeted the Texas side again, which caused many ranchers along the Rio Grande "to suspend agriculture and to remove their stocks of cattle from the fertile valleys on this side of the river to the parched and arid country in the adjoining Mexican States of Tamaulipas and Nueva [sic] León."[10] The mobility of Lipan raiders set a whole landscape in motion as formerly sedentary rancheros abandoned their homesteads in advance of raiding Indian columns. The Lower Lipans harnessed their geographic knowledge to sustain their independence, attacking on both sides in search of precious resources. They then sought out refuge either in the deserts or—increasingly—on the other side of the new political border. This was a dangerous game. As remarkable as they may have been at surviving and overcoming adversity, the border witnessed a significant militarization following the U.S.-Mexico War, which threatened to change the balance of power.

The Mexican state as well as local governments had worked for a generation to instill militarism in Mexico's northern citizens. Many Americans who rattled their sabers in the lead-up to the U.S.-Mexico War imagined Mexicans in the North as victims who cowered in the face of overwhelming Indian power. They imagined that power in the borderlands was a zero-sum game with clear-cut winners and losers. One side took all, and the other side trembled in fear as they passively watched their haciendas and villages burn.[11] This was not the case. Beginning with the institution of the Civil Militia in 1823, Mexican volunteerism inspired many norteños to protect their homes from outside invaders. Then, in the wake of the North American invasion, Mexican vecinos formed militias throughout the country, enlisting in the newly created National Guard units in 1846. In the North, alongside the older presidial companies, these volunteer militias found themselves charged with pushing back the Indian threat. Acting together to win the frontier, the National Guard was an important inculcator of a growing sense of regionalism in the North.

After the war, a new Mexican resolve to take control of the frontier was manifested clearly when a Liberal norteño, Mariano Arista, was promoted from commander of the Northern Army to secretary of war (he would go on to serve briefly as president of the republic). Under his stewardship, Mexicans constructed military colonies in 1848 all along the river. The government then invited immigrant tribes from U.S. Indian Territory to form additional colonies. The same treaty that allowed Papicua, Coacoochee, and John Horse to bring their disaffected tribes to Coahuila also listed the Indians who could not and would not be admitted "de paz" (in peace) in Coahuila. Among these were the "barbarous" tribes who could never become citizens or vecinos, such as the Lipans, since they refused to take on the trappings of civilization and dedicate themselves to labor and sedentary agriculture. Instead they would be hunted down and removed from Mexican territory. The vecino militias, presidial companies, tribus emigradas, and military colonists alike had many victories over Indian raiders in the ensuing years, not just losses.[12] For generations the violent terms of intercultural exchange had gone both ways: slavery and captivity had brought Mexicans into Indian culture and vice versa. Norteños now hoped to turn Indian relations into a one-way street with their new military institutions. Nevertheless, Lipan incursions into Coahuila remained a problem. Most likely this was because they could now cross the border to refuge, as was the case when a Upper Lipan band attacked San Fernando de Rosas, leaving a dead soldier and several dead animals in their wake. Into the fall, attacks continued to increase as Indians used the "strategy of entrance and exits" common of the "nomads'" tactic of survival in Coahuila.[13]

At least some Upper Lipans saw this tactic as increasingly dangerous. Some Lipans might have realized that the Mexicans now had the resolve to finish them off, and they sought some sort of arrangement with them instead. As a result, Dátil from the Painted Wood Band, which lived along the border of Coahuila and Texas, was instrumental in seeking out peace with the Mexicans. His first attempt occurred in 1845, when he traveled to Santa Rosa with ten warriors and two women to solicit peace. The historian Martha Rodríguez refers to Mexican attempts to assimilate Dátil as a "guerra cultural," and at least this time it did appear that Dátil was coming around to Mexican terms. "Firing their guns in joy and intoning their customary songs," they arrived in the main plaza of Santa Rosa from their camps in the Sierra del Carmen in Texas. These Indians were hardly unfamiliar, as they were from the group that had inhabited Mexico near El Remolino on and off since 1751. They also had intimate knowledge of the land since they had traversed and lived on it for many years, during which time they had maintained friendships with "the Mexican people, and in particular those of the frontier." Aware of the growing animosity to Lipans in both Texas and Mexico, they must have sought to reestablish themselves near their old homelands. Nor was Dátil's band the only group of Lipans seeking refuge across the line. Another western group under the chief Venego showed up a few years later.[14]

It does not seem that they made much headway in these initial attempts. But in 1850 Dátil once again turned the rusted wheels of diplomacy and appealed to the Mexicans for peace through a captive taken from the village of La Zarca. The sub-inspector of the frontier, Manuel Maldonado, agreed to forward Dátil's request for peace to Mexico City and asked the Lipans to await the response patiently.[15] Many Mexicans believed, however, that the Lipans' overtures of peace were once again a "trick" that would win them a reprieve while they regrouped and prepared to make war. Many Mexicans groaned that they were tired of the Lipans, and they hated them for always coming into their territory to ask for peace after plundering them and leading their enemies to their ranches. This time the Liberals in charge of the national capital found the resolve to reject the Painted Wood Lipans' offer, citing not only their "bad faith" but also the fact that their request for peace had provoked considerable grumbling among the officer corps.[16] In addition, the commanders knew that some Lipan warriors, perhaps of a different band, had been spotted around Guerrero acting in conjunction with Mescaleros. The Mescaleros outnumbered them, but the presence of Lipans among Indian enemies was always alarming. All too often they had led Mexicans' enemies to their towns and ranches. The officers recommended sending out a force of two hundred men to fight these Indians, even as Dátil's application for peace pended in Mexico City.[17] Soon thereafter, Coacoochee, who had just returned from U.S. Indian Territory with one hundred kindred black, black Indian, and Seminole immigrants, received instructions to deliver the bad news to the Lipans. The Mexican government had rejected their entreaty for peace. Arista then demanded that Coacoochee cut off all communication with them.[18]

Denied peace with Mexico and alienating their erstwhile Texan allies, many Lipans kept crossing the border. They effectively dipped into both populations for resources before retreating to sparsely-populated deserts on the other side where troops could not reach them. This was a dangerous gambit, but only if authorities on either side of the river could begin working together. The national treaty between Mexico and the United States absolutely forbade military forces from crossing over to chase down errant Indians without explicit permission—and the Lipans were certainly aware of this fact since they demonstrated impressive gall in some of their raids. In March of 1851, Upper Lipan bands fell upon the pastures of Fort Duncan, killing and butchering a number of cattle and driving off even more across the river. Secure that nobody would cross over to chastise them, the Indians then made their camp so close to the river on the Mexican side that some of the animals waded across the river and back to the pastures at Fort Duncan.[19] The Upper and Lower Lipans alike made war in Texas just as they had in Mexico for decades; they stole from the Texas settlements and sold the goods across the river, contributing to a blossoming trade in illicit goods, particularly in Villa de Rosas and San Fernando in northern Coahuila.[20]

But if this pattern of raiding on both sides promised booty, it was also incredibly risky. Lipans were remarkable survivors, but they lived in considerable peril, and almost all sources indicate that Lipan numbers diminished dangerously in the nineteenth century. When Indian agent John H. Rollins visited a Lipan camp in Texas he found that in the intervening years the male population of the tribe had been greatly reduced. He surmised that the Lipans had only 250 warriors (indicative of dwindling numbers, though not a scientific count). Rollins also noticed a disproportionate number of children and elderly at the Lipan camp. If his numbers and observations were accurate at all, they hinted at a demographic collapse among the Lipan men. By Rollins's reckoning, the number of Lipan warriors had decreased 75 percent since 1820, which likely reflected a growing reality. The near-constant plundering in Texas and Mexico and sometimes the Comanches took a heavy toll on the warriors of the tribe. Agent Rollins predictably saw their way of life as doomed. He offered the opinion that their survival as a tribe completely depended on the shelter and resources that Texas could offer them.[21]

As a result of the increasing precariousness of their situation, some western bands of Upper Lipans became desperate to enter into a permanent treaty with Mexico on whatever terms possible. Datíl was particularly persistent, and he began crossing borders again—putting mobility to a different, more strategic and diplomatic use. He started talks with the Mexicans for the third time in 1852 and professed interest in returning the Lipans to their roots. By going back to Mexico, he said, they were returning to the "land where they were born."[22]

Datíl's Painted Wood Band had long inhabited the area near El Remolino, but that year another group of Lipans approached the Mexican officers as well. In October, an Upper Lipan chief named Coyote traveled to the border, alerting the Mexicans that at least one group of Lipans who had long lived on the Texas side now wished to immigrate to

Mexico. Rodríguez points out the importance of when this application for peace occurred—in the fall, when the buffalo had begun to retreat and the hunting season was coming to an end. Although this may have been a "trick of peace," Coyote's band of Lipans nevertheless pulled out all the stops in their efforts to make a treaty with the Mexicans. They even resorted to a tactic that showed their willingness to acquiesce to the heavily gendered terms of peace demanded by the Mexicans. Coyote dispatched the tribeswomen Manuelita, Jesusa, and Jaunita to visit San Fernando, seek out Manuel Maldonado, and solicit peace. The meaning of the women's diplomacy was unmistakable; they were a symbol of peace widely understood by all fronterizos that had a genealogy dating to early colonial times. As the women of the tribe approached the vecinos, their gender signified that Coyote's band wanted to come up with a new, peaceable arrangement for coexistence.[23] The women were familiar to the vecinos as well since Maldonado knew them all by name.

The female peace commissioners said they would accept all the conditions the Mexicans imposed if only they would allow them to return to Mexico. They had even resolved among themselves to die in Mexico. Most surprisingly, the emissaries signaled that they would turn over their children and families to the Mexicans "before they would leave the country in which they were born."[24] This was the greatest concession they could make to gain peace, as the Mexican commanders were especially interested in taking charge of the next generation of Lipans before they were corrupted by the errant ways of their "bárbaro" ancestors. Such a sacrifice likewise pointed to the intimacy that Lipans and Mexicans shared—despite a good deal of distrust and dislike on both sides. The Lipans knew exactly what was entailed in a Mexican upbringing. The commanders took their willingness to hand the children over as a sign that the Lipans were at last ready to submit to their program of civilization and transform themselves into productive mexicanos and mexicanas, to settle down and lay down roots. Still, Mexicans had long pardoned past indiscretions, and leniency had all too often brought tragedy in its wake. Further, the military colonies had largely fallen into disrepair and disrepute by this point, so the inhabitants of the frontier knew the duty would fall to them if things turned out badly.[25]

Perhaps the federal government recognized this latest "trick of peace." In November, Maldonado received a new directive from the central government. The Lipans would not be granted peace, and they were instead to be pursued "as if they were enemies of the Mexicans."[26] The phrase "as if they were enemies" betrayed the fact that the Lipans were not the same as the Comanches in Coahuila: their history with norteños was intimate and intertwined. At least for some mexicanos, they were not enemies. Accordingly, a number of Lipan men repeatedly returned to Rosas and a few other points after the authorities rejected their petition for peace. Well known to the vecinos of Rosas, they visited with women and children to play on the sympathies of the villagers and to trade their furs. The vecinos of Rosas welcomed them back and even agreed to make a new application for peace on their behalf—though in offering their glove, they concealed an iron fist. If ever the Lipans ran afoul of the townsfolk again, they swore they would "finish them off" once and for all. They would not be betrayed again, even if they intended to continue enjoying licit and illicit trade with them. Maldonado himself was not so sure about the new war that the higher-ups in Mexico City hoped he would make against Lipans. He griped about the central directive against them since he had neither the horses nor the men necessary to carry it out effectively. To Maldonado's mind there were more important matters to tend to up North. Nevertheless, he promised to do what he could to confront Lipans when and if they ever returned from Texas.[27]

The Conservative Interregnum

Coyote's Lipans stayed in Texas for a season, but then something happened that allowed them to sue for peace with Mexico once again. Luckily for this band, a revolution was in the offing hundreds of miles south of the frontier. Even as Coyote received the news that Mexico City had rejected the Lipan women's petition for peace and retreated to Texas, Antonio López de Santa Anna—in exile in Turbaco, Colombia—sailed to Mexico to overthrow the Supreme Government for one last time. In 1853, Santa Anna ascended to a final term as president at the head of yet another Conservative revolution. This time he overthrew the Liberals and ruled under the title "His Highest Serenity" (*su altimisa serinidad*). Santa Anna's new, highly centralized government recast the states as military departments, reined in the autonomy of the regional military officers, and generally upset the practices put in place by the Liberals who had ruled Mexico since 1850.[28] Conservatives were not so likely to bend to the demands for autonomy in the North—an autonomy that all too often meant dealing with the Indians on deadly terms. As a result, Indians gained more power and could again deploy mobility to their great advantage.

This Conservative revolution at the federal level allowed the Lipans another chance to cross the border and try to win peace. Probably Coyote understood that Centralist and Conservative politicians were much more sympathetic to mobile, unassimilated Indians than Arista and his recently deposed Liberal regime. Ever since the war with Texas, Santa Anna had proven his mettle by protecting the sovereignty, independence, and liberty of Mexico from Anglo designs. This often resulted in odd alliances between Mexican officials and people whom the Texans considered enemies: runaway slaves and independent Indians in particular. As we have seen repeatedly, these alliances often hurt the interests of vecinos in the North.

Nevertheless, even as the dust settled from Mexico's most recent revolution—and despite grave misgivings among some vecinos—Coyote put in yet another application at Rosas for peace. Onofre Díaz, inspector of the eastern military colonies, forwarded this petition to the Supreme Government, and the Lipan band soon won the peace treaty they desired.[29] Interestingly, some vecinos in the North actually came out in support of the peace—and not just in San Fernando, which had long prospered from trade (illicit and otherwise) with the Lipans. Other towns wanted peace as well but not because they thought harmony would at last reign on the frontier and that Lipans would honor their obligations. Some supported the peace treaty out of fear. Many Coahuiltecans did not think a war against Upper Lipans was winnable, since that tribe was so "astute and war-like."[30] They feared the escalated bloodshed and robbery that characterized times of war. And they were tired of forming militias to chase Lipans into the deserts beyond the Santa Rosa Mountains while their crops languished in the fields and their wives and children stayed at home, exposed on the desolate frontier. For his part, the alcalde of Gigedo reckoned that the only peace the frontier had known since 1813 occurred during seasonal truces with the nearby Lipans. When the vecinos and Upper Lipans were at peace, the only attacks the Coahuiltecan pueblos suffered came from the Comanches—according to the alcalde anyway.[31] If the vecinos chose war with the Lipans, another nearby alcalde opined, the immobile presidial colonies and vecinos could never catch up to this "audacious and fierce" enemy who knew how to ford the river to the other side quickly and effectively.[32] Since these Lipans were masters of the northern Mexican deserts and knew every watering hole in the foothills of the Santa Rosa Mountains, some Mexicans doubted that they could ever truly pacify them. Better to join with them, and just maybe they would provide assistance in their ongoing war with the Comanches.

The vecinos were still suspicious of Lipans, but there were other ways to deal with them. The alcalde of Músquiz suggested an extreme form of vigilance over the tribe if they established themselves in Coahuila permanently. He believed that they needed to stay in one place and be carefully monitored. He said that the Lipans could be issued a unique brand for their *ganado mayor* (horses and cattle) and a uniform consisting of a red cloth and *sombrero de palmeta* to be worn at all times that would set them apart from the "barbarous" Indians. The key was to keep them separated, so that they would not make disastrous alliances. Certainly, the "passage of time" would destroy the customs of the Lipans, some said—but this was only of secondary concern to most vecinos. More important, they would stop playing one side against the other, bringing on the wrath of the Texans, and leave their herds alone.[33]

As evidenced by these voices for peace—and as the historian Luis Alberto García has argued—not all norteños shared the same capacity for violence as those who manned the military colonies and presidial companies.[34] The idea that norteño civilization was predicated on violence is something of a stereotype. Nevertheless, there were certainly angry voices that reacted to the news of peace with disgust. The military towns of Nava and Guerrero did not share the same forgiving attitude as their civilian neighbors. The vecinos of both places wanted to maintain the tougher line that Mariano Arista had sought to enforce before the change in government. The municipal president of Nava thought that violently reducing them and putting them to work forcibly was the only way to win a meaningful peace with the Lipans.[35] His counterpart in Guerrero was even more adamant, claiming that the Lipans routinely committed crimes while at peace and that articles found in their camps indicated that they had actually committed some of the raids blamed on the Comanches. In referring to past infractions, he called the Lipan application for peace an "engaño de la paz" (sham peace). Not surprisingly, these towns had the most invested in the newly militarized frontier. Guerrero had been founded as a military colony and probably did not enjoy much illicit trade with the Lipans. The townspeople wanted to reduce the Lipans violently to make room for frontier enterprise. They had also seen too much sham peace; Guerrero sat on the Lipans' most-trodden raiding path.[36]

Notwithstanding the opinion of the people of Guerrero and Nava, Coyote's band received the peace they solicited, and in early January

1854, many Upper Lipans crossed back into Mexico, leaving behind their camps along the Pecos River on the Texas side. They established themselves in the neighborhood of San Fernando, near the Seminole camp at El Nacimiento.[37] For the time being, peace with the Lipans prevailed. Many norteños, especially those in Guerrero and Nava, would have preferred that the federal government butt out and allow the local inhabitants to come up with their own solutions and pursue the Lipans until they no longer menaced the frontier. Not all Mexican frontier towns so vehemently opposed the Indians, however. Lipans nurtured different relationships with different towns across the Mexican North. In the end, Coyote's Lipans had masterfully played off yet another government—the new Conservative one in Mexico City—against the local governments to pursue their own agenda and guarantee their refuge in Mexico. As far as the Conservatives were concerned, rather than reducing Lipans to civilization and Christianity through war, they would to do it through peace.[38]

"A Den of Marauders"

But many Lipans did not intend to stay in one place and give up their accustomed mobility. Inevitably, Lipans continued to raid in Texas, maybe even those from the Painted Wood Band that had established itself in Coahuila. At least one band apparently still raided in the area surrounding Guerrero as well, taking captives and animals from that military colony in the winter of 1853.[39] The commander of Fort Duncan expressed his eagerness to dispatch a force of soldiers to punish the Upper Lipan camp on the other side of the river to his Mexican counterpart that winter. But Maldonado would not tolerate this violation of Mexico's sovereignty, and he would not allow a force of American troops on his country's soil—especially to punish a group granted peace by the federal government. The commander of Fort Duncan fumed, and he spoke of his desire "to punish this common enemy and remove him from the area," convinced that the Indians harmed interests on both sides.[40] Luckily for the Upper Lipans recently established in Coahuila, not everyone saw things this way, and relations between the authorities on both sides of the river remained frosty.

Given the intransigence of Mexican officials, Indian raids would not be the only problem to haunt the northern Mexican frontier. Another threat to the security of vecinos would soon cast a dark shadow. Texans were not likely to sit by idly as Lipans raided in their state and then found

refuge on the other side. Texans itched to cross over the border and punish the Lipans. Indeed, Indian raids into Texas did pick up in the early
1850s as Upper Lipans, Seminoles, Black Seminoles, and a few other
tribes found official refuge but little in the way of resources under the
Conservative government of Mexico. Fifteen years before, some Lipans
had ravaged the North of Mexico and found refuge in Texas. Now, the
Upper and Lower Lipans alike took the opposite tack, raiding on the U.S.
side of the border and finding shelter in Mexico.[41]

The Lower Lipans saved their worst depredations for the area surrounding Laredo, where they could easily ford the river to Mexico after
a raid.[42] Aware of the feebleness of the federal forces in Texas, the citizens of Webb County at last wrote to Governor Elisha Marshall Pease.
These Lipans were just too quick for the regular infantry or the distant
riflemen company, so the Texans needed soldiers who could match the
speed and mobility of the raiders. They put in a request for a force of not
less than two hundred volunteers from Bexar, Nueces, Star, Hidalgo, and
Cameron Counties to muster into a company of Rangers that could deal
with the Lipans.[43] A number of prominent Texans along the river began
calling openly for the Lower Lipans' genocide, now considering dras-
tic measures to finish off their onetime allies.[44] If the Mexicans would
not keep them on their side of the river, some Texans figured their only
option was to destroy the tribe root and branch when they caught them
in Texas. To many Texans, genocide seemed the most likely solution to
the problem of Indians slipping back and forth across a border that they
could not regulate.

With Texans talking openly of the Lower Lipans' extermination
around Laredo, a group of Lipans farther west (perhaps Upper Lipans)
stood accused of a particularly gruesome spate of murders in spring
1854. First, a Tejano farmer and his wife went missing in the area surrounding Fredericksburg, likely taken captive. Around the same time,
Indians—who the Texans also figured were Upper Lipans—killed a Mr.
Williams who lived on the Medina, raped and murdered his wife, and
captured his children.[45]

The most notorious raid blamed on the Lipans occurred in May 1854
outside of Fredericksburg. The fateful day of the crime began normally
enough as the farmer James Forrester was engaged in conversation with
his German neighbor. Then something very odd happened. A cow came
galloping up to the men, its sides pierced through with several arrows.
Forrester's German neighbor went home to get his gun to help Forrester
fend off any attackers. Then ten or fifteen minutes later three very heavily

armed "Indians" approached the door of the house and called for the farmer. Forrester asked them what they wanted and only received a confused answer. He then tried to scatter them but to no avail. Instead he was mortally wounded by a rifle bullet. The man's terrified wife ran to examine her husband's fallen body when the attackers knocked her across the head, flooring her instantly. The raiders then killed the two Forrester girls and the baby and took the boy captive. At some point they scalped the farmer who lay dead in the doorway with a hatchet. Forrester's wife managed to drag herself away and then encountered the neighbor who had gone for help. They joined with yet another neighbor and then journeyed to Fredericksburg, arriving around two o'clock in the morning, to alert the authorities. Acting on Forrester's wife's information, a troop of one hundred soldiers led by two Lipan scouts went on the trail of the murderers the following morning. One of these scouts was the Lower Lipan John Castro. Whether or not Castro knew that the Comanches or Tonkawas were the real instigators of the crime, he still managed to hurry the members of Chiquita's Lower Lipans across the border to Mexico before the posse could catch up to them.[46] Their escape to the other side of the river certainly made them look guilty, even if they were not.

In the aftermath of this newest tragedy, frontier Texans held a round of public meetings in San Antonio, Castroville, and Leona. The gathered Texans once again put ethnic cleansing on the table, threatening to begin a vigilante war of extermination against the Lipans since the frontier was in such a "state of lamentable exposure."[47] The *Indianola Bulletin* reported yet more depredations that summer authored by either the Comanches or the "Lipans who live in Mexico."[48] Governor Pease at last heeded the request for a force of volunteers to patrol the borderlands. He sent out Blanco River native James Hughes Callahan at the head of a company of Rangers in July, charging him with clearing the Blanco and Colorado Rivers of Indians.[49]

As long as the Lipans crossed the river in advance of their pursuers, they could continue raiding with impunity. And thanks to Coyote's treaty, western Lipans now had a home base near Villa de Rosas. These Indians were well aware of the border, and they made good use of the advantages it presented. Even if they did not commit the crimes in central Texas, Upper Lipan raiders based in Coahuila still gave plenty of cause for offense. According to one witness, they regularly plundered on the Texas side and then crossed over outside of the military's reach. They would then, rather infamously, bring the horses they stole from

Texas "down to the river to water and bathe them in the full view of the owners." The owners could do nothing, "as it is contrary to the treaty to cross over and chastise the thieves," complained the *Texas State Times*. The Mexican authorities were no help either. This same newspaper continued: "If the Government of Mexico will not restrain these Indians our own Gov. should take steps to do so. In the event it fails the people of Texas will be compelled to take the matter into their own hands. They can and will cross over and break up this den of marauders."[50] A week later, the same paper further fanned the flames: "If Mexico has the right to keep these savages near our border, to steal our property and kill our citizens, we also have an equal right to pursue them into their hiding places and visit retributive justice upon them—and we will do it."[51] William L. Marcy, U.S. secretary of state, himself became involved in the fray; he wrote to Juan Almonte, Santa Anna's representative to the United States, informing him that he did not approve of Mexico's sheltering and employment of Seminoles and Lipans.[52] The intense period of raiding continued throughout the summer and fall of 1855 with the western Hill Country suffering the greatest violence.[53]

As long as Mexico offered refuge to the western Lipans, Texans threatened to violate the border. They would go after their enemies, hunting them down, and finding their "den"—which they knew lay somewhere near Remolino or San Fernando, where Lipans had established themselves one hundred years earlier. Would Mexico continue to offer them refuge in the face of such pressure and threats to their sovereignty? The Texans certainly hoped not. And to that effect, James Callahan at the head of a large company of Rangers patrolled the western borderlands in search of errant Lipans and Seminoles into the late summer of 1855, filling in for the otherwise occupied federal army. But he knew that he could never properly chastise the Upper Lipans as long as they slipped the bonds of Texas and found refuge in Coahuila. As summer turned into fall, rumors circulated that Callahan had begun to make secret preparations to cross the Rio Grande illegally and find the Lipans in their "dens" in northern Coahuila.[54]

Now Mexicans were faced with an even greater threat to their security, one brought on by a generation of authorities and politicians offering refuge to Coyote, Dátil, other Lipans, the Seminoles, Kickapoos, and even runaway slaves. Francisco Castañeda successfully put together a militia to meet the Texans should they violate Mexican sovereignty in pursuit of the Indians. Ultimately, this Texan force that Mexican spies had spotted on the other side of the border did not intend to cross the river without permission. (This force actually wanted to help Mexican Liberals overthrow the Conservative government.) If Callahan had a plan coming together to cross over the border furtively, it was still in the offing. And even though Castañeda demonstrated that vecinos could form militias and capably defend themselves from invaders, the norteños were still spooked. They feared the damage that Lipans caused in Texas and felt their own security threatened as a result—not necessarily because of Indians this time but because of Texas volunteers who threatened to invade if Mexico did not address the problem of illicit border crossers.[55]

Then something momentous happened—a revolution that brought Liberals to power in the center of the country and in the North. Liberal armies removed the Conservative Santa Anna from the presidency and spread political power out and away from Mexico City. This event is covered in greater depth in the next chapter, but suffice it to say, most vecinos felt that the political winds had at last changed in their favor. Concerned that Texan filibusterers were about to violate their territory, in September 1855 the vecinos of Santa Rosa (now Músquiz) petitioned the new Liberal governor of Nuevo León, Santiago Vidaurri, to make war on the Lipans. At last, it looked like the Lipans might succumb to the perils of play-off diplomacy. Viduarri had just seized power in Monterrey as part of the national Revolution of Ayutla and aimed to center power in the North, away from Mexico City. Meanwhile, many Mexicans had grown tired of the Lipan presence in Coahuila—especially now that they threatened to bring on the wrath of the Texans. The frontier went on alert time and time again, fearful that a filibuster would materialize on the Texan side. Civilian pursuits suffered since farmers, ranchers, vaqueros, and nearly all men over the age of sixteen had to stop what they were doing and take up arms against Indians as well as filibusterers.[56] At last, they had a friend holding the reins of power.

But, surprisingly, Vidaurri roundly rejected this proposal, saying it was "absolutely necessary to keep the peace," and he expressly forbade anyone from working with the Texans and crossing the border into that state in pursuit of them.[57] Vidaurri took a hard line against the Texans and their demands for Lipan blood in order to bolster his image as a Mexican patriot, especially in the throes of the Revolution of Ayutla. Surely he feared that by kowtowing to the Texans, his reputation might suffer and he would give his political enemies ammunition. The issue of

FIGURE 9. Santiago Vidaurri presided over the increasing regionalism that characterized the era of La Reforma in the Mexican North. LOT 3112, no. 57 [P&P], Library of Congress Prints and Photographs Division, Washington, D.C. 20540 USA.

refuge was too tied up with that of national sovereignty. Many officers in the North had staked their patriotism on protecting runaways in a bold affront to Texas.

On about September 23, yet another rumor surfaced. This time, officials on the Mexican side learned that a large number of Texan volunteers intended to cross the river to pursue Coyote's Lipans. According to the rumor (*la voz pública*) a large group of Texan volunteers had made a camp near the Arroyo Seco, ready to cross the river and invade Coahuila. In the wake of this new information, the Mexican authorities gathered the Lipan captaincillos in Coahuila to forbid them from crossing the river and stirring up trouble while the emergency persisted. If the rumor of a Texan invasion turned out to be true, the Lipan women and children would have to retreat to Santa Rosa (Músquiz), leaving only the warriors, who the Mexicans hoped to press into service to defend Mexico from Texan invaders alongside vecinos, military colonists, and presidial soldiers.

Captain Manuel Menchaca then assumed command of the line. He ordered vecino militias to muster at a significant distance from Piedras Negras and Eagle Pass in order to ensure that townspeople would not know about the Mexicans' military preparations. Menchaca's commander then told him to keep the fact that Lipans had been removed from San Fernando to Santa Rosa secret.[58] For the time being, Texans— not Lipans—were the biggest threat. But both the vecinos and their officers knew that Lipans were the cause of the growing international tensions.

The conditions of play-off diplomacy employed by Lipans changed in the aftermath of the U.S.-Mexico War as Mexicans as well as Texans demonstrated a new military resolve. Dátil's and Coyote's efforts to create a refuge in Mexico were intended to ensure their continued existence among a people with whom they had long carried on a troubled intimacy. Lipan attempts at immigration failed at first, but the ascension of Santa Anna to power one last time in 1853 allowed the Lipans a reprieve. After making peace with Mexico, the somewhat reduced Upper Lipan bands of Dátil and Coyote continued crossing the border from a newly constructed refuge in Mexico, reserving most of their considerable raiding for the Texans. These Indians knew that the Texans were hamstrung; they could not cross the border so long as the government welcomed Indians into Mexico and gave them protection. Nor could the Texans count on the cooperation of norteños, some of whom shared the Texans' antipathy to the Lipans but whose authorities trusted the officials and citizens on the Texas side of the border even less. The Texans and the norteño officials found themselves in a stalemate regarding the issue of cross-border Lipan raiders, despite the fact that they harmed both of their interests.

Intimate geographic and cultural knowledge of the borderlands had afforded Lipans the ability to traverse South Texas and northern Mexico in search of resources and the best circumstances for themselves for generations. But how much longer they could maintain their independence by crossing the borderlands and stealing from Mexican and Texan herds alike was an open question. As the borderlands became the "bordered lands," a chilly wind blew over the North. Mexicans and Texans realized that rather than accuse each other and look through the Indians to see villains on the other side, their common problem was, in fact, the Indians themselves. When Texan volunteers threatened to cross over and find the Lipans in their "dens"—with or without official permission— they manifested the greatest threat yet to the vecinos' security and Mexico's sovereignty over its northern frontier. The Callahan Raid of 1855, launched by Rangers from Texas into Mexico that fall, would ultimately break this stalemate. It would also test the limits of liberty that Indians could find by crossing the border.

9 / Sacrificed on the Altar of Liberty: Regionalism and Cooperation in the Age of Vidaurri

Historians often talk about how borders have "soft" and "hard" periods, employing these terms to explain the porosity or rigidity of dividing lines. Boundaries can be elastic or static, flexible or stiff, or—as Adelman and Aron have written—"borderlands" can become less fluid "bordered lands." In instances where governments secure borders successfully, "gatekeeper states" emerge and the people-in-between find their options curtailed and their lives hemmed in. Others, such as Rachel St. John, have nuanced this historical trajectory, arguing that borders harden and soften for different people at different times.[1] In keeping with the spirit of this revision, I argue below that the power of the state to control movement across the international border did not result in hardening; instead I employ a different metaphor. Successful state control of the border was most broadly expressed through the effective filtering of the dividing line. Effective states could decide who could come in, where, when, and how. Rather than a gate, I imagine the border as a sieve operated by the state and its deputies.

I have shown that the border could be both hard and soft at the same time. Runaway slaves, marauding Native raiders, and fleeing debt peons could cross over the post-1848 line with relative ease and find protection on the other side as long as no extradition treaty was in place and harsh feelings between Texas and Mexico remained. Vigilantes, bounty hunters, slave hunters, and filibusterers, on the other hand, aroused immediate suppression when they came across the line. If the border was indeed a line of liberty, then Mexican officials actively sought to crush those who threatened that liberty in the interest of pursuing national sovereignty. Immigrants and runaways could establish themselves in Mexico, and by merely stepping onto Mexican soil many found freedom. Filibusterers, or land pirates, and Native raiders hostile to Mexico, however, found that Mexican soil sapped their vitality and endangered their health. How effectively Mexican territory protected allies and endangered enemies reflected the sovereignty and relative strength of the state at its distant frontier.

For most officials who served on the frontier from the dawn of independence through the 1850s, granting asylum to refuge seekers did not contradict the larger project of protecting national integrity. In fact, these two meanings of the border were mutually reinforcing. After all, if there was slavery in Texas and freedom in Mexico, protecting liberty across the line reinforced the sovereignty of national law on a distant frontier where the state's "vision" was myopic at best.[2] But what happened when these two meanings of the border—as a line of refuge and as a limit of national authority—ran up against one another? This chapter suggests that at least for some groups, previous arrangements along the border changed in the interests of national security in the 1850s.

Until the Revolution of Ayutla removed Conservatives from power in Mexico in 1855, Texans and Mexicans could expect to come to loggerheads over issues involving border crossers, refuge, and asylum. Ever since Santa Anna's great embarrassment at San Jacinto in 1836, many Mexican politicians—and the officers who carried out their fiats in the borderlands—made it a point to distinguish themselves from the Texans. Conservatives and Centralists who ruled Mexico from 1835 to 1855, with only a brief interruption or two, kept up an antagonistic stance against the Texans—whether Tejano or Anglo—and expected their deputies on the northern frontier to do the same. Because of uncooperative authorities on either side of the border, the line hardened against most Texans and softened for many who sought asylum. This policy was not necessarily in sync with the desires of vecinos of course.

When the seasoned Liberal and ascendant caudillo Santiago Vidaurri assumed power in Nuevo León (and then quickly annexed the state of Coahuila), Texans thought that their days of border strife might at last come to an end. They hoped that a new era of cooperation and prosperity could at last soften the border for them and restrict the movement of the troublesome mobile people whom this book has treated. Some from within Vidaurri's new regime likewise supported a new start in international relations. Yet Vidaurri could not give in to the Texan filibusterers and retain legitimacy in the eyes of his fellow Liberals in Mexico City, so his ascension to office was not quite the sea change that many expected. For that reason, Texan vigilantes and volunteers (primarily Anglos) resorted to the old policy of trying to effect change and carry out ad hoc diplomacy through force majeure when they made no headway through the normal channels. When they illegally crossed the border, they found that the new norteño regime reacted in a very similar way to the old regime. The Liberals, like their Conservative predecessors, mustered the frontier's defenders in the name of liberty and territorial integrity against foreign pirates. They fought in the name of the nation—but much more important, when they mustered to the frontier's defense they protected their local sovereignty and regional power base.

Yet defending the honorable name of México was at least partially a rhetorical practice. This chapter looks below the surface of the patriotic proclamations against raiders and examines the new routes that Liberals in the North of Mexico pioneered toward international cooperation and transborder harmony. The Liberals in Monterrey realized that as long as they continued antagonistic policies they would always be susceptible to illegal invasions from abroad. National sovereignty on the frontier, ephemeral and far from complete when the Liberals assumed office in 1855, hung in the balance as filibusterers constantly threatened to cross over. As a result, Liberals continued the Conservatives' practice of rebuffing international pirates in order to maintain territorial sovereignty into the late 1850s. To do otherwise would be treachery against the nation.

Behind the scenes, however, something began to change. Some norteños strengthened the ties they had shared with Tejanos since at least the Spanish colonial period. Some began to cooperate—not in an official or public capacity usually, but in an ad hoc, quiet, and secret way—in light of the pressure that the mostly Anglo bands of filibusterers brought to bear on the international border. Maintaining power and establishing sovereignty on the frontier encouraged the Liberals to come to terms with the Texans if they wanted to remain in control. If they sacrificed the liberty of some border crossers in the process, then it was in the greater cause of territorial integrity, regional autonomy, and transnational harmony. Thus did the meaning of the border as a limit of state power come to contradict, and sometimes trump, its significance as a line of liberty.

A Wind Sweeps the North

In 1855, the Revolution of Ayutla ended Santa Anna's chokehold on Mexican politics, and the broad political reforms associated with this upheaval swept through the north of the country just as they did through the Valley of Mexico. The Revolution of Ayutla was the final removal of Santa Anna from power, and—despite a major setback in the 1860s—the ultimate triumph of Liberalism in Mexico. By May 1855, the former secretary of the governor in Nuevo León, Santiago Vidaurri, took charge of the revolutionary current and assumed the position of the frontier's leading Liberal. He and his small entourage of advisers and allies implemented the Plan de Monterrey to overthrow the longtime ally of Santa Anna, General Jerónimo Cardona, in the capital of Nuevo León and implement much greater regional autonomy. Vidaurri's forces, dubbed the Ejército de la Restaración de Libertad, captured Monterrey in May, and two months later they took command of the plaza of Saltillo. From the other side of the river, Texans cheered on his successes.[3] They felt certain that Vidaurri's influence could at last thaw relations between northeastern Mexico and Texas, and they dreamed of powerful men on both sides of the border working together to find solutions to common problems. They especially hoped to find a solution to the challenges posed to both sides by the plague of unauthorized border crossers.

Cooperation with the Texans had the potential to ease tension on the border and make the frontier a more peaceable place. International commerce could flourish, agriculture might at last take off, laborers would stay in their place, and Mexicans and Texans might come up with a bilateral solution to the nettlesome problem of cross-border Native raiders, runaway slaves, and fugitive debt peons. One man in particular, the Danish-born colonel Emilio Langberg, is important to the early history of transborder cooperation between elites in the wake of the Revolution of Ayutla. Langberg served as the inspector of the Chihuahua military colonies in the 1840s, but he left Mexico in the aftermath of Santa Anna's resurgence in 1853. He visited San Antonio and Austin and then, in April, traveled to New Orleans, where he married a local beauty. By late spring he was back in Coahuila to take charge of five hundred men as the Liberals turned the tide against the Conservatives in the North. Langberg soon became an important member of Vidaurri's entourage, and he pursued an easy course with the Texans, even seeking to enlist them in the Liberal cause in Mexico. Langberg made such quick friends with the Texans because he evinced a certain affinity for southern culture. He chose a bride in New Orleans, and he moved fluidly in the company of planters and other southern gentlemen and women. During a visit to San Antonio in early 1855 he left quite an impression on genteel society. He charmed the city's upper set and even pulled out a violin at one point to entertain his hosts.[4] While in San Antonio, he also must have convinced some Texans to join the Liberals and lend military assistance to the revolution in the North.

But Mexicans walked a very fine line between working with their neighbors to the north and looking like they were cozying up to a colossal power that had long bullied them. Such assistance imperiled the freedom of Mexican officials to follow their own course and maintain their national independence. After all, just a few short years earlier, in 1851, the filibusterer José María de Jesús Carvajal's fortunes had foundered on the rocky shores of Texas volunteerism.[5] Then, in July 1855, when Langberg traveled from San Antonio to the border at the head of a force of mostly white Texan volunteers who hoped to join the Plan de Monterrey, a very alarmed Vidaurri made Langberg dismiss the Rangers immediately. Back in San Antonio there were some who whispered that the new caudillo had arrested the prominent Texan and alleged slave hunter, William Henry, when he requested a private conference with Vidaurri to talk the matter over.[6]

As much as the northerners may have sought political change, they did not want Texas's aid lest they appear treacherous. Vidaurri was already something of a suspicious character, and the Mexican national newspaper *Siglo xix* even reprinted a pernicious rumor that his Liberal forces were made up "in the most part of Americans." The editor chastised Vidaurri for this alleged antinational behavior, adding the admonition that "the admission of an auxiliary from a foreign army would be considered a crime of high treason." Fortunately, Vidaurri had an opportunity to respond to these charges in the columns of the same newspaper. He confirmed that Americans had indeed wanted to join his forces, but he declared that he had roundly rejected their offers.[7]

If a military alliance was not forthcoming, Texans looked instead for diplomatic options to bring them closer to the new Liberal authorities in Nuevo León and Coahuila, sounding out some ideas with their new friend, Emilio Langberg. Just a few months after Vidaurri successfully concluded the revolution, a panel of "the most respectable citizens" from San Antonio wrote to Langberg. They complained about the problem of runaway slaves from Texas—and in particular Bexar County—and they hoped that the new government would be more receptive to their pleas for cooperation than Jerónimo Cardona, Vidaurri's Conservative predecessor. They spelled out their plan for the friendly colonel. First, they asked him to count the number of African Americans in Mexico. Second, they requested that he collect them and hand them over to a specially appointed posse that would be waiting on the Texas side of the Rio Grande. The panel from San Antonio knew that there would be complications involved in this solution and agreed to cover any debts that runaway slaves may have incurred in Mexico (it was not uncommon for runaways to go into debt themselves on Mexican ranchos and haciendas). In exchange, the men from Bexar offered to round up all of the runaway debt peons who had taken up residency in San Antonio and hand them over to authorities in Mexico.[8] As we have already seen, the Texans would be only too glad to do this.

In the hope of fostering international cooperation and making the frontier a place where elites could do business and fulfill their dreams for the area, Langberg heard the panel out. He thought that the proposals were reasonable and recommended them to Vidaurri. He insisted that the Mexicans cease their protection of runaway slaves and errant tribesmen like the Lipans in order to end the "guerra sorda" (cold war) that existed between Texans and northeastern Mexicans. But Vidaurri did not appreciate how the panel of respectable citizens from San Antonio implied they would use force if the Mexicans did not heed their demands. Undaunted, Langberg still defended the Texans. Even if the Texans made good on their threat of violence, compelling the National Guard militias to "meet force with force," Langberg insisted that Vidaurri "still must recognize the justice that the state of Texas has in pursuing their blacks and evil-doers just like we should be able to reclaim our peons and property in Texas."[9]

Langberg suggested cooperation because when he looked at the frontier he saw disorder and delinquency. Nothing could advance as long as border crossers continued to manipulate the two states and cross to refuge, out of reach of the authorities on the other side. Further, routinely rounding up vecinos, taking them away from their ranch and farm work, and mustering them into militias to fight slave hunters and filibusterers did not help develop the Mexican frontier into the agricultural dynamo that so many norteño elites assumed it could become. When a raid threatened, the vecinos had to stop what they were doing, stay within the limits of the jurisdiction, and volunteer at the barracks.[10] The volunteers (or conscripted men if not enough vecinos enlisted) formed local militias whose actions were coordinated by the regional authorities. Most men between the ages of sixteen and fifty fought in these militias, even jornaleros (peons) and criados. Most lower-class men found themselves exclusively barred from service in places that had more manpower, but they fought in Coahuila.[11]

Mustering vecinos to the defense of the frontier may have buttressed the power of regional caudillos, but it did nothing for northern agriculture. Too many people left their fields untended while they served. Further, when peons enlisted they caused additional problems. First, the authorities had to pay their amos a salary in their absence. Second, debt peons sometimes enlisted so that they might run away or escape to Texas.[12] Such was the case with Juan Alvarado from Salinas who entered service and then abandoned the militia when the National Guard camped near Saltillo. Unfortunately for this peon, his amo was suspicious and sent his libro de cuentas to the authorities in Saltillo. They located Alvarado, stripped him of his arms, and returned him to his amo. Another runaway from the same master was also discovered after he had deserted the troops and wandered off.[13] In short, mustering the vecinos (and sometimes their peons) into campaigns to fight the Texans caused massive disruptions to the local economy.

But even more important than harming agricultural progress, Texan filibusterers were problematic for another reason. Mexico's very sovereignty and independence hung in the balance when Texans threatened the use of force against them. In light of the most recent threat from the panel in San Antonio, Langberg wondered whether the African Americans on the frontier were worth all of the protections guaranteed to them by Vidaurri's predecessors. They were a cause of great insecurity since the threat of a slave raid from Texas always loomed on the horizon. "It would be unfortunate indeed to expose the entire frontier to an invasion to defend these men when our own interests are hurt in this business," he baldly stated to Vidaurri. Further, he opined, Texas slaves "were treated with more consideration [by their masters] than we treat our own peons." Finally, some African Americans—especially those who joined the Black Seminoles at Nacimiento in the 1850s—had a reputation for criminality in the 1850s, earning Vidaurri's personal reprimand on at least one occasion.[14]

So cooperating with the Texans carried the taint of treason and compromised the independence and liberty of the Mexican North. But many vecinos did so anyway, as they felt the draw of economic incentive from the north much more strongly than they did the pull of the state from the south. Further, Langberg did not wish to trade security in the north for lofty principles when he felt that it was more expedient for both sides to turn over the fugitives and learn how to cooperate. He also feared an invasion from Texas for another reason. It might unite the entire country of Mexico, then in the throes of civil war, against a foreign threat. Maybe

Mexicans would put their differences aside if a foreign invasion material-ized. If this turned out to be the case, Langberg figured, the Revolution of Ayutla would ultimately fail and the Liberals might be blamed for all the bloodshed and strife.[15] Vidaurri must not have seen things this way, though, for he rejected the proposal, saying that any such arrangement with the Texans would have to go through national diplomatic channels. Further, he reiterated, if the Texans invaded to recover runaway slaves or horses stolen by Indians, the Mexican militias would "repel force with force."[16]

Even though Langberg felt a certain affability with the respectable citizens of San Antonio, neither he nor Vidaurri could concede to the bullying of the committee. Consequently, another attempted extradi-tion deal came and went, and the Mexicans again resolved to "meet force with force" if the citizens of Bexar entered Mexico to recover runaway slaves and stolen horses. Indeed, when William Henry (interestingly, a grandson of Patrick) entered Mexico to slave hunt in August, he and his thirty-five companions were jailed for a month.[17] Just as it had for a generation, conflict continued to characterize international relations for a variety of reasons—the most important being that Mexicans did not want to appear sycophantic and weak before their powerful inter-national neighbors. Soon enough they got their opportunity to flex their muscles before the Texans once again. But it would be Indians-in-between, not debt peons or African Americans, who at last brought on the most violent confrontation between filibusters and vecino mili-tias defending their national integrity and, even more important, their regional independence.

The Callahan Raid

When the Mexicans failed to cooperate, a long threatened invasion of Mexico by 111 Texas volunteers camped on the Leona River at last materialized on October 1, 1855. That day, Texas Ranger captains James Hughes Callahan of Blanco, William Henry of San Antonio, and Nat Benton of Seguin arrived at Eagle Pass in search of the Upper Lipan Apaches who they assumed had authored a number of outrages and murders over the preceding months, including the Forrester murders. Their corps of volunteers were at or near the end of their three month terms in the Rangers, and they resolved to cross over the border and find the Indians near their camps at San Fernando de Rosas. The vecinos of Piedras Negras watched warily as these volunteers gathered across the river, making their preparations to cross.[18] William Henry, recently released from Mexican prison, met up with Callahan at the Leona and joined the expedition—perhaps to hunt for slaves.[19]

Callahan blamed not just Indians but also Mexican officials when he made the reason for his filibuster explicit before the assembled citizens of Eagle Pass and read off his pronouncement. He named a litany of complaints against the Lipan Apaches to justify his imminent filibuster in front of what must have been a large, cheering crowd. He told the gathering townspeople that he did not intend to rest until he had exterminated all of the warriors in that band of "savages"—permanently ending their ability to steal Texas livestock, imperil Texas lives, and ford the Rio Grande quickly to escape persecution. He added in his pronouncement that he would do this whether the Mexican government approved his course of action or not.[20] Thus, Callahan and his company justified the volunteers' violation of the border as an illegal but morally sanctioned raid.

Later that night, William Henry and a small cadre of volunteers approached two Mexican skiff operators, signaling to the rowers that they needed their services. Just a few moments later, "eight or ten" Texan volunteers hidden near the river appeared and took possession of the boats, obliging the rowers at gunpoint to take them upriver two miles. When they arrived there they met the rest of the force, over one hundred men in total. One or two volunteers guarded the skiff operators so they would not run off and alert the authorities while the rest of the volunteers crossed the river—an operation that lasted through the night and into the next day. The fact that they crossed over in this remote area, El Paso de Las Adjuntas, confirms that they did not have permission from the alcalde of Piedras Negras, as Callahan and Henry later claimed.[21] The Texans faced enormous complications while crossing this many men, but eventually the captains rallied their men and rode off in the direction of the dusty little town of San Fernando de Rosas about twenty miles to the southwest. The Texans knew that this was where the Upper Lipans (and not a few runaway slaves) escaping Texas had taken up residence.

Upon learning that the Texans had overtaken the skiffs, Manuel Menchaca, an officer on the Mexican side of the river, sprang into action. He immediately moved all of the vecinos of Piedras Negras to the barracks in order to defend themselves in case the Texans attacked the town. He then left Piedras Negras to follow the instructions given to him by Emilio Langberg to muster two hundred men from the surrounding district into National Guard units.[22] With two hundred men under his command and even more coming to meet him, Menchaca learned from the alcalde of Piedras Negras that the Texans intended to take San Fernando. He began his march to a spot known to the Mexicans as La Maroma, where the San Antonio River and Río Escondido intersect. There he planned to meet the Texans, cutting them off en route to San Fernando.[23]

Meanwhile, Callahan's men had just begun to close in on San Fernando from the nearby Río Escondido when, at 2:30 in the afternoon of October 3, Menchaca's men materialized out of the thin desert air. They had the advantage, but the Texans nevertheless resolved to meet the Mexican force, and battle commenced. Callahan's men dismounted and held a line firm opposite the large force of Mexican volunteers and military colonists. Some Texans swore that three or four "Indian Chiefs," who were almost certainly Lipans, fired the first volley.[24] The Mexicans held the center, and the Texans failed to outflank them, losing five men in the process. Outmaneuvered, the filibusters had no choice but to make a hasty retreat. They ran back about three hundred paces toward the banks of a small creek that branched off from the Río Escondido. As they scattered, a few vecinos gave pursuit, firing at them as they fled. Captain Miguel Patiño led the charge, killing two Texans. He continued the chase, even as the disorganized Texan volunteers found cover along the creek. He only retreated when the Texans shot his horse out from under him. As the sun sank into the western desert, five Texans died from the wounds they suffered in the skirmish. These unfortunate men bled out into the Mexican soil, dying alongside the imperiled Texans hidden along the banks of the little creek's furrow, anxiously awaiting sunset.[25]

At last, when dusk settled and the battle concluded, the Mexicans retreated to San Fernando to reload and resupply themselves. They had, over the course of the engagement, run out of munitions. The remaining Texans evacuated under cover of dark, leaving behind a number of six-shooters, a few rifles, around twenty saddled horses, and some blankets and smaller articles.[26] Among the scattered effects they left behind was one particularly curious item. It was a suspicious paper, which the Mexican citizen Florencio Rodríguez discovered a bit later and handed over to Captain Menchaca. It was a letter written in English, with no signature or addressee. It did, however, include a map of San Fernando and the surrounding area. In fact, this hand-drawn map showed the best route to the dusty little pueblo, and someone had even translated part of the text into Spanish.[27]

FIGURE 10. View of Fort Duncan, Texas, engraved during the U.S. Boundary Commission of 1849–1857. View of Fort Duncan, near Eagle Pass. 1857. From Rice University. http://hdl.handle.net/1911/35476.

At the end of the day, the Mexican force had won a resounding victory over the filibusters, suffering only four dead and three lightly wounded.[28] The Texans, nursing their wounds, retreated to Piedras Negras and took command from the alcalde. Once there, they fortified themselves along the dock, passing their dead and wounded (around thirty-eight in all) on skiffs to the other side of the swollen river. The Americans at Fort Duncan offered at least some assistance, even though the filibusters did not have their government's permission to raid Mexico. Callahan reportedly turned down an offer by Captain Sidney Burbank to help them evacuate. The troops moved four pieces of artillery in front of the dock opposite Piedras Negras to give the impression that they intended to protect their countrymen's retreat.[29] While the Texans waited in Piedras Negras, they almost certainly looted, and they stampeded twenty horses to the other side of the river.[30] But they were trapped with their backs against the river. They were in a desperate situation, and on October 6, William Henry wrote to Captain Patiño to ask for peace. He insisted that the Texans had only come to chase and punish the Lipans and "anyone else who might have helped them in the robberies and murders recently committed in Texas." He assured the Mexican people of his "friendship" and said that he personally found it "repugnant to spill Mexican blood."[31] This plea fell on deaf ears, however. The Mexican forces were now back in action and on their way to Piedras Negras, and the force had grown considerably. Another captain, Felipe Torralba, had joined Menchaca, bringing Coacoochee in addition to fifty other Seminoles and blacks with him. Now the number of Mexicans under arms and in pursuit of the Texans approached five hundred.[32]

Then tragedy befell the hapless vecinos of Piedras Negras. As the military detachments under Evaristo Madero and Miguel Patiño began to close in on Piedras Negras, the Texans set fire to the town in order to cover their retreat.[33] The evacuated vecinos watched the tragedy unfold from the safety of the nearby cliffs. They saw plumes of smoke, and some claimed they heard the sound of a cannonade. Later they would testify that the artillery at nearby Fort Duncan helped cover the filibusters' retreat. There is no doubt that the soldiers from Fort Duncan had positioned four cannons opposite Piedras Negras to give the impression they would help, but the Americans insisted that they did not actually fire their guns. Whatever the case, the blaze consumed Piedras Negras and destroyed the possessions of nearly every vecino in that town. Among those who lost everything in the fire were impoverished vecinos, including Mexican cartmen who lost the tools of their trade. A mulatto fiddler named Pedro Tauns, who later served as star witness in the claims made against the U.S. government, said that that he, like many others, lost his home.[34] Regrettably, the vecinos would have to wait twenty years for the joint boundary commission of 1873 to address their claims.[35]

Only when the Texans had securely forded the river—thanks in large part to the blaze they set—did Emilio Langberg at last show up in Piedras Negras. Both the Texans and the Mexicans had a lot of questions for the colonel. The Texans claimed that he had invited them to cross the border and had then double-crossed them (perhaps Langberg himself had even authored that suspicious map found in the abandoned camp near the banks of the Río Escondido). Mexican sources confirm that Langberg gave the order to let the Texans cross unopposed, and he had also ordered the militias not to engage the volunteers until they reached the interior of the country. He had also ordered the Lipan Apaches moved away from San Fernando and had their men put under arms. Langberg certainly knew that the Texans were up to something, and he probably laid his own devious plans, trying to set up a trap.[36] Further complicating things, Langberg had not been present for either the battle at La Maroma or the burning of Piedras Negras. He was in Monclova, far to the south, when the news that the Texans had invaded Mexico at last reached him on October 4.[37] He finally arrived at Piedras Negras on the ninth, a day or two after the Texans had finished evacuating in advance of the Mexican forces.[38] Suspiciously, upon meeting up with Menchaca, Langberg immediately ordered him to hand over the hand-drawn map.[39]

For suggesting cooperation rather than conflict with the Texans, Langberg may already have been something of a suspicious character. His behavior following the Callahan Raid only confirmed his reputation for treachery. Witnesses later recounted that Langberg seemed nervous upon his arrival in Piedras Negras and did not stay around the neighborhood of Piedras Negras and Fort Duncan for long. Langberg left his troops with Manuel Leal and crossed the river with a small escort the day he arrived—and he did this even though the volunteers still sat across the river in plain sight of Piedras Negras, threatening to cross over again. He stayed in the area for fifteen days, but for the first five or six nights he and his escort stayed at the ranch of a friend, Pedro Arrañaga, about a league from Eagle Pass.[40] When Langberg at last screwed up the courage to face the music and return to Piedras Negras, the commander of Fort Duncan, James Callahan, and another "influential" Texan visited him. Menchaca, who was present at this meeting, described it as a very heated exchange. Menchaca could not understand much English, but he could easily read the angry attitude of Callahan. He also heard Callahan say to Langberg, translated into Castellaño, "Pues por que camino habian de ir cuando no habia otro" (We took this road because there was no other).[41]

It is impossible to know whether Langberg actually invited filibusterers into Mexico, undermining Mexican sovereignty in the process. Meanwhile, the anger evinced by the Texan captains of the expedition did not dissipate any time soon. A few months later, Agapito Cárdenas, municipal president of the ayuntamiento of San Fernando de Rosas, visited San Antonio. While there, he heard Callahan's second-in-command, presumably William Henry, in the main plaza, swearing that Langberg had tricked them. According to Henry, he had promised to give them safe passage to pursue criminals and runaways across the border when the Liberals took control of the frontier.[42] It is impossible to know if this was Langberg's plan. In any case, his superiors soon stripped him of his commission and brought him up on charges for "anti-nacional" behavior before relocating him to the center of the country. A few years later he died, far from the frontier and deep in the heart of Mexico, sacrificing his life to defend Maximilian's imperial reign.[43]

Langberg's perceived treachery did not dampen the spirits of the norteños. The Mexicans amply demonstrated that they could repel force with force. They did not shrink before the Texans when they invaded their territory, threatened their independence, their sovereignty, and their very liberty. But as was the case with any successfully repulsed raid, the victors could not savor their victory for long. Another round of rumors soon swept across the northern frontier as Texans in both San Antonio and along the Brazos River threatened to put together another force—a bigger one this time, composed of at least five hundred men. Again, the Mexicans called together the National Guard, armed the vecinos, and readied the militias. They were not out of the woods yet. Their liberty still imperiled, the Mexicans, Vidaurri claimed, had two thousand men at arms, ready to meet the new threat.[44]

The National Guard units became the guardians of liberty and regional integrity in the North. They protected authorized border crossers in Mexican territory and repulsed illicit raiders, shoring up their territorial sovereignty in the trade. Vidaurri praised the norteños' defense of the nation against outside aggressors and their defense of Mexican soil against unauthorized transgressors with their blood. He commended the vecinos as the nation's greatest patriots. He congratulated his paisanos for securing the border and defeating the filibusterers. Despite their lack of resources and despite the tragedy that had befallen the inhabitants of Piedras Negras, the Mexican forces had fulfilled their duties admirably. Their "patriotism and valor" had achieved the happiest results, and the frontier caudillo lauded his subordinates for acting bravely "under the honorable name of *México*."[45] Written for a national audience, Vidaurri's gestures toward Mexican patriotism may have been something of a performance. Whatever the case, the vecinos had certainly protected the Liberal regime and its regionalist politics as well—in an area known for its anti-Centralism.

The Liberals' victory was still fresh, and a foreign invasion could have ended it before it reached maturity. When Vidaurri heard rumors of a second invasion, he not only mustered vecinos again in defense of the frontier but also called off attacks by Liberal armies on other Mexicans. He asked Juan Alvarez, the ranking general in the Liberal army, to cease the attack on Matamoros and instead try to get the opposing army there to join him to fight off foreign invaders.[46] Fortunately for him the second attack never materialized. But had it come Vidaurri would have been ready to meet it with a Liberal army.

Vidaurri next made a complaint to U.S. Secretary of State Marcy, attributing the Callahan Raid to slave hunters (probably incorrectly), who were under no circumstances allowed to enter Mexican territory and spoil its sovereignty over the frontier. In a letter republished by *Siglo xix*, Vidaurri wrote that it was because Mexico "professed the principle of liberty of the slaves and the abolition of slavery ever since it became independent" that filibusters had scorned its laws. The Liberal revolution, Vidaurri stipulated, promised to end slavery in all of its hideous forms (although Vicente Guerrero had in fact already outlawed the practice in Mexico over twenty-five years earlier). In an ironic twist of fate, the causes of anti-imperialism and liberty for African Americans became joined. Blacks may have been troublesome, but protecting them offered an opportunity for Vidaurri, his minions, and the vecinos of the frontier to prove their patriotism by rebuffing raiders and protecting Mexican soil.[47]

In the end, the raid was not really about capturing African Americans—although surely some members of the Texan force hoped to do some slave hunting as they approached San Fernando. In Texas as well, many understood the raid as a confrontation about runaway slaves. Maybe even some of the vecinos in Piedras Negras thought the intended object of the raid was to capture runaway slaves. They were, after all, familiar with runaways crossing the border and through their town. Just a few weeks after the raid, some Mexicans in Piedras Negras took up a runaway slave and sent him back to the Texas side. "We can guess why they did that," Ed Burleson wrote to John S. Ford, describing the chastising effect the raid had on the Mexicans on the other side of the border.[48] The feelings of vecinos toward border crossers were complicated. While many were ready to defend their homes, it is unlikely that many felt compelled to defend the runaways in their midst. Nevertheless, Callahan had intended the raid—at least primarily—to end the transborder ways of the Lipan Apaches and to punish them for their crimes against Texas. Vidaurri soon realized this and sought to do something about it rather than risk another invasion from disgruntled Texans.

Gracias a Dios

The Upper Lipans found that the Mexicans would not accept their cross-border ways for much longer. This owed something to the fact that Lipan raids into Texas did not cease in the wake of the Callahan Raid—even though Emilio Langberg had hired someone to keep an eye on the

Lipans, paying him twenty-five pesos monthly.[49] The next spring, 1856, Colonel Edward Jordan, an Anglo who, interestingly enough, joined Vidaurri's army, wrote to the great caudillo from Laredo. He informed him that the fronterizos on both sides of the river were very well disposed toward him but that the Lipans were still causing problems. The time had arrived, said Jordan, for Vidaurri to champion their common cause if the settlers on the Texas side of the river were going to respect the border and keep their volunteers in check. Jordan informed Vidaurri that doing something about the Lipans might also endear him to his own countrymen in Mexico. "The Mexicans on both sides, just like the Americans, are very displeased with these *bichos* [bugs]," Jordan said, in reference to the Lipan Apaches.[50] Shortly after Jordan's letter, Daniel Ruggles from Fort McIntosh also wrote to Vidaurri, asking if he would allow the U.S. military to send a force over the border to "exterminate" the Lipans in Mexico. He asked Vidaurri to join in the expedition to confirm the "friendship" between the two governments.[51] The pressure continued to mount on Vidaurri's new government as the Lipans carried on terrorizing the debt peons at the larger ranches in South Texas at the end of 1855 and into the spring of 1856.[52] These attacks alarmed the new Liberal government, then struggling mightily to assert its legitimacy over the frontier. Vidaurri had deftly co-opted the Callahan raid to his cause, scapegoating Langberg so as not to offend the Texans. But another invasion from Texas could imperil the authority of the new Liberal government of the North.

Vidaurri made a brutal, practical decision to cooperate but on the norteño's own terms. He sacrificed the Upper Lipans near San Fernando and (probably Lower) Lipans near Gigedo to ensure that Mexico retained all of its territory, that the Mexican North remained free from Texan invasion, and that he, personally, held on to power in the region. Lipans were transformed from an authorized to an unauthorized presence on Mexican territory, and therefore they found Mexican sovereign soil harmful to their health in very short order. At last, Vidaurri chose cooperation—in at least some form—and took a somewhat reconciliatory course with the Texans, explicitly blaming the "política mezquina" (short-sightedness) of his Conservative predecessor, Jerónimo Cardona, for making peace with the Lipans. The Lipans had fooled the authorities too many times, he wrote to one of his officers, and "they are more pernicious when they live under the shadow of peace than when they are at war; they even make arrangements with other hostile tribes." Indeed, Vidaurri continued, "it is not consistent with natural law that peaceful men be made the plaything of the Lipans' barbarie." Not only did the Lipans rob the frontier of its scarce fortune. They had committed the greater crime of endangering Mexico's independence and spoiling the new caudillo's regional domination when they instigated an attack from Texas the year before.[53]

Vidaurri bowed to Texan pressure in order to stabilize his government, the border, and international relations since cooperation had the power to smooth relations and relax tensions along a border that separated one side starkly from the other. Conceding to the Texans that the Lipans mocked their promises and lived only from "rapine, robbery, and blood," he began to write openly of their "extermination." He concluded: to avoid the "repetition of the events at Río Escondido and Piedras Negras, [events that] had no other origin than the wickedness of the Lipans," the Indians were to be removed from the frontier in order to fulfill a "debt imposed by humanity." In this about-face Vidaurri saw a silver lining; if the Mexicans ended Lipan raids into Texas, perhaps the Americans could at last be persuaded to end the Cayuga and Comanche raids into Mexico in the absence of Article 11, which Santa Anna had allowed the United States to buy its way out of the year before.[54] Vidaurri even dreamed that the Texan authorities might crack down on arms dealers in their state who supplied weapons to Indians (and others) who raided in Mexico.[55]

Rather than blame Texas pirates and the filibusterers, who destabilized the border with unauthorized violence, Vidaurri placed the responsibility for the troubles squarely on Lipans seeking refuge in Mexico. Bowing to regional and Texan pressures, he sacrificed them to ensure the independence and security of the Mexican North, and he mustered the vecinos into their National Guard units yet again to take them on. Importantly, the militias acted without help from Texas. Not only would the victory be a Mexican one without help from the Texans, but the noreteños would dominate the terms of peace with the Lipans as well. Vidaurri, unlike the Texans, still believed the Lipans could be "civilized," but he believed that the militias would have to sacrifice the male warriors of the tribe to ensure this outcome. He wanted the women and children, uncorrupted by warriors, captured and imprisoned rather than murdered. The Lipan men—those troublesome warriors who continued raiding on either side of the border to ensure their independence—would be sacrificed on the altar of frontier civilization to ensure that Mexican territory would remain free of Texas pirates.

In order to achieve these felicitous results the commanders under Vidaurri engineered a daring plan to demonstrate sovereign Mexican control of its territory and against illicit raiders. The National Guard split its militias into two discrete campaigns, one led by Pablo Espinosa (Langberg's replacement) and the second captained by Juan Zuazua, the great hero of the Revolution of Ayutla and, later, the French intervention. The two hundred men under Espinosa planned to approach Gigedo and surprise the Lipan bands camped there. Zuazua's contingent sought to strike another Lipan camp in northern Nuevo León. Both officers received orders to surprise the Lipan camps, hold the Indians captive, and ask them to compose lists of all the captaincillos who were absent most frequently. The vecinos would then arrest these Lipan chiefs and captains and bring them and their families to Monterrey to face a tribunal. If the Lipans would not comply, Vidaurri authorized Espinosa and Zuazua to use force and take their entire camps captive.[56]

Espinosa mustered 175 eager men into his force (the village of Guerrero refused to participate), which then marched toward Gigedo. As the militias approached the Lower Lipan camp, Espinosa encountered the captaincillos Lemus Castro and El Perico outside the main settlement. He plied them with liquor and incorporated them into his company, but they would not give up the names of the Lipans who raided in Texas and Nuevo León. So on March 19 at eight o'clock in the morning, the Mexican forces took the Lipan camp near Gigedo by surprise. The vecino militia gained the high ground over the camp quickly and disarmed the warriors as they came out of their tents without firing a shot. Even though some warriors cried that it would be better to die than give up their arms, the vecinos nevertheless apprehended them quickly. Espinosa accused the captured Lipans of committing robberies in Texas, searched their camp, and found some articles plundered from the other side of the border. As a result of this discovery, he arrested the entire settlement. All told, the force captured 20 warriors, 30 women, and 9 children, as well as 104 horses and a good number of muskets.[57] More prisoners soon joined them. Vidaurri called on the authorities of the nearby villages to arrest any Lipans they encountered in or around their towns and to shoot any who resisted on the spot. The authorities followed these orders to the letter and soon apprehended renegade Lipans in the towns of San Fernando de Rosas, Nava, and Allende.[58]

The Lipans were not ready to give up completely. A party of troops from Espinosa's command volunteered to take the booty captured from the Lipan camp back to the town of Allende. On their way, they encountered unexpected resistance from their captives. As the Mexicans slowly carted their plunder toward town, a Lipan named Cojo approached the

convoy in disguise. When he got within shooting distance of the carts-
men, he pulled out a bow and fired an arrow at them. He missed his
mark, only hitting the wheel of a wagon, but the militiamen guarding
the convoy responded to the attack instantly and shot the Lipan dead.
Cojo's obstinacy demonstrated to Espinosa the "imperative necessity of
[the Lipans'] complete extermination" since they were prepared to fight
to the death. Further, it was only the "civility" of the Mexican forces
that kept the vecinos from killing all of the Lipans "as they deserved."[59]
There were a great number of vecinos under his command chomping at
the bit to visit revenge upon Lipans. The norteños had grown very tired
of putting up with them and hoped to rid themselves of their troublesome presence. At last the vecinos found themselves in sync with official
policies. For his part, Espinosa hoped that the defeated prisoners would
be conducted from Monterrey to San Juan de Úlua or some other island
fortress where they would be forced to work to earn their living—and
kept far away from the frontier where they had caused so much tension
with Texas and so much unhappiness among the local residents.[60] Some
Mexicans raised on the frontier agreed with the Texans on the question
of genocide, even if their commanders still imagined that the Lipans
could be of some use to Mexico.

Espinosa rendezvoused with Miguel Patiño and handed over the
Lipan prisoners. Their new jailer forced them to march on toward the
interior, but when the convoy arrived at the point known as Gracias a
Dios something terrible happened. A soldier named Julian Salinas, who
was in the vanguard and in charge of the prisoners, saw that the women
prisoners had begun to mutiny. He made a horrific accusation, alleging
that these Indian women began cutting the throats of their own children.
Salinas and the other troops tried to stop the women from performing
this "horrible act," but they said they had no choice except to open fire on
the prisoners if they wanted to save the children. The troops killed all of
the men and seventeen of the women prisoners, including a small girl—
although Patiño claimed that the small girl had died at the hand of her
own mother. In the end, only sixteen prisoners survived, all children.[61]

The foremost historian of Nuevo León, Isidro Vizcaya Canales, has
written briefly on the alleged filicide at Gracias a Dios and offers a plausi-
ble explanation for the incident. He believes that the justification offered
up by Patiño for the slaughter was merely a pretext for opening fire on
the prisoners. The troops had already shown a willingness to revenge
themselves on Lipans, to shoot first and ask questions later. When a warrior and two women prisoners in the charge of Captain José María Flores

attempted to escape the day before, the captain did not hesitate to murder them on the spot.[62] The vecino militiamen, most of whom came from Nuevo León, had little love for the Lipan Apaches and may well have sought any excuse to get rid of them once and for all.

But was there some truth to the claim? Would the Lipan women actually turn on their own children and commit this most horrible atrocity? And even if they did not actually carry this terrible act through, why did they threaten it? For their part, the Lipan women surely knew that it was primarily the children the Mexicans wanted. They had learned this in the stalled peace process a few years before, when Coyote had escorted so many women to Rosas to try to make peace with the Mexicans. Women and children uncorrupted by their warrior fathers held the key to reducing the Lipan Apaches. Mexicans, officers and vecinos alike, most likely considered the men expendable; they were beyond saving, and there was little room for them in a peaceful, civilized, agricultural Mexico. The women of the tribe were fully aware that the end goal of the Mexicans was to reduce the tribe to sedentary civilization—and the women of the band may have threatened to kill their children if they were not released. They saw the children as a bargaining chip and were willing to threaten them in order to maintain their independence. They knew what the Mexicans wanted, and they knew that by intimating that they might murder their own children they threatened to dash any hopes for reducing the uncorrupted youth to a sedentary, peaceful existence in Mexican society. After all, the Mexicans had long been interested in civilizing Indians and adding them to their scarce frontier populations. Children, if tutored in Mexican ways, might yet become productive members of society and laborers on a population-scarce frontier. Maybe one Lipan woman killed her child to avoid this fate.

In any case, even if the women were merely making a threat, it resulted in a terrible tragedy. Most likely the vecinos failed to recognize the women's gambit, believing these "uncivilized" people were capable of such a terrible act. Accordingly, they gave in to their baser, murderous impulses. It did not take much to send the Indian-hating militiamen over the edge. Therefore, the Lipans were cut down where they stood. Savagery triumphed—but in the name of civilization.

These tragic events did not mark the end of the story, however. As Espinosa's bungled operation came to a bloody conclusion outside of Gigedo at Gracias a Dios, the second force commanded by Zuazua sprang into action. Zuazua left Lampazos with 160 men drawn from the nearby towns and marched toward the Sabinas River and San Fernando, where a large band of Upper Lipans made their camp. The troops saw the Indians rustling horses in the neighborhood and a few Indians even turned themselves in, but the militias treaded lightly, waiting until the next day before striking. Then, when dawn broke over the eastern plains on March 22, a section of Zuazua's forces marched into the camp. They caught the Indians unprepared, as they were packing up their rancherías when Zuazua's citizen army materialized in the early morning mist. The warriors ran out of their tiendas to see what was happening, and Zuazua's troops immediately set upon them, managing to disarm most of them. He had less luck than Espinosa in this regard, however. Despite his best efforts, fifteen or twenty warriors managed to escape and join a detached band of Indians rustling animals nearby.[63]

As the Mexican force began to take the Lipan families into custody, the escaped Lipans emerged from a forest on an unguarded side of the camp. The Indians hoped to save the children from capture in one daring maneuver, surely aware that they represented a bargaining chip with the authorities. They were unsuccessful in their ploy but ran off before the Mexicans could capture them, resolving to die before becoming captives. Zuazua had not expected the degree of resistance he encountered. So great was the Lipans' solidarity that he decided it was pointless to explain to them he only intended to apprehend the guilty. In his opinion, the entire camp was too concerned about losing their "liberty" to listen to reason. Their freedom—to raise their children as they desired, to cross the border and play one side against the other to procure horses, cattle, and supplies, to continue in the traditions of their ancestors—was now greatly imperiled. They could not be mollified, so Zuazua ended up marching all ninety-four Lipan prisoners to the rendezvous with Miguel Patiño.[64]

This would not be a peaceful convoy either. The soldiers put in charge of the prisoners quickly found themselves subject to a great number of insults hurled at them by the Lipan captives. The prisoners raised a terrible row, abusing the soldiers, crying, and protesting bitterly. They complained that they would only like the opportunity to take their own lives. They claimed that God was clearly angry with the Lipans since he had not even allowed the handful of captured warriors to die an honorable death in defense of their children, women, and horses.[65]

Their Mexican captors had other problems too. The escaped warriors remained at large and were harassing the troops from the rear. Zuazua responded by dispatching a Lipan captive to find the warriors and tell them that if they did not surrender the Mexicans would kill all of the women and children they had imprisoned, ending any opportunity for their culture to continue. If the warriors did not turn themselves in at the Hacienda del Alamo, they would only have themselves to blame for their bands' complete cultural and physical extermination. Instead, the warriors called Zuazua's bluff, aware that the Mexicans most likely intended to assimilate the captured children as criados, not exterminate them. They remained apart, doing damage in the surrounding area, killing at least three people, and taking an eight-year-old Mexican boy captive. A day later, Zuazua's troops stumbled upon the dead bodies of the captive's parents in a "disgraceful condition." They looked upon this latest atrocity with revulsion and, almost certainly, growing hatred. The vecinos who made up this militia came for the most part from Lampazos, and they were boon companions to Juan Zuazua, a lifelong Indian fighter. As a result, they had very little compassion for their prisoners, and they were convinced that these were the same Indians who had robbed and killed their countrymen for years.[66]

Then, on the same night as the battle, tragedy struck again. Under the cover of dusk, several of the Lipan warriors who had escaped approached the camp. The Lipan prisoners held captive by the Mexican militias quickly learned that their salvation was near, and several threw themselves upon the guards in an open revolt. The guards responded in kind, meeting force with force, opening fire on the entire line of prisoners. Zuazua said that he could do nothing to avert the massacre. A large number of troops were "disgusted" with the tolerance that Mexicans had shown the Lipans in the past and showed little restraint when putting down the rebellion. They massacred the Indians. When the smoke cleared, thirty-six Indians lay dead, alongside two Mexican guards. Despite the slaughter, Zuazua defended the vecinos' actions. The Lipans would "give up anything before death," he said, and the troops had comported themselves bravely—if also a little overzealously. He went on to recommend the volunteers' behavior throughout the campaign, singling out some for special praise.[67] At long last, the attitudes of vecinos and their officials regarding the border-crossing troublemakers was in sync, and the massacre went unpunished. The violence reflected the vecinos' growing hatred of Lipans—the way they imperiled the independence of the Mexicans, the way they brought Texan raiders upon them, and the way that they had taken captives and animals from the Mexican fronterizos for generations. The vecino militias were an intensely local and, now under Vidaurri, regional institution. Their actions represented regional desires as well a break with the old Centralist habit of granting amnesty to Lipan fugitives. At last, the Mexicans could forcibly assimilate Indian captives—women and children—and make them adapt to their culture, not the other way around. Norteños would no longer be captive to the Indians.

Vidaurri regretted that so many Indians had been killed during these campaigns. The practice of statecraft, even in the Mexican North where belonging had long been predicated on masculine violence against outside raiders, still had room for the incorporation of outsiders. Lipans might have been transformed into citizens in an area that saw its absolute population shrink dramatically in the decades following independence. For this reason, northern officials felt deep ambivalence on the question of whether Lipans were welcomed on Mexican soil. In this new era, increasingly desirous of peace and given to regionalism over localism, something had changed irrevocably in the face of irregular pressure from Texas. Even the great caudillo went on record, saying that the Lipans possessed an "almost indomitable ferocity." He was pleased, meanwhile, that so many of the children were being brought to him, and he was hopeful for their transformation once they were removed from their relatives and surroundings. What to do with them remained something of an open question. Traditionally, Indian captives became servants in Mexican villages, but Vidaurri may have hoped to transform them into vecinos away from their homeland and memories of the bitter past. He wrote to Mexico City, asking if he could send the captured children to the *hospicios* (orphanages) of the capital and Guadalajara. They would learn a trade and at last "become useful to themselves and society" if they returned to the North afterward. Meanwhile, the children, women, and a few captured warriors who survived the massacre remained imprisoned in Monterrey.[68]

The murder of Lipans on Mexican soil expressed a new statecraft on the northern frontier in at least three ways. It ejected unauthorized border crossers who threw into question Mexico's sovereignty over its frontier. It resulted in cooperation with the Texans, if in an informal way, and this new attitude potentially represented a new day in international relations. Finally, it brought vecinos together to defend their territory and sovereignty from outside raiders, thereby tying themselves to their region and demonstrating their loyalty to the state government—a significant development in an area known for its libertarianism and calls for greater autonomy. By expelling raiders, the vecino militiamen protected the border even though they lived many miles away from it. At last they were in agreement with official policies. When they killed unfriendly

Indians, they vigorously filtered the border, removing transgressors in the name of the patria and in defense of their homes. They demonstrated a resolve to control their territory, transforming it into a lethal environment for illicit border crossers and some mobile peoples—similar to what they had done with Callahan the year before. Surely this attitude aligned much better with the attitudes of the frontier vecinos than the seemingly irrelevant dictates of Mexico City Conservatives. This is what liberty meant to them.

Lipans were not passive victims of this bloodshed; they openly contested the new order that vecinos hoped to apply to the border by suppressing movement across it. The Lipans who escaped Zuazua remained elusive and continued to cross the frontier with impunity, using the border for leverage just as they always had. Daniel Ruggles, from Fort McIntosh, proposed a joint venture to "exterminate" them. This joint venture never materialized, however, as the Mexican commanders still refused to follow orders from Texan officials.[69] Without cooperation or the will to mount a second large-scale campaign, the Lipans continued to cross the poorly manned border with impunity. More than a month after the massacres, Patiño was still chasing down escaped warriors with vecinos from Morelos and Rosas. He once caught up to their camp and got close enough to learn that there were only fifteen or twenty warriors in the group. Then he discovered something even more startling. The majority of this group of mobile Indians were women and children—an especially tempting target for the Mexicans who still hoped to reduce them.[70] In the end, although both Vidaurri and Ruggles had agreed to pursue "the most prompt extermination or reduction of these Indians," independently of one another, Vidaurri had to concede that capturing the remainder would be impossible. He told Ruggles that he had done all he could.[71] In the aftermath, a large number of women, children, and captives remained afoot, traveling with a handful of warriors who had survived the Mexican ambush, crossing back and forth. They would continue to do so for at least another generation, although at least one group would suffer another massive blow in 1859.[72] Their liberty had been imperiled, but it had not been snuffed out.

This move toward cooperation—even if carried out in an ad hoc way— reflected northern vecino attitudes and immensely pleased the Texans. Perhaps it even foreshadowed a new phase in international relations, but the Liberals did not represent an immediate revolution in cross-border relations. They would continue to fight against Texans when they felt their sovereignty and regional integrity were threatened. But they had also seen that international cooperation with the Texans—if carried out in a way that did not compromise their independence—could get healthy results. Already, as the historian Luis Alberto García has argued, budding relationships between norteños on both sides of the border—like the one between Vidaurri and Santos Benavides for instance—began to close the gap between Tejanos and mexicanos. They saw that their shared cultural identity actually led them to a similar conclusion about the problems that haunted both sides of the border, especially mobile Indian raiders, arms, and stalled enterprise.[73] Now some Tejanos began to look approvingly at their neighbors and the efforts they had made to achieve cooperation across the line.

The Tejanos were pleased in the aftermath of these massacres, and a shadow that had long loomed over the borderlands began to dissipate. Juan Long, an American married to a relative of Vidaurri's, wrote to the caudillo that he was glad to see that the Mexican "nation was going in the right direction," further indicating the tightening ethnic and kinship bonds that transcended the border. He even told Vidaurri that the United States should follow the example of the Mexicans and halt Comanche raids into Mexico once and for all. Vidaurri had also pleased his own paisanos, Long informed the great caudillo. The norteños' great pleasure was manifested most openly by the vecinos of Ciénegas, Coahuila, who wrote to Vidaurri to thank him for having allowed the fronterizos to avenge so many years of "spilled blood and shed tears" when he ordered the Lipans crushed in 1856. The inhabitants of the region pledged their eternal gratitude.[74] Not long before, many vecinos had thought that their only option with the Lipans was to agree to peace on their terms.

By sacrificing the Lipans, Vidaurri, his subordinates, and the vecino militias had guaranteed their own independence, a conviviality with Tejanos across the borderlands, and the Liberals' continued political hold on the frontier. They had demonstrated that Mexican soil was deadly to unauthorized border crossers, and they had greatly reduced the possibilities and promise of mobility—at least for one group of transborder people. They had also ensured their own liberty—at the expense of the Lipans' liberty. The Lipans, unperturbed, continued to cross the borderlands in search of liberty and the best options for themselves. Increasingly, their search for liberty would run up against the dangers of Mexican volunteerism and patriotic regionalism. As a result, they found the soil of their old homeland ever more poisoned against them.

The vecino militias that made up the new National Guard were extremely important. Organized at the state level and funded by taxes, duties, and smuggling, they were a bulwark of norteño patriotism. They ensured the continued independence of northern Mexico and buttressed regional rule under the Liberals. When they rid themselves of Texan filibusterers in 1855 and when they struck out against the Lipan Apaches in 1856, they proved invaluable in the defense of the region, especially once their goals aligned with official policy. They demonstrated sovereignty in an area that was always strapped for cash, manpower, and resources. Mustered into militias, carrying out murder, and defending their homes from outside invaders, they ensured the North's territorial sovereignty and their own autonomy. The vecinos did their commanders' bidding to make sure that when illicit and unauthorized border transgressors crossed into Mexico they greatly imperiled their own well-being. Gathering at the clarion call of la patria, vecino militias reinforced the meaning of the border as a line of sovereignty and territorial integrity. Like the border's meaning as a limit of liberty, this meaning also bubbled up from below. Vecinos shouldered muskets instead of plows when the state beckoned. They kept their country's soil free from outside invaders, whether pirates or Indians, and they protected their own independence and liberty to follow their destinies unperturbed by troublesome outsiders. Although they did this in the name of Mexico, they were even more interested in defending their autonomy, their regional institutions, and the recently ascendant Liberal political regime. Theirs was an intensively regionalist patriotism—one that transcended the mere localism that had predominated in the Mexican North for centuries.[75]

But despite the way their raids inspired patriotism and statecraft in the Mexican North, the Texans may have won a small victory. Maybe the ad hoc diplomacy of force majeure practiced by stateless volunteer militiamen from Texas had at last achieved its objective—at least in a roundabout way. After all, the Callahan Raid, which sought to punish Lipan Apaches, brought on the massacres carried out by Pablo Espinosa and Juan Zuazua at Gracias a Dios and outside Lampazos. But the important part is not that the vecinos acted because of Texan threats; it is that the vecinos acted independently to take care of a common problem. They had also acted in concert to rid their home of a major threat. At last, the days of localism were giving over to a growing sense of regionalism in the North. In the end, the Mexicans and Texans had come up with a common solution to the problem of raiding Lipans when diplomacy by normal means failed. They had cooperated, just not by acting in union.

Filibusters, as I show in the conclusion, continued to sully Mexican soil—but this massacre was a first step toward cooperation with Texans.

The move toward greater regional autonomy also signaled a new direction for international policy in the North. The vecinos, left to their own devices, went against the old policy of granting refuge to the enemies of the Texans when they murdered Lipan Apaches in large numbers. The vecinos alongside their heroic commanders could finally chart their own course to cooperation with the Tejanos and even the Anglo Texans on the other side of the border—free from the interlopers in Mexico City who had kept the frontier in a state of flux for a generation. At last, the frontier might know peace, independence, and liberty from the dictates of distant, unresponsive authorities. In this sense, the Vidaurri regime and the National Guard inculcated a growing sense of regional patriotism in the Mexican Northeast. Norteños alone would decide who could exist on Mexican soil and who could not.

Acting in accordance with the wishes of local vecinos, who largely detested the Lipans (and only incidentally in accordance with the wishes of the Texan filibusterers), the new regime fulfilled the northerners' desire for liberty and autonomy. For too many decades the Centralists had ruled the North, enforcing edicts handed down from the Supreme Government with very little concern for or understanding of conditions on the ground at the frontier. With the Liberals now firmly in charge, the new commanders of the frontier immediately began to put practical measures in place to ensure peace along the border. Frontier vecinos escaped the tyranny of the central government and forged their own solutions based in regional realities alongside Tejanos and Anglo Texans. International harmony could not endure as long as Texans and other invaders threatened constantly to disrupt the peace. Many vecinos wished for "the good relations that need to exist between two nations that find themselves divided only by a small stretch from each other," as the disgraced Emilio Langberg once put it.[76] With the Liberals taking charge, the vecinos and their popular commanders were at last free to come up with their own regional solutions to the pressing problems presented by meddlesome officials that had for too long separated them from Tejanos and Anglos on the other side. In the end, the border softened against Texas but not because of official edicts handed down from the central government. It was because it was what the vecinos wanted. This is what liberty looked like for northern vecinos; and it was indeed predicated on stripping others of the independence they found through mobility.

Conclusion: Mobility Interrupted

The common ground of Indian murder had great power. It could build bridges across cultures and between peoples and even transcend national divides. The Lipans were just one of many mobile peoples who invested heavily in the U.S.-Mexico border, however, and others continued to cross to refuge and cause international strife. The Lipans themselves soon recovered from the blow that the norteño vecinos dealt them in 1856. The massacres of the Lipans in Mexico may have ingratiated the Liberal officers to the Tejanos who lived on the left bank of the river, to the local vecinos, and maybe even to the Anglo Texans. It even helped fuel the birth of a regional, norteño, identity. But try though they might in the decades to come, the Mexicans could still never rid themselves of the Lipans' troublesome presence.[1]

In 1861, just six years after Gracias a Dios, the Lipans made their triumphant return to western Coahuila, where they forced tribute from the exposed colonia of Resurrección. The little village, founded in 1859, was the latest in the long series of colonization schemes that involved offering asylum in exchange for securing and populating the distant frontier. Located in an area known as a *"madriguera* [den] of savages," the colonia asserted state sovereignty over a distant corner of the frontier where Mexican law had little effect and Comanches and Lipans held sway. But the migration to this frontier outpost was not composed of peaceful Indians or blacks this time. Instead, immigrant Tejano families from Bexar County made up the bulk of the new colony's population. These men and women who crossed the line to take up residence at Resurrección were far less objectionable. Still, they found conditions in Mexico dangerous, insecure, and ultimately unbearable. Like so many who had come before them, they did not find things all that much better on the other side of the border—especially when a band of around a hundred Lipans (far from exterminated as Vidaurri claimed) came after their town en masse in February 1861. The Indians stole most of the former bejareños' animals and carried many of the townsfolk's children off into captivity. In a heartbreaking repetition of earlier events, many of the townsfolk discovered that they had traded one form of insecurity for another, and many families abandoned the town, dispersing to more established areas along the frontier.[2]

If Lipans still caused trouble on the frontier, so too did African Americans, who continued to cross the international line with impunity. Just a few years before the Lipan attack on Resurrección, the 1857 Constitution signaled the great triumph of the Revolution of Ayutla. It also enshrined in Mexican law the well-rehearsed policy of granting refuge to blacks who crossed the border. Well into the Civil War era, blacks found freedom after "having set foot in the Republic" of Mexico, as the national law declared.[3] Behind the scenes, however, Vidaurri and his Liberal ilk sought out a form of tacit cooperation with the Texans that betrayed the spirit of the new constitution. The governor of Nuevo León y Coahuila hoped to defuse the many problems caused by the proximity of Nacimiento de los Negros to the border—especially after another rumor of a slave hunt into Coahuila surfaced in spring 1859.[4] This alarming news seriously disrupted life on the frontier as the vecinos on the haciendas surrounding Guerrero abandoned their work and took up arms—in part to defend the fugitives and also, more important as far as they were concerned, to guard their homes against foreign invaders. Almost certainly some grumbled as they received instructions to stay put in their jurisdiction. As we saw in chapter 5, the vecinos were not exactly enamored of black Indians and runaway slaves. Nor could the vecinos' property be spared in the effort this time around, and they had to lend their horses, weapons, and munitions to the cause and—more specifically—to the notoriously resource-poor officers cobbling together a military response to the pirates' threat.[5] The alcalde of Sabinas Hidalgo readied a list of all the citizens ages sixteen to sixty in his municipality capable of bearing arms, who would be forced to "volunteer" if not enough vecinos enlisted. It was a just cause, however; the alcalde wrote that if was "an exemplary punishment of the *osadía* [arrogance] of the

Texans [and] . . . the most just measure one could undertake."[6] But such patriotic pronouncements could be hollow when families stayed home on the exposed frontier and fields lay fallow.

Fortunately, no repetition of the Callahan Raid occurred, and the Texans stayed put on their side of the river. Nevertheless, the authorities at last gave in to the irregular diplomacy practiced by Texan pirates, filibusterers, and slave hunters just as they had in 1856. They moved the Black Seminoles at Nacimiento de los Negros—in addition to all the blacks who worked at the surrounding ranches—inward, to the Hacienda de los Hornos, deep within the state of Coahuila.[7] The Black Seminoles, who for decades had found liberty through mobility, deeply resented this forced migration, and they never stopped yearning for their old farmsteads. Within months of the U.S. Civil War breaking out, they thought that the moment had arrived to return home and petitioned the government of Nuevo León y Coahuila to allow them to go back to Nacimiento de los Negros. Vidaurri's secretary quickly wrote back that this would be impossible. Their return would surely invite the jealousy (*codicia*) of Texan adventurers, which might very well "alter the relations of both countries" and affect adversely "the peace along the frontier." Further, the vecinos would have to remain in a "state of war-like readiness" to take on slave hunters if the blacks returned, mustering into their National Guard units to protect them, leaving their crops and dependents behind to languish.[8] In order to cooperate with the Texans and to ensure that agricultural enterprise on the frontier would advance, Vidaurri sacrificed the liberty of the blacks just as he had the Lipans.

The internalization of the Black Seminoles and their friends revealed the new practicality that the Liberals brought to the frontier. Going against high-minded national principles, Vidaurri even made some headway on the contentious matter of runaway slaves—in an unofficial capacity of course, since the new constitution expressly forbade comity when it came to this sensitive issue. It turned out that Vidaurri was not above returning runaway slaves to their "owners" to fund his caudillo wars, as long as he and Texan planters came to their agreements quietly. Vidaurri may very well have considered slavery "irrational" and railed against it in public (just as he did against debt peonage). But after failing in his bid to take over San Luis Potosí, his war chest ran low on funds and he offered to deal in runaway slaves. It was supposed to be a secret. Nevertheless, a Texas newspaper published the rumor and called his overtures "a move in the right direction."[9] The following year Vidaurri made preliminary arrangements with the governor of Texas,

Hardin Richard Runnels, for an extradition treaty—long the holy grail of Texan diplomatic overtures to Mexico.[10] The treaty would cover runaway slaves, runaway debt peons, and cross-border thieves and rustlers, as well as agitators. During the Civil War, the authorities in Matamoros even struck a deal with the Texans to return runaway slaves, something unimaginable in the decades after the Texans' revolt. This deal clearly violated the spirit of the Liberal Republican partisans fighting for control of Mexico, a party to which Vidaurri ostensibly belonged.[11]

Just as the tacit cooperation with the Texans against the Lipans did little to stop their cross-border ways, neither did Vidaurri's strategies actually stop blacks from crossing the border to freedom. The poor little town of Resurrección, so recently devastated by the Lipans, attracted at least one black man in search of a country where he might find liberty. Unfortunately for those townsfolk, lightning would strike a second time that year. Around the middle of November, a posse of about forty armed men from Texas illicitly crossed the border into Mexico in search of the Lipan Apaches and decided to ferret out runaway slaves since they found themselves on the other side of the line anyway. The Texans heard a rumor that a runaway had escaped to Resurrección and was hiding there. The Texans approached the village and ordered the vecinos to turn over the black man. The townsfolk demonstrated courageous resolve, and their leader, Manuel Leal, refused the Texans' demand. Despite the vecinos' pluck, the invaders would not be put off. Before they rode off to the east, the Texans swore to return with a hundred reinforcements waiting for them at Moras.[12] The entire town, still mourning the loss of so many cattle and children in the Indian raid earlier that year, packed up in the wake of this latest threat and dispersed. Commander Vicente Garza put together a force of vecinos to go after the Texans hunting the Lipan Apaches in Coahuila, but instead of Indians he encountered the large train of immigrants abandoning Resurrección, pushing all of their possessions in front of them, en route to new homes in safer places. Pleading with the scared and heartbroken vecinos, Garza managed to persuade about twenty of the fifty families to return only after he swore to dispatch a company of riflemen to watch over them.[13]

All too often, the old dynamics of attack and counterattack in defense of asylum seekers and Mexican soil raised the border against outside transgressors. The Liberals may have hoped to break this pattern, but so long as outside threats continued to imperil the frontier they could not do it. Garza, who fumed about the attack on Resurrección, responded in the only way possible for someone who professed a great love for his patria. He demanded that future attacks against Mexican populations meet a military force to demonstrate that Mexico could conserve intact "its dignity and national honor." Filibusterers and raiders, Garza bristled, compromised "the respectability, interests and credibility of Mexico." Pirates needed to face punishment for "violating the national integrity." He further railed that asylum seekers, including blacks, must receive the protection they sought in Mexico if the law promised it to them and if Mexico hoped to maintain its independence from international bullies.[14] There were few soldiers to spare, of course, and it once again fell on the beleaguered "sons of the state" to guard the frontier. The authorities expected the vecinos to continue mustering in, holding the line, and defending national integrity—at least so long as the government's penury continued.[15] In the final analysis, force remained the only possible answer to invasion from Texas, and beset vecinos had to abandon whatever they were doing to defend their homes.

It could be no other way. Despite the efforts to achieve comity and cooperation and despite removals and massacres, the border still invited transgression from people seeking to escape Texas. Notwithstanding the hostile attitudes of the vecinos toward Indians and the more liberal attitudes of the new class of officers who commanded Nuevo León y Coahuila toward Texans, the Mexicans simply could not turn back this tide. Even though the political atmosphere had changed, the border still functioned as a limit of liberty—too much time and effort had been spent marking Mexican territory off from Texas over the previous three decades. Nor did things get any better in the years that followed for the officers who, like Emilio Langberg before them, desired peace and harmony along the frontier and were prepared to sacrifice the liberty of border crossers to ensure it. Terrible social and political turmoil continued to characterize the lower Rio Grande during the U.S. Civil War and the French Intervention, creating yet more opportunities for mobility. People crossed the border in droves during these years of renewed warfare, seeking refuge and causing all sorts of trouble. The most common border crossers were Tejanos who escaped Confederate Texas in order to join the Union forces that showed up along the Rio Grande in 1863. Some mobile Tejano and mexicanos even enlisted to fight alongside that old enemy of the Texans, Juan Nepumuceno Cortina. Vidaurri may have sought to cozy up to the Confederates, once even making the startling suggestion that he wished to join the southern states in their rebellion. Despite these efforts toward international cooperation, however, the new borders created by the Mexican Republic, the French, the Union, and Confederate Texas during

FIGURES 11 AND 12. The Kickapoos returned to Mexico during the U.S. Civil War. The above photos were taken when they visited the court of Emperor Maximilian in Mexico City. Getty Research Institute, Los Angeles (2000.R.22) photo by Auguste Merille and Getty Research Institute, Los Angeles (95.R.70) photo by François Aubert.

these tumultuous war years created an enormous amount of movement among refuge seekers, opponents of the Confederacy, former slaves, and many others.[16]

The Kickapoos also came back to Mexico during the Civil War to escape the Confederacy, returning after an absence of over ten years. A Kickapoo envoy visited the court of Maximilian soon after their arrival. But like the Lipans before them, they soon became notorious for raiding in Texas from hideouts in Mexico. In the late 1860s and into the 1870s, these Indians habitually plundered stock in Texas and took refuge near Remolino, Coahuila.[17] Alongside non-Native rustlers operating across the border, these raiders pushed the United States and Mexico toward a diplomatic impasse, and some figured that war loomed on the horizon once again. Adding fuel to the fire, General Raynald MacKenzie heeded the protests of ranchers in Texas and crossed over the border to punish the Kickapoos in 1873, killing many and, of course, violating Mexican sovereign territory. Like so many filibusterers who came before him, he raised hackles and wounded national pride amongst the Mexicans when he transgressed the border—although there was no citizen militia on the Mexican side to meet him this time as there might have been a generation before. MacKenzie's raid recalled the old volunteer pressure that filibusters had put on Mexico, although this time a national institution, the U.S. Army, carried out the irregular diplomacy of force majeure, perfected by volunteer Texan militiamen in the 1850s. This raid also once again brought into open conflict the many diverse meanings that different people associated with the international border. For the Indians, it was a line of refuge and liberty. For the Mexicans, it was a line of national sovereignty. For the Texans, it was a steel trap that protected their enemies and forbade their entrance. The MacKenzie Raid signaled only one major change in this old struggle. This time it was a newly energized, expanded, and strengthened federal army fresh from defeating the Confederacy that composed the party of land pirates who crossed into Coahuila and found the Kickapoos in their hideouts. The state had at last arrived at the borderlands, and at least at first it adapted to ad hoc diplomacy carried out through force majeure and pioneered by Texas volunteers.[18]

This was an unsustainable situation, and ultimately cooler heads prevailed. The United States and Mexico opened diplomatic channels to avoid a war that could only have ended disastrously for the latter. In the 1870s, the nations agreed to investigate the border in an official capacity. The U.S. boundary commission and the Comisión Pesquisdora uncovered a large number of problems that had plagued the borderlands for a generation and wrote at great length about them. Finally, in the 1880s, after the boundary commission finished its work, the United States and Mexico agreed to a series of extradition agreements. Criminals, Indians, rustlers, and others would continue to cross into Mexico where they expected to find refuge, but it would now be easier for the national state on either side to send troops after them.[19]

The extradition treaties of the early 1880s did not portend an ultimate end to Native American cross-border mobility. Nor did the treaty betoken a time when the state would at last call the shots and shore up the border's meaning as an end of liberty, erasing once and for all the creative work that a generation of mobile peoples had put into reimagining the international boundary. Mexico still offered refuge to Native Americans seeking to escape the United States. After all, the Kickapoos and Black Seminoles, to this day, have villages in northern Coahuila, at Nacimiento, where the Sabinas once watered the crops of their ancestors. Nor did either of these groups ever assimilate properly; they have maintained their own cultural identity and cross-border ways as an expression of liberty. By the turn of the century, Nacimiento de los Negros was thriving, though it possessed something of an unsavory reputation and Mexicans in charge of the section often looked at it disparagingly. Not many blacks who lived there, said the Mexicans, practiced Catholicism or even spoke Spanish. Furthermore, many blacks crossed back and forth between Nacimiento and Bracketsville in Texas, where the Black Seminoles' barracks were located. Naturally, Nacimiento also still served as a haven for criminals and fugitives. In contrast, the authorities found the Kickapoos' settlement nearby much more peaceable. Nevertheless, Nacimiento de los Negros continued to prosper as a node in a transnational network maintained by a special group of black Indians and their friends whose ethnic presence along the lower Rio Grande can still be felt to this day.[20] Their neighbors, the Kickapoos, also maintain a transnational existence. Today their casinos are located in Texas, and at the same time a good number of them call northern Coahuila home.

International borders have continued to offer opportunity for Native peoples. In the 1880s, the United States at last divided up Native claims in the North American West and forced other Indians onto reservations, ending the mobility that so many had used to maintain their independence for decades. Finally, the newly energized post–Civil War national government yoked the vast grasslands and plains of the West, so conducive to mobile lifestyles, to the industrial East. But even in the wake of this great transformation, the international border did not cease lending leverage to Native Americans looking to cross boundaries to gain advantages for themselves. No better example exists than that of the Yaquis, who during their revolts against the consolidating Mexican state under Porfirio Díaz in the late 1800s and early 1900s, crossed over to work in the United States to fund their ongoing war effort against Díaz's *rurales*.[21] Native Americans, more than any other group, kept up the old meaning of the border as a line of refuge against grasping national states that sought to erase old Native American geographies and belittle Native conceptions of sovereignty and territoriality. For Indians, the border remained a staging ground that sat right in the middle of territory they had mastered.

This book has examined the origins of the international line as a limit of liberty, refuge, and even opportunity. There is no neat ending to this story. The border did not lose these meanings as states worldwide consolidated their power in the late nineteenth century over mobile peoples and nomads. The great national events of the late nineteenth century—the growth of the state on both sides of the border under the Republicans on one side and the Liberals on the other—only served to federalize patterns, practices, and violent acts along this borderline that had pedigrees dating back decades. So in this sense, the borderlands of the eastern Rio Grande remained apart, unique, and subject to their own local dynamics. But this finding presents another problem. Historians of borderlands often caution that when borderlands tell stories of very particular places, they do not fit into any larger story at all. Instead, their histories leave us with a patchwork of diverse places that do not conform to historical processes observed in other sites around the world. How, then, can these histories be of any significance it they do not bear comparison across time and space? And, on a related note, if borderlands histories do not conform to national narratives, then do they have their own turning points and narratives that correspond with other histories? Borderlands studies have left too many strands unwoven.[22]

Unfortunately, I must admit that I found the search for endings elusive. But I would like to make a suggestion in response to these criticisms of the field. Maybe there is something essential to borderlands histories, and we could test the findings in this book against studies made in other parts of the world. This book has uncovered a praxis of mobility toward political ends that predated the arrival of dividing lines and remained in place long after governments drew their boundaries. The borderland

FIGURE 13. "Peon Refugees on the Banks of the Rio Grande." The Rio Grande continued to beckon people across well into the twentieth century if not beyond. Here a mother and her children hope to cross the river and escape the excesses of the Mexican Revolution. LC-F81–2024 [P&P], Library of Congress Prints and Photographs Division, Washington, D.C. 20540 USA.

that lay along the eastern terminus of the Rio Grande conducted a great amount of movement as soon as different peoples began bumping into one another in the 1820s. The coming of the border in 1848 only encouraged greater mobility since, to put it simply, everyone knew where the dividing line was from that point forward. In tracing the history of transnational movement along this stretch of frontier, I have sought to bridge the gap between borderlands and "bordered lands" histories. Instead of closure, I found continuity. A narrative of today's border crossers' great ancestors comes into focus when seen from the vantage point of the stories related above. If we move away from a trend in borderlands history that has put too much focus on elites and instead look at borders from the bottom up, we might find similar practices of transborder mobility with an unbroken past in other places around the world. But we are still left with the problem of endings.[23] Maybe there never is an end to mobility—and this is something that makes borderlands essentially different from hinterlands. In subsequent decades, or even centuries, hundreds, thousands, millions more followed in the wake of the mobile peoples whose stories filled the pages of this book.

Mobile peoples defined this history, and states—usually the heroic actors in national narratives—struggled to keep up with them. In the nineteenth century, mobile peoples transformed a limit that governments intended to mark one territory off from another into a line of opportunity, economic mobility, and even social stability. Borders are designed with the end goal of keeping people in place, but for the people described here this was clearly not the case. This border actually had the contradictory effect of encouraging movement across it. Of course, transnational mobile peoples provoked outrage on either side of the border when they crossed—a sort of knee-jerk reaction to unauthorized cross-border mobility. Many people, then as now, felt that those who crossed borders without proper authorization somehow invaded their sovereign territory and made the state look ineffective. Mexico, as we saw above, could do little to stop the flows across its border, which greatly troubled its sovereignty at the frontier. So it offered refuge to some mobile peoples and demonized others—filibusterers and horseback Native raiders chief among them—in an effort to filter the border and express statecraft and at least a modicum of control over a distant frontier. Mexican officials may have been clever to use mobile people for nation building at the frontier in an effort to raise borders, but this was not effective border control as we think of it today. Mexico never became—to borrow Willem Van Schendel's term, "a gatekeeper state." [24]

We believe that as states and markets consolidate their hold over territories, the ultimate stroke in their domination is to cordon off one place from another. The power of the state lay in its ability to separate people, to make dividing lines, and to define who we are versus who they are. But borders, in fact, very rarely completely seal off one people from another, and maybe the "gate" is not the best metaphor for borders. The U.S.-Mexico border invited transgression since its very inception—even before the nebulous borderlands that bestrode the Nueces River eventually coalesced into a supposedly rigid national border. Once this border gained traction, it did not effectively barricade one space from the other. It did the opposite. Maybe this was the reason Mexicans often sought to plug transnational flows of people into their own state-building projects rather than pointlessly try to stop them.

Transnational mobility was the consequence of drawing stark dividing lines. Once enough people invested in the fiction of borders, they began to see major differences on either side of the divide. This was creative work, the result of a synergy produced between the people who made borders and the people who lived by them. But if distinctions created by borders were, in reality, an effect of state persuasion and performance working in tandem with the imaginations of people who bought into fantasies of difference created by imaginary lines, then there were still real consequences. If things were so different on the other side, why not cross over once life became overly stifling? The Mexican state—or rather, the officials, diplomats, and bureaucrats who invested in that state in the early to mid-nineteenth century—spared little effort in demonstrating their nation's immense difference from the Yankees on the other side. Those "*norteamericanos*" who inhabited the vast expanses of Texas on the other side of the Nueces and later the Rio Grande had strange ideas about race, servitude, and independence.[25]

We should remember these attitudes in our current age, the age of NAFTA—where some historians seek to imagine a new history of the continent that draws together Mexico, Canada, and the United States. When Mexicans referred to Anglos and even Tejanos as North Americans they wanted to set themselves apart. We might also want to exercise caution if we are to read a common history back on the continental mass that lay north of the Isthmus of Panama (and oddly includes neither Central America nor the Caribbean). Not everybody wanted to join forces with the northern colossus. Once Liberals came to power in the 1850s they veered closer to the "North Americans" who inhabited the vast reaches on the other side of the river, but they had terrible difficulty reversing all of the work that Mexican officials and mobile peoples had put into investing the international border with significant meaning separating Mexico from Texas and, later, the United States. Ever since, Mexico has remained apart. Its northern boundary is one of the most notable and rigid borders in the world. The border continues to separate two highly asymmetrical states, but it also continues to encourage movement across it as a result—even if today most of those flows of people go in the opposite direction.

This is the one thing that has changed more than anything else since the time period considered in this book. The international ebb and flow across the border has become increasingly unidirectional. This book has told the many stories of people who crossed the border not into the United States but out of the United States and into Mexico to find refuge. They may have crossed back and forth, but generally, as I have demonstrated, they spent a good deal of time in Mexico. I hope that my argument has denaturalized the seemingly inevitable flow of people from the

Mexican bank to the U.S. bank of the Rio Grande. But certainly from the postbellum period forward, many more human waves lapped the shores of Texas than those of Mexico. Border crossers into the United States imagined that opportunity could be found on the other side, just as their runaway peon ancestors did, and they crossed en masse from 1848 on. Later waves of Mexican migrants continued the creative work that so many mobile peoples of the nineteenth century put into reimagining the border, turning it from a line of national sovereignty into one of international liberty. Transborder Mexican workers who cross into the United States today have their roots (and, of course, their routes) in the nineteenth century. Runaway peons began crossing into the United States to escape debt and poverty in Mexico as early as the 1830s. After the coming of the border in 1848, they crossed in much larger numbers into Texas—and later the greater United States—engineering a "great system of roaming" in the trade. This system has only expanded across time and space. After the Civil War they notoriously headed into San Antonio on trains meant to carry cargo and then deserted their amos there, but they never stopped coming.[26] This network of laborers escaping Mexico to seek better opportunities on the other side has only grown across time and space—reaching from deep Texas into California, Chicago, and, most recently, New York City.

When we think of the border today, we do not think of state power but of the many violations of the state's supposed monopoly over power, violence, and movement at the international line. Hence the great anxiety felt by nationalist critics of globalization. We might see fences—more and more every year it seems. We might also see guard towers. We might even see citizen militias trying to protect their territory from outside "invaders" (of course, these days those citizen militias are more likely to be found on the U.S., not the Mexican, side of the border). But maybe these signs point to the state's weakness, its inability to lend the border the meaning it is supposed to have, that globalization happened long ago and there is little we can do to stop it.

This is not to say that the U.S.-Mexico border is ineffective in cordoning off one area from another. One only needs to look at the international fence separating Tijuana from San Diego. The southernmost points of San Diego are well-surveyed plains, buttressed by watchtowers and institutional edifices. The Mexican side, meanwhile, positively pushes up against the wall: buildings, walls, traffic, and, of course people fill the space of the city to its very limit, pushing against the border fence, hopeful of spilling over onto the other side. Most of that leakage is stopped—but not all of it. Enough people make it across, then keep in contact with family, friends, and peoples on the other side, building transnational networks that seep through the holes that develop in border fences and in the tunnels burrowed beneath them. These chains and networks remain in place, continuing to lend meaning to the border in ways that contradict the efforts of nation-states to build fortresslike walls and towers at their territorial limits.

So the border is still a line of liberty, although these days we might translate the term "liberty" into something more akin to "economic opportunity." In order to maintain autonomy, control of one's destiny, and to better the life of one's community, many must cross the border into a different national space. In the brave new world of the twenty-first century—simultaneously heavily bordered and oddly borderless—the meaning of the border as a line of opportunity is alive and well. Maybe even too alive and well, depending on who you ask. For many, crossing the line of liberty is no longer even an opportunity. It has become more like a duty. It is difficult to imagine that many Mexican schoolchildren dream of the day when they will cross illegally into the neighboring country, ferreted across the border by unscrupulous coyotes, and abandoned in deserts with meager, or no, supplies of food and water. Then, once on the other side, they must constantly live in fear of detection, deportation, and humiliation. But then again there have always been limits to the liberty people found by crossing the border.

NOTES

Introduction

1. Anderson, *The Conquest of Texas*, 118–20, 129; Reséndez, *Changing National Identities*, 57–58; Smith, *From Dominance*, 178–79.

2. *Gaceta del Gobierno de Tamaulipas*, June 26, 1841.

3. *Gaceta del Gobierno de Tamaulipas*, June 26, 1841; Anderson, *The Conquest of Texas*, 180, 192; Peña, *Lós bárbaros*, 84–88; Campbell, *Gone to Texas*, 177; Everett, *Texas Cherokees*, 114–15.

4. For the supposed neutrality of "exit" versus "voice" or resistance, see Hirshman, "Exit, Voice, and the State"; Brubaker, "Frontier Theses," 12–17.

5. See, e.g., Alcée Louis la Branche to John Forsyth, June 7, 1839, NARA Dispatches from U.S. Ministers to Texas, T728 Roll 1; Van Schendel, "Spaces of Engagement," 41.

6. "Bordered lands," see Adelman and Aron, "From Borderlands to Borders."

7. On border crossers and opportunity in the eastern borderlands, see Valerio-Jiménez, *River of Hope*; Schwartz, *Across the Rio*; Truett, *Fugitive Landscapes*; González Quiroga, "Los inicios"; Mora-Torres, *The Making of the Mexican Border*. For similar processes in the borderlands farther west, see Delgado, *Making the Chinese Mexican*; St. John, *Line in the Sand*; Jacoby, *Shadows at Dawn*; Meeks, *Border Citizens*; Martínez, *Troublesome Border*.

8. Kelley, "Mexico in His Head."

9. Works dealing with the immigrant tribes in Mexico include Mulroy, *Freedom on the Border*; Porter, *The Black Seminoles*, 137–75; Porter, "The Seminole in Mexico," 1–36; Rodríguez, *La Guerra*, 203–14; Vizcaya Canales, *Tierra de guerra viva*; del Moral, *Tribus olvidadas*; Miller, *Coacoochee's Bones*; Latorre and Latorre, *The Mexican Kickapoo Indians*.

10. See also Van Schendel, "Spaces of Engagement," 19; Adelman and Aron, "From Borderlands to Borders"; Díaz, *Border Contraband*; Katz, *The Secret War in Mexico*; Hu-Dehart, *Yaqui Resistance*.

11. Hämäläinen and Truett, "On Borderlands." "Great system of roaming," in Comisión Pesquisidora, *Reports of the Committee of Investigation*, 402–3.

12. For norteño attitudes, see Garza, *Breve historia de Nuevo León*; Herrera Pérez, *Breve historia de Tamaulipas*; Santoscoy, *Breve historia de Coahuila*; Torget, *Seeds of Empire*.

13. DeLay, *War of a Thousand Deserts*.

14. McGuinness, *Path of Empire*. The scholarship on race, populism, and nationalism in Latin America is vast. See, e.g., Knight, "Racism, Revolution, and Indigenismo."

15. Van Schendel, "Spaces of Engagement," 45; Baud and Van Schendel, "Toward a Comparative History," 218.

16. Garza, *Breve historia de Nuevo León*; Herrera Pérez, *Breve historia de Tamaulipas*; Santoscoy, *Breve historia de Coahuila*; Weber, *The Mexican Frontier*; Knight, *Mexico*, vol. 2; Valerio-Jiménez, *River of Hope*. For incorporation of the North in the late nineteenth century, see Nugent, *Spent Cartridges of Revolution*; Alonso, *Thread of Blood*; Vanderwood, *The Power of God*. For Texan identity, see Ramos, *Beyond the Alamo*; Reséndez, *Changing National Identities*, esp. chap. 5.

17. *Gaceta del Gobierno de Tamaulipas*, June 26, 1841; Campbell, *An Empire*, 25–27, 31; Francisco Pizarro Martínez to Secretario de Estado de Despacho de Relaciones, March 1, 1833, SRE, Cuaderno 5–16–8599.

18. Cornell, "Citizens of Nowhere," 351–74; For alternative points of view, see Schwartz, *Across the Rio to Freedom*; Baumgartner, "The Line of Positive Safety," 71–96; Jacoby, "The Alternative Borderlands," 209–39.

19. For the role Tejanos played in the winning of independence and beyond, see Ramos, *Beyond the Alamo*, 134–65; the essays in Poyo, *Tejano Journey*; Valerio-Jiménez, *River of Hope*, 130–34; Montejano, *Anglos and Mexicans*, Introduction.

20. Smith, *Dominance to Disappearance*, 3–9; Valerio-Jiménez, *River of Hope*, 25–29.

21. Valerio-Jiménez, *River of Hope*, 17–19; Ramos, *Beyond the Alamo*, 18; Tijerina, *Tejanos and Texas*, 5.

22. Alonzo, *Tejano Legacy*, 55; Valerio-Jiménez, *River of Hope*, 21, 27, 30–31, 35. This ethnic disappearance could also have been caused by disease, assimilation, or even the abolition of racial categories in official census reports after Mexican independence.

23. Valerio-Jiménez, *River of Hope*, 17–19.

24. On the isolation of these distant locations, see Reséndez, *Changing Identities*, 45–46, 53.

25. Tijerina, *Tejano Empire*, xx–xxi; Tijerina, *Tejanos and Texans*, 5–6.

26. Britten, *Lipan Apaches*, 169.

27. Ramos, *Beyond the Alamo*, 58, 67–69.

28. Ramos, *Beyond the Alamo*, 79.

29. Santoscoy, *Breve historia de Coahuila*, 106–7.

30. Tijerina, *Under the Mexican Flag*, 83–84.

31. Reséndez, *Changing Identities*, 40–41.

32. Ramos, *Beyond the Alamo*, 90–91. For a detailed analysis of Tejano, Coahuiltan, and Mexican attitudes toward Anglo settlers in Texas, see Torget, *Seeds of Empire*, esp. chaps. 2, 3, and 4.

33. Resdéndez, *Changing Identities*, 40–41; Ramos, *Beyond the Alamo*, 90–91.

34. Britten, *Lipan Apaches*, 173; Ramos, *Beyond the Alamo*, 69–72.

35. On social space, see Certeau, *The Practice of Everyday Life*; Lefebvre, *The Production of Space*; Yi-fu Tuan, *Space and Place*; David Ludden, "Presidential Address: Maps in the Mind and the Mobility of Asia; Juliana Barr, "Geographies of Power," 5–46.

1 / La Frontera del Norte

1. Capitán de la Companía de la Bahia to Mateo Ahumada, July 25, 1829, BCAH, Bexar Archives Microfilm, Roll 82.

2. On Indians in the northern frontier during the colonial period and beyond, see Weber, *The Mexican Frontier and the Spanish Frontier*. See Knaut, *The Pueblo Revolt of 1680*, for the term "buenos mexicanos."

3. Minor, *The Light Gray People*, 66–67, 72.

4. For the role of independent Indians in the making of the U.S.-Mexico borderlands on a regional scale, see Hämäläinen, *The Comanche Empire*; DeLay, *War of a Thousand Deserts*. I thank Brian DeLay for helping me think through these historiographical questions.

5. Britten, *Lipan Apaches*.

6. Britten, *Lipan Apaches*, xv; Minor, *Turning Adversity to Advantage*; Vizenor, *Manifest Manners*.

7. Minor, *The Light Gray People*, 18–20, 67–69 (quote on p. 31).

8. Weber, *Mexican Frontier*, 43–68; Weber, *The Spanish Frontier*, 171–75; Britten, *Lipan Apaches*, 129–99; Hämäläinen, *The Comanche Empire*, 107–41.

9. On the borderlands during the revolution, see Britten, *Lipan Apaches*, 173–75; Anderson, *The Conquest of Texas*, 44–58; Smith, *Dominance to Disappearance*, 97–106.

10. Here I use "creole" to denote the community of New World-born Euro-Americans that acted as a buffer between native peoples and the mother country. See Chasteen, "Americanos," 66–95, 153–55.

11. Smith, *Dominance to Disappearance*, 111.

12. Hämäläinen, *The Comanche Empire*, 183–87; Anderson, *The Conquest of Texas*, 19–22.

13. Minor, *The Light Gray People*, 68–69.

14. Reséndez, *Changing National Identities*, 15–22.

15. Gaspar López to José Felix Trespalacios, September 18, 1822 [note originally dated August 19], BCAH, Bexar Archives, Roll 72; Britten, *Lipan Apaches*, 177–78; Minor, *The Light Gray People*, 68.

16. My historicization of the term "civilization" was inspired by Mehta, *Liberalism and Empire*, esp. chap. 3; see Weber, *Bárbaros: Spaniards and Their Savages*, 15–20.

17. Hämäläinen, *The Comanche Empire*, 186; Hérnandez, *Mexican-American Colonization*, 34, 77, 90; Vizcaya Canales, *Tierra de guerra viva*, 25–26; José Manuel Herrera to capitán general de las provencias de oriente y occidente, August 17, 1822 [copy by Anastacio Bustamente, Saltillo, September 18, 1822], BCAH, Eberstadt Collection, William A Buckner Papers, Box 3J451.

18. The scholarship on Indian power and mobility in the west before and after the arrival of Euro-American frontiers is growing. See, e.g., Calloway, *One Vast Winter Count*; Hämäläinen, *The Comanche Empire*; White, *The Middle Ground*; Brooks, *Captives and Cousins*. On power and mobility, see esp. DeLay, *War of a Thousand Deserts*; LaDow, *The Medicine Line*.

19. On alternative geographic epistemologies in theory, see David Ludden, "Presidential Address: Maps in the Mind and the Mobility of Asia," 1057–78; Weber, *The Spanish Frontier*, 11. On the problems mobile people represented to states, see Scott, *The Art of Not Being Governed*.

20. Minor, *The Light Gray People*, 68.

21. José Manuel Herrera to capitán general de las provencias de oriente y occidente, August 17, 1822, [copy made by Anastacio Bustamente, Saltillo, September 18, 1822], BCAH, Eberstadt Collection, William A Buckner Papers, Box 3J451.

22. Ramón Músquiz, Felipe Enrique Neri, et al. to Eugenio Navarro, April 21, 1824, BCAH, Bexar Archives, Roll 76.

23. Vizcaya Canales, *Tierra de guerra viva*, 26–28; Santoscoy, *Breve historia de Coahuila*, 161–62.

24. Santoscoy, *Breve historia de Coahuila*, 161–63; on violence and character on the Mexican frontier, see Nugent, *Spent Cartridges of Revolution*; Alonso, *Thread of Blood*.

25. Hämäläinen, *The Comanche Empire*, 191–93 (quote on p. 192); Smith, *Dominance to Disappearance*, 119.

26. Viszaya Canales, *Tierra de guerra viva*, 31; Hämäläinen, *The Comanche Empire*, 252.

27. Berlandier, *Journey to Mexico*, 248–49.

28. Vizcaya Canales, *Tierra de guerra viva*, 31–32.

29. Vizcaya Canales, *Tierra de guerra viva*, 33; Minor, *The Light Gray People*, 70.

30. Vizcaya Canales, *Tierra de guerra viva*, 32, 35; for the language of family, see Hernández, *Mexican-American Colonization*, 25, 35, 64.

31. Vizcaya Canales, *Tierra de guerra viva*, 34, 35; Garza, *Breve historia de Nuevo León*, 132.

32. José de La Garza to comandante general de Coahuila y Tejas, March 7, 1829, BCAH, Bexar Archives, Roll 120.

33. Vizcaya Canales, *Tierra de guerra viva*, 40.

34. Rodríguez, *La guerra*, 140–41, 144.

35. *Mercurio del Puerto de Matamoros*, May 29, 1835.

36. *Mercurio del Puerto de Matamoros*, May 29, 1835.

37. Spicer, *Cycles of Conquest*, 281; Weber, *The Mexican Frontier*, 152. On seasonal grants of peace as a nomadic tactic to maintain independence, see Rodríguez, *La guerra*, 115–38.

38. For the role of blacks and Latino/as in the revolt, see Campbell, *An Empire for Slavery*, 33–34; Campbell, *Gone to Texas*, 116–19; Ramos, *Beyond the Alamo*, 81–133.

39. Herrera Pérez, "Reflexiones de una década." Ramos, *Beyond the Alamo*, 136–38, on Bexar County.

40. Herrera Pérez, *El norte de Tamaulipas*, 58–62, for more on the role played by Indians in the northeastern frontier.

41. Minister of Texas to John Forsyth, August 27, 1836, NARA, Dispatches from U.S. Ministers to Texas, 1836–1845, Vol. 1, July 18, 1836–July 5, 1842, NARA, Roll 1 T728.

42. Weber, *The Mexican Frontier*, 94–97. On bows and arrows, see García, *Guerra y frontera*, 49.

43. DeLay, *War of a Thousand Deserts*; Hämäläinen, *The Comanche Empire*. The great Comanche Empire had substantial horse wealth at its foundation. DeLay's

argument about the politics of revenge motivating raiding is a little less convincing than Hämäläinen's fundamentally economic one.

44. "Treaty between Texas and Lipan Indians," January 8, 1838, TIP, Vol. 1.

45. For a similar case of a boundary separating people from resources from those without and the many effects of that contrast, see Sahlins, *Boundaries*.

46. Truett, *Fugitive Landscapes*.

2 / Racial Fault Lines

1. Alberdi, *Bases y puntos de partida*, 14–17.

2. Everett, *The Texas Cherokees*, 27–29 (quote on p. 27); Smith, *Dominance to Disappearance*, 115–16.

3. Nugent, *Spent Cartridges of Revolution*; Alonso, *Thread of Blood*; Peña, *Los bárbaros del norte*.

4. José de la Garza to Antonio Elozua, January 8, 1828, BCAH, Bexar Archives, Roll 110; Sr. Comandante Militar de Nacagodoches to Comandante General de Coahuila y Tejas, February 5, 1828, BCAH, Bexar Archives, Roll 111.

5. The term "frontier of inclusion" was coined by Mikesell, "Comparative Studies in Frontier History," 62–74; Weber and Rausch, *Where Cultures*, xx; Weber, *The Mexican Frontier*, 278; for another example in Latin America using the "frontier of inclusion" model, see Black, *The Frontier Mission*, 161.

6. Everett, *The Texas Cherokees*, 40.

7. Reséndez, *Changing National Identities*, 48–49; Smith, *Dominance to Disappearance*, 115–16.

8. Pulte and Altom, "The Mexican Cherokees," 35–37.

9. After the "cultural turn" race became a paramount concern of historians of Latin America. For a representative sample of this scholarship, see the essays in Appelbaum et al., *The Idea of Race*; McGuinness, *Path of Empire*; Knight, "Racism, Revolution, and Indigenismo." For an interpretation of Mexican immigration policy and race, see Hérnandez, *Mexican American Colonization*, 31–32, 38.

10. For "soft racism," see Saxton, *The Rise and Fall of the White Republic*, 260–62; Sales, *The Slumbering Volcano*, 29–31. For a classic study on the mutability of racial categories in Latin America, see Gutiérrez, *When Jesus Came*, 193–206, 285–92.

11. Hernández, *Mexican American Colonization*, 60–62; Knight, *Mexico*, vol. 2, 329–30.

12. *Texas Sentinel*, January 15, 1840; Anderson, *The Conquest of Texas*, 76–77, 94, 112, 119–20; Smith, *Dominance to Disappearance*, 134, 139, 156.

13. D. W. Smith to John Forsyth, July 1, 1836, NARA, Consuls in Matamoros, Microcopy Vol. 281; Everett, *The Texas Cherokees*, 80–81 (quote on p. 81).

14. Anderson, *The Conquest of Texas*, 164–68.

15. D. W. Smith to John Forsyth, January 6, 1837, NARA, Consuls in Matamoros, Microcopy Vol. 281.

16. Anderson, *The Conquest of Texas*, 411 n.

17. *Texas Sentinel*, January 15, 1840 [refers to an earlier event]; Anderson, *The Conquest of Texas*, 177–79; Smith, *Dominance to Disappearance*, 166–67; Clarke, *Chief Bowles and the Texas Cherokees*, 80–81.

18. R. A. Trio to Alceé La Branche, February 13, 1838, NARA, Dispatches from U.S. Ministers to Texas, 1836–1845, Roll 1 T728.

19. On the Cherokees, see Reagan, "The Expulsion of the Cherokees," 38–46; Clark, *Chief Bowles*; *Texas Sentinel*, January 15, 1840; Everett, *The Texas Cherokees*, 87; David Lamar to David G. Burnet, A. S. Johnston, Thomas J. Rusk, Houston, June 27, 1839, TIP, vol. 1 p. 68; Alceé La Branch to John Forsyth, June 7, 1839, and March 5, 1840, NARA, Dispatches from U.S. Minsters to Texas, July 18, 1836–July 5, 1842, Roll 1 T728.

20. Everett, *The Texas Cherokees*, 108–9.

21. Anderson, *The Conquest of Texas*, 179; del Moral, *Las tribus olvidadas*, 31–32. Ujiya found a colony of Maroons at San Cranto, discussed below; see *Cherokee Advocate*, June 26, 1845, reprinted in *Chronicles of Oklahoma*, 36–41.

22. D. H. Smith to John Forsyth, January 1, 1840, NARA, Consuls in Matamoros, Microcopy Vol. 281.

23. *Texas Sentinel*, February 19, 1840.

24. On the turbulent republic, see Torget, *Seeds of Empire*, chap. 5.

25. *Texas Sentinel*, quote from June 13, 1840. On the Cherokees, see also *Texas Sentinel*, April 8, 1840; December 16, 1840; January 16, 1841; and January 30, 1841,

26. Thomas Farrow Smith to Anson Jones Warren, Fannon County, April 22, 1842, p. 126, TIP, Vol. 1.

27. Torget, *Seeds of Empire*, chaps. 3, 4; Ramos, *Beyond the Alamo*, chap. 3.

28. *Atalaya*, [Ciudad Victoria, Tamaulipas], March 7, 1835

29. *Atalaya*, November 26, 1836.

30. *Texas Sentinel*, January 25, 1840.

31. Mariano Arista to Ministro de Guerra, January 24, 1840, fs. 225–28, SEDNA, Vol. 1544.

32. Mariano Arista to Ministro de Guerra, February 20, 1840, fs. 229–30, SEDNA, Vol. 1544; Ministro de Guerra to Arista, March 16, 1840, fs. 234–35, SEDNA, Vol. 1544.

33. Mariano Arista to Ministro de Guerra, January 24, 1840, fs. 225–28, SEDNA, Vol. 1544.

34. Saxton, *The Rise and Fall of the White Republic*, 226–27; Nugent, *Spent Cartridges*; Alonso, *Thread of Blood*.

35. Mariano Arista to Ministro de Guerra, January 24, 1840, SEDNA, Vol. 1544, fs. 225–28.

36. Everett, *The Texas Cherokees*, 115.

37. Ujiya, *Cherokee Advocate*, 36–41; Everett, *The Texas Cherokees*, 114–16; Pulte and Altom, "The Mexican Cherokees," 35–37.

38. Francisco Pizarro Martínez to foreign minister in Washington, February 22, 1836, fol. 52, AEMEUA SRE, L26 E12; Reséndez, *Changing Identities*, 207–8; Smith, *Dominance to Disappearance*, 150–51.

39. D. H. Smith to John Forsyth, January 1, 1840, NARA, Consuls in Matamoros, Microcopy 281.

40. Rafael de la Fuente to the secretary of the governor of Coahuila, May 5, 1841 in *Gaceta del Gobierno de Tamaulipas*, June 26, 1841; Anderson, *The Conquest of Texas*, 118–20, 129; Alceé Louis La Branche to John Forsyth, June 7, 1839, NARA, Dispatches from U.S. Ministers to Texas, 1836–45, Roll 1 T728, July 18, 1836, to July 5.

41. *Gaceta del Gobierno de Tamaulipas*, June 26, 1841 [reprints Rafael de la Fuente to governor of department Monclova, May 5, 1841]

42. "Tratado de Paz entre Espopogne Imaya, Jefe de la Tribu Mascogue Dalgi y el Gobierno Mexicano para Establecerse en el Rio Sabinas, 1843," December 22, 1843; and "Lista Que Comprende Las Tribues Que Dalgi Ymaya a Nombre de Espopogne Ymaya Pone A Disposición Del Supremo Gobierno De La República, Diciembre De 1843," in Rodríguez, *Historias de resistencia y exterminio*, 159–62.

43. *Gaceta del Gobierno de Tamaulipas*, June 26, 1841 [Copy of letter: Rafael de la Fuente to governor of department Monclova, May 5, 1841].

44. Tocqueville, *Democracy in America*, 345–47.

3 / "Impatient for the Promised Freedom"

1. Torget, *Seeds of Empire*, 98–137; Campbell, *An Empire for Slavery*, 10–35.

2. Smithwick, *Recollections of Old Texas Days*, 36–37.

3. I thank Alice Baumgartner and her paper, "Fugitive Slaves, Free Soil, and the Contest over Sovereignty in the U.S.-Mexico Borderlands, 1829–60," presented at the Remaking North American Sovereignty Conference in Banff, Alberta, July 2015, for this observation.

4. Schwartz, *Across the Rio to Freedom*; Kelley, "Mexico in His Head," 709–23; Jacoby, "The Alternative Borderlands," 209–39; Jacoby, *The Strange Career of William Ellis*; Baumgartner, "The Line of Positive Safety," 71–96.

5. Cornell, "Citizens of Nowhere," 351–74. Cornell writes that a number of African Americans faced imprisonment in Mexico and that Mexican officials did not fulfill the promise of freedom for runaway slaves. Mexicans may not have had the resources to do everything they could for runaway slaves, but I found quite a contrasting attitude in my research.

6. Green, *The Mexican Republic*, 119; Campbell, *An Empire for Slavery*, 25–26.

7. José María de Letona to S. Aguirre, May 25, 1831, AGEC, Siglo XIX, C51 F9 E2 2F; Campbell, *An Empire for Slavery*, 26–27.

8. Ramos, *Beyond the Alamo*, 98.

9. Raptor: Ramón Músquiz to Comisario de Policía de Gonzales, June 6, 1832, BCAH, Bexar Archives, Roll 150; Músquiz to Green DeWitt and Ezekial Williams, March 27, 1832, BCAH, Bexar Archives, Roll 150; Músquiz to Gaspar Flores, Bexar, BCAH, Bexar Archives, Roll 150; DeWitt to Músquiz, May 30, 1832, BCAH, Bexar Archives, Roll 150; Torget, *Seeds of Empire*, 97–136.

10. José Miguel de Arciniega to Músquiz, June 12, 1832, BCAH, Bexar Archives, Roll 150; Torget, *Seeds of Empire*, 129.

11. Torget, *Seeds of Empire*, 131.

12. Ward, "Pre-Revolutionary Activity," 214; Lack, *The Texas Revolutionary Experience*, 183–207; Howe, *What Hath God Wrought*, 666.

13. Henson, *Juan Davis Bradburn*, 94–97. Interestingly enough, another slave, Harriett, tried to help Travis escape after his imprisonment by Bradburn.

14. Juan José Hernández to Músquiz, May 18, 1832, BCAH, Bexar Archives, Roll 150.

15. See Torget, *Seeds of Empire*, chap. 3.

16. Ezekial Hays to Manuel Mier y Terán [copy and translations into Spanish by Jorge Fisher, Matamoros, 10 August 1831], BCAH, Bexar Archives, Roll 150.

17. Barr, *Black Texans*, 14–15; Bishop, "LAW OF APRIL 6, 1830," *Handbook of Texas Online* (http://www.tshaonline.org/handbook/online/articles/nglo1), accessed November 1, 2013.

18. Campbell, *An Empire for Slavery*, 29. On resistance from the Texas-Coahuila congress, see Torget, *Seeds of Empire*, 131–36.

19. Francisco Pizarro Martínez to Mexican Charge of Affairs, February 8, 1832, AEMEUA, Leg. 20, Exp. 9.

20. Letter reprinted in Howren, "Cause and Origins of the Decree of April 6, 1830," 395–98.

21. Francisco Pizarro Martínez al encargado de los negocios de los EUA, February 2, 1832, AEMEUA, Leg. 20, Exp. 9.

22. Pizarro to José María Tornel, Feb 24, 1832, SRE, AEMEUA, Leg. 20, Exp. 9.

23. Manuel de Mier y Terán to Pizarro Martínez, February 3, 1831, SRE, AEMEUA, Leg. 20, Exp. 9.

24. Application of Andrés Dortola to Seccíon de Gobierno, February 8, 1825, fs. 28–29, AGN, Gobernación, C 58 E 12; For gradual emancipation of slavery in Veracruz, especially around Jalapa, see Caroll, *Blacks in Veracruz*; Bennett, *Africans in Colonial Mexico*; Schwartz, *Across the Rio to Freedom*, 8.

25. Lundy, *A Circular*, 14.

26. Herrera Pérez, *Breve historia de Tamaulipas*, 58–65, 87–88; Herrera Casasús, *Raíces africanas*, 52, 54; Valerio-Jiménez, *River of Hope*, 32–33, tables. For a model of creolization and hispanicization of Africans in Veracruz, see Carroll, *Blacks in Veracruz*, 112.

27. Report to Ciudad Victoria, November 14, 1845, AHMAT, Fondo Justicia, Caja 34, Exp. 10; Census, August 23, 1841, f. 214, AGN, Archivo Cartas de Seguridad, GD 129 Vol. 16; Lundy, *Travels*, 43.

28. Census, August 23, 1841, fol. 214, AGN, Archivo Cartas de Seguridad, GD 129 Vol. 16.

29. Census, August 23, 1841, fol. 214, AGN, Archivo Cartas de Seguridad, GD 129 Vol. 16; Lundy, *Travels*, 147.

30. Lundy, *Travels*, 119.

31. Lundy, *Travels*, 160–62.

32. Lundy, *Travels*, 143, 151–52; Lundy, *A Circular*, 7, 10; Valerio-Jiménez, *River of Hope*, 57. For examples of black thought on freedom, see Holt, "The Essence of the Contract," 33–60; Foner, *Reconstruction*, 102–6; Scott, *Degrees of Freedom*, 118–21.

33. Valerio-Jiménez, *River of Hope*, 281–82; Salazar, "La historia del oro blanco," 87–92. For interpretive community, see Kelley, "Mexico in His Head" 709–23; Blassingame, *The Slave Community*.

34. Pizarro Martínez to Secretario de Estado de Despacho de Relaciones, March 1, 1833, SRE, Folder 5–16–8599.

35. Addington, "Slave Insurrections in Texas," 411; Campbell, *An Empire for Slavery*, 10–35; Kelley, *Los Brazos de Dios*, 100–101.

36. On revolt and flight during the revolution, see Addington, "Slave Insurrections in Texas," 412; Campbell, *An Empire for Slavery*, 10–35; Kelley, "Mexico in His Head," 15; Tyler, "Fugitive Slaves in Mexico," 2.

37. *Diario del Gobierno de la República de Mexico*, November 28, 1836. As late as 1854 Juan Almonte retained two "free men of color" as servants, William Turley Blake and Augustine Watts. See William S. Marcy to Juan N. Almonte, July 28, 1854, NARA, Notes to the Foreign Legations in the United States from the Department of State, Roll 70.

38. Schwartz, *Across the Rio to Freedom*, 24–25.

39. Tyler, "Fugitive Slaves," 2; R. M. Potter, "Escape of Karnes and Teal," 73–78.

40. *Clarksville Northern Standard*, May 22, 1844.

41. Nance, *After San Jacinto*, 232–33.

42. Kelley, "Mexico in his Head," 712–13. My understanding of bottom-up alternative geographic epistemologies owes much to de Certeau, *The Practice of Everyday Life*; Soja, "The Socio-Spatial Dialectic," 207–25; Tuan, *Space and Place*; Hahn, *A Nation under Our Feet*, 13–62. On "territorialities," see Hogue, *Metis and the Medicine Line*, 5–6.

43. Comandante de Mier to Pedro Ampudia: testimony of Eduardo Ros (an Anglo-African), April 14, 1840, fs. 51–52, SEDNA, Vol. 1544; Mariano Arista to Ministro de Guerra, May 7, 1840, f.130, SEDNA, Vol. 1544.

44. *El Universal 1848–1855*, April 28, 1850 [Mexico City]; *El Monitor Republicano*, May 21, 1847 [Mexico City].

45. Vasconcelos, *La Raza Cósmica*.

46. *El Universal, 1848–1855*, February 11, 1849.

47. *El Monitor Republicano*, May 21, 1847.

48. Mariano Arista to Juan Manuel Maldonado, October 17, 1850, fs. 926–28, FCMO AGEC, Ficha 825 C8 F2 E27 F138 *(tribus de paz)*; Antonio Juáregui to Maldonado, November 5, 1852, AGEC, FCMO, C20 F1 E9 1F.

49. Nance, *After San Jacinto*, 127–28.

50. Lack, "The Córdova Revolt," 89–109.

51. Nichols, *Now You Hear My Horn*, 36.

52. McCutchan, *Mier Expedition Diary*, 67–70.

53. Enderle, "Plaza pública y discurso regionalista," 43–73.

54. Herrera Pérez, "Reflexiones de una década de frontera indefinida," 338–40; Valerio-Jiménez, "Neglected Citizens and Willing Traders," 251–96; Reséndez, *Changing National Identities*, 117–23, on the dual draw of Mexican institutions and American capital for those in the borderlands.

55. Johnson, *Soul by Soul*, 135–61, for how whiteness was constructed out of the slave market.

56. Stapp, *The Prisoners of Perote*, 43–44; Chapman, *The News from Brownsville*, 23, says that some merchants took up a subscription to help the suffering prisoners.

57. De Shields, *Border Wars of Texas*, 193.

58. Stapp, *The Prisoners of Perote*, 55.

59. *Spirit of the Times*, May 16, 1846.

60. "Proyecto de la ley constitucional de garantias individuales," *Siglo xix*, February 14, 1849; my thanks to Alice Baumgartner for the reference.

61. I never found the evidence that Sarah Cornell did, proving that Mexican authorities returned runaways to their masters and imperiled their freedom: Cornell, "Citizens of Nowhere," 351–74.

62. José Antonio Quintero to Secretaría de Relaciones Exteriores, November 27, 1839, f. 230, AGN, Archivo Cartas de Seguridad, GD 129 Vol. 16; José María Bocanegra to the governor of the state of Tamaulipas, December 18, 1843, f. 74, AGN Archivo Cartas de Seguridad, GD 129 Vol. 37; José Ignacio Gutiérrez to Bocanegra, January 25, 1844, f. 75, AGN Archivo Cartas de Seguridad, GD 129 Vol. 37.

63. Jesús Cárdenas to Mariano Arista, August 30, 1849, fs. 76–77, SEDNA, Vol. 3072; Arista to General De la Vega, August 29, 1849, fs. 81–83, SEDNA, Vol. 3072.

64. Rómulo Díaz de la Vega to Arista, August 18, 1849, fs. 43–45, SEDNA, Vol. 3072.

65. Jesús Cárdenas to Ministro de Relaciones Exteriores, February 14, 1849, fs. 132–133, SRE, LE 1094; *El Bien Público* [Matamoros], June 18 1849.

4 / A "Great System of Roaming"

1. Rafael Vidaurri to Eugenio García, April 30, 1834, BCAH, Bexar Archives, Roll 163.

2. "Remitido," *El Latigo de Tejas* [Matamoros], August 19, 1844.

3. Reséndez, *The Other Slavery;* Kiser, *Borderlands of Slavery,* chap. 3; Smith, *Freedom's Frontier,* chap. 3.

4. On "Indian" peons in Mexico, *San Antonio Daily Express,* June 25, 1860; Montgomery, *Eagle Pass,* 34–35; James Gadsden to Luis de la Rosa, [without date, 1854–1855?], SRE, cuaderno 6-18-42. On ethnic origins: Knight, *Mexico: The Colonial Era,* 131–37; Weber, *The Spanish Frontier,* 91–97; Brooks, 124–28. On Tlaxcalans: Santoscoy, *Breve historia de Coahuila,* 44–55; Valerio-Jiménez, *River of Hope,* 35–37, 58–64.

5. The scholarship on Mexican peonage is still sparse. Besides Reséndez, see Knight, *Mexico,* vol. 2, 98–102; Knight, "Mexican Peonage," 41–74; Bauer, "Rural Workers in Spanish America," 43–48. For a comparative study in the near-Mexican North, see Cross, "Debt Peonage Reconsidered," 473–95. On peon armies, see Van Young, "Beyond the Hacienda," 230–31. Kiser, *Borderlands of Slavery,* was going to press as I finished my final draft.

6. Herrera Pérez, "El Clan Fronterizo," 25–61.

7. Brooks, *Captives and Cousins,* 240–47. See *Siglo xix,* July 23, 1852, and July 22, 1854, for two late examples of shepherds exposed to attacks in Nuevo León.

8. Harris, *A Mexican Family Empire,* 228–29.

9. Lamar, "From Bondage to Contract," 293–327.

10. Harris, *A Mexican Family Empire,* 207–30, esp. 228–29. Quote from Winders, *Mr. Polk's Army,* 180.

11. Mora-Torres, *The Making of the Mexican Border,* 154–59; Delay, *The War of a Thousand Deserts,* 317–18; González Quiroga, "Los trabajadores mexicanos," 127. My thanks to Andrés Reséndez for his insight on the passing of debt.

12. Olmsted, *A Journey through Texas,* 334–35.

13. José María G. Cuellar to Secretaría del Gobierno, April 15, 1856, AGENL, Militares, C121; Santos Benavides to Vidaurri, March 9, 1856, Vidaurri Correspondence, AGENL.

14. *La Sociedad, Periódico Político y Literario* [Mexico City], June 17, 1858.

15. Winders, *Mr. Polk's Army,* 180–81.

16. Romero, *A Study of Subjects,* Vol. 1, 507–11; Winders, *Mr. Polk's Army,* 180.

17. *Texas State Times,* June 24, 1854, refers to 25 cents a day as the typical wage.

18. Thompson, *Recollections of Mexico,* 7.

19. *Siglo xix,* November 12, 1850; *El Universal* [Mexico City], February 11, 1849, April 28, 1850, March 19 and 25, 1851, and October 21, 1852; *La Sociedad, Periódico Político y Literario* [Mexico City], June 17, 1858.

20. On the intensely capitalistic nature of American slavery, see Johnson, *River of Dark Dreams;* and Baptist, *The Half Has Never Been Told.*

21. Which is of course exactly what allowed the system to function in a republican society. For racial dimensions of American republicanism, see Morgan, *American*

Slavery, American Freedom, 316–37; Saxton, *The Rise and Fall of the White Republic*, 41–45; David Roediger, *The Wages of Whiteness*, 43–64.

22. *El Universal 1848–1855*, March 8, 1849.

23. Adelman and Aron, "From Borderlands to Borders," 815–16.

24. González Quiroga, "Los trabajadores mexicanos," 127.

25. González Quiroga, "Los inicios de la migración laboral," 350; José María Girón to Zachary Taylor, June 10, 1846, BCAH, Matamoros Archives, 2Q279, Volume LV; José María Girón to Zachary Taylor, June 17, 1846, BCAH, Matamoros Archives, 2Q279, Volume LV; Ford, *Rip Ford's Texas*, 214–15; "Remitido," August 19, 1844, *El Latigo de Tejas*.

26. Winders, *Mr. Polk's Army*, 184; May, "Invisible Men," 463–77.

27. Chapman, *The News from Brownsville*, 18–19.

28. González Quiroga, "Los inicios de la migración laboral," 351; Ford, *Rip Ford's Texas*, 214–15.

29. *Siglo xix*, January 10, 1856.

30. This evidence is drawn from, SRE folder no. 7-12-63 and was collected by Alice Baumgartner—to whom I am very grateful for sharing it with me.

31. DeLay, *War of a Thousand Deserts*, 297–311; Hernández, *Mexican American Colonization*, 97–165. For more examples of migration, see *Corpus Christi Star*, September 19, 1848; September 26, 1848; and October 31, 1848. For debt peonage in wider political discourse, see Kiser, "A 'charming name for a species of slavery.'"

32. *Corpus Christi Star*, September 19, 1848; September 26, 1848; and October 31, 1848.

33. *Texas State Gazette*, September 30, 1854.

34. Ford, *Rip Ford's Texas*, 214.

35. *Southwestern American*, May 12, 1852; Montgomery, *Eagle Pass*, 34.

36. Thompson, *Recollections of Mexico*, 7; Montgomery, *Eagle Pass*, 36–8, 143.

37. Olmsted, *A Journey through Texas*, 334–35.

38. Olmsted, *A Journey through Texas*, 333. See *El Latigo de Tejas*, extra, June 26, 1849, for the printed declaration.

39. *Southwestern American*, November 17, 1852; Ford, *Rip Ford's Texas*, 215; Fornell, "Texas Filibusterers," 411–28; Shearer, "The Callahan Expedition, 1855," 431–51; Tyler, *Santiago Vidaurri*; Chance, *Carvajal*, 87–94.

40. Furber, *The Twelve Month Volunteer*, 210–11; Harris, *A Mexican Family Empire*, 219; Denning, *Mechanic Accents*.

41. "Remitido," August 19, 1844, *El Latigo de Tejas*.

42. Emilio Langberg to Santiago Vidaurri, September 1, 1855, AGENL, Vidaurri Correspondence; González Quiroga, "Los inicios de la migración laboral," 352.

43. Valerio-Jiménez, *River of Hope*, 185–87.

44. González Quiroga, "Los trabajadores mexicanos," 127.

45. Coronel Clark to the Alcalde of Matamoros, September 26, 1846, BCAH, Matamoros Archive, 2Q279, Volume LIII.

46. Díaz, *Border Contraband*, 23–24; Valerio-Jiménez, *River of Hope*, 263.

47. *El Constitutional* [Tamaulipas], September 16, 1848.

48. Testimony of Andrés García in Nuevo Laredo, July 25, 1873, f. 91, SRE, LE 1590.

49. Montejano, *Anglos and Mexicans*, 18–19; Testimony of Agustín Díaz, Nuevo Laredo, July 3, 1873, f. 183, SRE LE 1590. A failed extradition treaty attempt dated

to 1850, but Texans found it unacceptable because it contained no provision for the return of runaway slaves.

50. Testimony of Andrés García, Nuevo Laredo, July 25, 1873, f. 93, SRE LE 1590.

51. Testimony of Cesario de Luna, Candela, June 28, 1873, f. 83, SRE LE 1590; Testimony of Lorenzo Dominguez, Piedras Negras, August 22, 1873, f. 100, SRE LE 1590; Testimony of Agustín Díaz, Nuevo Laredo, July 3, 1873, f. 83, SRE LE 1590.

52. Testimony of José Mara Ramírez, Piedras Negras, August 22, 1873, fs. 99–100, SRE LE 1590.

53. On Chapa Guerra, see Mariano Arista to Ministro de Relaciones, February 14, 1850 [copy made February 18, 1850], fol. 30, AEMEUA, Leg. 32, Exp. 3; Luis de la Rosa to John M. Clayton, February 26, 1850 [copy, March 4, 1850] AEMEUA, Leg. 32, Exp. 3; Report: "Sobre emisiones del punto llamado el Ranchito y asesinato del C. Juan Chapa Guerra" [1872], f. 27, SRE, Fondo Comisión Pesquisidora del Norte, Caja 4.

54. Testimony of Clemente Zapata, Nuevo Laredo, July 25, 1873, fs. 93–94, SRE, LE 1590.

55. Testimony of Lorenzo Guevara, Nuevo Laredo, August 22, 1873, f. 98 SRE, LE 1590.

56. Testimony of André García, Nuevo Laredo, July 25, 1873, f. 91, SRE, LE 1590.

57. Testimony of José María García, Sabinas Hidalgo, June 21, 1873, f. 79, SRE, LE 1590.

58. Testimony of Luciano Ramírez, Matamoros, September 24, 1873, fs. 200–201, SRE, LE 1590.

59. Testimonies of C. Luis Ramos and Andrés Escamilla, Nuevo Laredo, July 2, 1873, fs. 182–185, SRE, LE 1590.

60. De la Rosa al Ministro de Relaciones Exteriores en Washington, (Reservada) August 27, 1851, f. 427, SRE, AEMEUA, L33 E1.

61. *El Constitutional,* November 25, 1850.

62. Francisco V. Fernandez to Ayuntamiento de Matamoros, July 31, 1848, AHMAT, Fondo Ilustre Ayuntamiento, C9 E35, Carpeta que encierra oficios de los Jueces de Policía.

63. Montgomery, *Eagle Pass,* 38–39.

64. *Boletín Oficial* (Monterrey), June 22, 1861.

65. *Siglo xix,* July 7, 1852.

66. *Siglo xix,* November 12, 1855.

67. *El Constitutional,* September 16, 1850 [reprints letter from Jésus Cárdenas to Jorge Hophannn, minstro de relaciones].

68. De la Rosa to Secretaría de Relaciones Exteriores, May 19, 1850, f. 112, AEMEUA, SRE, L32 E2; *El Constitutional* September 16, 1850, and September 30, 1850.

69. *Goliad Express,* July 4, 1857.

70. *El Constitutional,* September 16, 1850.

71. Katz, "Labor," 7–8. Katz also argues that conditions on northern haciendas greatly liberalized during the Porfiriato due to increased competition for laborers, and with the opportunities in railroads and mining in addition to the cross-border labor market (31–36). See also Katz, *The Secret War in Mexico.*

72. Ayuntamiento of Matamoros to Ayuntamiento of Nuevo Laredo, June 21, 1850, f. 236, SRE, LE 1595; de la Rosa to Minister of Foreign Relations, May 19, 1850, f. 112, SRE, AEMEUA, L32 E2.

73. Katz, "Labor."

74. Comisión Pesquisidora, *Reports of the Committee of Investigation*, 402–3.

75. Comisión Pesquisidora, *Reports of the Committee of Investigation*, 403.

5 / Warriors in Want

1. Nicolas Mendoza to Señor Comandante Militar de Monterrey, February 16, 1850; Nicolas Mendoza to Comandante General de Nuevo León, May 18, 1850; AGENL, Militares Caja 57; Miller, *Coacoochee's Bones*, 127–29.

2. Mulroy, *Freedom on the Border*, 57–107; Porter, *The Black Seminoles*, 137–75; Porter, "The Seminole in Mexico," 1–36; Rodríguez, *La guerra*, 203–14; Santoscoy, *Breve historia de Coahuila*, 205–208; Vizcaya Canales, *Tierra de Guerra Viva*, 185–205, 212–17; del Moral, *Tribus olvidadas de Coahuila*; Miller, *Coacoochee's Bones*, 139–73.

3. Juan Manuel Maldonado to Antonio Juáregui, July 24, 1850, fs. 851–852, AGEC, FCMO, Ficha 825, C8 F2 E27 F138.

4. Contract written up by Maldonado in San Fernando, July 24, 1850, f. 849, AGEC, FCMO, C8 F2 E27 F138; Minister of War, October 17, 1850 [copy], fs. 927–928, AGEC, FCMO, Ficha 825, C8 F2 E27.

5. Juáregui to Arista, July 27, 1850, f. 861, AGEC, FCMO, Ficha 825, C8 F2 E27 F138.

6. Maldonado to Juáregui, October 26, 1850, f. 941, AGEC, FCMO, Ficha 825, C8 F2 E27 F138.

7. Maldonado to Juáregui, November 20, 1850, fs. 1012–1014, AGEC, FCMO, Ficha 825, C8 F2 E27 F138.

8. Juáregui to Arista, December 27, 1850, fs. 1036–1037, AGEC, FCMO, Ficha 825, C8 F2 E27 F138; Arista to Juáregui, December (illegible date), 1850, AGEC, FCMO, Ficha 1134, C10, F8 E112 1F.

9. Maldonado to Juáregui, July 13, 1850, AGEC, FCMO, Ficha 805, C8 F1 E7 2F.

10. Maldonado to Juáregui, October 2, 1850, AGEC, FCMO, fs. 939–942, C8 F2 E27 F 138; Laura to Governor of Nuevo León, October 18, 1850, AGENL, Concluidos.

11. Porter, *The Black Seminoles*, 35.

12. Alcalde de Músquiz to governor of Coahuila, March 8, 1852, SRE, LE 1596.

13. Maldonado to Juáregui, September 11, 1852, AGEC, FCMO, Ficha 1953, C19 F3 E20 3F, for a typical report on Comanche raiders.

14. Juáregui and José María García to Secretary of War, June 30, 1852, fs. 115, 119, SEDNA, Vol. 3157; *Texian Advocate*, January 3, 1852.

15. Mulroy, *Freedom on the Border*, 71, 109.

16. On traveling to Mexico City in 1852, see Robles to Juáregui, May 28, 1852, AGEC, FCMO, Ficha 1785, C17 F4 E31 2F; Robles to Juáregui, May 4, 1852, AGEC, FCMO, Ficha 1762, C17 F1 E18 1F.

17. Maldonado to Juáregui, July 18 [contains copy of Wilson to Maldonado, July 16, 1851], AGEC, FCMO, Ficha 1486, C14 F4 E 53 9F; Robles to Juáregui, August 14, 1851, AGEC, FCMO, Ficha 1519, C14 F6 E86 1F.

18. Coacoochee to governor of Nuevo León, October 20, 1853, AGENL, Militares, Caja 96.

19. Coacoochee to governor of Nuevo León, no date, AGENL, Militares, Caja 96.

20. Maldonado, Rosas, to Juáregui, August 4, 1851, AGEC, FCMO, Ficha 1507, C14 F5 E77 3F. On capture of assimilated Comanches, see Maldonado to Juáregui, August (date illegible), 1851, AGEC, FCMO, Ficha 1232, C14 F3 E74 3F.

21. Coacoochee to governor of Nuevo León, no date, AGENL, Militares, Caja 96.

22. For an example of this oft-used term, see Arista to the Minister of War, February 20, 1840, fs. 229–230, SEDNA, Vol. 1544.

23. Juáregui to Arista, December 27, 1850, fs. 1035–1036, Ficha 825, AGEC, FCMO, C8 F2 E27 F138.

24. Juáregui to Arista, December 29, 1850, fs. 1035–1036, AGEC, FCMO, Ficha 825, C8 F2 E27 F138, AGEC, FCMO; Maldonado to Juáregui, December 17, 1850, fs. 1035–1036, AGEC, FCMO, Ficha 825, C8 F2 E27 F138.

25. "Apreciaciones del Ayuntamiento de Cuatro Ciénegas al Gobierno del Estado sobre los Seminoles y su Jefe Gato del Monte," reprinted in Rodríguez, *Historias de resistencia y exterminio*, 176–78.

26. Maldonado to Juáregui, August 13, 1850, fs. 894–895, AGEC, FCMO, Ficha 825, C8 F2 E27 F138.

27. For sartorial differences, see Mulroy, *Freedom on the Border*, 68, and pictures on 90–91.

28. "Decree of Corecuchi [sic]," March 28, 1851 reprinted in Rodríguez, *Historias de resistencia y exterminio*, 107.

29. Maldonado to Juáregui, August 13, 1850, fs. 889–890, and Maldonado to Juáregui, August 26, 1850, f. 1891, AGEC, FCMO, Ficha 825, C8 F2 E27 F138.

30. Alcalde de Músquiz to Doroteo Nava, December 21, 1852, SRE, LE 1596.

31. Alcalde de Músquiz to governor of Coahuila, September 6, 1852, SRE, LE 1596.

32. Juáregui, Moras, to Minister of War, July 27, 1850, f. 861, AGEC, FCMO, Ficha 825, C8 F2 E27 F138.

33. Alcalde de Músquiz to Pablo Espinosa, July 10, 1854, SRE, LE 1596.

34. Deutsch, *No Separate Refuge*, 38.

35. Maldonado to Juáregui, July 13, 1850, AGEC, FCMO, C8 F1 E7 2F, AGEC, FCMO; Governor of Coahuila to Juáregui, November 5, 1850, fs. 961–962, AGEC, FCMO, Ficha 825, C8 F2 E27 F138.

36. Governor of Coahuila to Santiago Rodríguez, August 10, 1850, f. 874, AGEC, FCMO, Ficha 825, C8 F2 E27 F138.

37. Alcalde de Músquiz to governor of Coahuila, April 12, 1852, SRE, LE 1595; Aguila to Santa Anna, Dec. 31, 1853, AGEC, FSXIX, C8 F14 E6 2F.

38. *La Unión* [Mexico City], 1853, p. 2; *El Republicano*, June 14, 1856.

39. Deutsch, *No Separate Refuge*, 48–49, on the way that the godparent system created community ties across kith and kin.

40. Alcalde Músquiz to Jesús Garza González, July 21, 1859, f. 55, SRE, LE 1596, for the Kickapoo Pedro Vidaurri; The preceptorship of the school changed hands from Juan Vidaurri to Juan Francisco Váldez in May 1856: Alcalde de Músquiz to governor, May 16, 1856, f. 16, SRE, LE 1596.

41. Maldonado, to Juáregui, December 7, 1852, AGEC, FCMO, Ficha 2068, C20 F5 E44 2F.

42. Maldonado to Juáregui, December 28, 1850, fs. 1052–1056, AGEC, FCMO, Ficha 825, C8 F2 E27 F138; Maldonado, Monclova Viejo, to Juáregui, January 16, 1851, AGEC, FCMO, Ficha 1167, C11 F3 E27 1F.

43. Ignacio Galán to Maldonado, September 10, 1850, AGEC, FCMO, Ficha 931, C9 F3 E40 10F; Maldonado to Juáregui, September 14, 1850, AGEC, FCMO, Ficha 931, C9 F3 E40 10F; Juáregui to Maldonado, September 24, 1850, AGEC, FCMO, Ficha 931, C9 F3 E40 10F.

44. Manuel Robles to Juáregui, January 3, 1851, f. 994, AGEC, FCMO, Ficha 825, C8 F2 E27 F138, records an early complaint about poverty after the governor told the Seminoles to muster into National Guard units.

45. Maldonado to Juáregui, March 27, 1851, AGEC, FCMO, Ficha 1302, C12 F6 E64 3F; Ayuntamiento of Guerrero to governor of Coahuila, April 4, 1851, AGEC, FSXIX, C3 F7 E6 1F.

46. Maldonado to Juáregui, March 30, 1851, AGEC, FCMO, Ficha 1311, C12 F6 E73 2F.

47. President of Ayuntamiento de Guerrero to Governor of Coahuila, March 4, 1851 [copy dated March 17], AGEC, FCMO, Ficha 1280, C12 F 3 E 42 3F; Rafael de la Fuente to Juáregui, Saltillo, March 17, 1851, AGEC, FCMO, Ficha 1280, C12 F 3 E 42 3F; Maldonado to Ayuntamiento of Guerrero, March 4, 1851, f. 41, SRE, LE 1596.

48. Juáregui to Maldonado, April 21, 1851, AGEC, FCMO, Ficha 1342, C13 F5 E25 3F.

49. Juáregui to Maldonado, May 31, 1851, AGEC, FCMO, Ficha 1432, C13 F15 E115 3F.

50. Maldonado to Juáregui, July 18, 1851 [contains copy of Wilson to Maldonado, July 16, 1851], AGEC, FCMO, Ficha 1486, C14 F4 E 53 9F; Robles to Juáregui, August 14, 1851, AGEC, FCMO, Ficha 1519, C14 F6 E86 1F.

51. Tomás Martínez Zulaica [alcalde de Rosas] to Juan José Galán, June [date illegible],1851, AGEC, FCMO, Ficha 1462, C14 F2 E 29 1F.

52. La Patria [Saltillo], July 19, 1851; Maldonado to Juáregui, AGEC, FCMO, July 15, 1851, Ficha 1477, C 14 F 3 E44 2F.

53. Maldonado to Juáregui, July 18, 1851 [contains copy of Wilson to Maldonado, July 16, 1851], AGEC, FCMO, Ficha 1486, C14 F4 E 53 9F; Robles to Juáregui, August 14, 1851, AGEC, FCMO, Ficha 1519, C14 F6 E86 1F; Maldonado to Juáregui, August 14, 1851, fs. 50–51, SRE, LE 1596.

54. On Papicua remaining behind: Maldonado to Juáregui, July 18, 1851, AGEC, FCMO, Ficha 1486, C14 F4 E53 9F; La Patria, August 9, 1851; Latorre and Latorre, The Mexican Kickapoo Indians, 263.

55. Maldonado to Juáregui, August 14, 1851, fs. 50–51, SRE, LE 1596.

56. Juan Zuazua to Santiago Vidaurri, April 30, 1853, AGENL, Militares, Caja 89.

57. Peña, Lós bárbaros del norte, 84–88. On Comanche raids into Nuevo León, see also DeLay, War of a Thousand Deserts, 75–76, 164, 175, 188.

58. Alcalde de Abasolo to governor of Coahuila, September 13, 1852 [copy September 27, 1852], AGEC, FCMO, Ficha 1979, C19 F5 E46 3F.

59. Governor of Coahuila to Juáregui, October 7, 1852, AGEC, FCMO, Ficha 1979, C19 F5 E46 3F. On Mescalero parties: Alcalde of Músquiz to senior prefect of the district, April 9, 1855 [Copy 1873], f. 120, SRE, LE 1596; Ujiya, Cherokee Advocate, 34; La Patria, September 25, 1852. On women in Comanche raiding parties, see Lehmann, Nine Years among the Indians, 168, 174.

60. Alcalde of Músquiz to Alcalde of Abasolo, October 4, 1852, f. 9, SRE, LE 1596; De la Fuente, governor of Coahuila, to Secretary of Defense, January 1, 1853 [copy February 10, 1853], f. 268, SEDNA, Vol. 3151; Maldonado to Secretary of Defense, February 10, 1853, f. 268, SEDNA, Vol. 3151; Rafael de la Fuente to Secretary of Defense, September 27, 1852, f. 268, SEDNA, Vol. 3151; Juáregui to Secretary of War, October 20, 1853, f. 271, SEDNA, Vol. 3151.

61. Alcalde de Músquiz to Doroteo Nava, December 21, 1852, f. 10, SRE, LE 1596.

62. First Constitutional Court of the Village of Mina to the Governor of Nuevo León, April 28, 1853 [copy August 15, 1873], f. 266, SRE, LE 1591.

63. Ramón Marcena to governor of Nuevo León, October 17, 1853, AGENL, Militares, Caja 96; Alcalde de Músquiz to prefecto de distrito, May 10, 1854, SRE, LE 1595.

64. Olmsted, *A Journey through Texas*, 345–46, 350–52.

65. *El Prisma*, October 14, 1857.

66. Santos Benavides to Vidaurri, February 20, 1859, Vidaurri Correspondence, AGENL; Felix Treviño to the governor, Salinas Victoria, N.L, February 19, 1859, AGENL, Militares, Caja 135.

67. Primero alcalde de Músquiz to Secretario del Gobierno, September 6, 1857, and September 28, 1857 [duplicated 1873], SRE, LE 1596; Mulroy, *Freedom on the Border*, 85–86, 107; Juan Zamora to Luis Villareal, August 18, 1858, AGENL, Militares, Caja 133.

68. Maldonado to Juáregui, January 2, 1851, f. 1038, AGEC, FCMO, Ficha 825, C8 F2 E27 F138.

69. *Western Texian*, November 18, 1852. For attempts made on John Horse in Coahuila, see Manuel Flores to the Governor's Secretary, Coahuila, September 27, 1851, AGEC, FSXIX, C9 E3 F5; Juan Manuel Maldonado, Rio Grande, to Ayuntamiento de la Villa de Guerrero, February 23, 1851, AGEC, FSXIX, C9 E3 F5; José Antonio Arredondo to the Commander at Fort Duncan, September 20, 1851, and September 21, 1851 [copy certified by Maldonado, Rosas], Governor's Papers, Folder 25, TSA; Mulroy, *Freedom on the Border*, 75; *Southwestern American*, November 24, 1852; Arredondo to Juáregui, November 5, 1852, AGEC, FCMO, Ficha 2033, C20 F1 E9 1F; Arredondo to Juáregui, November 5, 1852, AGEC, FCMO, Ficha 2033, C20 F1 E9 1F, AGEC, FCMO; Maldonado to Juáregui, September 27, 1852, AGEC, FCMO, Ficha 1575, C14 F10 E 142 1F.

70. Maldonado to Juáregui, June 21, 1853, AGEC, FCMO, Ficha 2213, C21 F14 E123 8F.

71. Mulroy, *Freedom on the Border*, 76.

72. Mulroy, *Freedom on the Border*, 73.

73. Langberg, *Itinerario*, 35.

74. Francisco Castañeda, to secretary of governor, Coahuila, October 5, 1854, AGEC, FSXIX, C8 F7 E9 3F.

75. Packet: Plaza de Monterrey, "Causa instruida contra los capitanes de caballeria D. Tomás Santa Cruz y Don Jesús María Chisman," April 18, 1856, fs. 8–9, AGENL, Militares, Caja 121.

76. Packet: Plaza de Monterrey, "Causa instruida contra los capitanes de caballeria D. Tomás Santa Cruz y Don Jesús María Chisman," April 19, 1856, f. 9, AGENL, Militares, Caja 121.

77. Vidaurri to Minister of development, colonization, industry and commerce, September 14, 1856, f. 108, SRE, LE 1596.

78. Francisco Treviño to Vidaurri, June 4, 1856, AGENL, Militares, Caja 124.

79. Francisco Treviño to Vidaurri, June 4, 1856, AGENL, Militares, Caja 124.

80. Manuel G. Bejan to Alcalde del Saltillo, December 12, 1860, AMS, Caja 103/1 E 118; Commander del Canton de Rio Grande to Vidaurri, May 24, 1861, f. 87, SRE, LE 1596; Mulroy, *Freedom on the Border*, 85–86, 107.

6 / The Line of Liberty

1. Olmsted, *A Journey through Texas*, 123–24. Olmsted wrote this volume to convince his audience of the evils of slavery and to champion the cause of the Free Soil

platform; William Carrigan also argues that the frontier of West Texas had a destabilizing effect on slavery, in "Slavery on the Frontier," 63–86.

2. Foner, *Free Soil, Free Labor, Free Men*; *San Antonio Daily Herald*, September 26, 1857.

3. Olmsted, *A Journey through Texas*, 123–24, 323–24.

4. Knapp, "Parliamentary Government," 65–87.

5. "Mexican Affairs," *Southwestern American*, November 17, 1852; Ford, *Rip Ford's Texas*, 250; Kelley puts the number nearer 4,000: "Mexico in His Head," 33.

6. Cornell, "Citizens of Nowhere," fn. 52.

7. "CENSUS AND CENSUS RECORDS," *Handbook of Texas Online* (http://www.tshaonline.org/handbook/online/articles/ulco1), accessed July 23, 2013; "SLAVERY," *Handbook*, (http://www.tshaonline.org/handbook/online/articles/ypso1), accessed July 23, 2013.

8. Campbell, *An Empire for Slavery*, 59; "Society with slaves": see Berlin, *Many Thousands Gone*, 93–109.

9. W. P. Reyburn to F. A. Hatch, November 21, 1859, House Ex. Doc. No. 52, p. 65, cited in Taylor, *An American-Mexican Frontier*, 33.

10. Campbell, *An Empire for Slavery*, 64, for an alternate viewpoint. On the pardo Llaneros, see Chasteen, *Americanos*, 127–30; and in Argentina, see Andrews, *The Afro-Argentines of Buenos Aires*.

11. *Clarksville Northern Standard*, November 11, 1854.

12. Petition to S. A. Maverick and the members of Bexar Delegation, December 20, 1851, TSA, Box 100–357.

13. Hudson, *Mistress of Manifest Destiny*.

14. On Jefferson's vision, see Johnson, *River of Dark Dreams*, 23–27; O'Sullivan, "Annexation," 7.

15. James Gadsdsen to Luis de la Rosa, [1854?], f. 42, SRE, Cuaderno 6–18–42; and "Circular to consuls of the United States acting under Exequaturs of the Republic of Mexico," June 25, 1854, Dispatches from United States Consuls in Matamoros, 1826–1906, NARA, microcopy 281, Roll 2, T18; Thomas Hirgan to William D. Marcy, November 25, 1854, Dispatches from United States Consuls in Matamoros, 1826–1906, NARA, microcopy 281, Roll 2, T18; de la Rosa to Secretaría de Relaciones Exteriores, May 19, 1850, f. 112, SRE, AEMEUA, Leg. 32, Exp. 2.

16. Thomas Hirgan to William D. Marcy, November 25, 1854, Dispatches from United States Consuls in Matamoros, 1826–1906, NARA, microcopy 281, Roll 2, T18; Cornell, 351–74.

17. Filación de Alejandro Tardé, Buenaventura, October 4 and 11, fs. 186–188, AGN, Archivo Cartas de Seguridad, Vol. 113.

18. Presidencia municipal de Nadadores to the secretaría de gobierno de Coahuila, January 12, 1853, AGEC, FSXIX, C1 F2 E6.

19. Knapp, "Parliamentary Government," 65–87.

20. William S. Marcy to Juan N. Alamonte, July 28, 1854, and November 21, 1855, Records of the Department of State, Dispatches from the United States Commissioners in Mexico, NARA, No. 99, Roll 69.

21. Thomas Hirgan to William D. Marcy, November 25, 1854, Dispatches from United States Consuls in Matamoros, 1826–1906, NARA, microcopy 281, Roll 2, T18.

22. Rippy, "Border Troubles," 91–111; Shearer, "The Carvajal Disturbances," 201–30; Chance, *Carvajal*.

23. *Defensor de Tamaulipas*, extra, June 26, 1849; Chance, *Carvajal*, 87–94.

24. An Ex-Member of the U.S. Senate to Luis de la Rosa, August 15, 1851, fs. 29–30, SRE, AEMEUA, Leg. 33, Exp. 1; An Ex-Senator of the United States to Percy Doyle, [copy dated and signed Luis de la Rosa], August 21, 1851, fs. 430–432, SRE, AEMEUA, Leg. 33, Exp. 1.

25. Santiago Vidaurri to Ayuntamiento of Matamoros, Monterrey, November 5, 1851, AHMAT, Caja 11, Exp. 24.

26. *Houston Telegraph and Texas Register*, September 5, 1851.

27. On the subversive will of runaways, see Johnson, *River of Dark Dreams*, 217–34; Rothman, *Slave Country*, 100, 109–10, 131, 157, for instances of runaways in open rebellion.

28. Johnson, *River of Dark Dreams*, 209–44.

29. Serapio Fragoso, secretaría del gobierno del Estado de Coahuila, to presidente municipal, Guerrero, August 15, 1851, AGEC, AMG, Caja 5, Exp. 54.

30. Jesús Castillón to the Secretary of the Governor of Coahuila, August 1, 1851, AGEC, FSXIX, Caja 8, Exp. 1.

31. *Nueces Valley* [Corpus Christi], March 18, 1854.

32. *Texas State Times*, March 15, 1856.

33. Johnson, *River of Dark Dreams*, 214.

34. *Dallas Herald*, June 21, 1856.

35. *Indianola Bulletin*, July 27, 1855.

36. *Washington Texas Ranger and Lone Star*, November 30, 1854.

37. *Washington Texas Ranger and Lone Star*, June 16, 1855.

38. *Southern Intelligencer*, April 27, 1859.

39. *LaGrange Monument*, October 16, 1850.

40. Olmsted, *A Journey through Texas*, 326.

41. *LaGrange Monument*, January 8, 1851.

42. For runaways from this region, see, e.g., *La Grange Texas Monument*, August 31, 1853, and October 19, 1853; *Texas State Gazette*, December 21, 1850, August 5, 1851, September 18, 1851, and March 26, 1853; *Washington Texas Ranger and Lone Star*, July 23, 1853; *Texas State Times*, September 15, 1855, and September 21, 1856.

43. *Houston Telegraph and Texas Register*, January 15, 1845; *Houston Telegraph and Texas Register*, January 22, 1845; *Indianola Bulletin*, May 31, 1855.

44. *Bastrop Advertiser*, March 14, 1857.

45. *Victoria Texian Advocate*, September 18, 1852.

46. *Gonzales Inquirer*, August 13, 1853.

47. *Victoria Texian Advocate*, June 12, 1852.

48. For a description of these towns, see Olmsted, *A Journey through Texas*, 240–66.

49. Olmsted, *A Journey through Texas*, 324.

50. Marcy, *Thirty Years*, 14–15; Frobel, *Seven Years of Travel*, 422.

51. *Texas State Gazette*, September 9, 1854, counts two drownings of runaways in one week, one near Eagle Pass and another farther downriver; see *Nueces Valley Weekly*, July 17, 1858.

52. Fuller, "Ben Kinchelow," 100–103; and *Houston Tri-Weekly* [no date: 1861?]; Reyburn to Hatch, November 21, 1859, House Ex. Doc. No. 52, p. 65, cited in Taylor, "Fugitive Slaves," 33.

53. Herrera Casasús, *Raíces africanas*, 71, cites *Noticas Estadística del departamento de Tamaulipas, formado por el Comisionado del Supremo Gobierno, agrimesnor e hidromensor D. Apolinar Márquez, 1852 s.p.i.*; for population of Matamoros: Cook, *Mexican Brick Culture*, 30.

54. Herrera Casasús, *Raíces africanas*, 71.

55. Johnson, *River of Dark Dreams*, 4–5, 31–38.

56. *El Rifle de Tamaulipas*, February 23, 1861, 6.

57. Vinson and Restall, *Black Mexico*; for an overview, see Vinson and Vaughn, *Afroméxico*.

58. *Texas State Gazette*, September 30, 1854.

59. Olmsted, *A Journey through Texas*, 326.

60. *Texas State Gazette*, October 12, 1850.

61. *San Antonio Daily Ledger*, August 16, 1861.

62. Montgomery, *Eagle Pass*, 139–40.

63. Johnson, *River of Dark Dreams*, 176–209; Johnson, "On Agency," 113–24.

64. Investigation by Primer Alcalde de Reynosa, March 8, 1853 [copy 1873], fs. 5–6, SRE, Fondo Comisión Pesquisidora del Norte, Caja 3, Exp. 13.

7 / Bordering on the Illicit

1. Investigation of the alcalde of Matamoros, August 1850 [copy 1873], fs. 1–3, SRE, Fondo Comisión Pesquisidora del Norte, Caja 3, Exp. 13.

2. Leonardo Espinosa to Sr. Juez del Primer Instancia, Matamoros, September 14, 1850, AHMAT, Justicia, Caja 35-A, Exp. 911.

3. The way that borders create contrasts has long been a theme of borderlands history. See, e.g., Sahlins, *Boundaries*. Also useful in thinking through national contrasts that manifest themselves at the border are many of the borderlands works already cited as well as Baumgartner, "The Line of Positive Safety," 71–96; Abraham and Van Schendel, "Introduction," 1–38.

4. "More Slaves Piloted to Mexico by Mexican Peons," *Indianola Bulletin*, May 31, 1855.

5. James Gasdsen, no date [probably 1854], f. 42, SRE, 6–18–42; On the Carvajal arrangements, see "Mexican Affairs," *Southwestern American*, November 17, 1852.

6. For a similar reading of a different situation see Baumgartner, "Positive Safety."

7. "Mexican Affairs," *Southwestern American*, November 17, 1852.

8. *Texas Ranger*, February 25, 1859.

9. For a similar argument related to lynching, see Carrigan, *The Making of a Lynching Culture*.

10. Hartley, *A Digest of the Laws of Texas*, 188, 784–85.

11. Directive from Peter Bell, September 17, 1851, BCAH, WPW, Correspondence Concerning the Texas Rangers, Vol. 2, 1851–1856, 2R291.

12. Juan Manuel Maldonado to the Ayuntamiento of Guerrero, September 23, 1851, AGEC, FCMO, C14 F9 E131.

13. Maldonado to president of the Ayuntamiento of Guerrero, February 23, 1851, AGEC, FSXIX, C9 F5 E3.

14. *LaGrange Texas Monument*, January 29, 1851.

15. *The Ranchero*, June 8, 1861.

16. Luis de la Rosa to John M. Clayton, March 1850, f. 43, SRE, AEMEUA, Leg. 32, Exp. 2. On the assault on Sanguijuela: José María Lacunza to Luis de la Rosa, February 12, 1850, fs. 15–16, SRE, AEMEUA, Leg. 28, Exp. 3; Santiago Rodríguez to the Minister of Foreign Relations, January 31, 1850 [duplicate], fs. 15–16, SRE, AEMEUA, f. 17, Leg. 28, Exp. 3; Luis Fernandez to José Andrés Cervera, January 31, 1850 [duplicate], fs. 15–16, SRE, AEMEUA, fs. 18–19, Leg. 28, Exp. 3.

17. Maldonado to Francisco Barela, January 24, 1850, AGEC, FCMO, Ficha 396, C5 F2 E20.

18. Barela to Manuel Maldonado, January 24, 1850 [copy January 28, 1850], AGEC, FCMO, Ficha 392, C5 F2 E16 5F; Barela to Maldonado, January 26, 1850 [copy January 28, 1850], AGEC, FCMO, Ficha 392 C5 F2 E16 5F.

19. Antonio Juáregui to Mariano Arista, Dec. 27, 1850, fs. 1036–1037, AGEC, FCMO, Ficha 825, C8 F2 E27 F138; Arista to Juáregui, December 26, 1850 [copy], AGEC, FCMO, Ficha 1134, C10 F8 E112 1F; Maldonado to Juáregui, January 24, 1851, fs. 979–982, AGEC, FCMO, Ficha 825 C8 F2 E27.

20. Juáregui to Arista, December 27, 1850, fs. 1036–1037, AGEC, FCMO, Ficha 825, C8 F2 E27 F138; *Texas Ranger,* date missing on microfilm, 1850; *Texian Advocate* [Victoria], November 7, 1850; Miller, *Coacoochee's Bones,* 133–35; Luther, *Ranger James Callahan,* 147.

21. Robert DuVal to Peter H. Bell, October, 20, 1850, CAH, WPW, Correspondence Regarding Texas Rangers 1846–1850 Vol. 1, 2R291; *Texas Ranger,* date missing, 1850; "Wild Cat," *La Grange Texas Monument,* December 4, 1850; *Victoria Texas Advocate,* November 7, 1850; Miller, *Coacoochee's Bones,* 133.

22. Olmsted, *A Journey through Texas,* 106.

23. Maldonado to the Ayuntamiento de la villa de Guerrero, September 26, 1851, AGEC, FSIX, C9; Declaration of the President of the Ayuntamiento of Guerrero, September 26, 1851, AGEC, FSXIX C9. For sources on invasion from Nuevo León, see AGENL, Militares, Caja 48.

24. Langberg, *Itinerario,* 30.

25. Alcalde of Laredo to Governor of Tamaulipas, January 17, 1850 [copy 1873], f. 239, SRE, LE 1595; Governor of Tamaulipas to the alcalde of Laredo, March 2, 1850 [copies 1873], f. 239, SRE, LE 1595.

26. Investigation of alcalde of Mier, July 7, 1851 [copy 1873], fs. 8–10, SRE, Fondo Comisión Pesquisidora del Norte, Caja 3, Exp. 13.

27. Campbell, *An Empire for Slavery,* 204–5.

28. Investigation of alcalde of Mier, July 7, 1851 [copy 1873], fs. 8–10, SRE, Fondo Comisión Pesquisidora del Norte, Caja 3, Exp. 13; Patterson, *Slavery and Social Death.*

29. Investigation of alcalde of Mier, July 7, 1851 [copy 1873], fs. 8–10, SRE, Fondo Comisión Pesquisidora del Norte, Caja 3, Exp. 13.

30. José María de la Garza al Ayuntamiento de Guerrero, January 16, 1850, AGEC, FSXIX, C1 F9 E2 1F; José María de la Garza, Nava, to Ayuntamiento de Guerrero, February 8, 1850, AGEC, FSXIX, C1 F9 E2 1F.

31. Testimony of Benjamin Thomas, Jesús Rodríguez, Vicente Garza, and Pedro Guerrero, witnesses Jesús Flores, A. Luis Benavides, J. Juan de la Garza, March 18, 1851, AGEC, FSXIX, C3 F8 E8 7F, FSXIX AGEC.

32. Testimony of Benjamin Thomas, Jesús Rodríguez, Vicente Garza, and Pedro Guerrero, witnesses Jesús Flores, A. Luis Benavides, J. Juan de la Garza, March 18, 1851, AGEC, FSXIX, C3 F8 E8 7F, FSXIX AGEC.

33. Manuel Flores to secretary of governor, June 27, 1851, AGEC, FSXIX, C6 F6 E3 2F.

34. The vecinos of the North and their attitudes to the Anglo Texans and slavery are hard to discern. Thus far we can only tell that many of the officials who manned the frontier until the Revolution of Ayutla tried to instill the twin causes of patriotism and abolitionism in their populations. And citizen militias offer the only evidence that these attempts were successful at all.

35. *El Constitutional* [Mexico City], December 6, 1851.

36. Justo Treviño, Investigation by juzgado del Primer Instancia del Distrito del Norte de Tamaulipas, January 1859 [1873], fs. 3–5, Fondo Comisión Pesquisidora del Norte, SRE, C3 E13.

37. Justo Treviño, Investigation by juzgado del Primer Instancia del Distrito del Norte de Tamaulipas, January 1859 [1873], fs. 3–5, Fondo Comisión Pesquisidora del Norte, SRE, C3 E13.

38. Montgomery, *Eagle Pass*, 36–40.

39. Montgomery, *Eagle Pass*, 36–40.

40. Hudson, *Mistress of Manifest Destiny.*

41. On early racial discourse in Texas, see Foley, *White Scourge,* 4–10; de León, *They Called Them Greasers.*

42. Olmsted, *A Journey through Texas,* 162–63.

43. Maldonado to Antonio Juáregui, March 7, 1850, AGEC, FCMO, C5 F6 E92 F3; Juáregui to Maldonado, March 18, 1850, AGEC, FCMO, C5 F6 E92 F3.

44. For "pelados," see *Southern Intelligencer,* January 6, 1858; for "sheep and stock," see *Texas State Times,* May 18, 1858.

45. *Gonzales Inquirer,* September 17, 1853.

46. *El Bejareño* [San Antonio], February 7, 1855.

47. Ramos, *Beyond the Alamo,* argues that Tejanos began to suffer a decline in the aftermath of the Texas secession. But the situation became more volatile and violent in the 1850s. My research confirms this periodization. I believe that a large influx of Mexicans and Anglos into the state during that decade also contributed to this uptick in violence. See chaps. 6 and 7 above.

48. Olmsted, *A Journey through Texas,* 163

49. Montejano, *Anglos and Mexicans,* 28–29; Hernández, *Mexican American Colonization,* 74–76. On the Gonzales convention to expel peons, see *Texas State Gazette,* September 30, 1854.

50. Petition to S. A. Maverick and the members of Bexar Delegation, December 20, 1851, TSA, Box 100–357.

51. Montejano, *Anglos and Mexicans,* 28–29; Olmsted, *A Journey through Texas,* 163–64; *Bastrop Advertiser,* March 14, 1857.

52. *Gonzales Inquirer,* August 13, 1853.

53. *Gonzales Inquirer,* September 17, 1853.

54. *Texas State Times,* September 27, 1856.

55. Lack, "Slavery and Vigilantism," 1–20.

56. *Texas State Gazette,* October 14, 21, and 28, 1854.

57. *Texas State Times,* October 7, 1854.

58. *Texas State Times,* October 14 and 21, 1854; Olmsted, *A Journey through Texas,* 163.

59. Comandante Subalterno de Nuevo Laredo to Gefe [*sic*] Político del Distrito del Norte de Tamaulipas, September 25, 1851 [copy 1873], f. 228, SRE, LE 1595.

60. *La Grange Texas Monument,* September 26, 1854.

61. *Bastrop Advertizer,* June 5, 1858, 2; italics in original.

62. Baumgartner, "Positive Safety," 71–96.

8 / "Not Even Seeming Friendship"

1. Minor, *Turning Adversity to Advantage.* On "shadow economy," see Minor, *The Light Gray People,* 75–76.

2. For the military roots of Indian independence, see DeLay, *War of a Thousand Deserts*; Hämäläinen, *The Comanche Empire*; Calloway, *One Vast Winter Count.*

3. Minor, *The Light Gray People,* 53, 55, 75, 111.

4. DeLay, "Independent Indians," 35–68.

5. On division between Upper and Lower Lipans, see Minor, *The Light Gray People,* 98; Britten, *Lipan Apaches,* 183; Schilz, *Lipan Apaches in Texas,* 471; Opler, "Lipan and Mescalero Apaches in Texas," 259; Sjoberg, "Lipan Apache Culture," 79; Maestas, "Culture and History," 326. In the context of the Texas Revolt, see Filisola, *Memoirs for the History of the War in Texas,* 161.

6. Britten, *Lipan Apaches,* 193; TIP Vol. 1, 164–65; Opler, "Lipan and Mescalero Apaches in Texas," 49; "A Testimonial of John Castro's Friendship for the People of Texas," March 28, 1843, in Barker and Williams, *The Writings of Sam Houston,* Vol. 1; Minor, *The Light Gray People,* 107.

7. Britten, *Lipan Apaches,* 196–99; TIP, Vol. 2, 38–41, 112–17; 336–38, 368–70, 411–12, 422–23.

8. Minor, *Turning Adversity to Advantage,* 153–55; Luther, *Ranger James Callahan,* 111.

9. *Corpus Christi Star,* October 10, 1848, 2.

10. *Nueces Valley,* May 25, 1850.

11. DeLay, *War of a Thousand Deserts,* and Hämäläinen, *The Comanche Empire,* masterfully demonstrate the way that independent Indians hijacked the borderlands. But in ascribing such agency to stateless raiders we should not overlook the strength of Mexican militias.

12. García, "A Medieval Frontier," 182–41; Peña, *Los bárbaros del norte,* 90–110; *La Patria,* November 9, 1850 [copy of contract with immigrant tribes signed by the Mexican minister of foreign relations].

13. Rodríguez, *La guerra,* 134.

14. Rodríguez, *La guerra,* 155–57(quote from July 1850); Minor, *Turning Adversity to Advantage,* 157, 170.

15. *La Patria,* August 3, 1850 [note from San Fernando de las Rosas, July 20, 1850]; Mariano Arista to Antonio Juáregui, September 6, 1850, AGEC, FCMO, Ficha 911, C9 F2 F.20 2F. Coacoochee, interestingly enough, acted as their advocate: Juan Manuel Maldonado to Francisco Castañeda, September 9, 1850 [copy San Fernando, September 9, 1850], AGEC, FCMO, Ficha 916 C9 F2 E25 4F; Maldonado to Ignacio Galán, September 9, 1850 [copy September 9, 1850], AGEC, FCMO, Ficha 916, C9 F2 E25 4F, AGEC, FCMO; Maldonado to Juáregui, August 15, 1850, AGEC, FCMO, Ficha 850, C8 F5 E52 3F, AGEC, FCMO. On the Painted Wood Band, see Minor, *The Light Gray People,* 108.

16. Maldonado to Juáregui, September 9, 1850, and Juáregui to Castañeda, September 9, 1850 [copy San Fernando, September 9, 1850], AGEC, FCMO, Ficha 916, C9 F2 E 25

4F; Galán to Maldonado, September 9, 1850 [copy San Fernando, September 9, 1850], AGEC, FCMO, Ficha 916 C9 F2 E 25 4F.

17. Maldonado to Juáregui, July 3, 1850, AGEC, FCMO, Ficha 784, C7 F9 E118 2F.

18. Arista to Juáregui, September 6, 1850, AGEC, FCMO, Ficha 911, C9 F2 E20 2F; Manuel Robles to Juáregui, February 19, 1851, AGEC, FCMO, C11 FC10 E 80 1F.

19. Maldonado to Juáregui March 22, 1851, AGEC, FCMO, Ficha 1296 C12 F5 E58 2F.

20. Minor, *Turning Adversity to Advantage*, 169–70.

21. John H. Rollins, May 8, 1850, Texas Agency, U.S. Bureau of Indian Affairs, letters received, 1847–1859, NARA, Reel 1; September 30, 1850, Texas Agency, U.S. Bureau of Indian Affairs, letters received, 1847–1859, NARA, Reel 1.

22. Maldonado to Júaregui, September 22, 1852, AGEC, FCMO, Ficha 1969 C19 F4 E35 26F.

23. Rodríguez, *Guerra*, 153, 71; Juliana Barr, *Peace Came in the Form of a Woman*, 35–42; Minor, *Turning Adversity to Advantage*, 170; Maldonado to Juáregui, October 21, 1852, AGEC, FCMO, Ficha 1969, C19 F4 E35 26F.

24. Maldonado to Juáregui, October 21, 1852, AGEC, FCMO, Ficha 1969 C19 F4 E35 26F.

25. Rodríguez, *Guerra,* 159–60.

26. Maldonado to Juáregui, November 24, 1852, AGEC, FCMO, Ficha 2041 C20 F3 E28 2F; Maldonado to Juáregui, December 4, 1852, AGEC, FCMO, Ficha 2066 C20 F5 E42 2F.

27. Maldonado, Nava, to Juáregui, December 11, 1852, AGEC, FCMO, Ficha 2072 C20 F6 E48 2F.

28. Warren, "The Damned Man," 33–35.

29. Onofre Díaz, Inspector General de las Colonias Militares de Oriente to Francisco Castañeda, March 26, 1853, AGEC, FCMO, Ficha 216, C21 F10 E71 32F, FCMO AGEC.

30. Félix Gonzáles, to Castañeda, May 27, 1853 [copy Castaneda June 21, 1853], AGEC, FCMO, Ficha 2161 C21 F10 E71 32F; Castañeda to Onofre Díaz, June 21, 1852, AGEC, FCMO, Ficha 2161, C21 F10 E71 32F.

31. Presidente of Morelos to Castañeda [copy Moral, June 21, 1853], AGEC, FCMO, Ficha 2161 C21 F10 E71 32F, FCMO AGEC; Matias Treviño to Castañeda, June 11, 1853 [copy Moral, June 21, 1853], AGEC, FCMO, Ficha 2161, C21 F10 E71 32F; Santos García to Castañeda, May 31, 1853 [copy June 21, 1853, by Castañeda], AGEC, FCMO, Ficha 2161, C21 F10 E71 32F.

32. Presidente of Morelos to Castañeda [copy Moral, June 21, 1853], AGEC, FCMO, Ficha 2161 C21 F10 E71 32F.

33. Gonzáles, Músquiz, May 27, 1853, to Castaneda, May 27, 1853 [copy Castañeda, June 21, 1853], Ficha 2161, AGEC, FCMO, C21 F10 E71 32F; Castañeda to Onofre Díaz, June 21, 1852, FCMO, AGEC, Ficha 2161 C21 F10 E71 32F.

34. García, "A Medieval Frontier."

35. José María de la Garza to Castañeda, June 6, 1853 [copy June 21, 1853], AGEC, FCMO, Ficha 2161 C21 F10 E71 32F.

36. José Andrés Cerera to Castañeda, May 25, 1853 [copy Moral, June 21, 1853], AGEC, FCMO, Ficha 2161, C21 F10 E71 32F; Rodríguez, *Guerra,* 168.

37. Santiago Vidaurri to Pablo Espinosa, March 11, 1856, f. 13 [copy March 12, 1856, by Galindo], SRE Folder 6-18-42.

38. Rodríguez, *Guerra,* 170–71.

39. José Alcorta to Ministro de Relaciones, Mexico City, November 4, 1853, f. 25, SRE, Exp. 1-2-488; Alcorta to Ministro de Relaciones, December 6, 1853, f. 33, SRE,

Exp. 1–2-488; Firzo (?) Castillon to Sr. Juez de Paz, Músquiz, August 15, 1853, fs. 116–118, SRE, LE 1596.

40. Maldonado to Juáregui, March 22, 1851, Ficha 1296, AGEC, FCMO, C12 F5 E58 F2.

41. "Had Capt. Callahan a Right to Enter Mexico?," *Texas State Times,* December 1, 1855; *Texas Ranger and Lone Star,* March 30, 1854.

42. *Texas Planter,* April 5, 1854, 2; *Texas Ranger and Lone Star,* March 30, 1854; Committee of José María Gonzales, H. P. Bee, Albino Treviño et al. to Elisha M. Pease, March 13, 1854, Office of the Governor of Texas, BCAH, WPW, Correspondence Concerning the Texas Rangers 1851–1856, Vol. 2; P. Bee to Governor Bee, March 13, 1854, and Pease to Edmund Davis, March 24, 1854, in Office of the Governor of Texas, BCAH, WPW, Correspondence Concerning the Texas Rangers 1851–1856, Vol. 2; *Texas Planter,* April 5, 1854, 2; *Texas Ranger and Lone Star,* March 30, 1854.

43. Davis to Pease, Laredo, March 13, 1854, pp. 159–63, TIP, Vol. 5.

44. See, e.g., H. P. Bee to E. M. Pease, Laredo, March 13, 1854, pp. 164–165, TIP Vol. 5; *Texas Ranger and Lone Star,* March 30, 1854.

45. *Gonzales Inquirer,* April 29, May 6, and May 13, 1854; "Had Capt. Callahan a Right to Enter Mexico?," *Texas State Times,* December 1, 1855.

46. *Gonzales Inquirer,* April 29, May 6, and May 13, 1854; on the identity of the assailants: Minor, *Turning Adversity to Advantage,* 165.

47. *Seguin Mercury,* June 3, 1855.

48. *Indianola Bulletin,* July 13, 1855.

49. Pease to J. H. Callahan, July 5, 1855, and Pease to Persifor F. Smith, September 5, 1855, BCAH, WPW, Correspondence Concerning the Texas Rangers, Vol. 2, 1851–1856; *Texas Ranger and Lone Star,* July 28, 1855; *Texian Advocate,* September 23, 1854.

50. *Texas State Times,* August 25, 1855.

51. *Texas State Times,* September 1, 1855.

52. William Marcy to Juan Almonte, January 8, 1855, NARA, Dispatches from the United States Commissioners in Mexico, No. 99, Roll 70.

53. Luther, *Ranger James Callahan,* 111.

54. Callahan to Edward Burleson, August 31, 1855, BCAH, Burleson (Edward Jr.), Papers, 1854–1861.

55. "Informacion de testigos practicada en averiguación de la conducta observada por el Estrangero Emilio Langberg en la epoca de la inbación [*sic*] tejana . . ." [Investigation of Emilio Langberg], May 17, 1856, testimony of Patiño, f. 10, AGENL, Militares, Caja 122.

56. Notification to Emilio Langberg, September 10, 1855, AGENL, Militares, Caja 115.

57. Notification to Emilio Langberg, September 10, 1855, AGENL, Militares, Caja 115.

58. Langberg to Manuel Menchaca, September 28, 1855 [copy May 30, 1856], in "Informacion de testigos practicada en averiguación de la conducta observada por el estrangero Emilio Langberg . . . ." Testimony of Pablo Espinosa and Pedro Gomez, f. 4, AGENL, Militares, Caja 122. Agapito Cárdenas and Manuel Menchaca knew about Langberg's plan to let the Texans pass; see testimony of Cárdenas from the same source.

9 / Sacrificed on the Altar of Liberty

1. Adelman and Aron, "From Borderlands to Borders," 814–41. On "gatekeeper state," see Van Schendel, "Spaces of Engagement," 55. St. John, *Line in the Sand,* for the hardening and softening of the border vis-à-vis various transgressors across time.

2. The metaphor of vision for the state comes from Scott, *Seeing Like a State.*

3. Peña, *Los bárbaros del norte,* 126–52; *Texas State Times,* September 1, 1855.

4. Cunningham and Hewitt, "A 'Lovely Land Full of Roses and Thorns,'" 407; *Texas State Times,* September 1, 1855.

5. Santiago Vidaurri to Ayuntamiento of Matamoros, November 5, 1851, AHMAT, Fondo Ilustre Ayunamiento, Caja 11, Exp. 14. On Carvajal's American auxiliaries, see "Later from the Rio Grande," *La Grange Texas Monument,* December 13, 1851; and for his problematic relations with Texan volunteers, see *Southwestern American,* November 17, 1852, December 29, 1852, January 5, 1853, and September 17, 1853, 2.

6. *Texas State Times,* September 1, 1855; "Informacion de testigos practicada en averiguación de la conducta observada por el Estrangero Emilio Langberg en la epoca de la inbación [*sic*] tejana . . . " [Investigation of Emilio Langberg], May 17, 1856, testimony of Agapito Cárdenas, f. 8; Testimony of Francisco Maldonado f. 7; Testimony of Miguel Patiño, f. 10, AGENL, Militares, Caja 122; Broadside (no title, no date), and Hanson Alsbery to Bennett Riddels, June 29, 1855, original in the Santiago Roel Papers, AGENL. My thanks to Miguel Ángel González Quiroga for this reference. *New York Times,* September 15, 1855, alleges that Langberg had struck a deal to return slaves in exchange for $80,000. There is, however, no other evidence of this.

7. *Siglo xix,* August 18, 1855. For more allegations, see *Siglo xix,* November 9, 1855, 4.

8. *Siglo xix,* November 12, 1855.

9. "Guerra sorda": Langberg to Vidaurri, August 16, 1855, AGENL, Vidaurri Correspondence; B. Lacoste, O. Evans, et. al. to Vidaurri, August 2, 1855, "Sobre la invasion de Piedras Negras," SRE, Fondo Comisión Pesquisidora, Cuaderno 10, Caja 3 Exp. 5; *Siglo xix,* November 12, 1855 [reprints from San Antonio committee]; *New York Times,* September 15, 1855. On recommendation of committee: Langberg to Vidaurri, September 1, 1855, AGENL, Vidaurri Correspondence. Last quote, from Langberg to Vidaurri, August 31, 1855, AGENL, Militares, Caja 115.

10. Pablo Espinosa to Sr. Alcalde de Guerrero, June 18, 1859, AGEC, FSXIX, C3, F6, E2, 2F; Espinosa to Sr. Alcalde de Guerrero, June 3, 1859, AGEC, FSXIX, C3, F5, E2, 2F.

11. Peña, *Los bárbaros del norte,* 97–112.

12. Dionisio Gonzáles to Governor of Nuevo León, July 11, 1848; and Perfecto Barbosa to Parás, August 22, 1848, and Perfecto Barbosa, Montemorelos, to Parás, August 22, 1848, AGENL, Militares, Caja 48; Secretaría de Gobierno, Monterrey, December 10, 1856, AGENL, Militares, Caja 127.

13. Estebán Gutiérrez, October 16, 1853, AGENL, Militares, Caja 96; Sr. Comandante del Department de Coahuila, October 18, 1853, AGENL, Militares, Caja 96.

14. Langberg to Vidaurri, September 1, 1855, AGENL, Vidaurri Correspondence; Mulroy, *Freedom on the Border,* 82.

15. Langberg to Vidaurri, August 31, 1855, and September 1, 1855, AGENL, Vidaurri Correspondence.

16. *Siglo xix,* November 12, 1855 [reprints Ignacio Galindo [secretary to Vidaurri] to Langberg, Monterrey, September 11, 1855].

17. Manuel Menchaca to Señor Comandante en Gefe de la sección de Coahuila, October 6, 1855, fs. 15–17; and Secretary of governor of Nuevo León to Sr. Coronel Don Emilio Langberg, comandante en gefe de la sección del Norte de Coahuila s/f, f. 7, SRE, Fondo Comisión Pesquisidora del Norte, Cuaderno 10, Sobre la Invasion de Piedras Negras, Caja 3, Exp. 5; Luther, *Ranger James Callahan,* 129.

18. Ashton, *Piedras Negras Claims*, 1–4. For earlier treatments of the Callahan Raid, see Shearer, "The Callahan Expedition, 1855," 430–51; and Tyler, "The Callahan Expedition of 1855: Indians or Negroes?," 574–85.

19. Luther, *Ranger James Callahan*, 125.

20. *Galveston Weekly,* October 17, 1855.

21. Langberg to editors of the *Bejareño*, October 24, 1855, AGENL, Militares, Caja 117; Manuel Menchaca, October 7, 1855 [copy Ignacio Galindo to Secretary of War and Marine, October 15, 1855], AGENL, Militares, Caja 117; *Siglo xix*, November 12, 1855, 3, reprints Vidaurri to Marcy [October 18, 1855]. Callahan insisted that he had written permission to cross and that the skiff owners were paid for their labor. See "Col. Langberg and His Letters," *Texas Ranger,* December 1, 1855, for the other side of the story. Luther argues differently, *Ranger James Callahan*, 138–39; Tom McDonald will likely sort this out in his forthcoming exhaustive treatment of James Callahan.

22. Langberg to Secretary of War, October 8, 1855, AGENL, Militares, Caja 117.

23. Langberg to editors of the *Bejareño*, October 24, 1855, AGENL, Militares, Caja 117; Manuel Menchaca, October 7, 1855 [copy Ignacio Galindo to Secretary of War and Marine, October 15, 1855], AGENL, Militares, Caja 117.

24. "Col. Langberg and His Letters," *Texas Ranger,* December 1, 1855. Pablo Espinosa would even employ Lipan Apaches to make arrows for Mexican troops: Pablo Espinosa to secretaría de Guerra, Monterrey, February 26, 1856, AGENL, Militares, Caja 120.

25. Statement of Manuel Menchaca, October 7, 1855 [copy Ignacio Galindo to Secretary of War and Marine, October 15, 1855], AGENL, Militares, Caja 117.

26. Menchaca, October 7, 1855 [copy Ignacio Galindo to Secretary of War and Marine, October 15, 1855], AGENL, Militares, Caja 117.

27. "Informacion de testigos practicada," May 17, 1856, testimony of Menchaca f. 3–4, Patiño, f. 10, Rodríguez, f. 11, AGENL, Militares, Caja 122.

28. Menchaca, October 7, 1855 [copy Ignacio Galindo to Secretary of War and Marine, October 15, 1855], AGENL, Militares, Caja 117,

29. Luther, *Ranger James Callahan*,148.

30. Report dated October 19, 1855 from San Antonio de Bejar, AGENL, Militares, Caja 117.

31. William Henry to Miguel Patiño, October 6, 1855, AGENL, Militares, Caja 117.

32. Menchaca to Langberg reprinted in *Siglo xix*, October 19, 1855 [original dated Múzquiz, October 4, 1855].

33. Tyler, "Indians or Negros"; Manuel Leal to sr. Comandante en gefe de la sección de Coahuila, October 8, 1855, AGENL, Militares, Caja 117; Cuartel General de Monterrey, October 8, 1855, AGENL, Militares, Caja 117.

34. Paper given by Francisco Javier Rodríguez Gutiérrez, "Algunos documentales para la historia de la funcación de Piedras Negras, 1848–1855," 14–15 [in author's posession]; Ashton, *Piedras Negras Claims*, 1–4.

35. Ashton, *Piedras Negras Claims*, 1, 31, 13; Emilio Langberg to Secretary of the governor, Monterrey, October 8, 1855, f. 17, SRE, Sobre la Invasion de Piedras Negras, Fondo Comisión Pesquisidora del Norte, Cuaderno 10, Caja 3, Exp. 5; *Siglo xix*, November 12, 1855.

36. "Col. Langberg and His Letters," *Texas Ranger,* December 1, 1855.

37. "Información de testigos practicada," May 17, 1856, Testimony of Miguel Patiño, fs. 9–10, and Agapito Cárdenas, f. 8, AGENL, Militares, Caja 122.

38. Testimony of Cárdenas, f. 8, AGENL, Militares, Caja 122.

39. Testimony of Menchaca, fs. 3–4; and Testimony of Patiño, f. 10, AGENL, Militares, Caja 122.

40. Testimony of Menchaca, fs. 2–3; and Testimony of Patiño, f. 10, AGENL, Militares, Caja 122. Tom McDonald, whose definitive biography of James Hugues Callahan is forthcoming, believes that Pedro Arrañaga probably lived on the Mexican side.

41. Testimony of Menchaca, f. 3, AGENL, Militares, Caja 122. Menchaca's account is suspicious in parts, and it is possible that Callahan was not in the area when Langberg returned.

42. Testimony of Cardenas, f. 8 (vuelto); AGENL, Militares, Caja 122.

43. "Edvard Emil Langberg" *Handbook of Texas Online,* http://www.tshaonline. org/handbook/online/articles/flapv, accessed July 21, 2015; Benavides, "Diálogo entre caciques."

44. Rumor of invasion after the Callahan Raid: *Siglo* XIX, November 16, 1855, 3; Caurtel general, October 8, 1855, AGENL, Militares, Caja 117.

45. Vidaurri to Ignacio Galindo, October 6, 1855, fs. 11–12, and Secretary of the governor, Monterrey, October 8, 1855, fs. 11–12, SRE, Sobre la Invasion de Piedras Negras, Fondo Comisión Pesquisidora del Norte, Cuaderno 10, Caja 3, Exp. 5.

46. *Siglo xix*, October 22 and October 23, 1855 [reprints Vidaurri to Juan Alvarez, October 6, 1855].

47. *Siglo xix*, November 12, 1855.

48. *Texas Ranger,* November 17, 1855.

49. Emilio Langberg to Secretaría de Guerra, Monterrey, October 22, 1855, AGENL, Militares, Caja 117.

50. Edward Jordan to Vidaurri, March 2, 1856 [copy Monterrey, March 16, 1856], SRE, 6–18–42.

51. Daniel Ruggles to Vidaurri, March 3, 1856 [copy, March 16 1856], SRE, 6–18–42.

52. Declaration of Victor Botello before J. E. Slaughter, s/f [copy March 15, 1856], SRE, 6–18–42; Manuel Robles to Vidaurri, May 15, 1856, f. 8, SRE, 6–18–42.

53. [Vidaurri], Monterrey, March 22, 1856, AGENL, Militares, Caja 121.

54. Vidaurri to Benito Juárez, March 16, 1856 [copy Juárez to Robles, April 7, 1856], f. 12, SRE, 6–18–42.

55. Vidaurri to Commander Fort Duncan, March 16, 1856 [copy July 2, 1856], f. 31, SRE, 6–18–42.

56. Vidaurri to Espinosa, Piedras Negras, March 11, 1856 [copy March 12, Galindo], f. 13, SRE, 6–18–42,.

57. Espinosa to Vidaurri, March 25, 1856 [copy March 25, 1856], AGENL, Militares, Caja 121; Vizcaya Canales, *Tierra de guerra viva,* 332–333.

58. *Gazeta de Saltillo,* Año III, no. 19, Santiago del Saltillo Número especial.

59. Espinosa to Vidaurri, March 20, 1856, AGENL, Militares, Caja 121.

60. Vizcaya Canales, *Tierra de guerra viva,* 332–33.

61. Patiño to Vidaurri March 21, 1856 [copy March 25, 1856], AGENL, Militares, Caja 121.

62. Vizcaya Canales, *Tierra de guerra viva,* 333.

63. Juan Zuazua to Vidaurri, March 27, 1856 [copy March 30, 1856], AGENL, Militares, Caja 121.

64. Zuazua to Vidaurri, March 27, 1856 [copy March 30, 1856], AGENL, Militares, Caja 121.

65. Zuazua to Vidaurri, March 27, 1856 [copy March 30, 1856], AGENL, Militares, Caja 121.

66. Zuazua to Vidaurri, March 27, 1856 [copy March 30, 1856] AGENL, Militares, Caja 121; Peña, *Los bárbaros del norte*, 82–84.

67. Zuazua to Vidaurri, March 27, 1856, [copy April s/f, 1856], AGENL, Correspondencia Alcaldes Primeros 1836–1859, Caja 10.

68. Vidaurri to Secretary of war and marine, April 13, 1856 [copy July 2, 1856], f. 28, SRE, 6–18–42.

69. Patiño to Espinosa, April 6, 1856 [copy April 20, 1856], AGENL, Militares, Caja 121; Ruggles to Francisco Treviño, April 5, 1856 [copy July 1, 1856], f. 39, SRE, 6–18–42.

70. Espinosa to Vidaurri, April 27, 1856 [copy July 2, 1856], f. 29, SRE, 6–18–42.

71. Vidaurri to Ruggles, April 7, 1856 [copy July 1, 1856], f. 29, SRE, 6–18–42.

72. Chebatah and Minor, *Chevato*, 3–6.

73. Luis Alberto García, "Santiago Vidaurri and Santos Benavides," personal paper in possession of author; Thompson, *Tejano Tiger*; Cerutti, *Economía de guerra y poder regional*; Tyler, *Santiago Vidaurri*; Ávila et al., *Santiago Vidaurri*; Benavides Hinojosa, *Santiago Vidaurri*; Gálvez Medrano, *Santiago Vidaurri*; Moseley, "The Public Career of Santiago Vidaurri"; Riley, "Santos Benavides: His Influence"; Thompson, *Vaqueros in Blue and Gray*; Hinojosa, *A Borderlands Town in Transition*, 58–59.

74. Vizcaya Canales, *Tierra de guerra viva*, 335.

75. García, "A Medieval Frontier."

76. *Siglo xix*, October 22, 1855, 2.

Conclusion

1. Perhaps the most famous massacre occurred outside of San Fernando, now renamed Zaragoza. The great Lipan shaman and apostle of peyote religion, Chevato, would witness this massacre before traveling with the other surviving Lipans to take up refuge with the Gileños in Arizona. But there are many other examples. Chebatah and Minor, *Chevato,* 32–39; Vizcaya Canales, *Tierra de guerra viva*, 399–400.

2. On the founding of Resurrección: fs. 160–163, SRE, 29–15–46, and f. 115, SRE, LE 1596; *Boletín Oficial*, August 3, 1858, and January 1, 1859. Indian attack: *Boletín Oficial*, November 30, 1861.

3. *Boletín Oficial*, October 21, 1861 [reprints Manuel G. Rejón to José Casciano].

4. Alcalde de Sabinas Hidalgo to secretary of governor Nuevo León y Coahuila, March 23, 1859, AGENL, Militares, Caja 135.

5. Pablo Espinosa to Sr. Alcalde de Guerrero, June 18, 1859, AGEC, FSXIX, C3, F6, E2, 2F; Espinosa to Sr. Alcalde de Guerrero, June 3, 1859, AGEC, FSXIX, C3, F5, E2, 2F.

6. Alcalde de Sabinas Hidalgo to secretary of governor Nuevo León y Coahuila, March 23, 1859, AGENL, Militares, Caja 135. On mustering vecinos under the 1846 and 1848 National Guard laws, see Peña, *Los bárbaros del norte*, 80–120.

7. Espinosa to Sr. alcalde primero de la villa de Guerrero, May 27 and May 29, 1859, AGEC, FSXIX, C3 F4 E7 F1; Espinosa to alcalde de la Villa de Guerrero, September 12,

1859, AGEC, FSXIX, C4 F1 E13 1F; Alcalde de Músquiz to prefect of Rio Grande, March 10, 1859, SRE, LE 1595.

8. Alcalde de Músquiz to prefect of Rio Grande, March 10, 1859, SRE, LE 1595; Secretaría del gobierno to Sr. alcalde de Músquiz, July 6, 1861, AGEC, Caja 10, Folder 121.

9. Vidaurri to Ignacio Galindo, November 7, 1858, fs. 5080–5082, AGENL, fondo Vidaurri, Correspondencia, Igancio Galindo-Santiago Vidaurri; I would like to thank Luis García for bringing this document to my attention. See also *Matagorda Gazette*, October 16, 1858, and December 25, 1858, for the rumors that Vidaurri would turn over runaways.

10. Correspondence of Hiram G. Runnels, January 8, 1859, San Antonio, TSA.

11. Tyler, "Fugitive Slaves," 11.

12. F. 74, SRE 29–15–46; *Boletín Oficial*, November 30, 1861; Sr. Alcade de Músquiz to secretary of the government, December 29, 1861, AGEC, Músquiz Archive, Box 10 Folder 121.

13. *Boletín Oficial*, November 30, 1861.

14. *Boletín Oficial*, November 30, 1861.

15. Vicente Garza to Sr. Secretario del Superior Gobierno del Estado, Monterrey, November 22, 1861; and Manul G. Rejón to Garza, November 22, 1861; and Vidaurri to minister of relaciones exteriors, December 11, 1861; all reprinted in *Boletín Oficial*, October 23, 1861.

16. Lavalle, *Una vecinidad efímera*, 78–90; Thompson, *Vaqueros in Blue and Grey*; Daddysman, *The Matamoros Trade*; William Seward to Mexican Legation, July 9, 1864, and Seward to Matías Romero, July 27, 1864, SRE, 10–21–73.

17. William Schuchardt to the Second Assistant Secretary of State, June 23, 1873, no. 106, NARA, Dispatches from the United States Consuls at Piedras Negras, MP/7157/M299 Roll 1.

18. On MacKenzie raid, see December 19, 1873, SRE, AEMEUA, Leg. 71 Exp. 6, among other sources.

19. On extradition treaties, see Samuel Truett, *Fugitive Landscapes*, 65–67.

20. Gilberto Crespo y Martínez to Secretaría de Relaciones Exteriores, February 29, 1892, fs. 32–33, SRE, 44–12–60.

21. Hu-Dehart, *Yaqui Resistance and Survival*.

22. Hämäläinen and Truett, "On Borderlands," 357–58.

23. Aron and Adelman, "From Borderlands to Borders," 814–41. For an argument about the essentialness of western places, see Limerick, *The Legacy of Conquest*.

24. Van Schendel, "Spaces of Engagement," 55.

25. For just a couple of examples among many, see Juan Almonte to William L. Marcy, October 18, 1855, AGENL, Militares, Caja 117; or SRE, Fondo Comisión Pesqusidora, Exp. 13, Caja 2, simply titled "invasión por fuerzas *norteamericanos* en 1848"; italics mine.

26. M. M. Morales, San Antonio, to Ciudadano ministro plenipotenciaro de la Republicana Mexicana en Washington D.C., January 7, 1870, f. 629, SRE, AEMEUA, Leg. 20, Exp. 1; Vice Consulado de la república Mexicana en San Antonio to Sr. Comandante General Del Quinto Districto Militar, Austin, November 8, 1869, f. 630, SRE, AEMEUA, Leg. 20, Exp. 1; Charles E. Morse, January 9, 1870, SRE, AEMEUA, Leg. 20, Exp. 1.

Bibliography

Archival Materials

AGEC. Archivo General del Estado de Coahuila, Saltillo.

AGEC, AMG. Archivo General del Estado de Coahuila, Fondo Archivo Municipal Guerrero, Saltillo.

AGEC, FCMO. Archivo General del Estado de Coahuila, Fondo Colonias Militares Orientales, Saltillo.

AGEC, FSXIX. Archivo General del Estado de Coahuila, Fondo Siglo XIX, Saltillo.

AGENL. Archivo General del Estado de Nuevo León, Monterrey.

AGN. Archivo General de la Nación, Mexico City.

AHMAT. Archivo Historico de Matamoros, Tamaulipas.

AM BEIN. Archivo Músquiz, Beinecke Library, Yale University, New Haven.

NARA. National Archives. Washington, DC, microfilm.

SEDNA. Archivo de la Secretaría de Defensa Nacional, Mexico City.

SRE. Archivo de la Secretaría de Relaciones Exteriores, Mexico City.

SRE, AEMEUA. Archivo de la Secretaría de Relaciones Exteriores, Mexico City, Archivo de la Embajada Mexicana en los Estados Unidos de América.

TSA. Texas State Archives, Austin.

TIP. Texas Indian Papers.

Published Works

Acuña, Rudolfo. *Occupied America: A History of Chicanos.* New York: Harper and Row, 1981.

Adelman, Jeremy, and Stephen Aron. "From Borderlands to Borders: Empires, Nation-States, and the Peoples in between in North American History." *American Historical Review* 104:3 (June 1999): 814–41.

Addington, Wendell G. "Slave Insurrections in Texas." *Journal of Negro History* 35:4 (October 1950): 408–34.

Alberdi, Juan B. *Bases y puntos de partida para la organización política de la República Argentina*. Buenos Aires: La Cultura Argentina, 1915.

Alonso, Ana. *Colonialism, Revolution, and Gender on the Northern Frontier*. Scottsdale: University of Arizona Press, 1995.

Alonzo, Armando C. *Tejano Legacy: Rancheros and Settlers in South Texas, 1734–1900*. Albuquerque: University of New Mexico Press, 1998.

Anderson, Gary Clayton. *The Conquest of Texas: Ethnic Cleansing in the Promised Land*. Norman: University of Oklahoma Press, 2005.

Andrews, George Reid. *The Afro-Argentines of Buenos Aires, 1800–1900*. Madison: University of Wisconsin Press, 1980.

Appelbaum, Nancy P., et al. *Race and Nation in Modern Latin America*. Chapel Hill: University of North Carolina Press, 2007.

Ashton, J. Hubley, counsel of the United States. *Piedras Negras Claims in the American and Mexican Joint Commission. Pedro Tauns and Others vs. the United States, Argument and Evidence for the United States*. Washington, DC: Department of Justice, 1872.

Ávila, Jesús, et al. *Santiago Vidaurri: La formación de un liderazgo regional desde Monterrey (1809–1867)*. Monterrey: Universidad Autónoma de Nuevo León, 2012.

Bales, Kevin. *Disposable People: New Slavery in the Global Economy*. Berkeley: University of California Press, 2004.

Baptist, Edward E. *The Half Has Never Been Told: Slavery and the Making of American Capitalism*. New York: Basic Books, 2014.

Barker, Eugene C., and Amelia W. Williams, eds. *The Writings of Sam Houston*. Vol. 1: 1813–1836. Austin: University of Texas Press, 1938.

Barr, Alwyn. *Black Texans: A History of African Americans in Texas, 1528–1995*. 2nd ed. Norman: University of Oklahoma Press, 1996.

Barr, Juliana. "Geographies of Power: Mapping Indian Borders in the 'Borderlands' of the American Southwest." *William and Mary Quarterly* 68:1 (January 2011): 5–46.

———. *Peace Came in the Form of a Woman: Indians and Spaniards in the Texas Borderlands*. Chapel Hill: University of North Carolina Press, 2007.

Baud, Michel, and Willem Van Schendel. "Toward a Comparative History of Borderlands." *Journal of World History* 8:2 (Fall 1997): 211–42.

Bauer, Arnold J. "Rural Workers in Spanish America: Problems of Peonage and Oppression." *Hispanic American Historical Review* 59:1 (February 1979): 34–63.

Baumgartner, Alice. "The Line of Positive Safety: Borders and Boundaries in the Rio Grande Valley, 1848–1880." *Journal of American History* 101:4 (March 2015): 1106–22.

Benavides Hinojosa, Artemio. "Diálogo entre caciques." In Artemio Benavides

Hinojosa, *Santiago Vidaurri: Caudillo del Noreste mexicano (1855-1864)*. Monterrey: Tusquets, 2012.

———. *Santiago Vidaurri: Caudillo del Noreste mexicano*. Mexico City: Tusquets, 2012.

———, ed. *Sociedad, milicia y política en Nuevo León, siglos xviii y xix*. Monterrey: Archivo General del Estado de Nuevo León, Gobierno del Estado, 2005.

Berlandier, Jean-Louis. *Journey to Mexico during the Years 1826 to 1834*. 2 vols. Translated by Sheila M. Holendorf, Josette M. Bigelow, and Mary M. Standifer, with an introduction by C. H. Muller. Botanical notes by C. H. Muller and Katherine K. Muller. Austin: Texas State Historical Association in cooperation with the Center for Studies in Texas History, University of Texas at Austin, 1980.

Bennett, Hermann. *Africans in Colonial Mexico*. Bloomington: Indiana University Press, 2003.

Berlin, Ira. *Many Thousands Gone: The First Two Centuries of Slavery in North America*. Cambridge, MA: Belknap Press of Harvard University Press, 1998.

Black, Nancy Johnson. *The Frontier Mission & Social Transformations in Western Honduras: The Order of Our Lady of Mercy, 1525-1773*. Leiden: Brill Academic Publishers, 1997.

Blackhawk, Ned. *Violence over the Land, Indians and Empires in the Early American West*. Cambridge: Harvard University Press, 2006.

Blassingame, John W. *The Slave Community: Plantation Life in the Antebellum South*. New York: Oxford University Press, 1972.

Bolton, Herbert E. "The Mission as a Frontier Institution in the Spanish American Colonies." *American Historical Review* 23:1 (October 1917): 41–80.

Bristol, Douglas W., Jr. *Knights of the Razor: Black Barbers in Slavery and Freedom*. Baltimore: Johns Hopkins University Press, 2009.

Britten, Thomas A. *The Lipan Apaches: People of Wind and Lightning*. Albuquerque: University of New Mexico Press, 2009.

Brooks, James F. *Captives and Cousins: Slavery, Kinship, and Community in the Southwest Borderlands*. Chapel Hill: University of North Carolina Press, 2002.

Brown, Charles Henry. *Agents of Manifest Destiny: The Lives and Times of the Filibusterers*. Chapel Hill: University of North Carolina Press, 1980.

Brubaker, Roger. "Frontier Thesis: Exit, Voice, and Loyalty in East Germany." *Migration World* 18:3–4 (1990): 12–17.

Calloway, Colin G. *One Vast Winter Count: The Native American West before Lewis and Clark*. Lincoln: University of Nebraska Press, 2003.

Campbell, Randolph B. *An Empire for Slavery: The Peculiar Institution in Texas, 1821–1865*. Baton Rouge: Louisiana State University Press, 1989.

———. *Gone to Texas: A History of the Lone Star State*. Oxford: Oxford University Press, 2004.

Carrigan, William D. *The Making of a Lynching Culture: Violence and Vigilantism in Central Texas, 1836–1916*. Urbana: University of Illinois Press, 2004

———. "Slavery on the Frontier: The Peculiar Institution in Central Texas." *Slavery and Abolition* 20 (August 1999): 63–86.

Carroll, Patrick J. *Blacks in Colonial Veracruz: Race, Ethnicity, and Regional Development.* Austin: University of Texas Press, 2001.

Cavazos Garza, Israel. *Breve historia de Nuevo León.* Mexico City: Fondo de Cultura Económica, 1994.

Ceceslki, David S. *The Waterman's Song: Slavery and Freedom in Maritime North Carolina.* Chapel Hill: University of North Carolina Press, 2002.

Cerutti, Mario. *Economía de guerra y poder regional en el siglo xix: Gastos militares, aduanas y comerciantes en los años de Vidaurri (1855-1864).* Monterrey: Archivo General del Estado de Nuevo León, 1983.

Certeau, Michel de. *The Practice of Everyday Life.* Berkeley: University of California Press, 1988.

Chance, Joseph E. *José María de Jesús Carvajal: The Life and Times of a Mexican Revolutionary.* San Antonio: Trinity University Press, 2006.

Chapman, Helen. *The News From Brownsville: Helen Chapman's Letters from the Texas Military Frontier, 1848-1852.* Edited by Caleb Coker. Austin: Texas State Historical Association, 1992.

Chasteen, John Charles. *Americanos: Latin America's Struggle for Independence.* New York: Oxford University Press, 2009.

Chebahtah, William, and Nancy McGown Minor. *Chevato: The Story of the Apache Warrior Who Captured Herman Lehmann.* Lincoln: University of Nebraska Press, 2007.

Clarke, Mary Whatley. *Chief Bowles and the Texas Cherokees.* Norman: University of Oklahoma Press, 1971.

Comisión Pesquisidora de la Frontera del Norte. *Reports of the Committee of Investigation Sent in 1873 by the Mexican Government to the Frontier of Texas. Translated from the Official Edition Made in Mexico.* New York: Baker and Godwin Printers, 1875.

Cook, Scott. *Mexican Brick Culture in the Building of Texas, 1800s–1980s.* College Station: Texas A&M University Press, 1998.

Cooper, Frederick. "Conflict and Connection: Rethinking African History." *American Historical Review* 95:4 (December 1994): 1516–1545.

Cope, R. Douglas. *The Limits of Racial Domination: Plebeian Society in Colonial Mexico City, 1660–1720.* Madison: University of Wisconsin Press, 1994.

Cornell, Sarah E. "Americans in the U.S. South and Mexico: A Transnational History of Race, Slavery, and Freedom, 1810–1910." PhD diss., New York University, 2008.

———. "Citizens of Nowhere: Fugitive Slaves and Free African Americans in Mexico, 1833–1857." *Journal of American History* 100:2 (September 2013): 351–74.

Cross, Harry E. "Debt Peonage Reconsidered: A Case Study in Nineteenth-Century Zacatecas." *Business History Review* 53:4 (Winter 1979): 473–95.

———. "Living Standards in Rural Nineteenth-Century Mexico: Zacatecas, 1820–1880." *Journal of Latin American Studies* 10:1 (1978): 1–19.

Cunningham, Bob, and Harry P. Hewitt. "A 'Lovely Land Full of Roses and Thorns': Emil Langberg and Mexico, 1835–1866. *Southwestern Historical Quarterly* 98:3 (January 1995): 387–425.

Daddysman, James W. *The Matamoros Trade: Confederate Commerce, Diplomacy, and Intrigue*. Dover: University of Delaware Press, 1984.

Davis, Graham. *Land! Irish Pioneers in Mexican and Revolutionary Texas*. College Station: Texas A&M University Press, 2002.

Dawon, Joseph, ed. *The Texas Military Experience*. College Station: Texas A&M University Press, 1995.

Dawson, Alexander. *Latin America since Independence: A History with Primary Sources*. 2nd ed. London: Routledge, 2015.

De Graaf, Lawrence B., Kevin Mulroy, and Quintard Taylor, eds. *Seeking El Dorado: African Americans in California*. Seattle: University of Washington Press, 2001.

DeLay, Brian. "Independent Indians and the U.S.-Mexican War." *American Historical Review* 112 (February 2007): 35–68.

———. *The War of a Thousand Deserts: Indian Raids and the us-Mexican War*. New Haven: Yale University Press, 2008.

De León, Arnoldo. *They Called Them Greasers: Anglo Attitudes towards Mexicans in Texas, 1821–1900*. Austin: University of Texas Press, 1983.

Delgado, Grace Peña. *Making the Chinese Mexican: Global Migration, Localism, and Exclusion in the U.S.-Mexico Borderlands*. Stanford: Stanford University Press, 2013.

Denning, Michael. *Mechanic Accents: Dime Novels and Working Class Culture in America*. New York: Verso, 1998 [1987].

De Shields, James T. *Border Wars of Texas: Being a Popular Account*. Tioga: Herald Company, 1912.

Deutsch, Sarah. *No Separate Refuge: Culture, Class and Gender on an Anglo-Hispanic Frontier in the American Southwest, 1880-1940*. New York: Oxford University Press, 1989.

Díaz, George T. *Border Contraband: A History of Smuggling across the Rio Grande*. Austin: University of Texas Press, 2015.

Enderle, Barrera. "Plaza pública y discurso regionalista en Nuevo León, 1848–1856." In Artemio Benavides Hinojosa, ed., *Sociedad, milicia y política en Nuevo León, siglos xviii y xix*, 43–73. Monterrey: Archivo General del Estado de Nuevo León, Gobierno del Estado, 2005.

Everett, Diana. *The Texas Cherokees: A People between Two Fires, 1890–1840*. Norman: University of Oklahoma Press, 1990.

Faulk, Odie B. "Projected Mexican Military Colonies for the Borderlands." *Journal of Arizona History* 9 (1968): 39–47.

Federal Writers Project. *Slave Narratives: A Folk History of Slavery in the United*

States from Interviews with Former Slaves, Texas Narratives. Part 2. St. Clair Shores: Scholarly Press, 1976.

Ferrell, Robert H. *Monterrey Is Ours! The Mexican War Letters of Lieutenant Dana, 1845-1847.* Lexington: University of Kentucky Press, 1990.

Filisola, Vicente. *Memoirs for the History of the War in Texas.* Austin: Eakins Press, 1985.

Foley, Neil. *White Scourge: Whites and Mexicans in the Making of Texan Cotton Culture.* Austin: University of Texas Press, 1999.

Foner, Eric. *Reconstruction: America's Unfinished Revolution, 1863-1877.* New York: Harper and Row, 1988.

———. *Free Soil, Free Labor, Free Men: The Ideology of the Republican Party before the Civil War.* New York: Oxford University Press, 1995 [1970].

Foos, Paul. *A Short, Offhand, Killing Affair: Soldiers and Social Conflict during the Mexican-American War.* Chapel Hill: University of North Carolina Press, 2002.

Ford, John Salmon. *Rip Ford's Texas.* Edited by Stephen B. Oates. Austin: University of Texas Press, 1963.

Fornell, Earl W. "Texas Filibusterers in the 1850s." *Southwestern Historical Quarterly* 59 (April 1956): 411–28.

Franklin, John Hope, and Loren Schweninger. *Runaway Slaves: Rebels on the Plantation.* New York: Oxford University Press, 1999.

Freyre, Gilberto. *The Masters and the Slaves: A Study in the Development of Brazilian Civilization.* New York: Random House, 1964 [1933].

Friends Intelligencer Association. *Friend's Intelligencer.* Vol. 10. Philadelphia: Wm. M. Moor, 1854.

Furber, George C. *The Twelve Month Volunteer: Or, the Journal of a Private Tennessee Regiment of Cavalry, in the Campaign, in Mexico, 1846–1847.* Cincinnati: J. A. & U. P. James, 1848.

García, Luis Alberto. *Guerra y frontera: El Ejército del Norte entre 1855 y 1858.* Monterrey: Anuario del Archivo General del Estado de Nuevo León, 2006.

———. "A Medieval Frontier: Warfare and Military Culture in Texas and Northeastern Mexico (1686–1845)." PhD diss., Dedman College, Southern Methodist University, 2013.

Gassner, John C. "African American Fugitive Slaves and Freemen in Matamoros, Tamaulipas, 1820–1865." Master's thesis, University of Texas, 2003.

Genovese, Eugene. *Roll Jordan Roll: The World the Slaves Made.* New York: Vintage, 1972.

———. *The World the Slaveholders Made.* New York: Pantheon Books, 1969.

Gibson, A. M. *The Kickapoos: Lords of the Middle Border.* Norman: University of Oklahoma Press, 1963.

Gilroy, Paul. *The Black Atlantic: Modernity and Double Consciousness.* Cambridge, MA: Harvard University Press, 1993.

Gómez, Laura E. *Manifest Destinies: The Making of the Mexican American Race.* New York: New York University Press, 2008.

González, Fernando Garza. *Una puerta al pasado: La historia de los dos Laredos.* Nuevo Laredo: s.n., 1998.

Green, Stanley C. *The Mexican Republic: The First Decade, 1823–1832.* Pittsburgh: University of Pittsburgh Press, 1987.

Greenberg, Amy S. *Manifest Manhood and the Antebellum American Empire.* New York: Cambridge University Press, 2005.

Gurza Lavalle, Gerardo. *Una vecindad efímera: Los Estados Confederados de América y su política exterior hacia México, 1861–1865.* Mexico City: Instituto Mora, 2001.

Guthrie, Keith. *History of San Patricio County.* Austin: Nortex, 1986.

Gutiérrez, Ramón A. *When Jesus Came, the Corn Mothers Went Away.* Stanford: Stanford University Press, 1991.

Gutiérrez Rodríguez, Francisco Javier. "Algunos testimonios documentales para la historia de la fundación de Piedras Negras, 1848–1855." Paper in possession of author, dated June 2008.

Hämäläinen, Pekka. *The Comanche Empire.* New Haven: Yale University Press, 2008.

Hämäläinen, Pekka, and Samuel Truett. "On Borderlands." *Journal of American History* 98:2 (September 2011): 338–361.

Hahn, Steven. *A Nation under Our Feet: Black Political Struggles from Slavery to the Great Migration.* Cambridge: Belknap Press of Harvard University Press, 2003.

Hardy, Dermot H., and Ingham S. Roberts. *Historical Review of South-east Texas: And the Founders, Leaders, and Representative Men of Its Commerce.* Chicago: Lewis Publishing Co., 1910.

Hartley, Oliver Cromwell. *A Digest of the Laws of Texas, to which is Subjoined an Appendix.* Philadelphia: Thomas, Cowperthwait, 1850.

Harris III, Charles H. *A Mexican Family Empire: The Latifundio of the Sánchez Navarros, 1765-1867.* Austin: University of Texas Press, 1975.

Hauge, Michel. *Metis and the Medicine Line: Creating a Border and Dividing a People.* Chapel Hill: University of North Carolina Press, 2015.

Hébert, Rachel Bluntzer. *The Forgotten Colony: San Patricio de Hibernia.* Burnet: Eakin Press, 1981.

Hedrick Basil C., J. Charles Kelley, and Carroll L. Riley, eds. *The North Mexican Frontier: Readings in Archaeology, Ethnohistory, and Ethnograpy.* Carbondale: Southern Illinois University Press, 1971.

Henson, Margaret Sweet. *Juan Davis Bradburn, a Reappraisal of the Mexican Commander of Anahuac.* College Station: Texas A&M University Press, 1982.

Hernández, José Ángel. *Mexican American Colonization during the Nineteenth Century: A History of the U.S.-Mexico Borderlands.* Cambridge: Cambridge University Press, 2012.

Herrera Casasús, Marís Luisa. *Raíces africanas en la población de Tamaulipas.* Ciudad Victoria: Universidad de Tamaulipas, Instituto de Investigaciones Históricas, 1998.

Herrera Pérez, Octavio. *Breve historia de Tamaulipas.* Mexico City: Fondo de Cultura Económica, 1999.

———. "El clan fronterizo: Genesis y desarollo de un grupo de poder político en el norte de Tamaulipas, 1821–1852." *Sociotam* 4:1 (1994): 25–61.

———. "Reflexiones de una década de frontera indefinida entre México y Estados Unidos (Texas) en el bajo Río Bravo." In Josefina Zoraida Vázquez, ed., *Historia y nación: Actas del Congreso en homenaje a Josefina Zoraida Vázquez.* Mexico City: Fondo de Cultura Económica, 1998.

Hietala, Thomas. *Manifest Design: Anxious Aggrandizement in Late Jacksonian America.* Ithaca: Cornell University Press, 1985.

Hinojosa, Gilberto Miguel. *A Borderlands Town in Transition: Laredo, 1755–1870.* College Station: Texas A&M University Press, 1983.

Hirshman, Albert O. "Exit, Voice, and the State." *World Politics* 31:1 (October 1978): 90–107.

Holt, Thomas C. "The Essence of the Contract." In Thomas C. Holt, Frederick Cooper, and Rebecca J. Scott, eds., *Beyond Slavery: Explorations of Race, Labor, and Citizenship in Postemancipation Societies,* 33–60. Chapel Hill: University of North Carolina Press, 2000.

Horsman, Reginald. *Race and Manifest Destiny: The Origins of American Racial Anglo-Saxonism.* Cambridge: Harvard University Press, 1981.

Howe, Daniel Walker. *The Political Culture of the American Whigs.* Chicago: University of Chicago Press, 1984.

———. *What Hath God Wrought: The Transformation of America, 1815-1848.* New York: Oxford University Press, 2009.

Howren, Alleine. "Cause and Origins of the Decree of April 6, 1830." *Southwestern Historical Quarterly* XVI (1913): 395–398.

Hu-Dehart, Evelyn. *Yaqui Resistance and Survival: The Struggle for Land and Autonomy, 1821-1910.* Madison: University of Wisconsin Press, 1984.

Hudson, Linda S. *Mistress of Manifest Destiny: A Biography of Jane McManus Storm Cazneau, 1807-1878.* Austin: Texas State Historical Association, 2001.

Huson, Hobart. *Refugio: A Comprehensive History of Refugio County from Aboriginal Times to 1953.* 2 vols. Woodsboro: Rooke Foundation, 1953, 1955.

Ignatiev, Noel. *How the Irish Became White.* London: Routledge, 1995.

Jacoby, Karl. "The Alternative Borderlands of William H. Ellis and the African American Colony of 1895." In Elliott Young and Samuel Truett, eds., *Continental Crossroads: New Directions in Borderlands History,* 209–39. Durham: Duke University Press, 2004.

———. *Shadows at Dawn: An Apache Massacre and the Violence of History.* New York: Penguin, 2008.

———. *The Strange Career of William Ellis: The Texas Slave Who Became a Mexican Millionaire.* New York: Norton, 2016.

Johanssen, Robert. *To the Halls of the Montezumas: The Mexican War in the American Imagination.* New York: Oxford University Press, 1985.

Johnson, Benjamin, and Andrew R. Graybill, eds. *Bridging National Borders in North America: Transnational and Comparative Histories.* Durham, NC: Duke University Press, 2010.

Johnson, Walter. "On Agency." *Journal of Social History* 37:1 (Fall 2003): 113–24.

———. *River of Dark Dreams: Slavery and Empire in the Cotton Kingdom.* Cambridge: Belknap Press of Harvard University Press, 2013.

———. *Soul by Soul: Life Inside the Antebellum Slave Market.* Cambridge: Harvard University Press, 1999.

Katz, Friedrich. "Labor Conditions on Haciendas in Porfirian Mexico: Some Trends and Tendencies." *Hispanic American Historical Review* 54:1 (February 1974): 1–47.

———. *The Secret War in Mexico: Europe, the United States, and the Mexican Revolution.* Chicago: University of Chicago Press, 1981.

Kavanagh, Thomas. *The Comanches: A History, 1706–1875.* Lincoln: University of Nebraska Press, 1996.

Kearney, Milo, and Anthony Knopp. *Boom and Bust: The Historical Cycles of Matamoros and Brownsville.* Austin: Eakin Press, 1991.

Kearney, Milo, Anthony Knopp, and Antonio Zavaleta, eds. *Further Studies in Rio Grande Valley History.* Vol. 6. Brownsville: University of Texas at Brownsville and Texas Southmost College, 2006.

———. *Studies in Matamoros and Cameron County History.* Brownsville: University of Texas at Brownsville and Texas Southmost College, 1997.

Kelley, Sean. *Los Brazos del Dios: A Plantation Society in the Texas Borderlands, 1821–1865.* Baton Rouge: Louisiana State University Press, 2010.

———. "Mexico in His Head: Slavery and the Texas-Mexico Border, 1810–1860." *Journal of Social History* 37:3 (2004): 709–23.

King, Duane H., ed. *The Cherokee Nation: A Troubled History.* Knoxville: University of Tennessee Press, 1979.

Kiser, Wlliam S. "A 'charming name for a species of slavery': Political Debate on Debt Peonage in the Southwest, 1840s–1860s." *Western Historical Quarterly* 45:2 (Summer 2014): 169–89.

———. *Borderlands of Slavery: The Struggle over Captivity and Peonage in the American Southwest.* Philadelphia: University of Pennsylvania Press, 2017.

Knapp, Frank A., Jr. "Parliamentary Government and the Mexican Constitution of 1857: A Forgotten Phase of Mexican Political History." *Hispanic American Historical Review* 33:1 (1953): 65–87.

Knight, Alan. "Mexican Peonage: What Was It and Why Was It?" *Journal of Latin American Studies* 18:1 (May 1986): 41–74.

———. *Mexico: The Colonial Era.* New York: Cambridge University Press, 2002.

————. "Racism, Revolution, and Indigenismo." In Richard Graham, ed., *The Idea of Race in Latin America: 1870–1940*. Austin: University of Texas Press, 1990.

Knight, Larry P. "Defending the Unnecessary: Slavery in San Antonio in the 1850s." *Journal of South Texas History* 15 (Spring 2002): 57–72.

Lack, Paul. "The Córdova Revolt." In Gerald Poyo, ed., *Tejano Journey: 1770–1850*, 89–100. Austin: University of Texas Press, 1996.

————. "Slavery and Vigilantism." *Southwestern Historical Quarterly* 4 (1981): 1–20.

————. *The Texas Revolutionary Experience: A Political and Social History, 1835–1836*. College Station: Texas A&M University Press, 1992.

LaDow, Beth. *The Medicine Line: Life and Death on a North American Borderland*. London: Routledge, 2002.

Lamar, Howard. "From Bondage to Contract: Ethnic Labor in the American West, 1600–1890." In Steven Hahn and Jonathan Prude, eds., *The Countryside in the Age of Capitalist Transformation: Essays in the Social History of Rural America*, 293–327. Chapel Hill: University of North Carolina Press, 1985.

Langberg, Emilio. *Itinerario de la Espedicion [sic] San Carlos a Monclova el Viejo Hecha por el Coronel D. Emilio Langberg*. Monterrey, 1851.

Lathrop, Barnes B., *Migration into East Texas, 1835–1860: A Study from the United States Census*. Austin: Texas State Historical Association, 1949.

Latorre, Felipe A., and Delores L. Latorre. *The Mexican Kickapoo Indians*. Austin: University of Texas Press, 1976.

Lefebvre, Henri. *The Production of Space*. Oxford: Blackwell, 1991.

Lehmann, Hermann. *Nine Years among the Indians, 1870–1879: The Story of the Captivity and Life of a Texan among the Indians*. Albuquerque: University of New Mexico Press, 1993.

Lewis, Archibald Ross, and Thomas Francis McGann. *The New World Looks at Its History*. Austin: University of Texas Press, 1963.

Lhamon, W. T. *Raising Cain: Blackface Performance from Jim Crow to Hip Hop*. Cambridge: Harvard University Press, 1998.

Limerick, Patricia Nelson. *The Legacy of Conquest: The Unbroken History of America's Past*. New York: Norton, 1987.

————. "Turnerians All: The Dream of a Helpful History in an Intelligible World." *American Historical Review* 100:3 (June 1995): 697–716.

————. "What on Earth Is the New Western History?" *Montana: The Magazine of Western History* 40:3 (Summer 1990): 1–64.

Littlefield, Daniel F., Jr. *Africans and Seminoles: From Removal to Emancipation*. Westport, CT: Greenwood Press, 1977.

Lott, Eric. *Love and Theft: Blackface Minstrelsy and the American Working Class*. New York: Oxford University Press, 1993.

Ludden, David. "Presidential Address: Maps in the Mind and the Mobility of Asia." *Journal of Asian Studies* 62:4 (November 2003): 1057–78.

Lundy, Benjamin. *A Circular, Addressed to Agriculturists, Manufacturers, Mechanics And C. on the Subject of Mexican Colonization.* Philadelphia: Published for the Author by J. Richards, 1835.

———. *The Life, Travels, and Opinions of Benjamin Lundy.* Philadelphia: William D. Parrish, 1847.

Luther, Joseph. *The Odyssey of Texas Ranger James Callahan.* Mount Pleasant, SC: Arcadia Publishing, 2017.

Maestas, Enrique Gilbert-Michael. "Culture and History of Native American Peoples of South Texas." PhD diss., University of Texas at Austin, 2008.

Maillard, N. Doran, *The History of the Republic of Texas, from the Discovery of the Country to the Present Time, and the Cause of Her Separation.* London: Smith, Elder, and Co., 1842.

Mallon, Florencia. "The Promise and Dilemma of Subaltern Studies: Perspectives from Latin American History." *American Historical Review* 95:4 (December 1994): 1491–1515.

Marcy, Randolph B. *Thirty Years of Army Life on the Border.* Philadelphia: J. B. Lippincott, 1963.

Martí, José. *Nuestra América.* In *Selected Writings.* New York: Penguin, 2002 [1891].

Martin, Justin. *Genius of Place: The Life of Frederick Law Olmsted.* Cambridge, MA: Da Capo Press, 2011.

Martínez, Oscar. *Troublesome Border.* Rev. ed. Tucson: University of Arizona Press, 2006.

Massey, Sarah R., ed. *Black Cowboys of Texas.* College Station: Texas A&M University Press, 2000.

Mauro, Frédéric. "Sistema agrario y régime de trabajo." *Historia Mexicana* 38:4 (1989): 842.

May, Robert E. "Invisible Men: Blacks in the U.S. Army during the Mexican War." *Historian* 49 (August 1987): 463–477.

———. *Manifest Destiny's Underworld.* Chapel Hill: University of North Carolina Press, 2002.

McCutchan, Joseph D. *Mier Expedition Diary: A Texan Prisoner's Account.* Austin: University of Texas Press, 1978.

McGuinness, Aims. *Path of Empire: Panama and the California Gold Rush.* Ithaca: Cornell University Press, 2007.

Meeks, Eric. *Border Citizens: The Making of Indians, Mexicans, and Anglos in Arizona.* Austin: University of Texas Press, 2007.

Mehta, Uday Singh. *Liberalism and Empire: A Study in Nineteenth-Century British Liberal Thought.* Chicago: University of Chicago Press, 1999.

Meining, David W. *The Shaping of America; A Geographical Perspective on 500*

Years of History. Vol. 2: *Continental America, 1800–1867.* New Haven: Yale University Press, 1993.

Mikesell, Marvin W. "Comparative Studies in Frontier History." *Annals of the Association of American Geographers* 50:1 (March 1960): 62–74.

Miller, Susan A. *Coacoochee's Bones: A Seminole Saga.* Lawrence: University of Kansas Press, 2003.

Mingus, Charles. *New Tijuana Moods.* New York: RCA Records, 1957.

Minor, Nancy McGown. *"The Light Gray People": An Ethno-History of the Lipan Apaches of Texas and Northern Mexico.* Lanham: University Press of America, 2009.

———. *Turning Adversity to Advantage: A History of the Lipan Apaches of Texas and Northern Mexico.* Lanham: University Press of America, 2009.

Montejano, David. *Anglos and Mexicans in the Making of Texas, 1836–1986.* Austin: University of Texas Press, 1986.

Montgomery, Cora. *Eagle Pass, or Life on the Border.* New York: Putnam, 1852.

Mora-Torres, Juan. *The Making of the Mexican Border: The State, Capitalism, and Society in Nuevo León, 1848–1910.* Austin: University of Texas Press, 2001.

del Moral, Paulina. *Tribus olvidadas de Coahuila.* Saltillo: Fondo Estatal para la Cultura y las Artes de Coahuila, 1999.

Morgan, Edmund S. *American Slavery, American Freedom: The Ordeal of Colonial Virginia.* New York: Norton, 1975.

Moseley, Edward H. "The Public Career of Santiago Vidaurri, 1855–1858." PhD diss., University of Alabama, 1963.

Mulroy, Kevin. *Freedom on the Border: The Seminole Maroons in Florida, Indian Territory, Coahuila and Texas.* Lubbock: Texas Tech University Press, 1993.

Nance, Joseph Milton. *After San Jacinto: The Texas-Mexican Frontier, 1836–1841.* Austin: University of Texas Press, 1963.

Nichols, James Wilson. *Now You Hear My Horn, the Journal of James Wilson Nichols, 1820–1887.* Austin: University of Texas Press, 2010.

Nugent, Daniel. *Spent Cartridges of Revolution: An Anthropological History of Namiquipa, Chihuahua.* Chicago: University of Chicago Press, 1993.

Oberste, William H. *Texas Irish Empresarios and Their Colonies.* Austin: Von Boeckmann-Jones, 1953; 2nd ed. 1973.

Olmsted, Frederick Law. *A Journey through Texas; or A Saddle-Trip on the Southwestern Frontier.* New York: Dix, Edwards, and Co., 1857.

Opler, Morris E. "Lipan and Mescalero Apache in Texas." In *American Indian Ethnohistory: Indians of the Southwest: Apache Indians, X.* New York: Garland, 1974.

Patterson, Orlando. *Slavery and Social Death: A Comparative Study.* Cambridge: Harvard University Press, 1982.

Pease, Donald E., and Amy Kaplan et al. *Cultures of United States Imperialism.* Durham: Duke University Press, 1994.

Peña, Luis Medina. *Los bárbaros del norte: Guardia nacional y política en Nuevo León, siglo xix*. Mexico City: Fondo de Cultura Ecónomica, 2015.

Pingenot, Ben E., ed. *Paso del Águila: A Chronicle of Frontier Days on the Texas Border as Recorded in the Memoirs of Jesse Sumpter*. Austin: Encino Press, 1969.

Porter, Kenneth W. *The Black Seminoles: A History of a Freedom-Seeking People*. Gainesville: University of Florida Press, 1996.

———. "The Seminole in Mexico, 1850–1861." *Hispanic American Historical Review* 31:1 (February 1951): 1–36.

———. "The Seminole Negro Indian Scouts, 1870–1881." *Southwestern Historical Quarterly* 55 (January 1952): 358–376.

Potter, R. M. "Escape of Karnes and Teal from Matamoros." *Quarterly of the Texas State Historical Association* 4 (October 1900): 73–78.

Prakash, Gyan. "Subaltern Studies as Postcolonial Criticism." *American Historical Review* 9:4 (December 1994): 1475–1490.

Pratt, Mary Louise. *Imperial Eyes: Travel Writing and Transculturation*. London: Routledge, 1992.

Pulte, William, and Kathy Altom. "The Mexican Cherokees and the Kickapoos of Nacimiento, Mexico: A Previously Unreported Relationship." *Journal of Cherokee Studies* 9:1 (Spring 1984): 35–37.

Quiroga, Miguel Ángel González. "Inicios de la migración laboral mexicana a Texas." In Miguel A. González Quiroga and Manuel Ceballos Ramírez, eds., *Encuentros en la frontera: Mexicanos y norteamericanos en un espacio común*. Mexico City: El Colegio de la Frontera Norte, El Colegio de México; Universidad Autonoma de Tamaulipas, 2001

———. "Los trabajadores mexicanos en Texas." In Miguel Ángel González Quiroga and Mario Cerutti, eds., *El Norte de México y Texas*. San Juan: Mixcoac, 1999.

Radding Murrieta, Cynthia. *Wandering Peoples: Colonialism, Ethnic Spaces, and Ecological Frontiers in Northwest Mexico*. Durham: Duke University Press, 1997.

Ramos, Raúl. *Beyond the Alamo: Forging Mexican Ethnicity in San Antonio, 1821–1860*. Charlotte: University of North Carolina Press, 2008.

Reagan, John H. "The Expulsion of the Cherokees from East Texas." *Texas Historical Quarterly* 1 (July 1897): 38–46.

Reséndez, Andrés. *Changing National Identities at the Frontier, Texas and New Mexico, 1800–1850*. New York: Cambridge University Press, 2005.

———. *The Other Slavery: The Uncovered Story of Indian Enslavement in America*. New York: Houghton Mifflin Harcourt, 2016.

Reynolds, Donald E. *Texas Terror: The Slave Insurrection Panic of 1860 and the Secession of the Lower South*. Baton Rouge: Louisiana State University Press, 2007.

Rice, L. L. *Freemen's Manual: A Campaign Serial of the Independent Democracy.* Vol. 1, no.1. Columbus: Published by the author, June 1, 1853.

Riley, John Denny. "Santos Benavides: His Influence on the Lower Rio Grande, 1823–1891." PhD diss., Texas Christian University, 1976.

Rippy, J. Fred. "Border Troubles along the Rio Grande, 1848–1860." *Southwestern Historical Quarterly* 23 (October 1919): 91–111.

———. "A Negro Colonization Project in Mexico, 1895." *Journal of Negro History* 6:1 (January 1921): 66–73.

Rodríguez, Martha. *Historias de resistencia y exterminio: Los indios de Coahuila durante el siglo xix.* Saltillo, Coahuila: CIESAS, 1995.

———. *La guerra entre bárbaros y civilizados: El exterminio del nómada en Coahuila, 1840-1880.* Saltillo: Centro de Estudios Sociales y Humanísticos,1998.

Roediger, David R. *The Wages of Whiteness: Race and the Making of the American Working Class.* Rev. ed. New York: Verso, 1999.

Romero, Matías. *Mexico and the United States: A Study of Subjects Affecting Their Political, Commercial, and Social Relations, Made with a View to Their Promotion.* Vol. 1. New York: G. P. Putnam's Sons, 1898.

Rothman, Adam. *Slave Country: American Expansion and the Origins of the Deep South.* Cambridge: Harvard University Press, 2005.

Sahlins, Peter. *Boundaries: The Making of France and Spain in the Pyrenees.* Berkeley: University of California Press, 1989.

St. John, Rachel. *Line in the Sand, A History of the Western U.S.-Mexico Border.* Princeton, NJ: Princeton University Press, 2011.

Salazar, Terrence J. "La historia del oro blanco en H. Matamoros, Tamaulipas." In Milo Kearney, Anthony Knopp, and Antonio Zavaleta, eds., *Studies in Rio Grande Valley History,* 87–92. Brownsville: University of Texas at Brownsville and Texas Southmost College, 2005.

Saldívar, Gabriel. *Los indios de Tamaulipas.* Mexico City: Instituto Panamericano de Geografía e Historia, 1943.

Sales, Maggie Montesinos. *The Slumbering Volcano: American Slave Ship Revolts and the Production of Rebellious Masculinity.* Durham: Duke University Press, 1997.

Santoro, Gene. *Myself When I Am Real: The Life and Music of Charles Mingus.* New York: Oxford University Press, 2001.

Santoscoy, María Elena, et al. *Breve historia de Coahuila.* Mexico City: Fondo de Cultura Económica, 2008.

Saxton, Alexander. *The Rise and Fall of the White Republic: Class Politics and Mass Culture in Nineteenth-Century America.* New York: Verso, 1990.

Schilz, Thomas F. *Lipan Apaches in Texas.* El Paso: Texas Western Press, 1987.

Schlereth, Eric. "Privileges of Locomotion: Expatriation and the Politics of Southwestern Border Crossing," *Journal of American History* 100 (2014): 995–1020.

Schoen, Harold. "The Free Negro in the Republic of Texas." *Southwestern Historical Quarterly* 41:1 (July 1937): 26–34.

Schwartz, Rosalie. *Across the Rio to Freedom: U.S Negroes in Mexico.* El Paso: Southwestern Historical Quarterly Monograph Series, 1974.

Scott, James C. *The Art of Not Being Governed: An Anarchist History of Upland Southeast Asia.* New Haven: Yale University Press, 2009.

———. *Domination and the Arts of Resistance: Hidden Transcripts.* New Haven: Yale University Press, 1990.

———. *Seeing Like a State: How Certain Schemes to Improve the Human Condition Have Failed.* New Haven: Yale University Press, 1998.

Scott, Rebecca J. *Degrees of Freedom: Louisiana and Cuba after Slavery.* Cambridge: Belknap Press of Harvard University Press, 2005.

Sellers, Charles. *The Market Revolution: Jacksonian America, 1815–1846.* New York: Oxford University Press, 1994.

Shearer, Earnest C. "The Callahan Expedition, 1855." *Southwestern Historical Quarterly* 54 (October 1951): 430–51.

———. "The Carvajal Disturbances." *Southwestern Historical Quarterly* 55 (October 1951): 201–30.

Shelton, Robert S. "On Empire's Shores: Free and Unfree Workers in Galveston, Texas, 1840–1860." *Journal of Social History* 40:3 (2007): 717–30.

Sjoberg, Andree F. "Lipan Apache Culture in Historical Perspective." *Southwestern Journal of Anthropology* 9:1 (Spring 1953): 76–98.

Slotkin, Richard. *Gunfighter Nation: The Myth of the Frontier in Twentieth-Century America.* Norman: University of Oklahoma Press, 1998.

Smith, F. Todd. *From Dominance to Disappearance: The Indians of Texas and the Near Southwest, 1786–1859.* Lincoln: University of Nebraska Press, 2005.

———. *Louisiana and the Gulf South Frontier, 1500–1821.* Baton Rouge: Louisiana State University Press, 2014.

Smith, Ralph A. "The Scalp Hunt in Chihuahua, 1849." *New Mexico Historical Review* 40 (April 1965): 117–40.

———. "The Scalp Hunter in the Borderlands." *Arizona and the West* 6 (Spring 1964): 5–22.

Smith, Stacy L. *Freedom's Frontier: California and the Struggle over Unfree Labor, Emancipation, and Reconstruction.* Chapel Hill: University of North Carolina Press, 2015.

Smithwick, Noah. *The Evolution of a State or Recollections of Old Texas Days.* Austin: H. P. N. Gammel, 1900.

Soja, Edward. "The Socio-Spatial Dialectic." *Annals of the Association of American Geographers* 70:2 (June 1980): 207–25.

Spicer, Edward H. *Cycles of Conquest: The Impact of Spain, Mexico, and the United States on the Indians of the Southwest, 1533–1960.* Tucson: University of Arizona Press, 1972.

Stapp, William Preston. *The Prisoners of Perote: Containing a Journal Kept by the Author, who was captured by the Mexicans, at Mier, Dec. 25, 1842, and released from Perote May 16, 1844.* Philadelphia: G. B. Zieber and Co., 1845.

Stephanson, Anders. *Manifest Destiny: American Expansion and the Empire of Right.* New York: Hill & Wang, 1995.

Tannenbaum, Frank. *Slave and Citizen: The Classic Comparative Study of Race Relations in the Americas.* Kansas City: Beacon Press, 1992 [1947].

Taun, Yi-Fu. *Space and Place: The Perspective of Experience.* Minneapolis: University of Minnesota Press, 1977.

Taylor, Paul Schuster. *An American-Mexican Frontier: Nueces County, Texas.* Chapel Hill: University of North Carolina Press, 1934.

Teja, Jesús F. de la. *San Antonio de Béxar: A Community on New Spain's Northern Frontier.* Albuquerque: University of New Mexico Press, 1996.

Thompson, E. P. *The Making of the English Working Class.* London: Penguin, 1980.

Thompson, Jerry D. *Cortina: Defending the Mexican Name in Texas.* College Station: Texas A&M University Press, 2007.

———. *Tejano Tiger: José de los Santos Benavides and the Texas-Mexico Borderlands, 1823–1891.* Forth Worth: Texas Christian University Press, 2017.

———. *Vaqueros in Blue and Grey.* Austin: State House Press, 2000 [1977].

Thompson, Waddy. *Recollections of Mexico: by Waddy Thompson Eq. Lt. Envoy Extraordinary and Minister Plenipotentiary of the United States at Mexico.* New York and London: Wiley and Putnam, 1846.

Tijerina, Andrés. *Tejano Empire: Life on the South Texas Ranchos.* College Station: Texas A&M University Press, 1998

———. *Tejanos and Texas under the Mexican Flag, 1821–1836.* College Station: Texas A&M University Press, 1994.

Tocqueville, Alexis de. *Democracy in America and Two Essays on the America.* New York: Penguin, 2002 [1831].

Torget, Andrew J. *Seeds of Empire: Cotton, Slavery, and the Transformation of the Texas Borderlands, 1800–1850.* Chapel Hill: University of North Carolina Press, 2015.

Truett, Samuel. *Fugitive Landscapes: The Forgotten History of the U.S.-Mexico Borderlands.* New Haven: Yale University Press, 2006.

Truett, Samuel, and Elliott Young, eds. *Continental Crossroads: Remapping U.S-Mexico Borderlands History.* Durham: Duke University Press, 2004.

Tucker, Philip Thomas. *Exodus from the Alamo: The Anatomy of the Last Stand Myth.* Havertown, MD: Casemate Publishers, 2010.

Turner, Frederick Jackson. "The Significance of the Frontier in American History." American Historical Association. Chicago World's Fair, 12 July 1893.

Turner, John Kenneth. *Barbarous Mexico: An Indictment of a Cruel and Corrupt System.* Ithaca: Cornell University Press, 2010 [1911].

Tutino, John. *From Insurrection to Revolution in Mexico: Social Bases of Agrarian Violence, 1750–1940.* Princeton: Princeton University Press, 1986.

Tyler, Ronnie C. "The Callahan Expedition of 1855: Indians or Negroes?" *Southwestern Historical Quarterly* 70 (April 1967): 574–585.

———. "Fugitive Slaves in Mexico." *Journal of Negro History* 57:1 (January 1972): 1–12.

———. *Santiago Vidaurri and the Southern Confederacy.* Austin: Texas State Historical Association, 1973.

———, ed. *The Slave Narratives of Texas.* Austin: State House Press, 1997.

Valdés, Carlos Manuel, Rodolfo Gutierrez F., and Adolfo Falcón Garza, eds. *Lectura de Coahuila.* Saltillo: Secretaría de Educación Pública de Coahuila, 1999.

Valerio-Jiménez, Omar S. "Neglected Citizens and Willing Traders: The Villas del Norte (Tamaulipas) in Mexico's Northern Borderlands, 1749–1846." *Mexican Studies/Estudios Mexicanos* 18:2 (Summer 2002): 251–96.

———. *River of Hope: Forging Identity and Nation in the Rio Grande Borderlands.* Durham: Duke University Press, 2013.

Van den Berghe, Pierre L. *The Ethnic Phenomenon.* New York: Elsevier, 1981.

Vanderwood, Paul. *The Power of God against the Guns of the Government.* Redwood City: Stanford University Press, 1998.

Van Schendel, Willem. *The Bengal Borderland: Beyond State and Nation in South Asia.* London: Anthem Press, 2004.

———. "Spaces of Engagement." In Willem Van Schendel and Itty Abraham, eds., *Illicit Flows and Criminal Things: The Other Side of Globalization.* Bloomington: Indiana University Press, 2005.

Van Young, Eric. "Beyond the Hacienda: Agrarian Relations and Socioeconomic Change in Rural Mesoamerica." *Ethnohistory* 50:1 (2003): 230–31.

Vasconcelos, José. *La Raza Cósmica.* Baltimore: Johns Hopkins University Press, 1997 [1925].

Vázquez, Josefina Zoraida. "La supuesta república del Río Grande." *Historia Mexicana* 36:141 (1986): 49–80.

———, ed. *México al tiempo de su guerra con Estados Unidos (1846-1848).* Mexico City: Fondo de Cultura Económica, 1997.

Vigness, David M. "Relations of the Republic of Texas and the Republic of the Rio Grande." *Southwestern Historical Quarterly* 57 (January 1954): 312–21.

———. "A Texas Expedition into Mexico, 1840." *Southwestern Historical Quarterly* 62 (July 1958): 18–29.

Vincent, Theodore G. "The Contributions of Mexico's First Black President, Vicente Guerrero." *Journal of Negro History* 86 (2001): 148–59.

Vinson III, Ben. *Bearing Arms for His Majesty: The Free-Colored Militia in Colonial Mexico.* Stanford: Stanford University Press, 2001.

Vinson III, Ben, and Matthew Restall. *Black Mexico: Race and Society from Colonial to Modern Times.* Albuquerque: University of New Mexico Press, 2009.

Vinson III, Ben, and Bobby Vaughn. *Afroméxico*. Mexico City: Fondo de Cultura Económica, 2004.

Vizcaya Canales, Isidro. *Tierra de guerra viva: Incursiones de indios y otros conflictos en el noreste de México durante el siglo xix, 1821–1855*. Monterrey: Academia de Investigaciones, 2001.

Vizenor, Gerald. *Manifest Manners: Narratives on Post-Indian Survivance*. Lincoln: University of Nebraska Press, 1999.

Ward, Forest E. "Pre-Revolutionary Activity in Brazoria County." *Southwestern Historical Quarterly* 64 (October 1960): 212–31.

Warren, Richard. "The Damned Man with the Venerated Plan: The Complex Legacy of Augustin Iturbide and the Iguala Plan." In Will Fowler, ed., *Celebrating Insurrection: The Commemoration and Representation of the 19th-Century Mexican Pronunciamientos*. Lincoln: University of Nebraska Press, 2012.

Weaver, John D. *The Brownsville Raid*. New York: Norton, 1970.

Weber, David. *Bárbaros: Spaniards and Their Savages in the Age of Enlightenment*. New Haven: Yale University Press, 2006.

———. *The Mexican Frontier, 1821–1846: The American Southwest under Mexico*. Albuquerque: University of New Mexicoy Press, 1982.

———. *The Spanish Frontier in North America: The Brief Edition*. New Haven: Yale University Press, 2009.

Weber, David J., and Jane M. Rausch, eds. *Where Cultures Meet: Frontiers in Latin American History*. Lanham: SR Books, 1994.

White, Richard. *"It's Your Misfortune and None of My Own."* Norman: University of Oklahoma Press, 1993.

———. *The Middle Ground: Indians, Empires, and Republics in the Great Lakes Region, 1650-1815*. New York: Cambridge University Press, 1991.

Wilentz, Sean. *Chants Democratic: New York City and the Rise of the American Working Class, 1788–1850*. New York: Oxford University Press, 1984.

Wilson, Cassandra. *Thunderbird*. New York: Blue Note Records, 2006.

Winders, Richard Bruce. *Mr. Polk's Army: The American Military Experience in the Mexican War*. College Station: Texas A&M University Press, 2001.

Wood, Gordon S. *An Empire of Liberty; A History of the Early Republic, 1790–1815*. New York: Oxford University Press, 2009 [2008].

Young, Elliott. "Red Men, Princess Pocahontas, and George Washington: Harmonizing Race Relations in Laredo at the Turn of the Century." *Western Historical Quarterly* 29 (Spring 1998): 48–85.

Index

To order or obtain more information on these or other University of
Nebraska Press titles, visit nebraskapress.unl.edu.